McCall's
SUPERB DESSERT
COOKBOOK

McCall's
SUPERB DESSERT
COOKBOOK

Mary Eckley,
Food Editor of McCall's

Random House / McCall's, New York

Library of Congress Cataloging in Publication Data
Main entry under title:

McCall's superb dessert cookbook.

Includes index.
1. Desserts. I. Eckley, Mary. II. McCall's magazine.
TX773.M15   641.8'6   77-90304
ISBN 0-394-41279-6

Manufactured in the United States of America
24689753

Design by Anne Lian
Illustrations by Lilly Langotsky

Contents

Introduction

Here, in our collection of more than 500 desserts, you'll find one for any occasion. From interesting "just family" desserts to the perfect ending to a little dinner for two, the choice is yours. All have been favorites of the *McCall's* reader, requested again and again through the years. And all have been tested in the *McCall's* kitchen to give you a great, fail-proof dessert collection on which to base your own repertory.

The old-fashioned desserts—cakes and pies, ice cream, custards, puddings and tarts—are all here, of course. But in line with today's preference for lighter desserts, we've given you a large selection of both simple and glamorous fruit desserts, not forgetting that short-cut to great distinction, fruit and cheese. Many of our recipes are for the people who, for the very special occasion, still like desserts rich with cream.

So, if you adore a superb and luscious shortcake bursting with berries, a flaky-crusted warm apple pie, a moist, very chocolaty chocolate cake, or a super-rich, creamy cheese cake and such, read on. Or if you're a light-dessert person, you'll find some great lower-in-calories, lower-in-fat ideas, to serve with style and imagination and to make your guests say, "Mmm, divine!"

Mary Eckley
McCall's Food Editor

PIES AND
SMALL PASTRIES

The making of a classic apple pie with a crisp, golden crust has long been the hallmark of a good cook—and today a luscious pie is easier than ever to create. Although we give directions for making and handling a flaky, light pastry, the fact is that the packaged pie-crust mixes available today are very good and act as quick and simple substitutes if you don't have the energy or inclination to tackle pastry from scratch.

And to fill the crusts you've created—mounds of fruit, cream and chiffon. Or, put pastry to other uses to make dumplings, tarts and turnovers—all old-fashioned and satisfying ways to end a meal.

Tips for Pie Bakers

1. Unless stated otherwise, we used sifted all-purpose flour to test our pastry recipes. This means that flour must be sifted before measuring. Use a set of standard measuring cups for measuring dry ingredients.

2. It's best to use a pastry cloth. Rub flour well into surface with palm of hand, then brush off any excess so that no additional flour is rolled into pastry.

3. A circle traced on pastry cloth or waxed paper is a helpful guide in rolling pastry to desired circumference. Or cut a sheet of waxed paper to desired circumference to use as a guide.

4. Use a stockinette cover for the rolling pin; it should be floured to keep pastry from sticking and tearing.

5. Another rolling trick: roll pastry between two sheets of waxed paper to desired circumference. Chill in waxed paper in refrigerator while preparing pie filling. Waxed paper peels easily from chilled pastry. No additional flour is used, making a more flaky pastry.

6. For a well-baked, browned bottom crust, select pie plates of heat-resistant glass (shiny metal pans do not bake bottom crusts as well) or use aluminum pans with dull finishes.

7. When baking a 2-crust fruit pie, place a square of foil on bottom of oven, directly under pie plate, to catch any juices that might bubble through crust.

Notes on Freezing Pies

TO FREEZE PIE SHELLS

Unbaked Pie Shells: Prepare pie shell as recipe directs. Prick pie shell that is going to be baked without filling. Freezer-wrap; label, and freeze.

Baked Pie Shells: Prepare and bake pie shell as recipe directs. Let cool completely on wire rack. Freezer-wrap; label, and freeze.

TO USE FROZEN PIE SHELLS

Unbaked Pie Shells: Preheat oven to 450F. Remove freezer-wrap. Immediately bake frozen pie shell about 20 minutes, or until golden-brown. Let cool completely on wire rack. Fill as desired.

If pie shell is going to be baked along with filling: Remove freezer-wrap. Let stand in refrigerator or at room temperature to thaw. Then fill as desired, and bake as specific recipe directs.

Baked Pie Shells: Preheat oven to 375F. Remove freezer-wrap. Heat solidly frozen pie shell 10 minutes, or until thawed. Cool completely on wire rack. Fill as desired.

Or remove freezer-wrap. Let stand at room temperature until completely thawed.

All Other Pie Shells: Let stand at room temperature to thaw. If necessary to bake pie shell, bake as specific recipe directs.

TO FREEZE PIES

Kinds to Freeze: Fruit pies, baked or unbaked, freeze best. You may also freeze chiffon pies, although filling may toughen slightly. Cream and custard pies do not freeze well.

Unbaked Fruit Pies: Prepare pie as recipe directs. Do not make slits in upper crust. Freeze pie, unwrapped, until firm.

Then wrap pie in freezer-wrap; label, and freeze.

Baked Fruit Pies: Prepare and bake pie as recipe directs. Cool completely on wire rack. Freezer-wrap; label, and freeze.

Chiffon Pies: Prepare pie as recipe directs; omit whipped-cream topping. Freeze pie, unwrapped, until filling is firm. Then wrap in freezer-wrap; label, and freeze.

TO SERVE FROZEN PIES

Unbaked Fruit Pies: Preheat oven to 425F. Remove freezer-wrap. Make slits in upper crust for steam vents. Bake about 1 hour, or until fruit is tender and crust is golden-brown.

If lightweight-aluminum-foil pie pans are used, place on cookie sheet during baking.

Baked Fruit Pies: Preheat oven to 375F. Remove freezer-wrap. Bake solidly frozen pies about 40 minutes, or until filling bubbles through slits in upper crust.

Chiffon Pies: Remove freezer-wrap. Let stand in refrigerator, to thaw, about 1 1/2 hours. Then top as desired.

Pastries and Shells

✥

FLAKY PASTRY FOR 2-CRUST PIE

2 cups sifted* all-purpose flour
1 teaspoon salt

¾ cup shortening or.⅔ cup lard
4 to 5 tablespoons ice water

* Sift before measuring.

1. Sift flour with salt into medium bowl.

2. With pastry blender, or 2 knives, using a short, cutting motion, cut in shortening until mixture resembles coarse cornmeal.

3. Quickly sprinkle ice water, 1 tablespoon at a time, over all of pastry mixture, tossing lightly with fork after each addition and pushing dampened portion to side of bowl; sprinkle only dry portion remaining. (Pastry should be just moist enough to hold together, not sticky.)

4. Shape pastry into a ball; wrap in waxed paper, and refrigerate until ready to use. Divide in half; flatten each half with palm of hand.

5. To make bottom crust: On lightly floured pastry cloth, using a stockinet-covered rolling pin, roll out half of pastry to an 11-inch circle, rolling with light strokes from center to edge and lifting rolling pin as you reach edge. As you roll, alternate directions, to shape an even circle.

6. If rolled piecrust is too irregular in shape, carefully trim off any bulge and use as patch. Lightly moisten pastry edge to be filled in. Gently press patch in place. Smooth seam with several light strokes of the rolling pin.

7. Fold rolled pastry in half; carefully transfer to pie plate, making sure fold is in center.

8. Unfold pastry, and fit carefully into pie plate. Do not stretch pastry. Trim bottom crust even with edge of pie plate.

9. Turn prepared filling into bottom crust.

10. To make top crust: Roll out remaining half of pastry to an 11-inch circle.

11. Fold in half; make several gashes near center for steam vents.

12. Carefully place pastry on top of filling, making sure fold is in center; unfold.

13. Trim top crust ½ inch beyond edge of pie plate. Fold top crust under bottom crust; press gently together, to seal. Crimp edges decoratively.

14. For a shiny, glazed top, brush top crust with 1 egg yolk beaten with 1 tablespoon water, or with 1 slightly beaten egg white, or with undiluted evaporated milk.

15. To prevent edge of crust from becoming too brown, place 1½-inch strip of foil around crust; bake as recipe indicates. Remove foil last 15 minutes of baking.

Makes enough pastry for an 8- or 9-inch 2-crust pie.

FLAKY PASTRY FOR 1-CRUST PIE

1 cup sifted* all-purpose flour
½ teaspoon salt

⅓ cup plus 1 tablespoon
    shortening or ⅓ cup lard
2 to 2½ tablespoons ice water

* Sift before measuring.

1. Sift flour with salt into medium bowl.

2. With pastry blender, or 2 knives, using a short, cutting motion, cut in shortening until mixture resembles coarse cornmeal.

3. Quickly sprinkle ice water, 1 tablespoon at a time, over all of pastry mixture, tossing lightly with fork after each addition and pushing dampened portion to side of bowl; sprinkle only dry portion remaining. (Pastry should be just moist enough to hold together, not sticky.)

4. Shape pastry into a ball; wrap in waxed paper, and refrigerate until ready to use. Flatten with palm of hand.

Makes enough pastry for an 8- or 9-inch pie shell, or top of 1½-quart casserole.

UNBAKED PIE SHELL

1. On lightly floured pastry cloth, using a stockinet-covered rolling pin, roll out Flaky Pastry for 1-Crust Pie to an 11-inch circle, rolling with light strokes from center to edge and lifting rolling pin

as you reach edge. As you roll, alternate directions, to shape an even circle.

2. If rolled piecrust is too irregular in shape, carefully trim off any bulge and use as patch. Lightly moisten pastry edge to be filled in. Gently press patch in place. Smooth seam with several light strokes of the rolling pin.

3. Fold rolled pastry in half; carefully transfer to 9-inch pie plate, making sure fold is in center.

4. Unfold pastry, and fit carefully into pie plate, pressing gently with fingertips toward center of plate. This eliminates air bubbles under crust and helps reduce shrinkage.

5. Fold under edge of crust, and press into upright rim. Crimp decoratively.

6. Refrigerate until ready to fill and bake.

BAKED PIE SHELL

1. Prepare Flaky Pastry for 1-Crust Pie; then make pie shell as directed in Unbaked Pie Shell.

2. Prick entire surface evenly with fork.

3. Refrigerate 30 minutes.

4. Meanwhile, preheat oven to 450F. Bake pie shell 8 to 10 minutes, or until golden-brown.

5. Cool completely on wire rack before filling.

OIL PASTRY FOR 2-CRUST PIE

2 cups sifted all-purpose flour
1 teaspoon salt
½ cup salad oil

1. Sift flour with salt into medium bowl.

2. Add salad oil, mixing well with fork.

3. Sprinkle 3 tablespoons cold water over all of pastry mixture, mixing well with fork.

4. If pastry seems too dry to hold together, add 1 to 2 tablespoons more salad oil, mixing well.

5. Divide pastry in half; form each into a ball. With palm of hand, flatten each ball slightly.

6. To make bottom crust: On wet counter top (so paper won't

slip), roll out half of pastry, between two sheets of waxed paper, to an 11-inch circle.

7. Peel off top sheet of paper; invert pastry into pie plate; peel off other sheet of paper.

8. Fit pastry carefully into pie plate; do not stretch.

9. Trim crust even with edge of pie plate. Turn prepared filling into bottom crust.

10. To make top crust: Roll out remaining half of pastry, between two sheets of waxed paper, to an 11-inch circle.

11. Peel off top sheet of paper; make several slits for steam vents. Invert pastry over filling; peel off paper.

12. Trim crust ½ inch beyond edge of pie plate. Fold top crust under bottom crust; crimp edge decoratively. Bake as specific recipe directs.

Makes enough pastry for an 8- or 9-inch 2-crust pie.

Note: We've included this recipe for oil pastry for those who are on a low-saturated fat diet. This pastry is also quite simple to make and to roll out.

OIL PASTRY FOR 1-CRUST PIE

1¼ cups sifted* all-purpose flour   *⅓ cup salad oil*
  ½ teaspoon salt

* Sift before measuring.

1. Sift flour with salt into medium bowl.

2. Add oil, mixing well with fork.

3. Sprinkle 2 tablespoons cold water over all of pastry mixture, mixing well with fork. If pastry seems too dry to hold together, add 1 to 2 tablespoons more salad oil.

4. Form pastry into a ball; flatten slightly.

Makes enough pastry for an 8- or 9-inch pie shell, or top of 1½-quart casserole.

UNBAKED PIE SHELL

1. On wet counter top (so paper won't slip), roll out pastry, between two sheets of waxed paper, to an 11-inch circle.

2. Peel off top paper; invert pastry into pie plate; peel off other sheet of paper.

3. Fit pastry carefully into pie plate, pressing gently with fingertips toward center of plate.

4. Trim crust ½ inch beyond edge of plate. Fold under edge of crust, and press into upright rim; crimp decoratively.

5. Fill with desired filling; bake as directed.

❈

BAKED PIE SHELL

1. Preheat oven to 450F. Prick entire surface of unbaked pie shell evenly with fork.

2. Bake 12 to 15 minutes, or until golden. Cool completely on wire rack before filling.

❈

UNBAKED GRAHAM-CRACKER PIE SHELL

1¼ cups graham-cracker crumbs
(about 18 crackers, crushed
with a rolling pin)

½ cup butter or regular
margarine, softened
¼ cup sugar
¼ teaspoon cinnamon

1. Combine all ingredients in medium bowl; blend with fingers, fork, or pastry blender.

2. Press evenly on bottom and side of 9-inch pie plate, not on rim. Set an 8-inch pie plate on top of crumbs; press firmly; remove pie plate. Refrigerate until ready to fill.

Makes 9-inch shell.

BAKED GRAHAM-CRACKER PIE SHELL

1. Make pie shell, above.

2. Preheat oven to 375F.

3. Bake 8 minutes, or until golden-brown. Cool on wire rack before filling.

Makes 9-inch shell.

COOKIE-CRUST PIE SHELL

1 cup sifted* all-purpose flour
1/4 cup sugar
1 teaspoon grated lemon peel

1/2 cup butter or margarine
1 egg yolk, slightly beaten
1/4 teaspoon vanilla extract

* Sift before measuring.

1. Preheat oven to 400F.
2. Combine flour, sugar, and lemon peel in medium bowl.
3. With pastry blender or 2 knives, cut in butter until mixture resembles coarse cornmeal.
4. Stir in egg yolk and vanilla.
5. Mix pastry, with hands, until well blended.
6. Pat evenly into 9-inch pie plate; make a small edge on rim.
7. Bake 10 minutes, or until light-golden. Cool on wire rack before filling.
Makes 9-inch shell.

VANILLA-WAFER PIE SHELL

1 pkg (4 3/4 oz) vanilla wafers
1/4 teaspoon nutmeg

1/3 cup butter or margarine, melted

1. Preheat oven to 300F.
2. With rolling pin, crush wafers between 2 sheets of waxed paper. Measure 2 cups crumbs.
3. Toss with nutmeg and butter until well mixed.
4. Press on bottom and side of 9-inch pie plate, not on rim.
5. Bake 10 minutes. Cool on wire rack before filling.
Makes 9-inch shell.

CHOCOLATE COOKIE CRUMB CRUST

½ pkg (8½ oz size) chocolate wafers

⅓ cup butter or margarine, melted
2 tablespoons sugar

1. Using a rolling pin, crush cookies between 2 sheets of waxed paper until very fine. (Or use blender or food processor to make crumbs.) Measure 1 cup.

2. Combine crumbs, butter and sugar in medium bowl; mix with fork or fingers until well combined.

3. Press evenly on bottom and side (not on rim) of pie plate. Refrigerate until ready to use.

Makes one (8- or 9-inch) pie shell.

The Fruit Pies

When the roadside stands and the supermarket bins are rich with fruits—the apple, the pumpkin, and the pear in autumn; rhubarb, berries, peaches, don't forget peaches, in spring and summer—then it's high time to bake our fruit pies. Bake them with one or two crusts, but do serve them warm from the oven. We like them with soft vanilla ice cream or an old-fashioned hard sauce.

❧

FROSTED APPLE PIE

1 pkg (9½ to 11 oz) piecrust mix
1 cup granulated sugar
2 tablespoons flour
1 teaspoon cinnamon
⅛ teaspoon nutmeg
¼ teaspoon salt
7 cups thinly sliced, pared tart
   cooking apples (2½ lb)
2 tablespoons lemon juice

2 tablespoons butter or regular
   margarine
1 egg yolk, slightly beaten

Frosting:
  1 cup confectioners' sugar
  1 tablespoon light corn syrup
  ½ teaspoon vanilla extract
  ½ cup chopped walnuts

1. Make pastry as package label directs. Shape into a ball. Divide in half; form each half into a round; then flatten each with palm of hand. On lightly floured pastry cloth, roll out half of pastry into a 12-inch circle.

2. Fold rolled pastry in half; carefully transfer to a 9-inch pie plate, making sure fold is in center of pie plate. Unfold pastry; fit carefully into pie plate. Refrigerate until ready to use.

3. Preheat oven to 425F. In small bowl, mix granulated sugar, flour, cinnamon, nutmeg and salt. In a large bowl, toss the apples with the lemon juice. Add sugar mixture to sliced apples; toss lightly to combine.

4. Roll out remaining pastry into 12-inch circle. Fold over in quarters; cut slits for steam vents.

5. Turn apple mixture into pastry-lined pie plate, mounding up high in center. Dot apples with butter cut in small pieces. Using

scissors, trim overhanging edge of pastry so it measures ½ inch from rim of pie plate.

6. Carefully place folded pastry so that point is at the center of filling and unfold. Using scissors, trim overhanging edge of pastry (for top crust) so it measures 1 inch from edge all around.

7. Moisten edge of bottom pastry with a little water. Fold top pastry under edge of bottom pastry. With fingers, press edge together to seal, so juices won't run out. Press upright to form a standing rim. Crimp edge.

8. Brush with egg yolk mixed with 1 tablespoon water. Bake 45 to 50 minutes, or until apples are fork-tender and crust is golden. Remove to rack; cool 30 minutes.

9. Make frosting: In small bowl, combine confectioners' sugar, corn syrup, 1 tablespoon water and the vanilla; mix until smooth. Spread over pie; sprinkle with nuts.

Makes 8 servings.

OLD-FASHIONED APPLE PIE

Omit frosting: serve pie slightly warm with vanilla ice cream.

❧

BRANDY APPLE PIE

10 cups (4 lb) pared, cored, thinly
    sliced tart apples
2 tablespoons lemon juice
1 jar (12 oz) apricot preserves
⅔ cup sugar
¼ cup cognac or brandy

3 tablespoons butter or margarine
1 tablespoon grated lemon peel
¼ teaspoon nutmeg
¼ teaspoon cinnamon
¼ cup golden or seedless raisins
1 unbaked 9-inch pastry shell

1. In small bowl, combine 2 cups sliced apples with lemon juice; toss lightly. Set aside.

2. Place remaining apples in medium saucepan, along with ¼ cup apricot preserves, ⅓ cup sugar, cognac, butter, lemon peel, spices, and raisins. Bring to boiling, stirring. Reduce heat and simmer, uncovered, stirring occasionally, 30 to 35 minutes, or just until applesauce consistency. Cool 30 minutes.

3. Preheat oven to 375F.

4. Pour warm applesauce mixture into bottom of unbaked pie shell. Arrange remaining apple slices, attractively, on top. Sprinkle with 3 tablespoons sugar.

5. Bake 25 to 30 minutes, or until pastry is golden-brown and

apple slices are tender and glazed. Transfer to rack.

6. In small saucepan, heat remaining apricot preserves with rest of sugar, stirring until preserves are melted. Remove from heat. Brush over top of apples.

7. Serve warm or at room temperature, with whipped cream or vanilla ice cream, if desired.

Makes 6 to 8 servings.

DUTCH APPLE PIE

9-inch unbaked pie shell

Topping:
⅔ cup sifted* all-purpose flour
⅓ cup light-brown sugar, firmly packed
⅓ cup butter or margarine

* Sift before measuring.

Filling:
2 lb tart cooking apples
1 tablespoon lemon juice
2 tablespoons flour
¾ cup granulated sugar
Dash salt
1 teaspoon cinnamon

1. Prepare pie shell; refrigerate until used.

2. Make Topping: Combine flour and sugar in medium bowl. Cut in butter, with pastry blender or 2 knives, until mixture is consistency of coarse cornmeal. Refrigerate.

3. Preheat oven to 400F.

4. Make Filling: Core apples, and pare; thinly slice into large bowl. Sprinkle with lemon juice.

5. Combine flour, sugar, salt, and cinnamon, mixing well. Toss lightly with apples.

6. Turn filling into unbaked pie shell, spreading evenly. Cover with topping; bake 40 to 45 minutes, or until apples are tender.

Makes 6 to 8 servings.

FRENCH APPLE PIE

1 pkg (10 or 11 oz) piecrust mix or
   pastry for 2-crust pie

Filling:
1/3 cup sugar
2 tablespoons flour
1 cup milk
3 egg yolks
1 tablespoon butter or margarine

1/2 teaspoon vanilla extract

2 lb tart cooking apples
1 tablespoon lemon juice
2 tablespoons butter or margarine
2 tablespoons sugar
   Dash nutmeg
3/4 cup apricot preserves
1 egg yolk

1. Prepare piecrust mix as packaged label directs. Form into a ball. On lightly floured pastry cloth, with a rolling pin covered with a stockinette, roll out two thirds pastry to form a 12-inch circle. Use to line a 9-inch pie plate; refrigerate with rest of pastry.

2. Make Filling: In small saucepan, combine 1/3 cup sugar and the flour; mix well. Stir in milk. Bring to boiling, stirring; reduce heat; simmer, stirring, until slightly thickened—1 minute.

3. In small bowl, beat 3 egg yolks slightly. Beat in a little of hot mixture; pour back into saucepan, beating to mix well. Stir in 1 tablespoon butter and the vanilla. Turn into bowl to cool.

4. Core, pare, and slice apples; sprinkle with lemon juice.

5. In medium skillet, heat butter with sugar and nutmeg. Add apple slices; sauté, stirring occasionally, until partially cooked— about 5 minutes. Remove from heat. Heat apricot preserves just until melted.

6. Preheat oven to 425F.

7. Turn filling into pie shell, spreading evenly. Arrange apple slices on top, mounding slightly in center. Spread with apricot preserves.

8. Roll out rest of pastry to form a 10-inch circle. With knife or pastry wheel, cut into 12 strips 1/2 inch wide.

9. Slightly moisten rim of pie shell with cold water. Arrange 6 strips across filling; press ends to rim of pie shell, trimming off ends if necessary.

10. Arrange rest of strips at right angle to first strips, to form a lattice.

11. Bring overhang of pastry up over ends of strips; crimp edge.

12. Mix yolk with tablespoon water; use to brush lattice strips, not edge.

13. On lowest shelf of oven, bake 35 to 40 minutes, or until pastry is golden. Cool. Serve slightly warm.

Makes 8 servings.

STRASBOURG APPLE PIE

½ pkg (11-oz size) piecrust mix	1 teaspoon ground cinnamon
2½ lb tart cooking apples	4 egg yolks
¾ cup sugar	½ cup heavy cream

1. Make pastry as package label directs for a 9-inch pie shell. On lightly floured surface, roll out into an 11-inch circle. Use to line a 9-inch pie plate. Fold under edge of crust, and press into an upright rim, about 1 inch high. Flute decoratively. Refrigerate.

2. Preheat oven to 350F.

3. Pare apples; slice into eighths. Arrange apples in pie shell in an attractive pattern. Sprinkle with ½ cup sugar combined with the cinnamon.

4. Bake 30 minutes. Meanwhile, in small bowl, beat together egg yolks, cream and remaining ¼ cup sugar.

5. Remove pie from oven. Pour egg-yolk mixture over the apples; return to oven. Bake 35 minutes, or until apples are tender and topping turns golden-brown. Serve slightly warm.

Makes 8 servings.

UPSIDE-DOWN APPLE PIE

Pastry:	2 tablespoons flour
1¼ cups unsifted all-purpose flour	½ teaspoon cinnamon
½ teaspoon salt	¼ teaspoon nutmeg
⅓ cup shortening	¼ teaspoon salt
1 egg	
1 tablespoon lemon juice	2 tablespoons butter or margarine, melted
Filling:	½ cup walnut halves
3 cooking apples (1 lb)	⅓ cup light-brown sugar, firmly
½ cup granulated sugar	packed

1. Make Pastry: Combine flour and salt in medium bowl. With pastry blender, cut in shortening until mixture resembles coarse cornmeal.

2. In cup, slightly beat egg with lemon juice. With fork, stir into flour mixture until pastry holds together. Form pastry into ball, and wrap in waxed paper or plastic film. Refrigerate until ready to use.

3. Make Filling: Pare, core, and thinly slice apples—there should be 3 cups. In large bowl, combine the apples, granulated sugar, flour, cinnamon, nutmeg, and salt.

4. Pour melted butter over bottom of 9-inch pie plate. Place walnuts, flat side up, in plate. Sprinkle with brown sugar.

5. Preheat oven to 375F.

6. Divide pastry in half. On lightly floured surface, roll out half of pastry to an 11-inch circle. Prick all over with fork. Fit into pie plate on top of sugar and nuts. Fill with apple mixture.

7. Roll out remaining pastry to a 10-inch circle; place on top of filling. Fold edge of top crust under bottom crust; press together, and crimp edge decoratively. Prick top crust in several places.

8. Place a sheet of foil under pie plate to catch juice. Bake 30 to 35 minutes, or until pastry is nicely browned. Cool in pie plate 5 minutes. Then invert on serving plate, and lift off pie plate. Serve warm.

Makes 6 to 8 servings.

To do ahead: Complete Steps 1 through 7. Refrigerate. Bake the pie about 45 minutes before serving.

❧

DRIED SCHNITZ (APPLE) PIE

1 pkg piecrust mix or pastry for 2-crust pie	1⅓ cups sugar
4 cups dried tart apples (schnitz)	1 teaspoon ground cinnamon
	¼ teaspoon ground cloves
2¼ cups warm water	Milk

1. Prepare pastry as packaged label directs; shape into a ball; wrap in waxed paper; refrigerate until ready to use.

2. In medium saucepan, cover apples with warm water; soak 30 minutes.

3. Bring to boiling; simmer, covered, just until soft—about 20 minutes.

4. Stir in sugar, cinnamon and cloves; cool 30 minutes.

5. Preheat oven to 425F.

6. On lightly floured surface, roll out half of pastry into an 11-inch circle. Use to line 9-inch pie plate; trim.

7. Turn apple mixture into pastry-lined pie plate.

8. Roll out remaining pastry into an 11-inch circle. Make several slits near center, for steam vents; adjust over filling; trim.

9. Fold edge of top crust under bottom crust; press together with fingertips; crimp edge decoratively. Brush surface lightly with milk.

10. Bake 40 to 45 minutes, or until crust is golden-brown and juices start to bubble through steam vents.

11. Cool on wire rack; serve slightly warm. Nice with vanilla ice cream.

Makes 8 to 10 servings.

FRESH APPLE-PEAR PIE

1 pkg (11 oz) piecrust mix
4 cups thinly sliced, pared ripe
    Bartlett pears (about 3 large
    pears, 1¾ lb)
3 cups thinly sliced, pared tart
    cooking apples (about 2 large
    apples, 1 lb)
2 tablespoons lemon juice

¾ cup light-brown sugar, packed
½ cup granulated sugar
⅛ teaspoon salt
3 tablespoons flour
½ teaspoon nutmeg
2 tablespoons butter or margarine
1 egg yolk

1. Make pastry as package directs for a 2-crust pie. On lightly floured surface, roll out half of pastry into an 11-inch circle. Use to line 9-inch pie plate; trim. Refrigerate, with rest of pastry, until ready to use.

2. Preheat oven to 400F.

3. In large bowl, combine the sliced pears and apples; sprinkle with lemon juice.

4. In small bowl, combine both kinds of sugar, salt, flour and nutmeg. Add to the fruit, tossing lightly to combine.

5. Turn into pastry-lined pie plate, mounding high in center; dot with butter.

6. Roll out remaining pastry into an 11-inch circle. Make several slits near center for steam vents; adjust over filling; trim.

7. Fold edge of top crust under bottom crust; press together with fingertips. Crimp edge decoratively. Brush with egg yolk beaten with 1 teaspoon water.

8. Bake 60 minutes, or until fruit is tender and crust is golden-brown. Cool partially on wire rack; serve warm.

Makes 8 servings.

✂

BLUEBERRY PIE

Pastry for 2-crust pie
2 pint boxes fresh blueberries
  (see Note)
1 tablespoon lemon juice
1 cup sugar
¼ cup all-purpose flour

¼ teaspoon ground cinnamon
⅛ teaspoon ground nutmeg
  Dash ground cloves
2 tablespoons butter or margarine
1 egg yolk

1. Shape pastry into a ball; divide in half. On lightly floured surface, roll out half of pastry into an 11-inch circle. Use to line a 9-inch pie plate. Refrigerate with rest of pastry until ready to use.

2. Preheat oven to 400F.

3. Gently wash berries; drain well. Place in large bowl; sprinkle with lemon juice.

4. Combine sugar, flour, cinnamon, nutmeg and cloves. Add to berries, and toss lightly to combine. Turn into pastry-lined pie plate, mounding in center. Dot with butter.

5. Roll out remaining pastry into an 11-inch circle. Make several slits near center, for steam vents. Adjust over filling; fold edge of top crust under bottom crust; press together, and crimp decoratively.

6. Beat egg yolk with 1 tablespoon water. Brush lightly over top crust.

7. Bake 45 to 50 minutes, or until juices start to bubble through steam vents and crust is golden-brown.

8. Cool on wire rack at least 1 hour. Serve slightly warm.

Makes 8 servings.

Note: Or use 2 packages (10-ounce size) frozen unsweetened blueberries, thawed.

✂

BEST CHERRY PIE

Pastry for 2-crust pie
2 cans (1-lb size) tart red
  cherries, packed in water
1 cup sugar
⅓ cup unsifted all-purpose flour
⅛ teaspoon salt

2 tablespoons butter or margarine
¼ teaspoon almond extract
¼ teaspoon red food color
  (optional)
1 egg yolk

1. Preheat oven to 425F. Make pastry. Wrap in waxed paper, and refrigerate until ready to use.

2. Drain cherries, reserving 1 cup liquid.

3. Combine sugar, flour, and salt; stir into cherry liquid in saucepan. Bring to boiling, stirring.

4. Reduce heat, and simmer 5 minutes. Mixture will be thickened. Stir in butter.

5. Add almond extract and food color. Add cherries; refrigerate, covered.

6. Roll half of pastry, on lightly floured surface, into an 11-inch circle. Fit into 9-inch pie plate; trim. Roll other half of pastry into an 11-inch circle. With knife or pastry wheel, cut eight ½-inch-wide strips.

7. Pour cooled cherry filling into pie shell.

8. Moisten edge of pie shell with cold water. Arrange 4 pastry strips across filling; press ends to rim of shell.

9. Place 4 pastry strips across first ones at right angles, to make lattice. Press ends to rim of shell.

10. Fold overhang of lower crust over ends of strips, to make a rim; crimp decoratively.

11. Lightly brush top, not edge, with egg yolk beaten with 1 tablespoon water.

12. Bake 30 to 35 minutes, or until pastry is nicely browned. Cool partially on wire rack; serve slightly warm.

Makes 6 to 8 servings.

CRANBERRY-APPLE PIE

1 pkg (11 oz) piecrust mix
4 large tart apples, pared, cored,
   and quartered (1½ lb)
2 cups fresh cranberries
1 cup sugar

2 tablespoons maple or maple-
   flavored syrup
3 tablespoons butter or margarine
   Milk or cream

1. Make and roll pastry as package label directs for a 2-crust, 9-inch pie. Preheat oven to 450F.

2. Line pie plate with bottom crust; fill with apple quarters.

3. In medium bowl, toss cranberries with sugar and maple syrup; mash cranberries lightly with fork. Pour over apples. Dot filling with butter.

4. Place remaining crust over filling, first making slits for steam vents. Moisten edge of bottom crust lightly with water; fold top-crust edge under lower crust, pressing firmly to seal. Crimp edge decoratively.

5. Brush top crust (not edge) lightly with milk or cream. Bake 15 minutes; reduce oven temperature to 375F; bake 30 minutes longer.

6. Let cool slightly on wire rack. Nice served warm with ice cream.

Makes 6 to 8 servings.

FRESH CRANBERRY LATTICE PIE

Pastry for 2-crust pie
3 cups fresh cranberries
2 tablespoons flour
2 cups sugar
1/4 teaspoon salt
2/3 cup boiling water
1 cup seedless raisins
2 teaspoons grated lemon peel
2 tablespoons butter or margarine
1 egg, beaten

1. On lightly floured surface, roll out half of pastry into an 11-inch circle. Use to line 9-inch pie plate; trim. Refrigerate, with rest of pastry, until ready to use.

2. Preheat oven to 400F.

3. Wash cranberries, removing stems.

4. Combine flour, sugar and salt in 3½-quart saucepan. Stir in cranberries, water, raisins and the grated lemon peel.

5. Cook, covered, over medium heat until cranberries start to pop—about 10 minutes. Remove from heat.

6. Add butter; place saucepan in bowl of ice cubes 20 minutes, to cool quickly.

7. Meanwhile, roll out other half of pastry into an 11-inch circle. With knife or pastry wheel, cut eight ½-inch-wide strips.

8. Turn cranberry-raisin filling into pie shell. Moisten edge of shell slightly with cold water. Arrange 4 pastry strips, 1 inch apart, across filling; press ends to rim of pastry. Place 4 pastry strips across first ones, at right angles, to make lattice. Press ends to rim of shell.

9. Fold overhang of lower crust over ends of strips, to make a rim. Crimp rim decoratively. Lightly brush pastry with egg.

10. Bake 45 to 50 minutes, or until crust is nicely browned. Cool partially on wire rack; serve slightly warm. (To carry, wrap in foil; reheat if necessary.) Nice with ice cream.

Makes 6 to 8 servings.

FRESH-FRUIT FLAN

Flan Shell:
1/4 cup butter or regular margarine,
    softened
3 tablespoons almond paste
2 tablespoons sugar
1/2 teaspoon grated lemon peel
1 egg white
3/4 cup sifted* all-purpose flour

1 cup strawberries, washed
    and hulled
1 cup blueberries, washed
1 cup seedless green grapes,
    washed and stemmed
2 small ripe peaches, peeled
    and sliced
1/2 cup apricot preserves
1 tablespoon kirsch
    Whipped cream

* Sift before measuring.

1. Make Flan Shell: Grease and lightly flour an 8-by-1½-inch round layer-cake pan.

2. In a medium bowl, with electric mixer at medium speed, beat butter with almond paste, sugar, and lemon peel until well combined.

3. Add egg white; beat at high speed until smooth. Gradually beat in flour until well blended. Turn into prepared pan; pat evenly over bottom and side. (If too soft to work with, refrigerate 10 minutes.) Refrigerate flan shell 1 hour or longer before baking.

4. Preheat oven to 300F. Bake shell 50 minutes, or until golden-brown. Let cool in pan on wire rack 15 minutes. Gently turn out onto rack, and let cool completely.

5. No more than 2 hours before serving: Mound strawberries in center of shell. Arrange blueberries, grapes, and peach slices around strawberries. (If standing longer than 2 hours before serving, fruit may make crust soggy.)

6. In small saucepan, heat apricot preserves over low heat just until melted. Stir in kirsch. Press through a sieve; spoon over fruit in shell. Refrigerate. Serve with whipped cream.

Makes 8-inch flan; 6 servings.

ะว

MINCEMEAT-APPLE PIE

1 pkg (11 oz) piecrust mix

Filling:
1 jar (1 lb, 12 oz) prepared
  mincemeat with brandy and
  rum (3 cups)

1 cup applesauce
1 cup diced, pared tart apple
1 can (4 oz) walnuts, coarsely
  chopped
1 egg yolk

1. In medium bowl, prepare piecrust mix as package label directs. Shape into a ball.

2. On lightly floured surface, roll out two thirds of pastry to 1/8-inch thickness. Fit into a 10-inch pie plate; trim overhang to 1 inch.

3. Roll out remaining pastry to a 12-inch circle. Cut with pastry wheel or a knife into 1/2-inch-wide strips.

4. Preheat oven to 400F.

5. Make Filling: In large bowl, combine mincemeat, applesauce, diced apple and walnuts. Turn into pie shell.

6. Moisten edge of shell slightly with cold water. Arrange 5 pastry strips, 1 inch apart, across filling; press ends to rim of shell. Place 5 strips diagonally across first ones, to make lattice; press ends to rim of shell. Fold overhang of lower crust over ends of strips, to make a rim. Flute rim.

7. Beat egg yolk with 1 tablespoon water. Brush over lattice top, but not on edge of pastry.

8. Bake 30 to 35 minutes, or until crust is nicely browned.

9. Let pie cool slightly on wire rack. Serve pie warm, with whipped cream or vanilla ice cream, if desired.

Makes 10 to 12 servings.

ะว

MINCEMEAT TART

1 pkg (11 oz) piecrust mix
1 jar (1 lb, 12 oz) prepared
  mincemeat with brandy

2 tablespoons brandy
1/4 cup sherry
1 egg yolk

1. Prepare pastry as package label directs. Shape into a ball; divide in half.

2. Preheat oven to 400F.

3. In large bowl, combine mincemeat, brandy and sherry; mix well.

4. On lightly floured pastry cloth or floured board, roll half of pastry to a 12-inch circle. Use to line a 9-inch tart pan with removable bottom. Trim edge.

5. Roll out second half of pastry to a 9-inch circle. Place tart pan on pastry. Using edge of pan as guide, with pastry wheel or sharp knife, cut around pan. Remove pan.

6. With pastry wheel, cut circle into eight triangles. From center, cut out and remove a circle 2 inches in diameter; discard along with one triangle.

7. Turn filling into pastry-lined pan, mounding slightly in center. On top, place seven pastry triangles, spoke fashion. Brush pastry triangles with egg yolk mixed with 2 teaspoons water.

8. Bake 40 to 45 minutes, or until pastry is golden. If not serving at once, cool completely on wire rack.

9. Refrigerate, wrapped in foil.

10. To serve: Preheat oven to 400F. Remove foil; heat in oven 20 minutes. Serve warm with vanilla ice cream or hard sauce, if desired.

Makes 8 servings.

LATTICE-TOP PEACH PIE

Pastry for 2-crust pie
6 cups thinly sliced, pared ripe
   peaches (about 2½ lb)
1 teaspoon lemon juice

¾ cup light-brown sugar,
   firmly packed
2 tablespoons flour
¼ teaspoon salt
¼ teaspoon cinnamon

1. On lightly floured surface, roll out half of pastry into an 11-inch circle. Use to line 9-inch pie plate. Refrigerate.

2. Roll out remaining pastry into a 12-inch circle. With knife or pastry wheel, cut fourteen ¾-inch-wide strips. Refrigerate, on waxed paper, until ready to use.

3. Preheat oven to 425F.

4. In large bowl, sprinkle peaches with lemon juice.

5. In small bowl, combine sugar, flour, salt, and cinnamon, mixing well.

6. Add to peaches, tossing lightly to combine.

7. Turn mixture into pastry-lined pie plate.

8. Moisten edge of shell slightly with cold water. Arrange 7 pastry strips across filling; press ends to rim of pastry.

9. Place 7 pastry strips across first ones, at right angles, to make lattice. Press ends to rim of shell.

10. Fold overhang of lower crust over ends of strips, to make a rim. Crimp decoratively.

11. Bake 45 to 50 minutes, or until peaches are tender and crust is golden.

12. Cool on wire rack.

Makes 6 to 8 servings.

PEACH AND BLUEBERRY PIE

2 tablespoons lemon juice
3 cups sliced, pitted, peeled
    peaches (2¼ lb)
1 cup blueberries
1 cup sugar
2 tablespoons quick-cooking
    tapioca
½ teaspoon salt
    Pastry for 2-crust pie
2 tablespoons butter or margarine

1. Sprinkle lemon juice over fruit in large bowl.

2. Combine sugar with tapioca and salt. Add to fruit, tossing lightly to combine. Let stand 15 minutes.

3. Meanwhile, preheat oven to 425F.

4. On lightly floured surface, roll out half of pastry into an 11-inch circle. Use to line 9-inch pie plate; trim.

5. Turn fruit mixture into pastry-lined pie plate, mounding in center; dot with butter.

6. Roll out remaining pastry into an 11-inch circle. Make several slits near center, for steam vents; adjust over filling; trim.

7. Fold edge of top crust under bottom crust; press together with fingertips. Crimp edge decoratively.

8. Bake 45 to 50 minutes, or until fruit is tender and crust is golden-brown.

9. Cool partially on wire rack; serve slightly warm.

Makes 6 to 8 servings.

PEACH AND GREEN-GRAPE PIE

9-inch baked pie shell
7 or 8 small fresh peach halves,
*   peeled*
1 cup seedless green grapes

1 cup apricot jam
¼ cup sherry
Dash salt

½ cup heavy cream, whipped

Glaze:
1½ teaspoons unflavored gelatine

1. Let baked pie shell cool.

2. Place peaches, cut side down, in bottom of cooled shell. Arrange grapes between peaches.

3. Make Glaze: Sprinkle gelatine over 2 tablespoons cold water; let stand, to soften.

4. In small saucepan, gently heat apricot jam; remove from heat.

5. Add gelatine mixture, stirring to dissolve gelatine. Stir in sherry and salt.

6. Pour glaze over peaches and grapes in pie shell.

7. Refrigerate pie until the glaze is set—about 2 hours.

8. Before serving, decorate pie with rosettes of whipped cream. Makes 6 to 8 servings.

PEACH STREUSEL PIE

½ cup light-brown sugar, packed
½ cup unsifted all-purpose flour
½ cup butter or regular margarine
2 lb ripe peaches (see Note)
*   9-inch unbaked pie shell*

½ cup granulated sugar
¼ teaspoon nutmeg
1 egg
2 tablespoons light cream
1 teaspoon vanilla extract

1. In bowl, combine brown sugar and flour; mix well. With pastry blender, cut in butter until mixture is like coarse crumbs. Preheat oven to 400F.

2. Wash peaches; peel; quarter; discard pits. Measure 4 cups peaches.

3. Sprinkle ½ cup crumb mixture over bottom of pie shell. Add peaches. Sprinkle with granulated sugar and nutmeg.

4. Beat together the egg, light cream and vanilla. Pour over peaches. Cover with the remaining crumb mixture.

5. Bake 40 to 50 minutes, or until top is golden-brown all over. Cool slightly. Serve warm, with cream, if desired.

Makes 6 servings.

Note: Or use 4 packages (12-oz size) frozen sliced peaches, thawed and drained. Sprinkle with 1 tablespoon granulated sugar (not ½ cup) and ¼ teaspoon nutmeg.

PEAR PIE WITH STREUSEL TOPPING

9-inch unbaked pie shell

Streusel Topping:
⅔ *cup sifted* all-purpose flour*
⅓ *cup light-brown sugar, firmly packed*
⅓ *cup butter or margarine*

* Sift before measuring.

Filling:
¼ *cup granulated sugar*
¼ *teaspoon ginger*
4 *teaspoons flour*
5 *ripe Bartlett pears (2 lb)*
4 *teaspoons lemon juice*
¼ *cup light corn syrup*

1. Prepare Pie Shell.

2. Make Streusel Topping: In small bowl, combine flour and sugar. Cut in butter, with pastry blender or 2 knives, until mixture is like coarse cornmeal. Refrigerate until ready to use.

3. Preheat oven to 450F.

4. Make Filling: Combine sugar, ginger, and flour; sprinkle about a third of mixture over bottom of pie shell.

5. Peel and core pears; slice thinly into bowl. Arrange half of pears in shell; top with a third of sugar mixture. Arrange remaining pears; top with remaining sugar mixture. Drizzle lemon juice and corn syrup over top.

6. Cover with Streusel Topping: bake 15 minutes. Reduce oven temperature to 350F, and bake 30 minutes.

Makes 6 to 8 servings.

ALMOND PEAR PIE

Custard Filling:
1 *pkg (3¼ oz) vanilla-pudding-and-pie-filling mix*
2 *cups milk*
½ *teaspoon vanilla extract*

½ *cup almond paste*
9-inch baked pie shell

1 *can (1 lb, 14 oz) pear halves, drained*
¼ *cup orange marmalade*
½ *cup heavy cream, whipped stiff with 2 tablespoons confectioners' sugar*
Candied red cherries (optional)

1. Make Custard Filling: Prepare pudding as package label directs, using 2 cups milk and the vanilla. Pour into medium bowl; place waxed paper directly on surface. Refrigerate until chilled—1 hour.

2. To assemble pie: Roll almond paste between two sheets of waxed paper into a 6-inch circle. Remove top sheet of paper. Invert paste onto bottom of baked pie shell; remove paper. Spread over chilled custard mixture.

3. Arrange pear halves around edge of pie. Brush pears with orange marmalade.

4. Fill pastry bag with number-6 star tip with whipped cream; pipe swirls between pear halves, and make a rosette in center of pie. Top with candied red cherries. Refrigerate for one hour before serving.

Makes 8 servings.

SPICED PLUM PIE

2 *tablespoons lemon juice*
4 *cups sliced, pitted, unpeeled purple plums (about 3 lb)*
1 *cup sugar*
2 *tablespoons quick-cooking tapioca*

½ *teaspoon cinnamon*
½ *teaspoon nutmeg*
Pastry for 2-crust pie
2 *tablespoons butter or margarine*

1. Sprinkle lemon juice over plums in large bowl.

2. Combine sugar with tapioca, cinnamon, and nutmeg. Add to plums, tossing lightly to combine. Let stand 15 minutes.

3. Meanwhile, preheat oven to 425F.

4. On lightly floured surface, roll out half of pastry into an 11-inch circle. Use to line 9-inch pie plate; trim.

5. Turn plum mixture into pastry-lined pie plate, mounding in center; dot with butter.

6. Roll out remaining pastry into an 11-inch circle. Make several slits near center, for steam vents; adjust over filling; trim.

7. Fold edge of top crust under bottom crust; press together with fingertips. Crimp edge decoratively.

8. Bake 45 to 50 minutes, or until plums are tender and crust is golden-brown.

9. Cool partially on wire rack; serve slightly warm.

Makes 6 to 8 servings.

RHUBARB PIE

Pastry for 2-crust pie
1½ cups sugar
⅓ cup unsifted all-purpose flour
4 cups fresh rhubarb, cut into
½-inch pieces (about 1¾ lb)

2 tablespoons butter or
margarine
Granulated sugar

1. On lightly floured surface, roll out half of pastry into a 12-inch circle. Use to line 9-inch pie plate; trim. Refrigerate, with rest of pastry, until ready to use.

2. Preheat oven to 400F.

3. In small bowl, combine 1½ cups sugar and flour; mix well.

4. Add to rhubarb in large bowl, tossing lightly to combine.

5. Turn into pastry-lined pie plate, mounding high in center; dot with butter.

6. Roll out remaining pastry into an 11-inch circle. Make several slits near center, for steam vents; adjust over filling; trim.

7. Fold edge of top crust under bottom crust; press together with fingertips. Crimp edge decoratively. Sprinkle with sugar.

8. Bake 50 to 55 minutes, or until rhubarb is tender and crust is golden-brown.

9. Cool partially on wire rack; serve slightly warm.

Makes 6 to 8 servings.

RHUBARB CUSTARD PIE

1 pkg (11 oz) piecrust mix
2½ cups unpared rhubarb, cut in
    1-inch lengths
1½ cups sugar
¼ cup flour

2 eggs, slightly beaten
2 teaspoons lemon juice
  Dash salt
2 tablespoons butter
1 tablespoon sugar

1. Make pastry as package directs. Handling gently, shape into ball. Divide in half; form each into a round, then flatten with palm of hand. On lightly floured pastry cloth, roll half of pastry into 12-inch circle. Roll with light strokes from center to edge, lifting rolling pin as you reach edge.

2. Place 9-inch pie plate on pastry circle (pastry should be 1 inch wider all around). Fold pastry in half and carefully transfer to pie plate, making sure fold is in center of pie plate. Unfold pastry and fit it carefully into pie plate, pressing gently with fingers, so pastry fits snugly all around. (Do not stretch.) Refrigerate. Preheat oven to 450F.

3. In large bowl, combine rhubarb, sugar, flour, eggs, lemon juice, salt. Turn into lined pie plate. Dot with butter.

4. Roll out remaining pastry into 12-inch circle. Fold over in quarters; cut slits for steam vents. Using scissors, trim overhanging pastry to measure ½ inch from rim of pie plate. Carefully place folded pastry so that point is at the center of filling, and unfold. Using scissors, trim overhanging pastry of top crust to measure 1 inch from edge all around.

5. Moisten edge of bottom pastry with a little water. Fold top pastry under edge of bottom pastry. With fingers, press edges together to seal, so juices cannot run out. Press upright to form a standing rim. Crimp edge decoratively.

6. Sprinkle with 1 tablespoon sugar. Bake at 450F for 10 minutes. Reduce heat to 350F; bake 30 minutes.

Makes 6 servings.

✷

RHUBARB-STRAWBERRY LATTICE PIE

1⅓ cups sugar
  ⅓ cup unsifted all-purpose flour
  2 cups cut-up fresh rhubarb, in
      1-inch pieces (about 1 lb)
  1 pint strawberries, washed,
      hulled and cut in half

1 pkg (11 oz) piecrust mix
1 tablespoon butter or margarine
  Milk
  Sugar

1. In large bowl, combine 1⅓ cups sugar and the flour. Add rhubarb and strawberries, tossing lightly to combine; let stand 30 minutes.

2. Prepare piecrust mix as package label directs. Shape into a ball; divide in half.

3. On lightly floured surface, roll out half of pastry into a 12-inch circle. Use to line 9-inch pie plate. Refrigerate, along with remaining pastry, until ready to use.

4. Preheat oven to 400F.

5. Roll out remaining half of pastry into a 10-inch circle. With knife or pastry wheel, cut into nine 1-inch-wide strips.

6. Turn rhubarb mixture into pastry-lined pie plate, mounding in center. Dot with butter.

7. Moisten rim of pastry slightly with cold water. Arrange five pastry strips, ½ inch apart, over filling; press ends to pastry rim. Place remaining strips across first ones at right angle, to make a lattice, and press to rim. Fold overhang of bottom crust over ends of strips, and crimp decoratively. Brush lattice top, but not rim, lightly with milk, and sprinkle with sugar.

8. Bake 50 minutes, or until crust is golden and juice bubbles through lattice.

9. Cool on wire rack. Serve warm, with ice cream, if desired.
Makes 6 to 8 servings.

✷

FREEZER FRESH-FRUIT PIES

Filling for Frozen Apricot Pie,
  Frozen Raspberry-Apple Pie,
  Frozen Peach-Blueberry Pie
  Frozen Spiced Plum Pie, below

1 pkg (11 oz) piecrust mix
2 tablespoons butter or margarine

To freeze filling:

1. Line a 9-inch pie plate with heavy-duty foil, making sure foil extends at least 6 inches above rim.

2. Make pie filling as recipe directs. Turn into pie plate; bring foil over top, to cover loosely. Freeze several hours, or until filling is firm.

3. Remove frozen, foil-wrapped filling from pie plate; cover top tightly with foil. Label, and return to freezer until ready to bake. Filling may be stored as long as six months.

To bake pie:

1. Preheat oven to 400F. On lightly floured surface, roll out half of pastry into an 11-inch circle. Use to line 9-inch pie plate; trim.

2. Remove filling from freezer; discard foil. Place filling in pastry-lined pie plate. Dot with butter.

3. Roll out remaining pastry into an 11-inch circle. Make several slits near center, for steam vents. Adjust over filling; trim. Fold edge of top crust under bottom crust; crimp edge.

4. Bake 45 to 50 minutes, or until crust is golden.

5. Cool partially on wire rack; serve slightly warm.

Makes 6 servings.

FROZEN APRICOT PIE

1 tablespoon lemon juice	*¼ cup granulated sugar*
4 cups sliced, pitted, unpeeled apricots (about 3 lb)	*2 tablespoons quick-cooking tapioca*
¾ cup light-brown sugar, packed	*½ teaspoon salt*

1. Sprinkle lemon juice over apricots in large bowl.

2. Combine both kinds of sugar with tapioca and salt. Add to apricots, tossing lightly. Let stand 15 minutes.

3. Follow directions, above, to freeze filling and bake pie.

FROZEN RASPBERRY-APPLE PIE

1 tablespoon lemon juice
2 cups thinly sliced, pared, cored
   tart cooking apples
2 cups raspberries

1 cup sugar
2 tablespoons quick-cooking
   tapioca
1/2 teaspoon salt

1. Sprinkle lemon juice over fruit in large bowl.

2. Combine sugar with tapioca and salt. Add to fruit, tossing lightly to combine well. Let stand 15 minutes.

3. Follow directions, above, to freeze filling and bake pie.

FROZEN PEACH-BLUEBERRY PIE

2 tablespoons lemon juice
3 cups sliced, pitted, peeled
   peaches (about 2 1/4 lb)
1 cup blueberries

1 cup sugar
2 tablespoons quick-cooking
   tapioca
1/2 teaspoon salt

1. Sprinkle lemon juice over fruit in large bowl.

2. Combine sugar with tapioca and salt. Add to fruit, tossing lightly to combine. Let stand 15 minutes.

3. Follow directions, above, to freeze filling and bake pie.

FROZEN SPICED PLUM PIE

2 tablespoons lemon juice
4 cups pitted, sliced, unpeeled
   purple plums (about 3 lb)
1 cup sugar

2 tablespoons quick-cooking
   tapioca
1/2 teaspoon ground cinnamon
1/2 teaspoon ground nutmeg

1. Sprinkle lemon juice over plums in large bowl.

2. Combine sugar with tapioca, cinnamon and nutmeg. Add to plums, tossing lightly. Let stand 15 minutes.

3. Follow directions, above, to freeze filling and bake pie.

⛣

DEEP-DISH APPLE PIE

Pastry for 1-crust pie
2 lb tart cooking apples
1 tablespoon lemon juice
1 cup sugar
3 tablespoons flour

$\frac{1}{2}$ teaspoon nutmeg
$\frac{1}{4}$ teaspoon cloves
1 egg yolk
$\frac{1}{2}$ cup heavy cream

1. Prepare pastry. Refrigerate, wrapped in waxed paper, until ready to use.

2. Preheat oven to 400F. Lightly grease 1$\frac{1}{2}$-quart casserole.

3. Wash apples; pare; core; slice thinly into large bowl. Sprinkle with lemon juice.

4. Combine sugar, flour and spices; gently toss with apples, mixing well. Turn into prepared casserole.

5. On lightly floured surface, roll out pastry into a 9$\frac{1}{2}$-inch circle. Fit over top of casserole; flute edge.

6. Make several cuts, 1 inch long, in center, for vents.

7. Brush lightly with egg yolk beaten with 1 tablespoon water; bake 50 to 60 minutes. Top should be golden-brown and apples tender. Remove from oven to rack. Pour cream into vents. Serve warm.

Makes 8 servings.

⛣

DEEP-DISH APPLE CIDER PIE

Filling:
1$\frac{1}{2}$ cups apple cider
1 to 1$\frac{1}{4}$ cups sugar
3 lb tart cooking apples
2 tablespoons lemon juice

2 tablespoons butter or
    margarine

Pastry for 1-crust pie
1 egg yolk

1. Make Filling: In large saucepan, combine cider and sugar; bring to boiling, stirring until sugar is dissolved. Boil, uncovered, 10 minutes.

2. Meanwhile, pare and core apples; cut into thin slices into large bowl. Sprinkle with lemon juice. Add to cider mixture; return to boiling over moderate heat, stirring several times. Lower heat; simmer, uncovered, 5 minutes, or just until apples are partially cooked.

3. With slotted spoon, lift apples out of syrup and into a round, 8¼-inch, shallow baking dish, mounding slices in center.

4. Return remaining syrup to boiling; boil, uncovered, 5 minutes. (Syrup should measure ½ cup.) Pour over apple slices; dot with butter.

5. Preheat oven to 400F.

6. On lightly floured surface, roll out pastry into an 11-inch circle. Fit over top of baking dish; flute edge. Make several slits in center for vents.

7. Beat egg yolk with 1 tablespoon water; brush over pastry. Bake 40 to 45 minutes, or until pastry is golden-brown and juice bubbles through slits.

8. Serve warm, with ice cream, light cream or hard sauce. Makes 6 to 8 servings.

DEEP-DISH APPLE-CRANBERRY PIE

1 pkg (11 oz) piecrust mix
2 cups fresh cranberries, halved
1½ cups sugar
¼ cup all-purpose flour
2 tablespoons maple or maple-
    flavored syrup

6 large tart apples (3 lb), pared,
    cored and sliced
¼ cup butter or margarine
1 egg yolk

1. Prepare pastry as package label directs for a 2-crust pie. Preheat oven to 400F.

2. In large bowl, mix cranberries with sugar, flour and maple syrup.

3. Add apple slices; toss lightly to mix well. Turn into 2-quart, shallow, oblong baking dish. Dot with butter.

4. On lightly floured pastry cloth or floured board, roll three quarters of pastry into rectangle 11 by 13 inches; trim edge. Fit over top of baking dish; fold edge under and flute edge. Make several slits in center of crust for vents.

5. Roll remaining pastry ⅛ inch thick. Using fancy cutter 2 inches long, cut out 12 leaves or ovals. Arrange three in each corner on top of pie.

6. Brush crust, but not edge, with the egg yolk, mixed with 2 teaspoons water.

7. Bake 40 to 45 minutes, or until pastry is golden-brown and juices bubble through slits.

8. Serve warm with ice cream or hard sauce.
Makes 8 servings.

✺

BRANDIED APPLE DEEP-DISH PIE

2 cans (1-lb, 4-oz size) pie-sliced
    apples
1 pkg (9½ to 11 oz) piecrust mix
¾ cup light-brown sugar
¼ cup currants

2 tablespoons sliced almonds
¼ cup brandy
¼ cup butter or margarine
Milk
Granulated sugar

1. Turn apple slices into a colander to drain.

2. Prepare piecrust mix as package label directs. Shape into a ball; wrap in waxed paper; refrigerate until ready to use.

3. Preheat oven to 400F.

4. In large bowl, combine apple slices, brown sugar, currants, almonds, and brandy; toss to mix well. Turn into 12-by-8-inch baking dish. Dot with butter.

5. On lightly floured surface, roll out pastry into a 14-by-10-inch rectangle. Fit over top of baking dish. Tuck edges under; flute decoratively, pressing against dish to seal.

6. Slash top in decorative design, for steam vents. Brush with milk; sprinkle lightly with granulated sugar.

7. Bake 30 to 35 minutes, or until crust is golden-brown and juice bubbles through cuts.

8. Cool in pan on wire rack. Serve warm, with light cream or vanilla ice cream.

Makes 8 servings.

✺

DEEP-DISH PEACH PIE

4 to 4½ lb fresh peaches
¼ cup lemon juice
1½ cups light-brown sugar
¼ cup unsifted all-purpose flour
⅛ teaspoon cloves

⅛ teaspoon cinnamon
½ cup heavy cream
¼ cup butter or margarine
Pastry for 2-crust pie
1 egg yolk

1. Peel and slice enough peaches to make 9 cups. Turn into large bowl. Add lemon juice; toss gently.

2. In small bowl, mix well sugar, flour, cloves, and cinnamon.

Sprinkle over peaches; stir until combined. Stir in cream. Turn into a 12-by-8-by-2-inch shallow baking dish. Dot with butter.

3. Preheat oven to 425F.

4. On lightly floured pastry cloth or board, roll out pastry to a 12-inch square. Cut into 1-inch-wide strips.

5. Arrange 4 strips lengthwise over peaches; arrange remaining strips across them, slightly on diagonal. Trim strips, pressing ends to edge of dish. If you wish, arrange leftover pastry strips, end to end, around edge of dish, to make a border.

6. Mix egg yolk with 1 tablespoon cold water; brush over pastry.

7. Bake 35 to 40 minutes, or until pastry is golden-brown and juice bubbles.

8. Let pie cool on wire rack about 30 minutes.

Makes 8 to 10 servings.

Note: To make pie with canned peaches, use 3 cans (1-lb, 14-oz size) sliced peaches. Drain peaches, reserving syrup. Reduce sugar to 1 cup and use ½ cup reserved syrup in place of cream.

DEEP-DISH PEAR PIE

2¼ to 2½ lb fresh pears
¾ cup light-brown sugar, packed
3 tablespoons flour
⅛ teaspoon salt
Dash ground cloves
Dash nutmeg
⅓ cup heavy cream

2 tablespoons lemon juice
2 tablespoons butter or margarine
Pastry for 1-crust pie
1 egg yolk
Heavy cream or vanilla ice cream

1. Halve pears lengthwise; scoop out core; cut a V shape to remove stems. Pare and slice to make 6 cups.

2. In small bowl, combine brown sugar, flour, salt, cloves, and nutmeg. Stir in ⅓ cup cream.

3. Place sliced pears in an 8¼-inch round, shallow baking dish or 9-inch deep-dish-pie plate (about 1¾ inches deep). Sprinkle with lemon juice; add cream mixture. With wooden spoon, stir gently until well mixed. Dot with butter.

4. Preheat oven to 400F.

5. On lightly floured surface, roll out pastry to an 11-inch circle. Fold in half; make slits for steam vents.

6. Place over fruit in baking dish, and unfold. Press pastry to edge of dish. For decorative edge, press firmly all around with thumb.

7. Lightly beat egg yolk with 1 tablespoon water. Brush over pastry.

8. Place a piece of foil, a little larger than baking dish, on oven rack below the one on which pie bakes, to catch any juices that may bubble over edge of dish. Bake pie 35 to 40 minutes, or until crust is golden and juice bubbles through steam vents.

9. Let pie cool on wire rack about 30 minutes. Serve warm, with heavy cream or ice cream.

Makes 6 to 8 servings.

Note: To make pie with canned pears, use 2 cans (1-lb, 13-oz size) sliced pears. Drain, reserving 2 tablespoons syrup. Make as above, reducing sugar to ½ cup and decreasing flour to 2 table-spoons. Add reserved syrup with the cream.

APPLE KUCHEN

1¼ cups sifted* all-purpose flour
¼ cup sugar
1½ teaspoons baking powder
½ teaspoon salt
¼ cup butter or margarine
1 egg, beaten
¼ cup milk
1 teaspoon vanilla extract
5 cups thinly sliced, pared tart
   apple

Topping:
¼ cup sugar
1 teaspoon cinnamon
¼ cup butter or margarine,
   melted

⅓ cup apricot preserves
Soft vanilla ice cream or
   whipped cream

* Sift before measuring.

1. Preheat oven to 400F. Lightly grease a 13-by-9-by-2-inch baking pan.

2. Into medium bowl, sift flour with ¼ cup sugar, the baking powder and salt. With pastry blender, cut in ¼ cup butter until mixture resembles coarse crumbs.

3. Add beaten egg, milk and vanilla, stirring with a fork until mixture is smooth—about 1 minute.

4. Spread batter evenly in bottom of prepared pan. Arrange apple slices, thin sides down and slightly overlapping, in parallel rows over the batter.

5. Make Topping: Combine sugar, cinnamon and melted butter. Sprinkle sugar mixture over the apple slices.

6. Bake 35 minutes, or until apple slices are tender. Remove to wire rack.

7. Mix apricot preserves with 1 tablespoon hot water. Brush over apple. Cut apple kuchen into rectangles, and serve warm, with ice cream or whipped cream.

Makes 12 servings.

꿍

FRESH-FRUIT KUCHEN

1¼ cups sifted* all-purpose flour
1½ teaspoons baking powder
½ teaspoon salt
¼ cup sugar
¼ cup butter or margarine
 1 egg, beaten
¼ cup milk
 1 teaspoon vanilla extract
 3 fresh plums, pitted and cut in
    eighths

 2 fresh peaches, peeled and
    sliced
 1 tart apple, thinly sliced
 1 cup seedless green grapes

Topping:
 ¼ cup sugar
  1 teaspoon cinnamon
 ¼ cup butter or margarine,
    melted
 ⅓ cup currant or red-raspberry
    jelly

* Sift before measuring.

1. Preheat oven to 400F. Lightly grease 13-by-9-by-2-inch metal pan.

2. Into medium bowl, sift flour with baking powder, salt, and sugar. With pastry blender or 2 knives, cut in ¼ cup butter until mixture resembles coarse cornmeal.

3. With fork, stir in egg, milk, and vanilla, mixing until smooth— about 1 minute. Spread batter evenly in bottom of prepared pan. Arrange plum, peach, and apple slices, slightly overlapping, in parallel rows over batter. Arrange grapes in rows between other rows of fruit.

4. Make Topping: Combine sugar, cinnamon, and melted butter; sprinkle over fruit.

5. Bake 35 minutes, or until fruit is tender. Remove to wire rack.

6. Beat jelly with 1 tablespoon hot water; brush over fruit.

7. To serve: Cut into rectangles while still warm. Top with whipped cream, if desired.

Makes 12 servings.

PEACH KUCHEN

Boiling water
2 lb ripe peaches, peeled and
    sliced (about 6); or 2½ pkg
    (10-oz size) frozen sliced
    peaches, drained
2 tablespoons lemon juice

Kuchen Batter:
1½ cups sifted* all-purpose flour
½ cup sugar
2 teaspoons baking powder
½ teaspoon salt
2 eggs

2 tablespoons milk
1½ tablespoons grated lemon peel
¼ cup butter or regular
    margarine, melted

Topping:
¼ cup sugar
½ teaspoon ground cinnamon
1 egg yolk
3 tablespoons heavy cream

    Sweetened whipped cream or
    soft vanilla ice cream

* Sift before measuring.

1. Pour enough boiling water over peaches in large bowl to cover. Let stand 1 minute to loosen skins; then drain, and plunge into cold water for a few seconds to prevent softening of fruit. With paring knife, pare peaches; place in large bowl.

2. Preheat oven to 400F. Sprinkle peaches with lemon juice to prevent darkening. Slice into the bowl; toss to coat with lemon juice; set aside.

3. Onto sheet of waxed paper, sift flour with the sugar, baking powder, and salt. In large mixing bowl, using fork, beat eggs with milk and lemon peel. Add flour mixture and melted butter, mixing with fork until smooth—1 minute. Do not overmix.

4. Butter a 9-inch springform pan, or a 9-inch round layer-cake pan. (If cake pan is used, kuchen must be served from pan.) Turn batter into pan; spread evenly over bottom. (At this point, kuchen may be refrigerated several hours, or until about ½ hour before baking.)

5. Combine sugar and cinnamon; mix well. Drain peach slices; arrange on batter, around edge of pan; fill in center with 5 peach slices. Sprinkle evenly with sugar-cinnamon mixture. Bake 25 minutes. Remove kuchen from oven.

6. With a fork, beat egg yolk with cream. Pour over peaches. Bake 10 minutes longer. Cool 10 minutes on wire rack.

7. To serve, remove side of springform pan. Serve kuchen warm, cut into wedges, with sweetened whipped cream or soft vanilla ice cream.

Makes 8 to 10 servings.

The Cream Pies

Cream, custard, meringue or chiffon—they're all delicious. Whether it's chocolate with a whipped-cream lattice or lemon hidden under fluffy meringue or just plain coconut, these are the crème de la crème. So they're rich, but have you ever tasted anything more delectable?

❈

VANILLA CREAM PIE

9-inch baked pie shell

Filling:
¾ cup granulated sugar
4 tablespoons cornstarch
½ teaspoon salt
3 cups milk
3 egg yolks, slightly beaten

1 tablespoon butter or margarine
2 teaspoons vanilla extract

Topping:
1 cup heavy cream
2 tablespoons confectioners'
    sugar
½ teaspoon vanilla extract

1. Prepare and bake pie shell; let cool.
2. Make Filling: In medium saucepan, combine granulated sugar, cornstarch, and salt; mix well.
3. Gradually stir in milk, mixing until smooth.
4. Over medium heat, bring to boiling, stirring occasionally; boil 1 minute, stirring.
5. Remove from heat. Stir half of hot mixture into egg yolks. Pour back into saucepan; mix well.
6. Return to boiling, stirring occasionally; boil 1 minute.
7. Remove from heat. Gently stir in butter and 2 teaspoons vanilla. Pour into pie shell.
8. Refrigerate at least 3 hours.
9. Make Topping about 1 hour before serving: With rotary beater, beat cream with confectioners' sugar and ½ teaspoon vanilla until stiff. Spread over filling.
10. Refrigerate 1 hour longer.
Makes 6 to 8 servings.

BANANA CREAM PIE

Prepare Vanilla Cream Pie. Let filling cool; pour half into pie shell. Slice 2 large ripe bananas on the diagonal; arrange over filling. Add rest of filling. Proceed as directed.

COCONUT CREAM PIE

Prepare Vanilla Cream Pie. Fold 1 cup flaked coconut into filling before turning into pie shell.

COFFEE CREAM PIE

Prepare Vanilla Cream Pie, combining 2 tablespoons instant coffee with the granulated sugar, cornstarch, and salt in filling. Reduce vanilla in filling to 1 teaspoon. Omit vanilla in topping.

STRAWBERRY CREAM PIE

Prepare Vanilla Cream Pie. Spread with whipped-cream topping. Wash 1 pint box fresh strawberries; drain; hull. Cut in half lengthwise. Insert strawberry halves in cream, pointed half showing, forming graduated circles on top of pie.

GLAZED PEAR CREAM PIE

9-inch baked pie shell

Filling:
1 pkg (3¼ oz) vanilla-pudding-and-pie-filling mix
2 egg yolks, slightly beaten
1¼ cups milk

½ cup crushed almond macaroons
1 tablespoon kirsch

1 can (1 lb, 14 oz) pear halves
½ cup red-currant jelly
Whipped cream

1. Prepare and bake pie shell; let cool completely.

2. Meanwhile, make Filling: Prepare pudding mix as package label directs, adding egg yolks and milk.

3. After pudding is cooked, add macaroons and kirsch; stir just until combined. Pour immediately into bowl; place sheet of waxed paper directly on surface. Refrigerate until chilled—about 3 hours.

4. Meanwhile, drain pears well on paper towels. Reserve ⅓ cup liquid. Pour liquid into small saucepan; bring to boiling; boil, uncov-

ered, 5 minutes, or until syrup is reduced to about 1 tablespoon. Remove from heat.

5. Stir in currant jelly; cook over low heat, stirring, until jelly is dissolved. Remove from heat, and cool slightly.

6. Using a sharp paring knife, make 5 cuts across rounded side of each pear half, being careful not to cut all the way through.

7. Brush each pear well with some of jelly mixture (if it becomes too thick, reheat), letting it run into the cuts. Refrigerate pears until well chilled. Set aside remaining glaze.

8. To assemble pie: Turn chilled filling into cooled pie shell. Arrange glazed pears, rounded side up, on filling, spoke fashion, with narrow ends meeting at center. Reheat remaining jelly mixture slightly; use to brush over pears. Decorate with whipped cream. Serve at once.

Makes 7 or 8 servings.

CHOCOLATE CREAM PIE

3/4 cup sugar
1/3 cup cornstarch
2 squares unsweetened
    chocolate, cut up
1/2 teaspoon salt
2 1/2 cups milk
3 egg yolks, slightly beaten

1/2 teaspoon vanilla extract
9-inch baked pie shell

Cream Topping:
1 cup heavy cream
2 tablespoons confectioners'
    sugar
1/2 teaspoon vanilla extract

1. In top of double boiler, combine the sugar, cornstarch, chocolate, and salt; mix well. Then gradually stir in the milk.

2. Cook, over boiling water, stirring, until the mixture is thickened—about 10 minutes. Cook, covered, stirring occasionally, 10 minutes longer.

3. Gradually stir half of the hot mixture into beaten egg yolks. Return to rest of mixture in double boiler; cook over boiling water, stirring occasionally, 5 minutes. Remove from heat; stir in vanilla. Pour chocolate filling into baked pie shell.

4. Refrigerate until well chilled—at least 3 hours.

5. Make Cream Topping 1 hour before serving. With rotary beater, beat cream with confectioners' sugar and vanilla until stiff. Spread over pie. Refrigerate.

Makes 6 to 8 servings.

BANANA SOUR-CREAM PIE

1½ cups sour cream
2 eggs
1 cup sugar
2 tablespoons cornstarch
1 teaspoon vanilla extract

3 ripe medium-size bananas
2 tablespoons lemon juice
9-inch baked or unbaked
    graham-cracker pie shell

1. In top of double boiler, heat sour cream over boiling water just until hot (cream will become thin).

2. In small bowl, beat eggs slightly. Combine sugar and cornstarch to mix well; stir into eggs. Stir in a little hot cream; mix well. Pour back into cream, stirring. Cook over boiling water, stirring occasionally, until thickened—15 to 20 minutes.

3. Remove from heat; add vanilla; cool.

4. Into shallow dish, slice bananas crosswise, about ¼ inch thick. Sprinkle with lemon juice to prevent darkening.

5. In bottom of pie shell, layer half of banana slices; cover with half of cooled filling; cover with rest of banana; top with rest of filling. Refrigerate until well chilled and firm—several hours or overnight. If desired, garnish with a little whipped cream before serving.

Makes 6 to 8 servings.

CHERRY-GLAZED CREAM PIE

9-inch baked pie shell

1 can (1 lb, 5 oz) prepared cherry-
    pie filling
1 teaspoon almond extract
1 pkg (3¼ oz) vanilla-pudding-
    and-pie-filling mix

2 cups milk
1 cup heavy cream
2 tablespoons confectioners'
    sugar
¼ teaspoon almond extract

1. Prepare and bake pie shell; let cool.

2. Combine cherry-pie filling and 1 teaspoon almond extract; mix well.

3. Spread 1 cup cherry mixture in bottom of pie shell, reserving rest of cherry mixture.

4. Prepare pie-filling mix as package label directs, using 2 cups milk; let cool 10 minutes.

5. Turn into pie shell, covering cherry layer. Refrigerate several hours, or until well chilled.

6. Spread reserved cherry mixture over top of pie.

7. Combine cream, confectioners' sugar, and ¼ teaspoon almond extract; beat, with rotary beater, until stiff.

8. Use to fill pastry bag with rosette tip. Make rosettes around edge of pie.

9. Refrigerate 1 hour longer, or until well chilled.

Makes 6 to 8 servings.

HONOLULU COCONUT PIE

Filling:
¾ cup granulated sugar
3 tablespoons cornstarch
   Dash salt
2 cups milk
3 egg yolks
¾ teaspoon vanilla extract
¼ teaspoon almond extract

9-inch baked pie shell

1 cup heavy cream
2 tablespoons confectioners' sugar
2 cans (3½-oz size) flaked coconut, or 2 cups grated fresh coconut

1. Make Filling: In top of double boiler, combine granulated sugar, cornstarch, and salt. Gradually stir in milk until smooth.

2. Cook over boiling water, stirring constantly, until mixture thickens. Cover, and cook 15 minutes, stirring several times.

3. In small bowl, beat egg yolks slightly. Stir ½ cup hot cornstarch mixture into egg yolks, mixing well. Pour back into top of double boiler; cook mixture 2 minutes longer, stirring constantly. Remove from heat.

4. Stir in extracts; turn into small bowl; cover. Cool to room temperature—about 1 hour.

5. Refrigerate until well chilled—at least 1 hour.

6. Meanwhile, make, bake, and cool pie shell. Also, whip cream with confectioners' sugar until stiff. Refrigerate, covered.

7. To assemble pie: Turn filling into pie shell. Sprinkle with half the coconut. Cover with whipped cream. Sprinkle remaining coconut over top. Serve at once, or refrigerate no longer than 1 hour.

Makes 8 servings.

BANANA COCONUT PIE

Slice two bananas; arrange in pie shell to cover bottom; cover with filling, as in Step 7.

LEMON MERINGUE PIE

Lemon Filling:
 1/4 cup cornstarch
 3 tablespoons flour
1 3/4 cups sugar
 1/4 teaspoon salt
 4 egg yolks, slightly beaten
 1/2 cup lemon juice
 1 tablespoon grated lemon peel

 1 tablespoon butter
 9-inch baked pie shell

Meringue:
 4 egg whites
 1/4 teaspoon cream of tartar
 1/2 cup sugar

1. Make lemon filling: In medium saucepan, combine cornstarch, flour, 1 3/4 cups sugar and the salt, mixing well. Gradually add 2 cups water, stirring until smooth.

2. Over medium heat, bring to boiling, stirring occasionally; boil 1 minute.

3. Remove from heat. Quickly stir some of hot mixture into egg yolks. Return to hot mixture; stir to blend.

4. Return to heat; cook over low heat 5 minutes, stirring occasionally.

5. Remove from heat. Gently stir in lemon juice, lemon peel and butter. Pour into pie shell.

6. Preheat oven to 400F.

7. Make Meringue: In medium bowl, with mixer at medium speed, beat egg whites with cream of tartar until frothy.

8. Gradually beat in sugar, 2 tablespoons at a time, beating after each addition. Then beat at high speed until stiff peaks form when beater is slowly raised.

9. Spread over lemon filling, carefully sealing to edge of the crust and swirling top decoratively.

10. Bake 7 to 9 minutes, or until the meringue is golden-brown. Let pie cool completely on wire rack—2 1/2 to 3 hours.

Makes 8 servings.

LIME MERINGUE PIE

Substitute ½ cup fresh lime juice and 1 tablespoon grated lime peel for lemon juice and lemon peel. Add a few drops green food color to filling, if desired.

BUTTERSCOTCH MERINGUE PIE

9-inch baked pie shell

Filling:
3/4 cup light-brown sugar, firmly packed
1/4 cup granulated sugar
1/3 cup cornstarch
1/2 teaspoon salt
2 1/2 cups milk
3 egg yolks, slightly beaten

2 tablespoons butter or margarine
1 teaspoon vanilla extract

Meringue:
3 egg whites, at room temperature
1/4 teaspoon cream of tartar
6 tablespoons granulated sugar

1. Prepare and bake pie shell; let cool.
2. Make Filling: In medium saucepan, combine brown sugar, 1/4 cup granulated sugar, the cornstarch and salt; mix well.
3. Gradually stir in milk, mixing until smooth.
4. Over medium heat, bring to boiling, stirring occasionally; boil 1 minute. Remove from heat.
5. Stir half of hot mixture into egg yolks, mixing well; pour back into saucepan.
6. Bring back to boiling, stirring occasionally; boil 1 minute longer. Remove from heat.
7. Stir in butter and vanilla; pour immediately into pie shell.
8. Meanwhile, preheat oven to 400F.
9. Make Meringue: In medium bowl, with portable electric mixer at medium speed, beat egg whites and cream of tartar until soft peaks form when beater is slowly raised.
10. Gradually beat in sugar, 2 tablespoons at a time, beating well after each addition. Continue to beat until stiff peaks form when beater is raised.
11. Spread meringue over warm filling, sealing to edge of crust.
12. Bake 7 to 10 minutes, or until meringue is golden.
13. Cool on wire rack, away from drafts, 1 hour before serving. Makes 6 to 8 servings.

ÇÇ

CHOCOLATE MERINGUE PIE

9-inch baked pie shell

Filling:
  3/4 cup sugar
  1/4 cup cornstarch
    2 squares unsweetened
        chocolate, cut up
  1/2 teaspoon salt
2 1/2 cups milk

  3 egg yolks, slightly beaten
  1/2 teaspoon vanilla extract
  1/2 teaspoon almond extract

Meringue:
    4 egg whites (1/2 cup), at room
        temperature
  1/4 teaspoon cream of tartar
  1/2 cup sugar

1. Prepare, bake pie shell. Let cool.

2. Make Filling: In medium saucepan, combine 3/4 cup sugar, the cornstarch, chocolate, salt; mix well.

3. Gradually stir in milk, mixing until smooth.

4. Over medium heat, bring to boiling, stirring occasionally; boil 1 minute. Remove from heat.

5. Stir half of hot mixture into egg yolks, mixing well; return to pan.

6. Bring back to boiling, stirring occasionally; boil 1 minute. Remove from heat.

7. Stir in vanilla and almond extract. Pour immediately into pie shell.

8. Preheat oven to 375F.

9. Make Meringue: In medium bowl, with portable electric mixer at medium speed, beat egg whites and cream of tartar until soft peaks form when beater is raised.

10. Gradually beat in sugar, 2 tablespoons at a time, beating well after each addition. Continue to beat until stiff peaks form when beater is raised.

11. Spread meringue over warm filling, sealing to edge of crust.

12. Bake 10 to 12 minutes, or until meringue is golden.

13. Cool on wire rack, away from drafts, at least 2 hours before serving.

Makes 6 to 8 servings.

❊

SOUR-CREAM MERINGUE PIE

9-inch unbaked pie shell

Filling:
1 cup light-brown sugar, packed
2 tablespoons flour
1 teaspoon ground allspice
1 cup sour cream
3 egg yolks, slightly beaten

2 tablespoons butter or
    margarine, melted
1 teaspoon vanilla extract
1 cup raisins

Meringue:
4 egg whites
1/4 teaspoon cream of tartar
1/2 cup granulated sugar

1. Make pie shell; refrigerate until ready to use. Preheat oven to 375F.

2. Make Filling: In large bowl, combine brown sugar, flour, all-spice, sour cream, egg yolks, melted butter, and vanilla; beat with rotary beater until smooth. Add raisins; mix well.

3. Pour into pie shell. Bake 45 to 50 minutes, or until tip of sharp knife inserted in center comes out clean.

4. While pie is baking, let egg whites in medium bowl warm to room temperature—about 1 hour.

5. Make Meringue: At medium speed, beat egg whites with cream of tartar just until soft peaks form when beater is slowly raised.

6. Add granulated sugar, 2 tablespoons at a time, beating well after each addition; continue beating until stiff peaks form.

7. Spread meringue over warm filling, carefully sealing to edge of crust. Bake 7 to 10 minutes, or until golden.

8. Let cool on wire rack at room temperature, away from draft, 1 hour. Serve slightly warm.

Makes 8 servings.

❊

LEMON CHIFFON PIE

9-inch baked pie shell or
    unbaked graham-cracker crust

4 egg whites
1 envelope unflavored gelatine
4 egg yolks
1/2 cup lemon juice

1 cup granulated sugar
1/4 teaspoon salt
1 tablespoon grated lemon peel
    Yellow food color (optional)
1 cup heavy cream
    Confectioners' sugar

1. Prepare and bake pie shell; let cool completely before filling. In large bowl, let egg whites warm to room temperature—about 1 hour.

2. Sprinkle gelatine over ¼ cup cold water, to soften; set aside. With wooden spoon, beat yolks slightly. Stir in lemon juice, ½ cup sugar, and the salt.

3. Cook, stirring, over hot, not boiling, water (water should not touch bottom of double-boiler top) until mixture thickens and forms coating on metal spoon—8 to 10 minutes.

4. Add gelatine; stir to dissolve. Add lemon peel, 2 drops color, if desired. Remove from water.

5. Turn into medium bowl; set in a larger bowl of ice cubes to chill, stirring occasionally, until as thick as unbeaten egg white— 10 minutes.

6. Meanwhile, beat whites at high speed until soft peaks form when beater is slowly raised (peaks bend slightly).

7. Beat in ½ cup sugar, 2 tablespoons at a time, beating after each addition. Beat until stiff peaks form when beater is raised.

8. With rotary beater, beat ½ cup cream until stiff. With wire whisk, gently fold gelatine mixture into whites just until combined. Gently fold in whipped cream. Mound high in pie shell. Refrigerate until firm—3 hours.

9. Beat ½ cup cream with 2 tablespoons confectioners' sugar until stiff. Turn into pastry bag with number-5 tip; make lattice on top, rosettes around edge.

Serves 8.

STRAWBERRY CHIFFON PIE

9-inch baked pie shell or
   unbaked graham-cracker crust

4 egg whites
4 egg yolks
1 tablespoon lemon juice

¼ teaspoon salt
1 cup granulated sugar
1 envelope unflavored gelatine
1 pint box fresh strawberries
1 cup heavy cream

1. Prepare and bake pie shell; let cool completely before filling. In large bowl, let egg whites warm to room temperature, about 1 hour.

2. In top of double boiler, beat egg yolks until frothy. Add lemon juice, salt and ½ cup sugar.

3. Place over hot water; cook, stirring, until thickened—about 7 to 8 minutes. Remove from heat.

4. Meanwhile, sprinkle gelatine over ¼ cup cold water in small bowl; let stand 5 minutes to soften. Then stir into egg mixture to dissolve.

5. Gently wash berries in cold water. Drain; hull. Set aside 6 whole berries for garnish.

6. In medium bowl, crush remaining berries with potato masher; add egg-gelatine mixture. Stir to mix well.

7. Set in a large bowl of ice cubes to chill; stir occasionally, until as thick as unbeaten egg white—10 minutes.

8. Meanwhile, beat whites at high speed until soft peaks form when beater is slowly raised. Beat in ½ cup sugar, 2 tablespoons at a time, beating after each addition. Beat until stiff peaks form when beater is slowly raised.

9. In medium bowl with rotary beater, beat ½ cup cream until stiff.

10. With wire whisk, gently fold gelatine mixture into whites just until combined. Gently fold in whipped cream. Mound high in pie shell. (If too thin to mound, refrigerate until slightly set—10 to 15 minutes.) Refrigerate until firm—3 hours.

11. Beat ½ cup cream with 2 tablespoons confectioners' sugar until stiff. Turn into pastry bag with number-5 tip; make lattice on top, rosettes around edge. Garnish with strawberries, if desired.

Serves 8.

RHUBARB CHIFFON PIE

4 cups cut rhubarb, in ½-inch pieces (about 1½ lb)	2 tablespoons sugar
1 cup sugar	9-inch baked pie shell
1 envelope unflavored gelatine	¾ cup heavy cream, whipped
4 eggs, separated	8 large strawberries

1. In large saucepan, combine rhubarb, 1 cup sugar, and 2 tablespoons water. Cook over medium heat, stirring, until sugar starts to dissolve. Cover, and cook, occasionally stirring gently, just until rhubarb is tender—about 10 minutes. Do not let boil, and be careful not to crush rhubarb when stirring.

2. Drain rhubarb in a strainer, reserving juice. Set aside ¼ cup of the juice in top of double boiler, to cool. Place the drained rhubarb in a medium bowl.

3. Return remaining juice to saucepan. Bring to boiling; boil, uncovered, until reduced to ½ cup—about 10 minutes. Combine with rhubarb in bowl.

4. Meanwhile, sprinkle gelatine over cooled juice in top of double boiler, to soften. Add egg yolks; beat until well blended. Cook over hot, not boiling, water, stirring constantly, until gelatine is dissolved —about 7 minutes.

5. Stir into rhubarb. Refrigerate, stirring occasionally, until consistency of unbeaten egg white—about 20 minutes.

6. In large bowl, with electric mixer at high speed, beat egg whites until stiff peaks form when beater is slowly raised. Gradually beat in 2 tablespoons sugar. Fold in rhubarb mixture just until combined. Turn into baked pie shell.

7. Refrigerate until firm—at least 2 hours. Just before serving, pipe whipped cream around edge. Garnish with strawberries.

Makes 6 to 8 servings.

BLACK BOTTOM PIE

9-inch baked graham-cracker pie shell	4 eggs, separated
	1 pkg (6 oz) semisweet chocolate pieces
1 tablespoon unflavored gelatine	1 teaspoon vanilla extract
1 cup sugar	¼ cup golden rum
½ teaspoon salt	¼ teaspoon cream of tartar
¼ cup cornstarch	½ cup heavy cream, whipped
2 cups milk	Chocolate curls, optional

1. Make pie shell. Cool completely on wire rack.

2. Sprinkle gelatine over ¼ cup cold water, to soften.

3. In saucepan, combine ½ cup sugar, salt, cornstarch; gradually stir in milk. Bring to boiling, stirring, until thickened.

4. In small bowl, beat egg yolks slightly; gradually stir in half the hot mixture; pour back into saucepan. Return custard to heat; cook, stirring, 2 minutes.

5. Remove saucepan from heat; measure 1½ cups custard. Add chocolate pieces and vanilla; stir until chocolate is melted; pour into pie shell. Refrigerate 45 minutes.

6. Add gelatine to remaining custard, stirring until gelatine dissolves. Cool to lukewarm. Add rum. Refrigerate mixture until it just begins to set.

7. In medium bowl, with portable electric mixer, beat egg whites

with cream of tartar, just until soft peaks form. Gradually beat in remaining ½ cup sugar, 2 tablespoons at a time, beating until stiff. Fold whites into rum-flavored custard; mound over chocolate mixture.* Refrigerate at least 6 hours. Garnish with rosettes of whipped cream, and chocolate curls, if desired.

Serves 8.

* If rum custard is too thin to mound, refrigerate to thicken slightly.

CRÈME DE MENTHE PIE

9-inch baked graham-cracker
pie shell

Filling:
2 envelopes unflavored gelatine
¾ cup milk
4 eggs, separated

½ cup sugar
⅛ teaspoon salt
⅓ cup green crème de menthe
¼ cup white crème de cacao
1 cup heavy cream
Green food color (optional)

1. Make Pie Shell. Cool completely on wire rack.

2. Make Filling: Sprinkle gelatine over milk in top of double boiler; let soften 3 minutes.

3. Add egg yolks, ¼ cup sugar, and the salt; beat with rotary beater or fork until well blended. Cook over boiling water, stirring constantly, about 5 minutes, or until gelatine dissolves and mixture thickens slightly and coats a metal spoon.

4. Remove double-boiler top from bottom. Stir crème de menthe and crème de cacao into custard mixture.

5. Set double-boiler top in bowl of ice cubes and water. Cool, stirring occasionally, 10 to 15 minutes, or until custard mixture is the consistency of unbeaten egg white.

6. Meanwhile, in medium bowl, whip cream. Refrigerate. Also, in large bowl, beat egg whites until soft peaks form when beater is slowly raised. Gradually beat in remaining ¼ cup sugar. Continue beating until stiff peaks form.

7. With rubber scraper or wire whisk, fold custard mixture into egg whites. Then fold in whipped cream and 1 or 2 drops food color, if desired, until mixture is just combined.

8. Turn into baked crumb crust. Refrigerate 3 hours, or until filling is firm.

9. Decorate with more whipped cream, if desired.

Makes 6 to 8 servings.

❧

EGGNOG PIE

Cookie Crust:
 1 pkg (4¾ oz) vanilla wafers
 ¼ teaspoon nutmeg
 ⅓ cup butter or margarine, melted

Eggnog Filling:
 2 tablespoons unflavored gelatine

2 cups eggnog
¼ teaspoon rum extract
1 cup heavy cream, whipped
 Nutmeg
 Whipped cream

1. Cookie Crust: Preheat oven to 300F. With rolling pin, crush wafers between 2 sheets of waxed paper. Measure 2 cups crumbs; toss with nutmeg and butter until well mixed. Press on bottom and side of 9-inch pie plate, but not on rim; bake 10 minutes. Cool on wire rack.

2. Filling: Sprinkle gelatine over 1 cup eggnog in top of double boiler; let stand 5 minutes, to soften. Then heat over hot—not boiling —water, stirring, until gelatine is dissolved. Remove from heat. Add rest of eggnog; stir until well mixed.

3. Refrigerate until mixture is as thick and syrupy as unbeaten egg white. With rotary beater, beat until frothy. Stir in rum extract. Then, with wire whip or rubber scraper, gently fold whipped cream into gelatine until well combined. Pour into cookie crust; refrigerate 3 to 4 hours, or until firm. Sprinkle with nutmeg. Garnish with 6 whipped-cream rosettes.

Makes 6 servings.

❧

NESSELRODE PIE

2 eggs
1 envelope unflavored gelatine
2 cups light cream
⅔ cup sugar
 Dash salt
1 tablespoon rum

½ cup bottled Nesselrode sauce

1 9-inch baked pie shell

½ cup heavy cream, whipped
½ square (1 oz) unsweetened
 chocolate

1. Make pie day before: Separate eggs, placing yolks in small bowl and whites in a large bowl. Let whites warm to room temperature.

2. Sprinkle gelatine over ¼ cup cold water in small bowl to soften.

3. In top of double boiler, heat cream slightly (do not boil); add ⅓ cup sugar, the salt and softened gelatine; heat, stirring to dissolve gelatine.

4. In medium bowl, beat egg yolks until thick; stir in some of cream mixture, mixing well. Return to rest of cream mixture in top of double boiler.

5. Place over boiling water; cook, stirring, until thickened—about 5 minutes. Refrigerate until syrupy and mixture just begins to set—takes about 1¼ hours (or set double boiler in bowl of ice, stirring occasionally, until it just begins to set). Stir in rum and ¼ cup Nesselrode.

6. Meanwhile, beat egg whites just until soft peaks form. Gradually beat in remaining ⅓ cup sugar, 2 tablespoons at a time. Continue beating until stiff peaks form when beater is slowly raised.

7. With wire whisk or rubber scraper, gently fold thickened egg-yolk mixture into whites, to combine well. Turn into pie shell. Refrigerate until well chilled and firm enough to cut—about 4 hours or overnight.

8. To serve, spread with a layer of whipped cream. Shave chocolate with vegetable parer over top. Decorate around edge with ¼ cup Nesselrode.

Makes 8 servings.

SHERRY CREAM PIE

3 eggs	½ cup sugar
1½ cups crushed (see Note) crisp chocolate cookies	1 cup milk
	⅛ teaspoon salt
¼ cup butter or regular margarine, melted	¼ teaspoon nutmeg
	½ cup sherry
1 envelope unflavored gelatine	1 cup heavy cream
¼ cup milk	

1. Make pie day before: Separate eggs, placing yolks in small bowl and whites in large bowl. Let whites warm to room temperature.

2. In medium bowl, combine cookie crumbs with butter; toss with fork to mix well. Turn into a 10-inch pie plate, patting evenly on bottom and side and up on edge to form a pie shell. Refrigerate at least 1 hour.

3. Sprinkle gelatine over ¼ cup milk in small bowl. Let stand 5 minutes to soften.

4. In top of double boiler, beat egg yolks slightly. Stir in sugar and 1 cup milk. Cook, stirring, over hot water, until slightly thickened —about 10 minutes. Add gelatine mixture, salt and nutmeg. Stir until gelatine is dissolved.

5. Gradually add sherry, stirring constantly. Refrigerate until mixture thickens and just begins to set.

6. Beat egg whites until stiff peaks form when beater is raised. Also, beat cream until stiff. With wire whisk or rubber scraper, fold whipped cream and custard mixture into whites, to combine well. Turn into pie shell.

7. Refrigerate overnight, or until firm enough to cut. Decorate top with more cookie crumbs or shaved chocolate, if desired.

Makes 8 servings.

Note: Crush cookies between two sheets of waxed paper with a rolling pin until very fine.

STRAWBERRY FLAN

Flan Shell:
- 1/4 cup butter or regular margarine, softened
- 2 tablespoons granulated sugar
- 3 tablespoons almond paste
- 1/2 teaspoon grated lemon peel
- 1 egg white
- 3/4 cup sifted* all-purpose flour

Rum Cream:
- 1 teaspoon unflavored gelatine
- 2 tablespoons granulated sugar
- 2 tablespoons flour
- Salt

- 1 egg yolk
- 1/2 cup milk
- 2 tablespoons rum
- 1 egg white, stiffly beaten
- 1/2 cup heavy cream
- 1 tablespoon confectioners' sugar
- 1 inch vanilla bean, scraped

- 1 1/2 pint boxes strawberries, washed and hulled
- 1/2 recipe Currant-Jelly Glaze, page 72

* Sift before measuring.

1. Make Flan Shell: Grease and lightly flour an 8-by-1 1/2-inch round layer-cake pan.

2. In a medium bowl, with electric mixer at medium speed, cream butter with 2 tablespoons granulated sugar, the almond paste, and lemon peel until well combined.

3. Add 1 egg white; beat at high speed until smooth. Gradually beat in 3/4 cup flour until well blended. Turn into prepared pan; pat evenly over bottom and side. (If too soft to work with, refrigerate 10 minutes.) Refrigerate 1 hour or longer.

4. Preheat oven to 300F. Bake shell 50 minutes, or until golden-brown. Let cool in pan on wire rack 15 minutes; then gently turn out onto rack, and let cool completely.

5. Make Rum Cream: In small saucepan, mix gelatine, granulated sugar, flour, and dash salt; mix well.

6. Beat egg yolk with milk and rum. Add to gelatine mixture; cook over medium heat, stirring constantly with wire whisk, until mixture is thickened and comes to boiling.

7. Pour into medium bowl; set bowl in pan of ice and water; let stand, stirring occasionally, until mixture begins to set—about 8 to 10 minutes. Fold in beaten egg white.

8. Beat cream with confectioners' sugar; fold into gelatine mixture. Stir in scraped vanilla bean. Spread evenly over flan shell. Refrigerate 30 minutes.

9. Arrange berries on rum cream in shell; brush with Currant-Jelly Glaze. Refrigerate until serving.

Makes 8 servings.

LEMON YOGURT PIE

2/3 cup boiling water
1 pkg (3 oz) lemon-flavored
   gelatine
1 tablespoon grated lemon peel
1 tablespoon lemon juice

2 containers (8-oz size) plain
   low fat yogurt

9-inch graham-cracker crust

Lemon slices (optional)
Fresh mint leaves (optional)

1. Pour boiling water over gelatine in medium bowl; stir to dissolve. Place in a large bowl of ice water; stir occasionally until slightly thickened, the consistency of unbeaten egg whites—about 20 minutes.

2. With wire whisk, beat in lemon peel, juice and yogurt until combined. Turn into graham-cracker crust.

3. Refrigerate 4 hours, or until well chilled and firm. To serve: Garnish with lemon slices and fresh mint.

Makes 6 to 8 servings.

STRAWBERRY YOGURT PIE

2 pkg (10-oz size) frozen sliced
  strawberries, thawed
1 envelope unflavored gelatine
  (see Note)

2 containers (8-oz size) plain
  low-fat yogurt
8-inch graham-cracker crust
Fresh strawberries (optional)

1. Drain ½ cup juice from strawberries into top of double boiler. Sprinkle gelatine over juice; let stand 5 minutes to soften.

2. Turn remaining strawberries and juice into a large bowl.

3. Place softened gelatine over boiling water in bottom of double boiler. Stir to dissolve gelatine. Stir into strawberries and juice.

4. Refrigerate until slightly thickened—consistency of unbeaten egg whites—about ½ hour. With wire whisk, fold in yogurt until well combined. Turn into pie shell.

5. Refrigerate until well chilled and firm enough to cut—about 8 hours or overnight (see Note). To serve, garnish with whole strawberries, if desired.

Makes 6 servings.

Note: To make pie set faster, use 1 ½ packages of gelatine.

SOUTHERN CHESS PIE

9-inch unbaked pie shell

1½ cups light-brown sugar, firmly
  packed
⅔ cup butter or regular
  margarine, softened
4 eggs

1½ teaspoons vanilla extract
1 cup dried currants
¾ cup coarsely chopped walnuts
  or pecans
Whipped cream, optional

1. Prepare pie shell. Refrigerate until ready to fill.

2. Preheat oven to 375F.

3. In bowl, with electric mixer at medium speed, beat sugar and butter until creamy.

4. Add eggs, one at a time, beating well after each addition. Stir in vanilla, currants, and nuts.

5. Turn into unbaked pie shell. Bake 40 to 50 minutes, or just until filling is set in center (shake pie gently; center should be firm).

6. Let cool on wire rack. If desired, serve garnished with whipped cream.

Makes 6 to 8 servings.

SLIPPED COCONUT CUSTARD PIE

9-inch baked pie shell

4 eggs
1 1/2 cups heavy cream
1 1/3 cups milk
1 can (4 oz) shredded coconut
1/2 cup granulated sugar
1 teaspoon vanilla extract
1/4 teaspoon coconut flavoring
1/4 teaspoon salt
2 tablespoons confectioners' sugar

1. Prepare and bake pie shell. Cool.
2. Preheat oven to 350F. Butter a 9-inch pie plate.
3. In medium bowl, with wire whisk or rotary beater, beat eggs slightly. Add 1 cup cream, the milk, 1 cup coconut, the granulated sugar, vanilla, coconut flavoring, and salt; beat until well mixed.
4. Pour into prepared pie plate. Place in shallow pan; pour cold water to about 1/2 inch around pie plate.
5. Bake 40 to 45 minutes, or until silver knife inserted in center comes out clean.
6. Remove pan from water. Let custard cool completely on wire rack; then refrigerate until well chilled—several hours or overnight.
7. Loosen custard from pie plate by carefully running a small spatula around edge and shaking plate gently. Holding plate just above rim of baked shell, carefully slip custard into shell.
8. Whip remaining cream with confectioners' sugar. Use to decorate edge of pie. Sprinkle cream with remaining coconut. (Toast coconut, if desired.)

Makes 6 to 8 servings.

CUSTARD PIE

Make as above, omitting coconut.

CONDENSED MILK CUSTARD PIE

3 eggs
½ teaspoon salt
1 teaspoon vanilla extract
1 can (14 oz) sweetened
   condensed milk

1½ cups hot water
1 (9-inch) unbaked pie shell with
   a high, fluted edge

Nutmeg

1. Preheat oven to 425F.

2. In large bowl, beat eggs; beat in salt, vanilla and condensed milk, mixing well. Blend in hot water until well combined.

3. Place pie shell on rack in middle of oven; pour in filling. Sprinkle top with nutmeg.

4. Bake 10 minutes. Reduce oven temperature to 300F. Bake 35 minutes or until a silver knife inserted into center comes out clean. Cool on wire rack, then refrigerate until well chilled.

Makes 6 to 8 servings.

COCONUT CUSTARD PIE

Add 1 cup flaked coconut to filling; bake as above.

OLD-FASHIONED PUMPKIN PIE

3 eggs
1 can (1 lb) pumpkin
½ cup light-brown sugar, packed
½ cup granulated sugar
1 teaspoon cinnamon
½ teaspoon ginger
¼ teaspoon nutmeg

⅛ teaspoon cloves
½ teaspoon salt
¾ cup milk
½ cup heavy cream

9-inch unbaked pie shell

Whipped-Cream Lattice (recipe
   follows)

1. Preheat oven to 350F. In large bowl, beat eggs slightly. Add pumpkin, sugars, spices, salt; beat until well blended. Slowly add milk and cream.

2. Pour into shell; bake 60 to 70 minutes, or until knife inserted in center comes out clean. Cool on rack. Just before serving, decorate pie with Whipped-Cream Lattice.

Makes 6 to 8 servings.

WHIPPED-CREAM LATTICE

1/2 cup heavy cream
1 tablespoon confectioners' sugar

1/4 teaspoon vanilla extract

1. Whip cream with sugar and vanilla until stiff.
2. Using cream in pastry bag with number-3 (large rosette) decorating tip, pipe cream in lattice design over top of pumpkin pie.

BRANDIED PUMPKIN PIE

9-inch unbaked pie shell

Filling:
1 cup canned pumpkin
1 cup evaporated milk, undiluted
1 cup light-brown sugar, packed
3 eggs, slightly beaten
1/4 cup brandy

1 teaspoon cinnamon
1 teaspoon nutmeg
1/2 teaspoon ginger
1/2 teaspoon mace
3/4 teaspoon salt

Heavy cream, whipped

1. Prepare pie shell. Preheat oven to 400F.
2. Make Filling: Combine pumpkin, milk and sugar in large bowl, blending until well mixed.
3. Stir in eggs, brandy, spices and salt; mix well.
4. Pour filling into prepared pie shell; bake 50 to 55 minutes, or until tip of sharp knife inserted in center comes out clean. Cool the pie on wire rack.
5. Just before serving, garnish pie with 6 to 8 rosettes of the whipped cream.
Makes 6 to 8 servings.

PUMPKIN PIE WITH CREAM CHEESE LATTICE

9-inch unbaked pie shell

Filling:
1 egg, slightly beaten
1 can (1 lb) pumpkin
1 can (14 oz) sweetened
    condensed milk
3/4 teaspoon cinnamon
1/2 teaspoon nutmeg

1/2 teaspoon salt

Lattice:
2 pkg (3-oz size) cream cheese,
    softened
2 tablespoons confectioners'
    sugar
1/4 cup light cream
    Preserved ginger

1. Prepare pie shell, using a piecrust mix, as package label directs, or using your own pastry. Refrigerate until used.

2. Preheat oven to 350F. Make Filling: In medium bowl, combine filling ingredients; stir until blended and smooth.

3. Turn into unbaked pie shell; bake about 1 hour, or just until tip of knife inserted in the center comes out clean.

4. Let pie cool completely on wire rack.

5. Make Lattice: With spoon, beat cheese and sugar in small bowl until fluffy. Gradually add cream, beating until light.

6. Using topping in pastry bag with number-3 (large rosette) decorating tip, pipe lattice effect over top of pie. Garnish cheese with bits of chopped ginger.

7. Refrigerate several hours, or until serving time.

Makes 8 servings.

BUTTERNUT SQUASH PIE

Filling:
3 eggs, slightly beaten
1/2 cup sugar
1/2 cup maple or maple-flavored
    syrup
1/2 teaspoon cinnamon
1/2 teaspoon ginger
1/2 teaspoon salt

2 pkg (12-oz size) thawed frozen
    winter squash, undrained*
1 cup light cream

9-inch unbaked pie shell

1/2 cup heavy cream, whipped
    Maple syrup

* Or substitute 3 cups canned
    pumpkin.

1. Preheat oven to 400F.

2. Make Filling: In large bowl, combine eggs, sugar, maple syrup, spices, salt, squash and light cream. Beat, with rotary beater, until mixture is smooth.

3. Turn most of filling into unbaked pie shell. Place on lowest shelf of oven; pour in rest of filling. Bake 55 to 60 minutes, or until filling is set in center when pie is gently shaken.

4. Let cool on wire rack. Serve pie slightly warm or cold. Garnish with whipped-cream rosettes drizzled with maple syrup.

Makes 8 servings.

BUTTERSCOTCH PECAN PIE

3 eggs
1 cup light corn syrup
⅛ teaspoon salt
1 teaspoon vanilla extract
1 cup sugar

2 tablespoons butter or regular
   margarine, melted
1 cup pecan halves

9-inch unbaked pie shell

Whipped cream

1. Preheat oven to 400F.

2. In medium bowl, beat eggs slightly. Add corn syrup, salt, vanilla, sugar, and butter; mix well. Stir in pecans. Pour into pie shell.

3. Bake 15 minutes. Reduce heat to 350F; bake 30 to 35 minutes, or until outer edge of filling seems set.

4. Let cool completely on wire rack. Just before serving, decorate with rosettes of whipped cream.

Makes 8 servings.

SOUTHERN PECAN PIE

9-inch unbaked pie shell

Filling:
4 eggs
1 cup sugar
1 cup light corn syrup
½ tablespoon flour

¼ teaspoon salt
1 teaspoon vanilla extract
¼ cup butter or margarine, melted
2 cups pecan halves

Whipped cream

1. Prepare the pie shell, and refrigerate.

2. Preheat oven to 350F.

3. Make Filling: In a medium bowl, with a rotary beater, beat the eggs well.

4. Add the sugar, corn syrup, flour, salt, and vanilla; beat until well combined.

5. Stir in butter and pecans, mixing well.

6. Turn into unbaked pie shell. Bake 50 minutes, or until the filling is set in the center when the pie is shaken gently.

7. Cool pie completely on a wire rack. Then chill it slightly before serving.

8. Just before serving, decorate pecan pie with whipped cream.
Makes 8 servings.

PEANUT-CARAMEL PIE

1/2 cup sugar
1 1/2 cups light corn syrup
1/4 cup butter or margarine
3 eggs, slightly beaten

1/2 teaspoon vanilla extract
1 cup salted peanuts, chopped

9-inch unbaked pie shell

1. Preheat oven to 350F.

2. In medium saucepan, combine sugar, corn syrup and butter; stir to mix well. Over medium heat, bring to boiling, stirring.

3. Slowly pour over beaten eggs in large bowl, stirring constantly. Stir in vanilla extract and the chopped nuts; mix well.

4. Pour filling into unbaked pie shell. Bake 45 minutes, or until mixture seems firm in center.

5. Cool on wire rack. If desired, serve with whipped cream or ice cream.

Makes 6 to 8 servings.

BLUM'S COFFEE-TOFFEE PIE

Pastry Shell:
1/2 pkg piecrust mix
1/4 cup light-brown sugar,
    firmly packed
3/4 cup finely chopped walnuts
1 square unsweetened chocolate,
    grated
1 teaspoon vanilla extract

Filling:
1/2 cup soft butter

3/4 cup granulated sugar
1 square unsweetened chocolate,
    melted and cooled
2 teaspoons instant coffee
2 eggs

2 cups heavy cream
2 tablespoons instant coffee
1/2 cup confectioners' sugar
Chocolate curls, page 346

1. Preheat the oven to 375F.

2. Make Pastry Shell: In medium bowl, combine piecrust mix with brown sugar, walnuts, and grated chocolate. Add 1 tablespoon water and the vanilla; using fork, mix until well blended. Turn into well-greased 9-inch pie plate; press firmly against bottom and side of pie plate. Bake for 15 minutes. Cool pastry shell in pie plate on wire rack.

3. Meanwhile, make Filling: In small bowl, with electric mixer at medium speed, beat the butter until it is creamy.

4. Gradually add granulated sugar, beating until light. Blend in cool melted chocolate and 2 teaspoons instant coffee.

5. Add 1 egg; beat 5 minutes. Add remaining egg; beat 5 minutes longer.

6. Turn filling into baked pie shell. Refrigerate the pie, covered, overnight.

7. Next day, make topping: In large bowl, combine cream with 2 tablespoons instant coffee and the confectioners' sugar. Refrigerate mixture, covered, 1 hour.

8. Beat cream mixture until stiff. Decorate pie with topping, using pastry bag with number-6 decorating tip, if desired. Garnish with chocolate curls. Refrigerate the pie at least 2 hours.

Makes 8 servings.

CHOCOLATE MOUSSE PIE

8- or 9-inch baked pie shell or graham-cracker pie shell

1⅓ cups semisweet-chocolate pieces

2 tablespoons sugar
4 eggs, separated
Whipped cream

1. Prepare and bake pie shell. Let cool.

2. In top of double boiler, combine chocolate, sugar, and ¼ cup water. Cook over hot, not boiling, water, stirring frequently, until chocolate is melted.

3. Remove from hot water; let cool slightly. Add egg yolks; stir until well combined.

4. Beat egg whites just until stiff. Fold into chocolate mixture until well combined. Turn into pie shell.

5. Refrigerate until well chilled—at least 6 hours. At serving time, decorate top with whipped cream.

Makes 6 to 8 servings.

Small Pastries

If you're counting calories, think small when you're thinking desserts.

Here are tiny pastries you might find arranged in tempting splendor on a pastry tray in a fine restaurant: bite-size pecan, lemon or fruit-filled tarts; jam-filled strips of Linzer Torte and miniature pies—all less than half the calories.

Of course, we've the usual flaky fruit turnovers and delicious warm dumplings for noncalorie counters. But whatever your choice, we think you'll agree that less was never more!

❧

FLUTED TART SHELLS

1. Prepare pastry for 2-crust pie, page 6.
2. Divide pastry in half; divide each half into 5 parts.
3. On lightly floured surface, roll each part into a 5-inch circle. Use each circle to line a 3-inch fluted tart pan, pressing pastry evenly to bottom and side of each pan; trim.
4. Prick each tart shell well with fork; refrigerate 30 minutes.
5. Meanwhile, preheat oven to 450F.
6. Bake shells, on large cookie sheet, 10 to 12 minutes, or until golden-brown.
7. Cool completely on wire racks; then carefully remove shells from pans. Fill as desired.

Note: For thicker shells, divide pastry in half; divide each half into 4 parts. Proceed as above.

Makes 8 or 10.

APPLE-MINCE TARTS

1 pkg (10 or 11 oz) piecrust mix
½ cup unsifted all-purpose flour
⅓ cup sugar
¼ cup butter or margarine
1½ cups prepared mincemeat

2½ cups thinly sliced, pared
    Golden Delicious, Cortland
    or Northern Spy apples (3)

Hard Sauce, page 351

1. Preheat oven to 400F.
2. Prepare piecrust mix as package label directs.
3. Divide pastry in half; divide each half into six parts.
4. On lightly floured surface, roll each part into a 4-inch circle. Use each circle of pastry to line 12 (2½-inch) muffin pans.
5. In small bowl, combine flour and sugar. With pastry blender or 2 knives, cut in butter until mixture resembles coarse crumbs.
6. Spoon 2 tablespoons mincemeat into bottom of each tart shell; cover with apple. Sprinkle each with 1 tablespoon crumb mixture.
7. Bake 30 to 35 minutes. Remove to wire rack; cool 15 minutes before removing from pans. Serve warm with Hard Sauce or whipped cream.

Makes 12 servings.

LEMON CURD TARTS

Filling:
3 eggs
2 tablespoons grated lemon peel
½ cup lemon juice

¾ cup butter, softened
1 cup plus 2 tablespoons sugar

8 (3-inch) or 12 (2½-inch)
    baked tart shells
½ cup heavy cream

1. Make Filling: In top of double boiler, beat eggs well with a fork. Add lemon peel and juice, butter, and 1 cup sugar; mix well till combined.
2. Place over simmering water (water should not touch bottom of double-boiler top); cook egg-lemon mixture, stirring constantly, about 15 to 20 minutes, or until mixture forms a thick coating on a metal spoon and mounds slightly.
3. Remove mixture from heat, and turn it into a bowl. Refrigerate the filling, covered, several hours, or until it is well chilled.

4. To serve: Divide the lemon filling into 8 tart shells.

5. In a small bowl, using a rotary beater, beat heavy cream with 2 tablespoons sugar until stiff. Decorate tarts with whipped cream, using a spoon or a pastry bag with decorating tip. Sprinkle whipped cream with grated lemon peel, if desired.

Makes 8 or 12 tarts.

LIME CURD TARTS

Substitute 1 tablespoon grated lime peel for the grated lemon peel, and ½ cup lime juice for the lemon juice. Tint a pale green, if desired, by adding 2 drops green food color.

PEAR MARMALADE TARTS

1 can (1 lb, 1 oz) pear halves	⅛ teaspoon cloves
½ cup sugar	12 (3-inch) baked tart shells
1½ teaspoons lemon peel	½ cup heavy cream, whipped
2 teaspoons lemon juice	

1. Drain pear halves; measure liquid. If necessary, add water to make 1 cup. In 3-quart saucepan, combine pear liquid and sugar.

2. Bring to boiling, stirring, until sugar is dissolved. Boil gently, uncovered, until syrup is thickened—about 10 minutes.

3. Meanwhile, chop pears finely in bowl. To syrup, add pears, lemon peel, juice, and the cloves. Cook, uncovered and stirring occasionally, over medium heat until consistency of marmalade— about 5 minutes.

4. Turn into bowl; refrigerate, covered, until cold, or until ready to use. (Can be made a day or two ahead of time.)

5. To serve: Fill tart shells with pear marmalade, 1 heaping tablespoonful for each. Top each with a spoonful of whipped cream.

Makes 12.

✂

DAMSON PLUM TARTS

1 pkg (11 oz) piecrust mix
¾ cup butter or regular margarine,
    softened
¾ cup sugar
    Dash salt

3 eggs
¾ cup damson plum preserves
½ teaspoon vanilla extract
¾ cup heavy cream, whipped

1. Prepare piecrust mix as package label directs. Divide pastry in half and each half into five parts.

2. On lightly floured surface, roll each part into a 5-inch circle; use to line 3½-inch fluted tart pans, pressing pastry evenly into pans; trim. Reroll and cut pastry trimmings to make two more tart shells. Refrigerate on cookie sheet until baking time.

3. Preheat oven to 350F.

4. In medium bowl, with electric mixer at medium speed, beat butter with sugar and salt until light. Add eggs, one at a time, beating after each addition until well blended. Add the damson plum preserves and vanilla extract, beating until they are well combined.

5. Fill each tart shell with ¼ cup filling. Bake 35 minutes, or until top is golden and puffed. (Filling shrinks as it cools.) Let tarts cool completely on wire rack.

6. To serve: Gently remove tarts from pans. Top each with a spoonful of whipped cream.

Makes 12.

✂

FRUIT TARTS

Tart Shells:
  ½ cup butter or regular
      margarine, softened
  ¼ cup sugar
  ¼ teaspoon salt
  1 egg white
1½ cups sifted* all-purpose flour

  Rum Cream, below

* Sift before measuring.

Fruits: whole strawberries, blueberries, red raspberries, sliced bananas, seedless green grapes, apricot halves, black cherries (fresh, frozen, or canned), canned small pineapple rings or tidbits

Apricot Glaze or Currant-Jelly Glaze, page 72

1. Make Tart Shells: In medium bowl, with fork, blend butter, sugar, salt, and egg white until smooth and well combined.

2. Gradually stir in flour, mixing until smooth.

3. For each tart, use 2 teaspoons dough. Press evenly into 2½- to 3-inch tart pans of assorted shapes and sizes. Set pans on cookie sheet.

4. Refrigerate 30 minutes.

5. Preheat oven to 375F. Bake tart shells 12 to 15 minutes, or until light golden. Cool in pans on wire rack a few minutes; then turn out, and cool completely before filling.

6. To fill tarts: Spoon several teaspoons of Rum Cream into each shell. Refrigerate.

7. Top with fruit. (Drain fruit very well before using.) Brush yellow or light fruit with warm Apricot Glaze and red or dark fruit with Currant-Jelly Glaze.

8. Refrigerate until ready to serve.

Makes 1½ dozen.

Note: If desired, make Tart Shells and Rum Cream day before. Then assemble tarts several hours before serving.

RUM CREAM

1 . teaspoon unflavored gelatine	2 tablespoons rum
2 tablespoons granulated sugar	1 egg white, stiffly beaten
2 tablespoons flour	½ cup heavy cream
Salt	1 tablespoon confectioners' sugar
1 egg yolk	1 inch vanilla bean, scraped, or
½ cup milk	½ teaspoon vanilla extract

1. In small saucepan, mix gelatine, granulated sugar, flour, and dash salt; mix well.

2. Beat egg yolk with milk and rum. Add to gelatine mixture; cook over medium heat, stirring constantly with wire whisk, until mixture is thickened and comes to boiling.

3. Pour into medium bowl; set bowl in pan of ice and water; let stand, stirring occasionally, until mixture begins to set—about 8 to 10 minutes. Fold in beaten egg white.

4. Beat cream with confectioners' sugar; fold into gelatine mixture. Stir in vanilla. Refrigerate until ready to use—at least 30 minutes.

Makes about 1½ cups.

CURRANT-JELLY GLAZE

½ cup red-currant jelly   1 tablespoon kirsch

1. In small saucepan, over moderate heat, stir currant jelly until melted. Remove from heat.
2. Stir in kirsch. Use warm, on tarts. (If glaze becomes too thick, reheat gently, and add a little hot water.)
Makes about ½ cup.

APRICOT GLAZE

½ cup apricot preserves

1. In small saucepan, over medium heat, stir apricot preserves until melted. (If preserves seem too thick, thin with ½ to 1 tablespoon hot water.)
2. Strain. Use warm, on tarts.
Makes about ½ cup.

MINIATURE COCONUT TARTS

Pastry:
1⅓ cups sifted* all-purpose flour
 ⅓ cup sugar
 ¼ teaspoon salt
 ¾ cup butter or margarine

* Sift before measuring.

1 egg, slightly beaten

Filling:
 1 egg
 1 can (3½ oz) flaked coconut
 ⅔ cup sugar

1. Make Pastry: Sift flour with ⅓ cup sugar and the salt into medium bowl. With pastry blender, cut in butter until mixture is like coarse crumbs. With a fork, stir in the beaten egg.
2. Knead slightly until mixture holds together. Wrap in waxed paper; refrigerate several hours, or until firm.
3. Preheat oven to 375F.
4. Make Filling: With fork, beat egg in small bowl. Add coconut and sugar; mix well.
5. For each tart, pinch off about 1 teaspoon chilled dough. Press into 2-by-½-inch tartlet pan, to make a shell ⅛ inch thick. Fill each with 1 teaspoon filling.
6. Bake tarts (about 24 at a time), set on cookie sheets, 12 minutes, or until coconut filling is golden-brown.

7. Place pans on wire rack; cool slightly. With small spatula, gently remove tarts from pans.

Makes about 4 dozen.

✠

PECAN TARTLETS

1 pkg (9½ or 11 oz) piecrust mix

Filling:
2 eggs
½ cup sugar
⅓ cup light corn syrup
2 tablespoons golden rum

1 teaspoon flour
½ teaspoon salt
½ teaspoon vanilla extract
2 tablespoons butter or regular margarine, melted
1 cup pecan halves

1. Prepare piecrust mix as package label directs. Divide in half. Using palms of hands, roll each half into a 15-inch-long roll. Cut roll into 15 pieces. Press each piece evenly into a shallow 2-inch tart pan, to line pan. Refrigerate while making filling.

2. Preheat oven to 350F.

3. Make Filling: In medium bowl, with rotary beater, beat eggs well.

4. Add sugar, syrup, rum, flour, salt, and vanilla; beat until well combined. Stir in butter and pecans, mixing well.

5. Spoon about 1 tablespoon filling into each pastry-lined pan.

6. Bake 15 to 20 minutes, or until filling is firm and golden.

7. Let tarts cool in pans on wire rack at least 10 minutes, or until completely cool.

Makes 30 tarts.

✠

MAIDS OF HONOR

1 pkg piecrust mix

Almond Topping:
⅓ cup egg whites (2 egg whites)
Dash salt
1 cup confectioners' sugar

1 cup ground blanched almonds
¼ teaspoon almond or vanilla extract

⅔ cup raspberry or strawberry jam

1. Make pastry as package label directs. Shape into a ball; divide in half.

2. On lightly floured surface, roll out one half into 12-by-10-inch

rectangle. With 3-inch round cookie cutter, cut into 12 circles. Fit each into a 2¼-inch muffin-pan cup. Repeat with rest of dough. Refrigerate.

3. Preheat oven to 350F.

4. Make Almond Topping: In medium bowl, with electric mixer, beat egg whites with salt until soft peaks form when beater is slowly raised. Gradually beat in sugar, 2 tablespoons at a time, beating well after each addition; continue beating until well blended and thick. Stir in almonds and extract.

5. Spoon 1 teaspoon jam into each pastry-lined muffin cup. Spoon about 1 tablespoon almond topping over jam.

6. Bake 25 to 30 minutes, or until topping is puffy and golden. Carefully remove from cups to wire rack; cool completely.

Makes 2 dozen.

APPLE-CIDER TURNOVERS

1½ pkg (11-oz size) piecrust mix

Filling:
 1 cup cider
½ cup granulated sugar
 4 cups sliced pared apple
⅓ cup seedless raisins
 1 tablespoon lemon juice

2 teaspoons cornstarch
¼ teaspoon cinnamon
2 tablespoons cider

2 tablespoons butter or
   margarine, softened
   Confectioners' sugar

1. Prepare pastry as package label directs; form into a ball; wrap in waxed paper; refrigerate until ready to use.

2. Make Filling: In large skillet, combine 1 cup cider and the granulated sugar. Bring to boiling, stirring to dissolve sugar. Add apple, raisins and lemon juice. Simmer gently, uncovered, 3 to 5 minutes, stirring occasionally.

3. In small bowl, combine cornstarch and cinnamon with 2 tablespoons cider; stir until smooth. Stir into apple mixture. Cook, stirring, until thickened and translucent—2 to 3 minutes. Let cool completely.

4. To make turnovers: Preheat oven to 425F. Divide pastry into eight parts on lightly floured pastry cloth; roll each part into a 7-inch circle. Moisten edge of each circle. Brush with butter. Spread about ¼ cup filling on half of each circle; fold over. Fold edge of bottom crust over top; crimp edges. Make three gashes in center for steam to escape.

5. Bake, on ungreased cookie sheet, about 30 minutes, or until golden-brown.

6. Cool partially on wire rack. Serve warm, sprinkled with confectioners' sugar.

Makes 8.

※

MARMALADE PIES

1 pkg (9½ or 11 oz) piecrust mix   Milk
1 jar (12 oz) orange marmalade   Granulated sugar

1. Preheat oven to 400F.

2. Make piecrust as package label directs. Divide dough into 8 parts.

3. On lightly floured surface, roll out each part into a 5-inch circle. Spoon 1½ tablespoons marmalade on half of each circle, leaving a half-inch edge. Moisten edge with water.

4. Fold other half over marmalade; press edges together with tines of fork, to seal. Brush lightly with milk. Sprinkle with sugar. Place pies on ungreased cookie sheet.

5. Bake 20 minutes, or until golden-brown.

6. With wide spatula, remove to wire rack. Cool slightly. Serve warm.

Makes 8.

※

FRESH STRAWBERRIES WITH STRAWBERRY SAUCE IN COOKIE SHELLS

1 quart fresh strawberries   Cookie Shells, below

Strawberry Sauce:
2 pkg (10-oz size) frozen
    strawberries, partially thawed

1. Wash berries; drain. Remove hulls. Refrigerate until serving.

2. Make Sauce: Press frozen strawberries through sieve, or blend in electric blender, covered, about 1 minute. Refrigerate until serving.

3. At serving time, place strawberries in Cookie Shells, dividing evenly. Pour strawberry sauce over berries, dividing evenly. Serve at once.

Makes 10 to 12 servings.

COOKIE SHELLS

1 pkg (12 oz) sugar-cookie mix   *1 egg*
1 teaspoon butter or margarine

1. Preheat oven to 375F. Prepare cookie mix as package label directs, using butter and egg. Divide dough into 12 balls.
2. On ungreased cookie sheets, pat each ball to make a 4-inch circle, leaving spaces between cookies. Bake four at a time (no more) about 7 minutes, or until golden and center is firm. Do not underbake.
3. Meanwhile, grease bottom of four (6-ounce) custard cups.
4. Let cookies cool on cookie sheet 1 minute. Then with broad spatula, remove one at a time and mold over bottoms of custard cups, to form a shell.
Note: Cookie shells may be made several days ahead, unless weather is very humid, and stored at room temperature in a closed tin container to keep crisp.

APPLE DUMPLINGS

1½ pkg (9½-to-11-oz size) piecrust   *¾ teaspoon ground cinnamon*
*   mix*   *6 large baking apples (4 lb)—*
3 tablespoons butter or   *   Rome Beauty, Northern Spy*
*   margarine, softened*   *2 tablespoons lemon juice*
3 tablespoons granulated sugar   *   Whole cloves*
1 tablespoon dark raisins   *1 egg yolk*
2 tablespoons chopped walnuts   *   Hard Sauce, page 351*

1. Make pastry as package label directs. Form pastry into a flat, 8-inch round; wrap in waxed paper; refrigerate.
2. In small bowl, combine 3 tablespoons butter, granulated sugar, raisins, walnuts and cinnamon; blend with fork. Core apples with corer. Pare apples and brush with lemon juice. Using spoon, fill hollows with raisin-walnut mixture.
3. Preheat oven to 425F. Grease well a shallow baking pan 15½ by 10½ by 1 inch.
4. On lightly floured pastry cloth or floured surface, divide pastry evenly into sixths. Form each piece into a round ball. Flatten each piece; then roll out from center into an 8½-inch square. Trim edges, using pastry wheel for decorative edge. Save trimmings.
5. Place an apple in center of each square; brush edges lightly

with water. Bring each corner of square to top of apple; pinch edges of pastry together firmly, to cover apple completely.

6. Reroll trimmings ¼ inch thick. With knife, cut out 24 leaves, 1¾ inches long and ¾ inch wide. Brush one end of each leaf lightly with water.

7. Press leaves on top of dumplings; put clove in center. Arrange in pan. Brush with yolk mixed with 1 tablespoon water. Bake, brushing once with juices in pan, 40 minutes, or until pastry is browned and apples are tender when tested with a wooden pick.

8. Meanwhile, make Hard Sauce.

9. With broad spatula, remove dumplings to serving dishes. Serve warm, topped with Hard Sauce.

Makes 6 servings.

GLAZED APPLE DUMPLINGS

Pastry for 2-crust pie
6 medium baking apples
6 tablespoons granulated sugar
½ teaspoon nutmeg

6 tablespoons butter or
    margarine, softened

Syrup:
    2 cups light-brown sugar,
        firmly packed

1. Make pastry; form into a ball. Wrap in waxed paper, and refrigerate until ready to use.

2. Pare and core apples.

3. Combine sugar and nutmeg.

4. On lightly floured surface, divide pastry into 6 parts.

5. Roll each part into a 7- to 9-inch circle or square.

6. Place apple in center of each. Fill hollow with 1 tablespoon sugar-nutmeg mixture and 1 tablespoon butter. Mold pastry around each apple, covering completely.

7. Place in 13-by-9-by-2-inch baking pan; refrigerate 30 minutes.

8. Meanwhile, preheat oven to 425F.

9. Make Syrup: In small saucepan, combine sugar with 1 cup water. Over medium heat, dissolve sugar, stirring. Bring to boiling; boil gently 5 minutes.

10. Spoon 1 tablespoon syrup over each dumpling; bake, uncovered, 10 minutes.

11. Remove from oven; pour remaining syrup over dumplings. Continue baking 25 to 30 minutes, basting occasionally with syrup, or until apples are tender.

12. Serve warm, with syrup spooned over, and with cream, if desired.

Makes 6.

❖

PEACH DUMPLINGS

2 cans (1-lb, 1-oz size) cling-peach
  halves
1 pkg (9½ to 11 oz) piecrust mix
3 tablespoons light-brown sugar

½ teaspoon nutmeg
6 teaspoons butter or margarine

Hard Sauce, page 351

1. Place peach halves on paper towels to drain. (You should have 12 halves.)

2. Prepare piecrust mix as package label directs. Shape into a ball; divide into sixths. On lightly floured surface, roll out each piece into a 6½-inch square. If desired, reroll any trimmings, and cut into small leaf shapes, for decoration.

3. Preheat oven to 425F. Grease a 13-by-9-by-2-inch baking pan.

4. Combine brown sugar and nutmeg.

5. Place a peach half in center of each pastry square. Sprinkle each with 1½ teaspoons sugar mixture, and top with 1 teaspoon butter and another peach half. Bring pastry up, covering peach completely, and press edges together, to seal. Decorate with pastry leaves, if desired. Arrange in prepared pan.

6. Bake 25 minutes, or until golden-brown. Serve warm, with Hard Sauce.

Makes 6 servings.

❖

PEAR DUMPLINGS

1½ pkg (11-oz size) piecrust mix
6 ripe (but not soft) pears (about
  2½ lbs)
¼ cup sugar

1 teaspoon ground cinnamon
¼ cup lemon juice
1 egg yolk
Custard Sauce, page 348

1. Preheat oven to 400F. Prepare pastry as package label directs. On lightly floured surface, divide pastry into seven parts. With a stockinette-covered rolling pin, roll six pieces of pastry into 7-inch squares.

2. Pare pears, leaving stems on. Combine ¼ cup sugar and the

cinnamon. Sprinkle each pear with lemon juice, then with cinnamon-sugar.

3. Slip center of a square of pastry over stem of each pear; mold pastry around pears, covering completely. Place in lightly greased shallow, 15½-by-10½-inch baking pan.

4. Roll remaining piece of pastry into a 9-inch circle. Using a 3-inch cookie cutter, cut out 3 rounds. Cut centers from each with a one-inch cutter. Reroll trimmings for three more rounds.

5. Slip a circle of pastry over each stem. Blend 1 egg yolk with 1 teaspoon water. Brush pastry with egg-yolk mixture. Bake 45 to 50 minutes.

6. Make Custard Sauce. Serve warm dumplings with chilled custard sauce.

Makes 6 servings.

Fabulous Fruit Tarts

You can adapt this flaky pastry crust and rich cream filling, given here, to any fruit you choose. Just top with colorful fresh fruit in season; in winter use canned or frozen fruit. The tart pan comes in all sizes: small individual ones, to one large enough to serve 12.

PASTRY FOR FABULOUS TARTS

1½ cups sifted* all-purpose flour
 ¼ cup sugar
 ¼ teaspoon salt

½ cup butter or regular
   margarine
1 egg

* Sift before measuring.

1. With fork, blend flour, sugar and salt in medium bowl, to combine well.

2. With pastry blender, cut in butter until it is in small particles —should be the size of small peas. Stir in egg; blend well.

3. Form into ball; refrigerate 1 hour, or until ready to roll out.

Makes enough pastry for one 10-, 11- or 12-inch shell; two 7½-inch shells; six 4- or 5-inch shells.

PASTRY FOR 9-INCH TART SHELL

¾ cup sifted* all-purpose flour
 2 tablespoons sugar
⅛ teaspoon salt

¼ cup butter or margarine
1 egg yolk

* Sift before measuring.

Follow directions for Pastry, above.

❖

PASTRY CREAM

⅓ cup sugar
⅛ teaspoon salt
1½ tablespoons cornstarch
1½ cups milk

3 egg yolks, slightly beaten
¾ teaspoon vanilla extract
½ teaspoon almond extract

1. In small saucepan, mix sugar, salt and cornstarch. Stir in milk.

2. Cook, stirring constantly, over medium heat until mixture thickens and begins to boil; boil 1 minute. Remove from heat.

3. Add a little hot mixture to egg yolks, mixing well. Return to pan.

4. Cook, stirring constantly, until mixture is thick and bubbly.

5. Stir in extracts. Let cool to room temperature—about 1 hour. Refrigerate, with waxed paper placed directly on surface, until well chilled.

Makes about 1⅔ cups.

Note: You may make the pastry cream a day ahead and refrigerate until ready to use. You can also make and bake the pastry shells a day or two ahead, but store at room temperature. Then, on day of serving, put them together with fruit and glaze as directed.

❖

PINEAPPLE-STRAWBERRY TART

Pastry for 12-inch shell page 80
2 cans (1-lb size) pineapple slices
    in syrup, chilled
About 12 large strawberries

Glaze:
    Pineapple syrup

1 tablespoon arrowroot or
    cornstarch
1 tablespoon lemon juice
    Yellow food color (optional)

2 times recipe Pastry Cream,
    above

1. Roll pastry on lightly floured pastry cloth to form a 14-inch circle. Lift into a fluted 12-inch pan with removable bottom in place. Press evenly to bottom and side all around. Trim pastry, if necessary. Prick all over with fork. Refrigerate until ready to bake.

2. Preheat oven to 400F. Bake pastry shell 15 minutes. Cool on wire rack.

3. Several hours before serving, gently remove outer rim from pastry, keeping shell on bottom. Place on serving platter.

4. Drain pineapple slices, reserving syrup. Place pineapple on

paper towels to drain very well. Wash and drain strawberries. Reserve 1 large berry for center. Remove hulls from rest. Slice hulled berries in half lengthwise.

5. Make Glaze: Measure ½ cup pineapple syrup into small saucepan. Add arrowroot; stir until dissolved. Add ½ cup more syrup and the lemon juice. Bring to boiling, stirring. Cook until thickened and translucent. Add a few drops of yellow food color. Refrigerate until cool.

6. Fill pastry shell with chilled pastry cream. Arrange strawberry halves around outside of shell and pineapple slices in center. Top with reserved berry. Brush pineapple and strawberries all over with glaze to cover completely. Refrigerate 1 hour to chill well.

Makes 10 to 12 servings.

KADOTA FIG TART

Pastry for 12-inch shell, page 80

4 cans (1-lb size) Kadota figs, chilled

Glaze:
  Fig juice

1 tablespoon arrowroot or cornstarch
1 tablespoon lemon juice

¼ cup light rum
2 times recipe Pastry Cream, page 81

1. Roll pastry on lightly floured pastry cloth to form a 14-inch circle. Lift into a fluted 12-inch pan with removable bottom in place. Press evenly to bottom and side all around. Trim pastry if necessary. Prick with fork all over. Refrigerate until ready to bake.

2. Preheat oven to 400F. Bake pastry shell 12 minutes. Let cool on wire rack.

3. Several hours before serving, gently remove outer rim from pastry, keeping shell on bottom.

4. Drain figs well, reserving juice.

5. Make Glaze: Measure ½ cup fig juice into small saucepan. Add arrowroot; stir until dissolved. Add ½ cup more fig juice. Bring to boiling, stirring. Cook until thickened and translucent. Stir in lemon juice. Refrigerate until cool.

6. Add rum to chilled pastry cream. Fill pastry shell with pastry cream. Arrange figs to cover pastry cream. Brush figs all over with glaze, to cover completely. Refrigerate 1 hour, to chill well.

Makes 10 to 12 servings.

Ω

FRUIT COMPOTE TART

Pastry for two 7½-inch shells,
    page 80

1 can (1 lb) pear halves, chilled
1 can (1 lb) pineapple slices,
    chilled
2 cans (1-lb size) whole apricots,
    chilled

Glaze:
½ cup liquid from fruit
1 teaspoon arrowroot or
    cornstarch
1 teaspoon lemon juice

Pastry Cream, page 81

1. Divide pastry in half. Roll each half on lightly floured surface to form a 9½-inch circle. Lift each into a fluted 7½-inch pan with removable bottom. Press evenly to bottom and side. Trim, if necessary. Prick all over with fork. Refrigerate until ready to bake.

2. Preheat oven to 400F. Bake pastry shells 15 minutes. Cool on wire rack.

3. About 1 hour before serving, gently remove outer rims from pastry, keeping shells on bottoms.

4. Drain fruits, reserving enough juice from each to make ½ cup in all.

5. Measure ¼ cup fruit juices into saucepan. Add arrowroot; stir until dissolved. Add ¼ cup more combined juices. Bring to boiling, stirring. Cool until thickened and translucent. Stir in lemon juice. Refrigerate until cool.

6. Fill pastry shells with chilled pastry cream. Arrange fruit to cover cream. Brush with glaze, to cover completely. Refrigerate 1 hour, to chill well.

Makes 2 tarts, 12 servings.

Ω

HONEYDEW-MELON-BALL TART

Pastry for a 9-inch Tart Shell,
    page 80

1 to 1½ large, ripe honeydew
    melons
Pastry Cream, page 81

Glaze:
½ cup apple jelly
1 tablespoon lemon juice
1 thin lemon slice

1. Roll pastry on lightly floured pastry cloth to form a 12-inch circle. Lift into a fluted 9-inch pan with removable bottom in place.

Press evenly to bottom and side; pastry should come halfway up the side. Pick with fork. Refrigerate until ready to bake.

2. Preheat oven to 400F. Bake pastry shell 15 minutes. Cool on wire rack.

3. About 1 hour before serving, gently remove outer rim from pastry, keeping shell on bottom.

4. Cut melons in half. Using a 2-inch ice-cream scoop, make melon balls. Drain on paper towels.

5. Fill pastry shell with chilled pastry cream. Arrange melon balls to cover pastry cream.

6. Just before serving, melt jelly over low heat; stir in lemon juice. Use to brush over melon balls. Garnish with a twist of lemon. Serve at once.

Makes 8 servings.

MELON MÉLANGE

Pastry for 9-inch Tart Shell,
page 80

4 cups assorted melon balls,
chilled (cantaloupe,
honeydew, watermelon)

Pastry Cream, page 81
2 tablespoons light rum

Glaze:
1/2 cup apple jelly
1 tablespoon lemon juice

1. Roll pastry on lightly floured pastry cloth to form a 12-inch circle. Lift into a fluted 9-inch pan with removable bottom in place. Press evenly to bottom and side; pastry should come halfway up the side. Prick with fork. Refrigerate until ready to bake.

2. Preheat oven to 400F. Bake pastry shell 15 minutes. Cool on wire rack.

3. About 1 hour before serving, gently remove outer rim from pastry, keeping shell on bottom.

4. Drain melon on paper towels.

5. Add rum to chilled pastry cream. Fill pastry shell with pastry cream. Arrange assorted melon balls over top.

6. Just before serving, melt jelly over low heat; stir in lemon juice. Use to brush over melon balls.

Makes 8 servings.

FRESH STRAWBERRY TART

Pastry for a 9-inch Tart Shell,
  page 80

2 pint boxes strawberries, chilled
Pastry Cream, page 81

Glaze:
³⁄₄ cup apple jelly
  1 tablespoon lemon juice

1. Roll pastry on lightly floured pastry cloth to form a 12-inch circle. Lift into a fluted 9-inch pan with removable bottom in place. Press evenly to bottom and side all around; pastry should come halfway up the side. Prick all over with fork. Refrigerate until ready to bake.

2. Preheat oven to 400F. Bake pastry shell 15 minutes. Cool on wire rack.

3. About 1½ hours before serving, gently remove outer rim from pastry, keeping shell on bottom.

4. Wash and hull strawberries; drain.

5. Fill pastry shell with chilled pastry cream. Arrange strawberries to cover pastry cream.

6. Make glaze: Melt jelly over low heat; stir in lemon juice. Use to brush over berries, coating completely. Refrigerate about 1 hour, to chill well.

Makes 8 to 10 servings.

ROYAL ANNE CHERRY TARTS

Pastry, page 67

2 jars (1-lb, 1-oz size) Royal Anne
  cherries

Glaze:
½ cup cherry juice

1 teaspoon arrowroot or
  cornstarch
1 teaspoon lemon juice

Pastry Cream, page 81

1. Divide pastry into 6 pieces. Roll each on lightly floured pastry cloth to form a 6-inch circle. Lift each into a fluted 4-inch pan with removable bottom. Press evenly to bottom and side. Trim pastry, if necessary. Prick with fork. Refrigerate until ready to bake.

2. Preheat oven to 400F. Bake pastry shells 15 minutes. Cool on wire rack.

3. About 1 hour before serving, gently remove outer rims from

pastry, keeping shells on bottoms.

4. Drain cherries, reserving juice. Gently remove pits, if desired.

5. Make Glaze: Measure ¼ cup cherry juice into small saucepan. Add arrowroot; stir until dissolved. Add ¼ cup more cherry juice. Bring to boiling; stirring. Cook until thickened and translucent. Stir in lemon juice. Refrigerate until cool.

6. Fill pastry shells with chilled pastry cream. Arrange cherries to cover cream. Brush cherries all over with glaze, to cover completely. Refrigerate 1 hour, to chill well.

Makes 6 servings.

GREEN-GRAPE TARTS

Pastry for six 4- to 5-inch
  shells, page 67
Pastry Cream, page
¾ lb seedless green grapes,
  washed, drained

Glaze:
½ cup apple jelly
1 tablespoon lemon juice

1. Divide pastry into 6 pieces. Roll each piece on lightly floured pastry cloth to form a 6-inch circle. Lift each into a fluted 4-to-5-inch pan with removable bottom in place. Press evenly to bottom and side all around. Trim pastry, if necessary. Prick all over with fork. Refrigerate until ready to bake.

2. Preheat oven to 400F. Bake pastry shells 15 minutes. Cool on wire rack.

3. About 1 hour before serving, gently remove outer rims from pastry, keeping shells on bottoms. Place each on a serving plate. Fill pastry shells with chilled pastry cream. Arrange grapes over top. Refrigerate if not serving at once. Just before serving, make Glaze: Melt jelly over low heat; stir in lemon juice. Use to brush over grapes. Serve at once.

Makes 6 servings.

PINEAPPLE-BLUEBERRY TARTS

Pastry for six 4-inch shells,
   page 67
3 cans (8¼-oz size) pineapple
   slices, chilled

Glaze:
½ cup pineapple syrup

1 teaspoon arrowroot or
   cornstarch
1 teaspoon lemon juice

Pastry Cream, page 81
¾ cup blueberries, washed
   and chilled

1. Divide pastry into 6 pieces. Roll each piece on lightly floured pastry cloth to form a 6-inch circle. Lift each into a fluted 4-inch pan with removable bottom in place. Press evenly to bottom and side all around. Trim pastry, if necessary. Prick all over with fork. Refrigerate until ready to bake.

2. Preheat oven to 400F. Bake pastry shells 15 minutes. Cool on wire rack.

3. About 1 hour before serving, gently remove outer rims from pastry, keeping shells on bottoms.

4. Drain pineapple, reserving syrup.

5. Make Glaze: Measure ¼ cup pineapple syrup into small saucepan. Add arrowroot; stir until dissolved. Add ¼ cup more pineapple syrup. Bring to boiling, stirring. Cook until thickened and translucent. Stir in lemon juice. Refrigerate until cool.

6. Fill pastry shells with chilled pastry cream. Arrange two pineapple slices on each. Put blueberries in center of each. Brush all over with glaze, to cover completely. Refrigerate 1 hour to chill well.

Makes 6 servings.

APPLE MAZARIN TART

½ pkg piecrust mix

5 medium baking apples (2 lb)
1 cup sugar
2 tablespoons lemon juice

Almond Filling:
6 tablespoons butter or regular
   margarine, softened
⅓ cup sugar

½ can (8-oz size) almond paste*
1 egg

Whipped cream

* Do not use prepared almond
   filling instead of almond paste.

1. Preheat oven to 450F.

2. Prepare piecrust mix as package label directs. On lightly floured surface, roll out to make a 12-inch round. Fit over an inverted 9-inch layer-cake pan (1½ inches deep), folding edge of pastry under to make even. Prick well with fork.

3. Bake, pastry side up, 8 to 10 minutes, or until golden-brown. Cool on wire rack. Invert pan on a cookie sheet; with knife, carefully loosen shell from pan; remove pan.

4. Meanwhile, pare apples; halve each, and core. In large skillet, combine 1 cup water, 1 cup sugar, and the lemon juice; bring to boiling. Add apples, cut side up, in a single layer; simmer, covered, 5 minutes. Turn apples, and simmer 5 to 10 minutes longer, or just until tender. With slotted utensil, remove apples, and place, cut side down, on paper towels, to drain. Cover the apples with plastic film, to prevent darkening, and let cool to room temperature.

5. Preheat oven to 350F.

6. Make Almond Filling: In small bowl, with electric mixer at medium speed, beat butter with sugar until light. Gradually add almond paste; beat until well combined. Add egg; beat until light and fluffy.

7. Place apples, cut side down, in pastry shell. Spoon filling between apples; spread lightly with spatula.

8. Fold a 32-by-12-inch piece of foil in half lengthwise three times, to make a 1½-inch-wide band. Wrap around outside of pastry shell; fasten with paper clip, pulling ends to fit snugly.

9. Bake tart 40 to 45 minutes, or until almond filling is puffed and golden-brown. Cool; loosen from cookie sheet with spatula; remove foil. Slide tart onto serving plate. Serve warm, with whipped cream. Or cool completely, and decorate with whipped cream.

Makes 8 servings.

TARTE TATIN
(Upside-down Apple Tart)

1 cup sugar
½ cup butter
8 medium (3 lb) baking apples
   (see Note)

½ pkg (11-oz size) piecrust mix
Sweetened whipped cream
Crystallized violets

1. In a medium-size heavy skillet, over medium heat, cook sugar, stirring constantly, until sugar melts and turns a very light-golden color.

2. Remove from heat; add butter, stirring until combined.

3. Turn syrup into a 1½-quart shallow baking dish (8¼-inch).

4. Pare, quarter, and core apples. Layer apples, rounded side down, in sugar mixture. Arrange a second layer, rounded side up, fitting apples together smoothly. Fill in any open spaces with apples.

5. Preheat oven to 450F.

6. Prepare piecrust mix as package label directs for a 1-crust pie. On lightly floured surface, roll pastry to form a 9-inch circle.

7. Arrange over apples; do not attach edge of pastry to rim of baking dish. Prick with fork to allow steam to escape.

8. Bake 35 to 40 minutes, or until crust is golden and apples are tender when pierced with fork.

9. Remove to wire rack to cool 15 minutes. Then invert into shallow serving dish, so that crust is on bottom and apples are on top.

10. Garnish with whipped cream and violets. Serve warm or cold. Makes 8 servings.

Note: Use Northern Spy or Winesap apples.

❧

PEAR TARTE TATIN
(Upside-down Pear Tart)

2 cans (1-lb, 14-oz size) pear
    halves
1 cup sugar
1 tablespoon butter
½ pkg piecrust mix (pastry for
    1-crust pie)

1 jar (9½ oz) marrons in syrup,
    drained (optional)
1 cup heavy cream, whipped and
    sweetened

1. Preheat oven to 450F.

2. Drain pears well. Cut each in half lengthwise; drain on paper towels.

3. To caramelize sugar: In large skillet, cook sugar over medium heat, stirring occasionally, until sugar melts and becomes a light-brown syrup.

4. Immediately pour into bottom of 8½-inch round baking dish. Arrange pears, rounded side down, spoke fashion, in caramelized sugar. Top with a second layer of pears, rounded side up, fitting pieces over bottom layer to fill open spaces.

5. Dot with butter. Bake, uncovered, 25 minutes, or just until caramelized sugar is melted.

6. Let stand in baking dish on wire rack until cooled to room temperature—about 1½ hours.

7. Meanwhile, prepare pastry, following package directions. On lightly floured surface, roll out to a 9-inch circle. Place on ungreased cookie sheet; prick with fork. Refrigerate 30 minutes.

8. Bake pastry at 450F for 10 minutes, or until golden-brown. Let stand on cookie sheet on wire rack until ready to use.

9. To serve: Place pastry circle over pears in baking dish. Top with serving plate; invert, and remove baking dish. Mound marrons in center. Serve with whipped cream.

Makes 6 to 8 servings.

Napoleon and Friends
(Puff Pastry Desserts)

In the land where these luscious pastries were born, a Napoleon is called a *mille-feuille* (a thousand leaves) to describe its countless flaky layers. It is made by arranging thin layers of puff pastry, one on top of the other, with layers of cream filling in between.

The same puff pastry forms the base for many delicious variations almost as famous: Palmiers, Papillons, Pinwheels, Fanchonettes, Cornets, the Pithiviers Torte. Directions are given for all of these, but we must warn you: take great pains and allow all the time necessary to make these delicate pastries.

❧

PUFF PASTRY

1 lb (4 bars) sweet butter, chilled
4 cups sifted* all-purpose flour

1 teaspoon salt
1 cup ice water

* Sift before measuring.

1. Cut each bar of butter in half lengthwise. On sheet of waxed paper, place side by side, to form a rectangle. Refrigerate until ready to use.

2. Sift flour and salt into large bowl. With fork, stir in ice water until well combined (dough will be dry). Now mix dough with hands until there are no traces of dry flour. Shape into a ball.

3. On unfloured surface, knead dough until smooth and elastic—about 10 minutes. Cover with towel; let rest 20 minutes (this relaxes dough so it is easier to roll).

4. On lightly floured pastry cloth with stockinet-covered rolling pin, roll out dough into a 20-by-6-inch rectangle. Place butter strips on half of dough, ½ inch from sides.

5. Fold other half of dough over butter; press edges together firmly, with rolling pin or fingertips, to seal. Refrigerate, wrapped in foil, 30 minutes.

6. With rolling pin, tap dough lightly several times, to flatten butter. On lightly floured pastry cloth, quickly roll out, lengthwise, into a 20-by-8-inch rectangle, pulling out corners to keep square. (When rolling, work from center out, with firm, even strokes, rolling over the sides, lightly, only when desired length and width have been reached.)

7. From short side, fold dough into thirds, making sure edges and corners are even; press edges firmly to seal. Refrigerate, in foil, 30 minutes.

8. Place dough on lightly floured pastry cloth, with folded side of dough at right. Starting from center, with quick, light strokes, roll out dough, lengthwise, into a 20-by-8-inch rectangle. (If butter breaks through pastry, brush spot very lightly with flour.) Fold in thirds, as above. Refrigerate, in foil, 30 minutes.

9. Repeat the rolling, folding, and chilling of dough 4 more times (6 times in all).

10. Keep dough refrigerated until ready to use. If using only half the pastry, as most of our recipes call for, freezer-wrap remaining dough, and store in freezer to use later.

Makes 2 pounds.

NAPOLEONS

1 recipe Puff Pastry, page 91
  Almond Cream, below

Decoration:
  ½ cup semisweet-chocolate
    pieces
  1 teaspoon shortening

2½ cups sifted* confectioners'
    sugar
2 tablespoons light corn syrup
1 teaspoon vanilla extract
¼ teaspoon almond extract

* Sift before measuring.

1. Line 4 cookie sheets with a double thickness of heavy brown paper. (Or use 2 cookie sheets and 2 trays.)

2. Remove pastry from refrigerator; divide into 4 equal portions. On lightly floured pastry cloth, with stockinet-covered rolling pin, roll out one portion at a time into a 15-by-9-inch rectangle, and place on a prepared cookie sheet. If necessary, quickly roll again to bring back to proper size. Refrigerate 30 minutes.

3. Make Almond Cream.

4. Preheat oven to 400F. Remove 2 cookie sheets of pastry from refrigerator. Prick well with fork; trim edges with sharp knife.

5. Bake 25 to 30 minutes, or until pastry is puffed and golden-

brown. Remove pastry, still on paper, to wire rack; let cool 5 minutes; then remove paper. Let cool completely.

6. Prick, trim, and bake remaining pastry rectangles. (If on trays, transfer to cookie sheets.)

7. When baked pastry layers are completely cool, carefully trim sides with very sharp or serrated knife, so layers are all the same size. Select the most even layer for top, and set it, puffed side up, on wire rack on tray, ready to be decorated.

8. Make Decoration: Place chocolate and shortening in small saucepan. Set pan in hot water to melt chocolate; stir to blend.

9. Meanwhile, make frosting: In top of double boiler, combine confectioners' sugar, corn syrup, extracts, and 2 tablespoons water. Cook over hot, not boiling, water, stirring constantly, until frosting is smooth and shiny and coats a wooden spoon.

10. Remove from hot water. Immediately pour frosting over top pastry layer on wire rack on tray; spread evenly.

11. With chocolate mixture in small pastry bag or metal pastry tube with small writing tip, pipe 7 lengthwise stripes, 1 inch apart, over frosting.

12. To make chevron effect, pull wooden pick crosswise through chocolate and frosting, at 1-inch intervals; alternate direction each time—left to right, then right to left. Set aside.

13. When Almond Cream is chilled, assemble Napoleon: Place an undecorated pastry layer, puffy side up, on serving tray; spread with one third of Almond Cream. Repeat with two remaining undecorated pastry layers and rest of cream. Top with decorated pastry.

14. Refrigerate at least 1 hour before serving.

15. To serve: With very sharp knife, cut in half lengthwise. Cut each half crosswise into 8 pieces.

Makes 16 servings.

ALMOND CREAM

1 envelope unflavored gelatine	6 egg yolks
4 cups milk	2 teaspoons vanilla extract
1 cup sugar	1 teaspoon almond extract
1/2 cup cornstarch	1 cup heavy cream
Dash salt	

1. Sprinkle gelatine over 1/4 cup milk; let soften.

2. Meanwhile, in medium saucepan, heat remaining milk until tiny bubbles appear around the edge of the pan.

3. In small bowl, combine sugar, cornstarch and salt; mix well.

Gradually stir into hot milk. Cook over medium heat, stirring, until mixture boils and is thickened.

4. Stir in gelatine; boil 1 minute.

5. In small bowl, beat egg yolks slightly. Gradually add a little hot mixture, stirring constantly. Add to hot mixture in saucepan; cook, stirring, until mixture boils. Remove from heat.

6. Stir in extracts; pour into large bowl. Place sheet of waxed paper directly on surface of filling. Refrigerate until chilled—2 to 3 hours.

7. Whip cream until stiff. Add to chilled mixture; beat with rotary beater just until smooth. Refrigerate 1 hour longer, or until ready to use.

Makes 5¾ cups.

PITHIVIERS TORTE

1 recipe Puff Pastry, page 91

Almond Filling:
1 can (4½ oz) blanched whole
    almonds, ground
1 cup sifted* confectioners' sugar
¼ cup softened butter or
    margarine

2 tablespoons light cream
1 teaspoon grated lemon peel
2 tablespoons dark rum

1 egg yolk
2 tablespoons confectioners'
    sugar
1 cup heavy cream, whipped

* Sift before measuring.

1. Line 2 cookie sheets with a double thickness of heavy brown paper.

2. Remove half of pastry from refrigerator. On lightly floured pastry cloth, with stockinet-covered rolling pin, roll pastry into a 10-inch square; place on prepared cookie sheet. Refrigerate 30 minutes.

3. Repeat with other half of pastry.

4. Make Almond Filling: In small bowl, combine all filling ingredients; with fork, mix to a smooth paste. Set aside.

5. Remove pastry squares from refrigerator. Invert a 9-inch round cake pan on one square, for bottom of torte. Using sharp knife, cut around pan to make a 9-inch circle. Prick pastry well with fork. Refrigerate 30 minutes.

6. Cut second pastry square into circle as above, for top of torte. Do not prick. With tip of sharp knife, cut notches, 1 inch apart, around edge of circle. Score surface into 8 wedges (do not cut all the way through).

7. Starting at center, score surface of each wedge with seven arcs, increasing in size, to make a spiderweb design. Refrigerate 30 minutes.

8. Preheat oven to 400F. Mix egg yolk with 1 tablespoon cold water. Brush on tops (not sides) of pastry circles.

9. Bake circles 15 minutes, or until pastry has puffed. Reduce heat to 350F; bake 30 minutes longer, or until golden-brown.

10. Remove to wire racks. With sharp knife, split each circle crosswise, to make 4 layers in all.

11. Arrange, cut side up, on cookie sheets; bake 5 minutes longer. Remove to wire racks; cool completely.

12. Sift confectioners' sugar evenly over patterned circle for top. Run under broiler, 3 inches from heat, 2 minutes, or just until sugar melts but does not burn.

13. Shortly before serving, assemble torte: Reserve patterned circle for top. Place a pastry circle, cut side up, on serving platter; spread with one third of the filling and then one third of whipped cream. Place another circle, cut side up, on first; spread with one third of filling and cream. Add third circle, cut side down; spread with rest of filling and cream. Then top with patterned circle.

14. To serve, cut into wedges.

Makes 10 to 12 servings.

PAPILLONS (BUTTERFLIES)

½ recipe Puff Pastry, page 91   Confectioners' sugar
½ cup granulated sugar

1. Line 2 cookie sheets with a double thickness of heavy brown paper. Remove pastry from refrigerator; divide into two equal portions.

2. Sprinkle a lightly floured pastry cloth with 2 tablespoons granulated sugar. With a stockinet-covered rolling pin, roll one portion of pastry to ¼-inch thickness; fold in half.

3. Sprinkle pastry cloth with 2 tablespoons granulated sugar. Roll pastry into an 11-by-6-inch rectangle; trim edges.

4. Cut rectangle crosswise into quarters; stack together, lightly brushing each with cold water.

5. With handle of wooden spoon, press firmly down the middle of pastry, making a slight indentation. Then cut crosswise into 10 (½-inch-wide) strips.

6. Twist each strip. Place on prepared cookie sheet, 2 inches apart; press ends to cookie sheet. Refrigerate 30 minutes.

7. Repeat with remaining pastry.

8. Preheat oven to 425F. Bake papillons 15 minutes. Reduce temperature to 350F; bake 10 minutes longer, or until golden-brown.

9. Remove to wire rack; let cool completely. Sprinkle with confectioners' sugar.

Makes about 20.

CORNETS (HORNS)

½ recipe Puff Pastry, page 91
1 egg white
    Granulated sugar

Filling:
 2 cups heavy cream

½ cup sifted* confectioners' sugar
½ teaspoon almond extract
1 teaspoon vanilla extract

* Sift before measuring.

1. Line 2 cookie sheets with a double thickness of heavy brown paper.

2. Remove pastry from refrigerator. On lightly floured pastry cloth, with stockinet-covered rolling pin, roll out pastry into an 18-by-12-inch rectangle; trim edges. Cut lengthwise into 12 strips, 1 inch wide.

3. For each cornet: Starting at tip of a cone-shape metal form, held tip down, spiral pastry strip upward around form, with each row overlapping the one below about ½ inch. Do not extend pastry beyond wide end of form. Moisten end of strip with a little water; press gently to seal.

4. Place cornets, sealed side down, 2 inches apart, on prepared cookie sheets. Refrigerate 30 minutes.

5. Preheat oven to 400F. Bake cornets 20 minutes.

6. Meanwhile, lightly beat egg white with 2 tablespoons water. Brush over baked cornets; sprinkle lightly with granulated sugar. Bake 5 minutes longer, or until golden-brown and glazed.

7. Carefully remove to wire rack; cool slightly. Then remove forms; let cool completely.

8. Make Filling: In medium bowl, beat cream with confectioners' sugar just until stiff. Gently fold in extracts. Use to fill cooled cornets. Serve at once.

Makes 12.

Note: To make your own cone forms: Using double thickness of heavy-duty foil, cut a 9-inch square; fold over to form a triangle. Then roll into a cone shape, 4 inches long and 1½ inches in diameter at widest part, leaving a small opening at narrow end. Fold top flap over, to make cone secure.

PALMIERS

½ recipe Puff Pastry, page 91   *½ cup sugar*

1. Line 2 cookie sheets with two thicknesses of heavy brown paper. Remove the puff pastry from the refrigerator.

2. Sprinkle lightly floured pastry cloth with ¼ cup sugar. On this, with a stockinet-covered rolling pin, roll out pastry into an 18-by-16-inch rectangle.

3. From short side, fold dough into thirds, making sure edges and corners are even; press edges firmly to seal. Refrigerate, wrapped in foil, for 30 minutes.

4. First sprinkling surface with 2 tablespoons sugar, repeat rolling, folding, and chilling dough.

5. Once again, roll out dough into an 18-by-16-inch rectangle; sprinkle surface with 2 tablespoons sugar. Fold in half crosswise; seal edges.

6. Fold short sides over to just meet in center. Moisten edges with water; press gently to seal. Fold each half again to meet in center. Then fold in half lengthwise, as if closing a book. Press long side firmly to seal. Refrigerate 30 minutes.

7. With sharp knife, cut dough crosswise into slices, ½ inch thick. Place flat, 2 inches apart, on prepared cookie sheets; separate folded edges of each slightly. Refrigerate 30 minutes.

8. Preheat oven to 400F. Bake palmiers 12 to 15 minutes. Turn over with wide spatula; bake 10 minutes longer, or until golden-brown and glazed.

9. Remove to wire rack; cool.

Makes about 16.

✂

PINWHEELS

½ recipe Puff Pastry, page 91

Glaze:
  1 cup confectioners' sugar

1½ tablespoons milk

2 tablespoons jelly or jam

1. Line 2 cookie sheets with a double thickness of heavy brown paper. Remove pastry from refrigerator; divide in half.

2. On lightly floured pastry cloth, with stockinet-covered rolling pin, roll out one portion into a 9-by-6-inch rectangle; trim edges. Cut rectangle into 6 (3-inch) squares.

3. In each square, make a 1½-inch slit from each corner toward center. Fold right-hand point of each corner to center, forming a pinwheel. Moisten with a little water; press gently to seal.

4. Place, 2 inches apart, on prepared cookie sheet. Refrigerate 30 minutes.

5. Repeat with remaining pastry.

6. Preheat oven to 450F. Bake pinwheels 15 minutes. Reduce temperature to 350F; bake 15 minutes longer, or until golden-brown. (If pastry browns too quickly, place a sheet of brown paper over top during last part of baking.) Remove to wire rack.

7. Make Glaze: Mix sugar with milk until smooth. Drizzle over warm pinwheels. Place ½ teaspoon jelly in center of each.

Makes 12.

✂

FANCHONETTES (LITTLE KERCHIEFS)

½ recipe Puff Pastry, page 91

Filling:
  1 cup sifted* confectioners' sugar
  2 egg yolks
  1 egg
  ¾ cup ground blanched almonds

* Sift before measuring.

1 tablespoon flour
¼ cup soft butter
  Dash salt
1 teaspoon almond extract

1 cup heavy cream, whipped stiff
  Currant or raspberry jelly

1. Remove chilled pastry from refrigerator; divide into two equal portions. On lightly floured pastry cloth, with a stockinet-covered rolling pin, roll out one portion to a 12½-by-8½-inch rectangle.

2. With 4-inch plain or fluted cookie cutter, cut out 6 pastry

rounds. (If you don't have a cutter, cover a 4-inch cardboard round with foil; lay it on dough, and cut around it.) Discard scraps.

3. Line 6 (3½-inch) tart pans or muffin pans with pastry rounds; prick well all over with fork. Refrigerate 30 minutes.

4. Repeat with remaining portion of dough.

5. Meanwhile, make Filling: In medium bowl, combine all filling ingredients; mix with fork until smooth. Set aside.

6. Preheat oven to 400F.

7. Remove chilled tart shells from refrigerator. Spoon 2 tablespoons filling into each. Arrange tart pans on cookie sheet.

8. Bake 15 minutes. Reduce temperature to 350F; bake 20 minutes. Cover tarts with brown paper; bake 10 minutes longer—or until pastry puffs. Filling will be richly brown.

9. Remove tarts from pans; cool completely on wire rack.

10. To serve: Fill pastry tube with whipped cream. Pipe five petals in center of each tart, to resemble flower. Spoon about ¼ teaspoon jelly in center of flower.

Makes 12.

Cheese Cakes and Other Cheese Desserts

All the world loves cheesecake. In fact, the main attraction at Lindy's, once one of New York's most famous restaurants, was its cheesecake. Though Lindy's is gone now, you can still enjoy what many think is the greatest cheesecake ever made. Try it along with the others in this chapter, equally great.

❉

LINDY'S FAMOUS CHEESECAKE

1 cup sifted* all-purpose flour
¼ cup sugar
1 teaspoon grated lemon peel
½ teaspoon vanilla extract
1 egg yolk
¼ cup soft butter or margarine

Filling:
5 pkg (8-oz size) soft cream
    cheese

* Sift before measuring.

1¾ cups sugar
3 tablespoons flour
1½ teaspoons grated lemon peel
1½ teaspoons grated orange peel
¼ teaspoon vanilla extract
5 eggs
2 egg yolks
¼ cup heavy cream

    Pineapple Glaze, below

1. In medium bowl, combine flour, sugar, lemon peel, and vanilla. Make well in center; add egg yolk and butter. Mix, with fingertips, until dough cleans side of bowl.

2. Form into a ball, and wrap in waxed paper. Refrigerate about 1 hour.

3. Preheat oven to 400F. Grease the bottom and side of a 9-inch springform pan. Remove the side from the pan.

4. Roll one third of dough on bottom of springform pan; trim edge of dough.

5. Bake 8 to 10 minutes, or until golden.

6. Meanwhile, divide rest of dough into 3 parts. Roll each part into a strip 2½ inches wide and about 10 inches long.

7. Put together springform pan, with the baked crust on bottom.

8. Fit dough strips to side of pan, joining ends to line inside completely. Trim dough so it comes only three fourths way up side of pan. Refrigerate until ready to fill.

9. Preheat oven to 500F. Make Filling: In large bowl of electric mixer, combine cheese, sugar, flour, lemon and orange peel, and vanilla. Beat, at high speed, just to blend.

10. Beat in eggs and egg yolks, one at a time. Add cream, beating just until well combined. Pour mixture into springform pan.

11. Bake 10 minutes. Reduce oven temperature to 250F, and bake 1 hour longer.

12. Let cheesecake cool in pan on wire rack. Glaze top with Pineapple Glaze. Refrigerate 3 hours, or overnight.

13. To serve: Loosen pastry from side of pan with spatula. Remove side of springform pan. Cut cheesecake into wedges.

Makes 16 to 20 servings.

PINEAPPLE GLAZE

2 tablespoons sugar
4 teaspoons cornstarch
2 cans (8¼-oz size) crushed
   pineapple in heavy syrup,
   undrained

2 tablespoons lemon juice
2 drops yellow food color, optional

Make Glaze: In small saucepan, combine sugar and cornstarch. Stir in remaining ingredients. Over medium heat, bring to boiling, stirring; boil 1 minute, or until thickened and translucent. Cool.

CHOCOLATE CHEESECAKE

Crumb Crust:
1 pkg (8½ oz) chocolate wafers
⅓ cup melted butter or margarine
2 tablespoons granulated sugar
¼ teaspoon nutmeg

Cheese Filling:
3 eggs
1 cup granulated sugar

3 pkg (8-oz size) cream cheese,
   softened
2 pkg (6-oz size) semisweet-
   chocolate pieces, melted
1 teaspoon vanilla extract
⅛ teaspoon salt
1 cup sour cream

1 cup heavy cream
2 tablespoons confectioners'
   sugar

1. Preheat the oven to 350F.

2. Make Crumb Crust: In electric blender or with rolling pin, crush chocolate wafers into fine crumbs. In a medium bowl, combine the wafer crumbs, melted butter, 2 tablespoons granulated sugar, and the nutmeg; mix until ingredients are well combined.

3. Press evenly over bottom and side (½ inch from top) of a 9-inch springform pan. Refrigerate crust until needed.

4. Make Cheese Filling: In large bowl of electric mixer, at high speed, beat eggs with 1 cup granulated sugar until light. Beat in cream cheese until mixture is smooth.

5. Add melted chocolate, vanilla, salt, and sour cream; beat until smooth.

6. Turn into crumb crust, and bake 1 hour, or until cheese cake is just firm when the pan is shaken gently.

7. Cool cheesecake in pan on a wire rack. Then refrigerate, covered, overnight.

8. Beat heavy cream with confectioners' sugar just until stiff. Remove the side of the springform pan.

9. Decorate cheesecake with the whipped cream, put through a pastry tube with a decorative tip.

Makes 16 servings.

RATNER'S FAMOUS MARBLE CHEESECAKE

Cookie Crust:
- ¾ cup sugar
- ½ cup soft shortening
- 1¼ cups plus 2 tablespoons cake flour
- 1 tablespoon beaten egg
- ⅛ teaspoon salt
- ⅛ teaspoon grated lemon peel
- 2 tablespoons packaged dry bread crumbs

Cheese Filling:
- 3½ pkg (8-oz size) cream cheese
- 1 container (8 oz) skim-milk cottage cheese (see Note)
- 1¼ cups sugar
- 3 eggs
- 2 tablespoons heavy cream
- 2 teaspoons vanilla extract
- 3 squares semisweet chocolate, melted

1. Make Cookie Crust: Preheat oven to 350F.

2. In large bowl, combine ¾ cup sugar, the shortening, cake flour, egg, 1½ teaspoons water, the salt, lemon peel. With electric mixer, beat at medium speed until well combined and dough leaves side of bowl.

3. Form dough into a ball. Fit onto bottom of a 9-inch springform pan, rolling lightly with rolling pin to make a smooth surface.

Trim pastry ⅛ inch from edge all around. Prick with fork to prevent shrinkage.

4. Bake 10 minutes. Remove from oven; cool on wire rack 15 minutes. Then lightly grease inside of side of springform pan. Sprinkle lightly with bread crumbs, and attach side to bottom of pan with cookie crust. Retrim crust, if necessary.

5. Meanwhile, make Cheese Filling: Increase oven temperature to 400F.

6. In large bowl, with electric mixer, combine cream cheese, cottage cheese, and sugar. Beat at medium speed until mixture is smooth and creamy.

7. Beat in eggs, one at a time, beating well after each addition. Beat in cream and vanilla.

8. Pour half of batter into prepared springform pan. Drizzle 2 tablespoons melted chocolate over batter. With finger, lightly swirl chocolate over surface.

9. Repeat with rest of batter and chocolate.

10. Bake 15 minutes. Remove to wire rack. Let cake cool 45 minutes. Heat oven to 350F.

11. Bake cake 25 minutes longer. Let cool completely on wire rack. Refrigerate several hours or overnight, if possible, before serving.

12. Gently remove side of springform pan before serving.

Makes 8 to 10 servings.

Note: If cottage cheese is moist, drain very well before using.

TEDDY'S CHEESECAKE

7 pkg (8-oz size) cream cheese, softened	6 eggs
	1 cup sour cream
1¼ cups sugar	1 jar (12 oz) pineapple topping

1. Preheat oven to 450F. Grease a 13-by-9-by-2½-inch baking pan.

2. In large bowl, with electric mixer at medium speed, beat cheese until smooth. Gradually beat in sugar.

3. Add eggs, one at a time, beating well after each addition.

4. Add sour cream; continue to beat until well blended and mixture is soft and creamy. Turn into prepared pan. Place in shallow pan; pour hot water to ½-inch level around pan of cheese mixture.

5. Bake 35 minutes, or until deep golden and set in center. Cool in pan on wire rack, then refrigerate overnight.

6. To serve: Loosen sides from pan with spatula; invert onto serving plate. Spread with pineapple topping.

Makes 24 servings.

McCALL'S BEST CHEESECAKE

Crust:
3/4 cup graham-cracker crumbs*
1 tablespoon sugar
1 tablespoon melted butter or
   margarine

* To make graham-cracker crumbs:
  With rolling pin, crush 10 graham
  crackers between 2 sheets of
  waxed paper.

Filling:
3 pkg (8-oz size) cream cheese,
  at room temperature
4 eggs
1 teaspoon vanilla extract
1 cup sugar

Topping:
2 cups sour cream
1 tablespoon sugar
1 teaspoon vanilla extract

1. Preheat oven to 375F.

2. Make Crust: In medium bowl, combine crumbs, sugar, and butter, mixing well.

3. Spread evenly over bottom of a 9-inch springform pan, pressing lightly with fingertips. Refrigerate while filling is prepared.

4. Make Filling: In large bowl of electric mixer, at medium speed, beat cheese until light.

5. Add eggs, vanilla, and sugar; continue beating until creamy and light.

6. Pour into crust in pan; bake 35 minutes.

7. Meanwhile, make Topping: In medium bowl, with wooden spoon, beat together cream, sugar, and vanilla.

8. Remove cheesecake from oven. Spread topping evenly over surface; bake 5 minutes.

9. Cool in pan, on wire rack. Then refrigerate 5 hours, or overnight.

10. To serve: Remove side of springform pan. Cut cheesecake into wedges.

Makes 10 to 12 servings.

‎❃

FRUIT-GLAZED CREAM-CHEESECAKE

Crust:
2½ cups packaged graham-cracker
    crumbs
¼ cup sugar
½ cup butter or regular
    margarine, softened

Filling:
3 pkg (8-oz size) cream cheese,
    softened

3 tablespoons grated lemon peel
1½ cups sugar
3 tablespoons flour
4 eggs
½ cup lemon juice

    Fruit Glazes, below
    Sour cream

1. Make Crust: In medium bowl, with hands or back of metal spoon, mix graham-cracker crumbs with ¼ cup sugar and the butter until well combined.

2. With back of spoon, press crumb mixture to the bottom and sides of a greased 12-by-8-by-2-inch baking dish or 3-quart shallow baking dish.

3. Preheat oven to 350F.

4. Make Filling: In large bowl of electric mixer, at medium speed, beat cream cheese, lemon peel, sugar, and flour until they are smooth and well combined.

5. Beat in eggs, one at a time. Beat in lemon juice.

6. Pour filling into crust-lined dish. Bake 35 to 40 minutes, or until center of filling seems firm when dish is shaken.

7. Cool completely on wire rack. Refrigerate 4 hours or overnight, or until very well chilled.

8. Meanwhile, make Fruit Glazes.

9. Divide surface of cheesecake into thirds. Spoon glazes, each in one third, over cheesecake. Refrigerate 1 hour.

10. To serve, cut into squares. Pass sour cream. Wonderful for a large buffet or dessert party.

Makes 12 to 16 servings.

FRUIT GLAZES

BLUEBERRY GLAZE

1 pkg (10 oz) frozen blueberries,
    thawed

1 tablespoon sugar
2 teaspoons cornstarch

1. Drain blueberries, reserving liquid. Measure liquid; add water, if necessary, to make ½ cup.

2. In small saucepan, combine sugar and cornstarch. Stir in reserved liquid.

3. Over medium heat, bring to boiling, stirring; boil 1 minute.

4. Remove from heat; cool slightly. Stir in blueberries. Cool completely.

PINEAPPLE GLAZE

1 tablespoon sugar
2 teaspoons cornstarch

1 can (8¼ oz) crushed pineapple, undrained

1. In small saucepan, combine sugar and cornstarch. Stir in pineapple.

2. Over medium heat, bring to boiling, stirring; boil 1 minute. Cool completely.

STRAWBERRY GLAZE

1 pkg (10 oz) frozen strawberries, thawed

1 tablespoon sugar
2 teaspoons cornstarch

1. Drain the strawberries, reserving ½ cup of the liquid.

2. In a small saucepan, combine sugar and cornstarch. Stir in reserved liquid.

3. Over medium heat, bring to boiling, stirring; boil 1 minute.

4. Remove from heat; cool slightly. Stir in strawberries; cool completely.

ॐ

CHERRY CHEESE PIE SUPREME

9-inch unbaked pie shell
1 can (1 lb, 5 oz) cherry-pie filling
4 pkg (3-oz size) cream cheese, softened
½ cup granulated sugar
2 eggs

½ teaspoon vanilla extract
1 tablespoon grated lemon peel
½ cup heavy cream
2 tablespoons confectioners' sugar

1. Preheat oven to 425F. Prepare pie shell.

2. Set aside ¾ cup cherry-pie filling. Spread remaining filling in unbaked pie shell.

3. Bake 15 minutes, or just until crust is golden-brown; remove to wire rack. Reduce oven temperature to 350F.

4. Meanwhile, in medium bowl, with electric mixer at medium speed, beat cheese with granulated sugar, eggs, and vanilla until smooth. Stir in lemon peel. Pour over hot cherry filling in pie shell.

5. Bake 25 to 30 minutes. Filling will be set in center.

6. Remove to wire rack; let cool completely. Spread reserved cherry filling on pie, leaving 1-inch margin around edge. Refrigerate until well chilled—about 1½ hours.

7. To serve: Beat cream with confectioners' sugar until stiff. Place in pastry bag with number-6 star tip. Pipe swirls around edge of pie.

Makes 8 servings.

BLUEBERRY CHEESE PIE SUPREME

Follow above recipe, substituting 1 can (1 lb, 5 oz) blueberry-pie filling for cherry-pie filling.

CHOCOLATE CHEESE PIE

Crust:
20 graham crackers
¼ cup butter or margarine, softened
¼ cup sugar

Filling:
1 cup evaporated milk, undiluted
1 pkg (6 oz) semisweet chocolate pieces
1 pkg (3 oz) soft cream cheese
¼ cup sugar

1. Make Crust: Place graham crackers between 2 pieces of waxed paper; roll, with rolling pin, to make fine, even crumbs. (Crumbs will measure about 1¾ cups.) Combine crumbs, butter, and sugar; blend, with pastry blender or fork, to mix well.

2. Using back of spoon or an 8-inch pie plate, press mixture evenly on bottom and side (not on rim) of 9-inch pie plate.

3. Make Filling: In ice-cube tray, freeze milk just until ice crystals form 1 inch in from edge of tray.

4. Meanwhile, melt chocolate pieces over hot, not boiling, water; let cool slightly.

5. In medium bowl, beat cream cheese and sugar with rotary beater till smooth. Add milk gradually, beating until thick and fluffy. Gradually beat in melted chocolate, blending well. Turn into pie shell; refrigerate, covered, overnight.

6. Garnish top with whipped cream, if desired.

Makes 8 servings.

ॐ

ITALIAN CHEESE PIE

Crust:
1 1/2 cups unsifted all-purpose flour
1 1/4 teaspoons baking powder
1/2 teaspoon salt
3 tablespoons butter or
    margarine, softened
1/4 cup sugar
1 egg

1/2 teaspoon vanilla extract
1/2 teaspoon grated orange peel
1 tablespoon orange juice or
    whisky

Filling: below
1 egg, separated

1. Make Crust: Sift flour with baking powder and salt.

2. In medium bowl, with electric mixer, beat butter with sugar and 1 egg until light and fluffy. Beat in vanilla, orange peel and orange juice.

3. Add half of flour mixture; with wooden spoon, beat until well blended. Add remaining flour mixture, mixing with hands until dough leaves side of bowl and holds together.

4. Turn out onto board; knead several times, to blend well. Set aside, covered.

5. Make Filling. Preheat oven to 350F.

6. Divide pastry in half. Roll one half between two sheets of waxed paper to an 11-inch circle. Remove top paper. Fit pastry into a 9-inch pie plate; trim to edge of plate. Brush with egg white.

7. Roll remaining pastry to 1/8-inch thickness. With pastry cutter, cut into ten strips, 1/2 inch wide.

8. Turn filling into lined pie plate. Place five pastry strips across filling, pressing firmly to edge of pie plate. Place remaining strips across first ones, to make lattice.

9. Reroll trimmings, and cut into 1/2-inch-wide strips. Place around edge of pie, and with fork, press firmly to pie plate.

10. Beat egg yolk with 1 tablespoon water; brush over crust. Place a strip of foil, about 2 inches wide, around edge of crust, to prevent overbrowning.

11. Bake about 50 minutes, or until top is golden-brown and filling is set.

12. Cool on wire rack. Then refrigerate until well chilled—8 hours or overnight.

Makes 6 to 8 servings.

FILLING

1 container (15 oz) ricotta
    cheese
3/4 cup sugar
3 eggs

1 1/2 teaspoons flour
1 teaspoon almond extract
2 tablespoons finely chopped
    citron

In a medium bowl, with portable electric mixer, beat ricotta cheese until it is creamy. Add sugar, eggs, flour, almond extract and citron; beat until well combined.

REFRIGERATOR CHEESE PIE

Graham-Cracker Crust:
  1 cup graham-cracker crumbs
  2 tablespoons sugar
  1/4 cup butter or margarine, melted

Filling:
  1/2 cup sugar

1 envelope unflavored gelatine
1/4 teaspoon salt
1 cup milk
2 eggs
1 tablespoon grated lemon peel
2 cups creamed cottage cheese

1. Make Graham-Cracker Crust: In small bowl, combine crumbs, sugar, and butter, stirring with fork to mix well. Reserve 1/4 cup mixture for topping.

2. With back of metal spoon, press rest of crumb mixture to bottom and side (not on rim) of a 9-inch pie plate. Refrigerate while preparing filling.

3. Make Filling: In small saucepan, combine sugar, gelatine, salt, milk, and eggs.

4. Over medium heat, cook, stirring constantly, until custard forms a coating on metal spoon—about 5 minutes.

5. Remove from heat; stir in lemon peel. Refrigerate until mixture mounds when dropped from spoon—about 45 minutes.

6. Turn into large bowl of electric mixer. Add cheese. At high speed, beat until light and fluffy—3 minutes.

7. If filling is slightly thin, refrigerate 10 minutes. Turn into crust. Sprinkle reserved crumb mixture around edge of pie.

8. Refrigerate until firm—about 3 hours.

Glazed Refrigerator Cheese Pie: Omit crumb topping. Spread chilled pie with one of the glazes in Fruit-Glazed Cream-Cheesecake, page 105. Refrigerate 1 hour before serving.

Makes 8 servings.

COEUR À LA CREME

2 pkg (8-oz size) cream cheese
½ cup sugar
1 cup heavy cream, whipped

Strawberries and Raspberries,
below

1. Line a heart-shape mold (about 6 inches in diameter and about 2 inches deep) with dampened cheesecloth, completely covering bottom and side of mold.

2. In medium bowl, let cream cheese stand at room temperature to soften—about 1 hour.

3. With wooden spoon, beat cheese with sugar until smooth. Beat in whipped cream, a small amount at a time, until mixture is light and smooth.

4. Turn into prepared mold, filling evenly. Smooth top with spatula. Refrigerate, covered, overnight, or until well chilled.

5. To serve, turn into a serving dish with a rim. Surround with Strawberries and Raspberries.

Makes 8 or more servings.

Note: This is a rather rich dessert; servings should be small.

STRAWBERRIES AND RASPBERRIES

1 pkg (10 oz) frozen strawberries,
   thawed
1 pkg (10 oz) frozen raspberries,
   thawed

1 tablespoon cornstarch
¼ cup kirsch

1. Drain fruits, reserving juice. Add water to juice to measure 1¾ cups.

2. In small saucepan, combine cornstarch and juice, mixing until smooth. Bring to boiling over medium heat, stirring constantly. Reduce heat, and cook 5 minutes, or until thickened and translucent. Let cool.

3. Add strawberries, raspberries and kirsch. Refrigerate, covered, overnight.

Makes 2½ cups.

Cream Puffs,
Éclairs and Variations

From a basic pâte à choux (cream puff dough) comes a myriad of fanciful desserts. Start with Cream Puffs and Éclairs—tender pastry on the outside, a rich, creamy custard within. Then go on to a Cream Puff Tower, Profiteroles or Les Religieuses (Little Nuns)—a luxurious assemblage of cream puffs and éclairs. The most elegant and regal of all is the Gâteau St.-Honoré, cream puffs with rich cream filling, glazed with caramel, standing on a base of puff pastry and decorated with "poufs" of whipped cream.

❦

CREAM PUFFS

Cream Puff Dough, below   *Chocolate Glaze, page 121*

Easy Custard Filling, page 120   *Confectioners' sugar*

1. Preheat oven to 400F. Make Cream Puff Dough.

2. Drop the dough by rounded tablespoonfuls, 2 inches apart, onto an ungreased cookie sheet.

3. Bake 35 to 40 minutes, or until puffed and golden-brown. Puffs should sound hollow when lightly tapped with fingertip.

4. Meanwhile, make Easy Custard Filling.

5. Carefully remove puffs to wire rack. Let cool completely, away from drafts.

6. Shortly before serving: Cut off tops of cream puffs with sharp knife. With fork, gently remove any soft dough from the inside.

7. Fill puffs with custard; replace tops. Frost tops with Chocolate Glaze, or sprinkle with confectioners' sugar. Serve soon after filling. (Filled puffs become soggy on standing.)

Makes 6 large puffs.

CREAM PUFF DOUGH

1/4 cup butter or regular margarine
1/8 teaspoon salt

1/2 cup unsifted all-purpose flour
2 large eggs

1. In small saucepan, combine 1/2 cup water, the butter, and salt. Bring to boiling over medium heat.

2. Remove from heat. Immediately, with wooden spoon, beat in flour all at once.

3. Return to low heat, and continue beating until mixture forms a ball and leaves side of pan.

4. Remove from heat. Add eggs, one at a time, beating hard after each addition until smooth. Continue beating until the mixture is shiny and breaks in strands.

Makes 6 large puffs or 8 medium-size puffs.

Note: To make double recipe of Cream Puff Dough: Make as above in medium saucepan, using 1 cup water, 1/2 cup butter or margarine, 1/4 teaspoon salt, 1 cup flour, and 4 eggs.

ÉCLAIRS

3/4 cup water
1/3 cup butter or regular margarine
1/8 teaspoon salt
3/4 cup all-purpose flour (sift
    before measuring)

3 large eggs
Rich Custard Filling, page 120
Double recipe Chocolate Glaze,
    page 121

1. Preheat oven to 400F. In medium saucepan, bring water, 1/3 cup butter and the salt to boiling. Remove from heat. Quickly add flour all at once. With wooden spoon, beat constantly over low heat until mixture forms ball and leaves side of pan. Remove from heat.

2. Using portable electric mixer or wooden spoon, beat in eggs, one at a time, beating very well after each addition. Continue beating vigorously until dough is shiny and satiny and breaks away in strands. Dough will be stiff and hold its shape.

3. Drop dough by rounded tablespoons 3 inches apart on un-greased cookie sheet. With spatula, shape into 4-by-1½-inch strips, rounding ends and slightly indenting sides. Bake 35 to 40 minutes, or until puffed and golden. Cool on rack. Meanwhile, make filling.

4. To fill: With sharp knife cut off tops of éclairs crosswise. Remove some of soft dough inside. Fill each with ¼ cup custard. Replace tops.

5. Make glaze. Spoon over éclairs, place on rack on tray. Serve at once or refrigerate.

Makes 8.

CREAM PUFF TOWER

Double recipe Cream Puff
    Dough, page 112

Filling:
  1 cup granulated sugar
 ¼ cup cornstarch

     Dash salt
2⅔ cups milk
  4 egg yolks
  1 teaspoon vanilla extract

  Confectioners' sugar

1. Make Cream Puff Dough. Preheat oven to 400F.

2. Drop dough by rounded tablespoonfuls, 2 inches apart, onto ungreased cookie sheet, to make 12 rounds.

3. Bake 35 to 40 minutes, or until puffed and golden-brown. Remove to wire rack; let cool completely.

4. Meanwhile, make Filling: In a heavy saucepan, combine granulated sugar, cornstarch, salt. Gradually stir in milk until smooth.

5. Cook the mixture, stirring constantly, until it thickens and boils; boil 3 minutes, stirring constantly.

6. In small bowl, beat egg yolks slightly. Stir ½ cup hot cornstarch mixture into egg yolks, mixing well. Pour back into saucepan. Cook 2 minutes longer, stirring constantly. Remove from heat.

7. Stir in vanilla. Turn into small bowl; cover. Cool to room temperature—about 1 hour.

8. Refrigerate until very well chilled—at least 1 hour.

9. To assemble puffs: With sharp knife, split in half; scoop out any filaments of soft dough. Fill bottom halves with about ¼ cup cream filling. Replace tops. Refrigerate.

10. To serve: Mound on a dessert plate, to make a tower. Sprinkle with confectioners' sugar.

Makes 12 servings.

Note: Instead of cream filling, you may use 1 package pudding-and-pie-filling mix, prepared as label directs; or any flavor ice cream; or sweetened whipped cream.

LES RELIGIEUSES (LITTLE NUNS)

Chocolate Cream, page 121
½ *pkg (11-oz size) piecrust mix*
Cream Puff Dough, page 112

1 *cup heavy cream*
¼ *cup confectioners' sugar*
½ *teaspoon vanilla extract*

1. Make Chocolate Cream.

2. Prepare piecrust mix as package label directs for one-crust pie. Divide into eighths. On lightly floured surface, roll each piece into a 4-inch circle. Invert a 6-ounce custard cup over each circle; trim pastry to edge of cup.

3. Fit each circle over outside of inverted custard cup; pinch in pleats, to fit snugly. Prick with fork. Refrigerate 30 minutes.

4. Preheat oven to 450F. Bake shells 10 to 12 minutes, or until golden-brown. Cool thoroughly on wire rack. Remove shells from cups.

5. Lower oven to 400F. Make Cream Puff Dough.

6. For puffs, drop dough by level teaspoonfuls, 1 inch apart, onto ungreased cookie sheet, to make 8 small rounds. For éclairs, place remaining dough in pastry bag with number-6 plain tip. Pipe, 1 inch apart, onto ungreased cookie sheet, to make 24 strips 2½ inches long.

7. Bake 30 minutes, or until puffed and a deep golden-brown. Remove to wire rack; let cool completely.

8. Beat cream with sugar and vanilla until stiff. Refrigerate, covered.

9. To assemble: With sharp knife, cut slice off top of each puff and éclair. Fill each with 2 teaspoons chocolate cream; replace tops.

10. Spoon remaining chocolate cream into tart shells, dividing evenly. Stand 3 éclairs in each shell, to form a pyramid; press tips together.

11. With whipped cream in pastry bag with number-2 star tip, pipe a rosette on bottom of each puff. Place a puff, cream side down, on top of éclairs in each shell. Decorate with remaining whipped cream. Refrigerate if not serving at once.

Makes 8 servings.

✿

STRAWBERRY PROFITEROLES

Cream Puff Dough, page 112
1 cup heavy cream
¼ cup confectioners' sugar
1 tablespoon golden rum

24 large strawberries, washed
*   and hulled*

Confectioners' sugar

1. Preheat oven to 400F. Make Cream Puff Dough.

2. Drop dough by rounded teaspoonfuls, 2 inches apart, onto ungreased cookie sheet, to make 24 puffs.

3. Bake 25 to 30 minutes, or until puffed and golden-brown Remove to wire rack; let cool completely.

4. Meanwhile, beat cream with ¼ cup confectioners' sugar until stiff. Stir in rum. Refrigerate, covered.

5. With sharp knife, cut a slice from top of each puff. Fill each with a rounded teaspoonful of whipped cream; press a strawberry into each; replace top. Refrigerate if not serving at once.

6. To serve: On each dessert plate, arrange 4 puffs. Sprinkle with confectioners' sugar.

Makes 6 servings.

✿

PROFITEROLES

Cream Puff Dough, page 112
2 pints strawberry ice cream or
*   other favorite flavor*

Chocolate Sauce, page 122
½ cup heavy cream, whipped
Chopped pistachios

1. Preheat oven to 400F. Make Cream Puff Dough.

2. Drop dough by rounded half teaspoonfuls, 1 inch apart, onto ungreased cookie sheet, to make 40 puffs.

3. Bake 20 to 25 minutes, or until puffed and golden-brown. Remove to wire rack; let cool completely.

4. Meanwhile, with large end of a melon-ball cutter or a 1-teaspoon measuring spoon, scoop ice cream into 40 balls. Place immediately in a chilled pan, and store in freezer.

5. Make Chocolate Sauce.

6. To assemble profiteroles: With sharp knife, cut a slice from top of each puff. Fill each with an ice-cream ball; replace top. (Place in freezer if not serving at once.)

7. To serve: Mound puffs in serving dish. Spoon chocolate sauce over top. Garnish with whipped cream and pistachios. For individual servings: In each dessert dish, mound 5 puffs. Spoon sauce over top. Garnish with whipped cream and pistachios.

Make 8 servings.

✥

MADELONS

Cream Puff Dough, page 112
½ cup heavy cream
2 tablespoons confectioners' sugar

½ teaspoon vanilla extract
¾ cup cherry preserves
   Confectioners' sugar

1. Preheat oven to 400F. Make Cream Puff Dough.

2. Place dough in pastry bag with number-6 star tip. Pipe, 2 inches apart, onto ungreased cookie sheet, to make 12 S shapes 3 inches long.

3. Bake 25 to 30 minutes, or until puffed and a deep golden-brown. Remove to wire rack; cool completely.

4. Meanwhile, beat cream with 2 tablespoons sugar and the vanilla until stiff. Refrigerate, covered.

5. To assemble madelons: With sharp knife, cut each S-shape puff in half lengthwise. Scoop out any filaments of soft dough.

6. Spoon 1 tablespoon cherry preserves into each bottom half, then a rounded tablespoon of whipped cream; replace top. Sprinkle with confectioners' sugar. Refrigerate if not serving at once.

Makes 12.

✥

MINIATURE CREAM PUFFS AND ÉCLAIRS

1. Preheat oven to 400F. Make Cream Puff Dough.

2. For cream puffs, drop dough by rounded teaspoonfuls, 2 inches apart, onto ungreased cookie sheet.

3. Bake until puffed and golden-brown—20 to 25 minutes.

4. Let cool completely on wire rack, away from drafts.

5. For éclairs, put cream puff dough into small pastry bag with round decorating tip, ½ inch in diameter. On an ungreased cookie sheet, press mixture in 2½-inch strips, 2 inches apart, using less pressure for center.

6. Bake 20 to 25 minutes, or until golden-brown.

7. Let cool completely on wire rack, away from drafts.

8. Fill with ice cream or cream filling. Sprinkle tops with confectioners' sugar or glaze with chocolate glaze or serve with chocolate or strawberry sauce.

Makes 35 cream puff shells or 35 éclair shells.

§3

GÂTEAU GLACÉ

½ pkg piecrust mix
  Cream Puff Dough, page 112
1 cup heavy cream
¼ cup confectioners' sugar
½ teaspoon vanilla extract

2 pints vanilla ice cream
  Candied violets and angelica
  (optional)
  Chocolate Sauce, page 122

1. Prepare piecrust mix as package label directs for one-crust pie. Shape into a ball.

2. On lightly floured surface, roll out pastry into an 8½-inch circle; trim to an 8-inch round. Place on back of 9-inch ungreased cake pan or small cookie sheet; prick well with fork. Refrigerate.

3. Preheat oven to 400F. Make Cream Puff Dough.

4. Place dough in pastry bag with plain tip about ½ inch in diameter. Pipe dough onto edge of pastry circle, to form a single border. Then pipe remaining dough into 8 small mounds, 2 inches apart, on ungreased cookie sheet.

5. Bake small mounds 35 minutes, or until puffed and golden-brown. Bake pastry shell 40 minutes, or until cream puff border is a deep golden-brown. Remove to wire rack; let cool completely.

6. Meanwhile, beat cream with confectioners' sugar and vanilla until stiff. Refrigerate, covered.

7. To assemble gâteau: With sharp knife, cut a slice off top of each puff. Fill each with a rounded teaspoon of whipped cream; replace top.

8. Spoon remaining whipped cream into pastry bag with number-6 star tip. Spacing evenly, pipe 8 rosettes on cream puff border of pastry shell. Gently top each rosette with a filled cream puff. Then pipe a rosette between each two cream puffs.

9. Spoon ice cream into center. Decorate rosettes and ice cream with bits of candied violet and angelica. Spoon about ½ teaspoon chocolate sauce on each puff. Serve immediately, with remaining chocolate sauce.

Makes 6 to 8 servings.

POLKAS

½ pkg (11-oz size) piecrust mix
  Cream Puff Dough, page 112

Cream Filling:
  1 pkg (3¾ oz) instant vanilla-
    pudding mix
1½ cups light cream
  ½ teaspoon vanilla extract
  ¼ teaspoon almond extract

Apricot Glaze:
  ½ cup apricot preserves

Fruit Topping:
  Drained canned mandarin
    orange sections
  Fresh or drained canned
    pineapple tidbits

1. Prepare piecrust mix as package label directs for one-crust pie. Divide into eighths. Shape each piece into a ball.

2. On lightly floured surface, roll out each pastry ball into a 3¼-inch round. Cut with 3-inch round scalloped or plain cutter, and place, 3 inches apart, on ungreased cookie sheet. Prick well with fork. Refrigerate.

3. Preheat oven to 400F. Make Cream Puff Dough.

4. Place dough in pastry bag with plain tip about ½ inch in diameter. Pipe dough on edge of each pastry circle, to form a single border.

5. Bake 30 to 35 minutes, or until a deep golden-brown. Remove shells to wire rack; let cool completely.

6. Meanwhile, make Cream Filling: In medium bowl, prepare pudding mix as package label directs, substituting the light cream for the milk and adding vanilla and almond extracts. Refrigerate, covered.

7. Make Apricot Glaze: In small saucepan, heat preserves, stirring, until melted. If too thick, thin with ½ to 1 tablespoon water; strain.

8. Assemble polkas: Spoon a rounded tablespoonful cream filling into each shell. Arrange fruit on top. Brush with glaze. Refrigerate until serving time.

Makes 8.

‰

GÂTEAU ST.-HONORÉ

1 1/2 pkg (10-oz size) frozen patty
    shells
  Rich Custard Filling, page 119
  2 tablespoons amber rum
  12 to 14 medium-size cream puffs

Caramelized Sugar:
1 1/4 cups granulated sugar

Cream Topping:
  2 cups heavy cream, chilled
  1/2 cup confectioners' sugar
  1 1/2 teaspoons vanilla extract

  Candied red cherries, angelica
  bits

1. Cover a cookie sheet with two thicknesses of heavy brown paper.

2. Remove patty shells from packages; let stand at room temperature 30 minutes, to soften.

3. Meanwhile, make Rich Custard Filling. Add rum; refrigerate.

4. On lightly floured pastry cloth, arrange patty shells, overlapping, in three rows of 3 shells each. Roll with rolling pin to make a solid pastry square, 12 by 12 inches. Press sides to make even. Fold dough into thirds, making three layers. Fold again in thirds to make square. Press edges to seal. Starting at center, roll out to a 12-inch circle.

5. Transfer to prepared cookie sheet; trim edges to make a cut edge all around. Prick entire surface with fork. Refrigerate 60 minutes.

6. Meanwhile, make double recipe Cream Puff Dough. Preheat oven to 400F.

7. Drop dough by rounded tablespoonfuls, 2 inches apart, onto an ungreased cookie sheet. Bake 30 to 35 minutes, or until puffed and golden-brown. Remove to wire rack; let cool.

8. Increase oven temperature to 450F. Bake round pastry base 15 minutes. Reduce heat to 350F, bake 15 minutes longer, or until puffed and richly browned. Remove from cookie sheet to wire rack.

9. Caramelize sugar: In medium skillet, place granulated sugar and 1/4 cup water; cook over medium heat until mixture forms a light-brown syrup—takes about 8 minutes. Then stir to blend. Remove from heat.

10. Meanwhile, make Cream Topping: Beat cream with confectioners' sugar and vanilla until stiff.

11. To assemble gâteau: Dip bottoms of cream puffs into caramel syrup; arrange around edge of pastry round to make border (cream puffs should touch each other). Use 12 to 14 puffs. (Any leftover puffs may be frozen.) Spoon rest of caramel syrup over tops of

cream puffs. Turn filling into center, spreading evenly.

12. Place whipped cream in pastry bag with number-6 star tip. Pipe all of the cream decoratively into center. Decorate with candied cherries and angelica. Refrigerate to chill well before serving—4 hours or longer.

Makes 12 to 14 servings.

Note: This dessert may be prepared day before and refrigerated overnight.

If desired, make filling again. Use to fill puffs just before assembling.

✂

EASY CUSTARD FILLING

1 pkg (3¼ oz) vanilla-pudding-
　　and-pie-filling mix
1½ cups milk
½ cup heavy cream

2 tablespoons confectioners'
　　sugar
½ teaspoon vanilla extract

1. Make pudding as package label directs, using 1½ cups milk.

2. Pour into medium bowl; place waxed paper directly on surface. Refrigerate until chilled—at least 1 hour.

3. In small bowl, combine heavy cream, sugar, and vanilla; with rotary beater, beat just until stiff. Then fold whipped-cream mixture into pudding until combined.

4. Refrigerate several hours, to chill well before using.

Makes 2 cups; enough filling for 6 large puffs or 36 miniature puffs.

✂

RICH CUSTARD FILLING

1½ cups milk
¼ cup sugar
1½ tablespoons cornstarch

2 egg yolks, slightly beaten
1 teaspoon vanilla extract
½ cup heavy cream, whipped

1. In small heavy saucepan, heat 1½ cups milk until bubbling around edge. Mix sugar and cornstarch; stir, all at once, into hot milk. Over medium heat, cook, stirring, until bubbling. Reduce heat; simmer 1 minute.

2. Beat a little of hot mixture into yolks. Return to saucepan;

cook, stirring, over medium heat until thickened. Add vanilla. Turn into bowl; refrigerate—with waxed paper on surface—1½ hours. Fold in cream.

Makes 2 cups.

❈

CHOCOLATE CREAM

¼ cup sugar
1 tablespoon cornstarch
  Dash salt
1 cup milk

1 pkg (6 oz) semisweet chocolate
  pieces (1 cup)
1 egg
1 tablespoon butter or margarine
½ teaspoon vanilla extract

1. In small saucepan, combine sugar, cornstarch, and salt. Gradually stir in milk; add chocolate.

2. Cook over medium heat, stirring constantly, until mixture boils; boil 1 minute. Remove from heat.

3. Lightly beat egg in small bowl. Gradually stir in a little hot mixture; then stir into rest of mixture in saucepan. Cook, stirring, until thick—about 2 minutes. Remove from heat; stir in butter and vanilla.

4. Cool to room temperature. Turn into bowl; refrigerate, covered.

Makes 1¾ cups.

❈

CHOCOLATE GLAZE

½ cup semisweet chocolate
  pieces
1 tablespoon butter or regular
  margarine

1 tablespoon light corn syrup
1½ tablespoons milk

1. In top of double boiler, combine the chocolate pieces, butter, corn syrup, and milk.

2. Place over hot, not boiling, water, stirring occasionally, until mixture is smooth and well blended. Let cool slightly before spooning over puffs or éclairs.

Makes ½ cup.

CHOCOLATE SAUCE

1 *pkg (6 oz) semisweet chocolate*   ¼ *cup light corn syrup*
     pieces (1 cup)   ½ *teaspoon vanilla extract*
½ *cup milk*

   1. In small saucepan, combine chocolate pieces, milk, and corn syrup; cook over medium heat, stirring constantly, until chocolate is melted and mixture is smooth.

   2. Remove from heat; stir in vanilla. Let cool at room temperature.

   Makes 1¼ cups.

CHILDREN'S PARTY DESSERTS

Put two or more children together and guess what? A party! Spur-of-the-moment gatherings can be given a glow of excitement by simple and quick desserts such as chocolate fondue, jelly-filled crêpes or little pastries. Larger gatherings may call for more elaborate concoctions, such as ice-cream cakes and fresh-faced cupcakes —but these too are easy to make and much less expensive than those from the bakery or ice-cream parlor.

And of course we include the very best party treat of all—the traditional, decorated party cake, made by Mother herself.

CAROUSEL BIRTHDAY CAKE

1 pkg yellow-cake mix (two layers)
1 pkg (5¾ oz) fluffy white frosting mix
¼ cup cranberry or cherry juice
10 animal crackers
Pastel-color jelly beans
Multicolor candy wafers
Cardboard circle, 3¼ inches across, covered with yellow construction paper
6 colored candy sticks
Name flags made of pink construction paper
Wooden toothpicks
8 pink or white candies

1. Follow the directions on the package of cake mix for preparing cake. Preheat oven as directed. Make cake following instructions for two 9-inch layers. Cool in pans 10 minutes.

2. To turn out of pans: Carefully run a spatula or paring knife around edge of cake pan to loosen cake. Invert over wire rack; shake gently, then lift off pan. Let cake cool completely.

3. Prepare fluffy white frosting mix, following the directions on the package. Measure ¼ cup cranberry or cherry juice and use this in the frosting for half the water called for to make a pink color.

4. Place a cake layer on a serving plate. With spatula, spread with ⅓ cup frosting. Then place the second layer on top. Frost cake all over, top and around side, with the rest of the frosting.

5. Place animal crackers all around side of cake in center.

6. Decorate around top and bottom on side of cake alternating jelly beans with wafers.

7. For tent: Measure cardboard and cut out circle. Cover with yellow paper. Insert candy sticks through circle, equidistant all around. Then arrange candy sticks in frosting, on a slant, to make it look like a tent.

8. With glue, attach flags with names lettered on them to toothpicks, then stick flags into the center of cardboard circle.

9. Last, put candles in the cake.

Makes 10 servings.

CHOCOLATE CUPCAKE FACES

4 squares unsweetened chocolate
2 cups sifted* all-purpose flour
1 teaspoon baking powder
1 teaspoon salt
¾ cup butter or margarine
1 cup sugar
4 eggs
6 tablespoons milk
1 teaspoon vanilla extract

1 cup finely chopped walnuts
1 pkg (6 oz) fluffy white frosting
    mix
Licorice laces
Candy corn
Life Savers
Semisweet chocolate pieces
Chocolate sprinkles

* Sift before measuring.

1. Melt chocolate over hot, not boiling, water; remove from hot water; let cool.

2. Preheat oven to 350F. Line 24 cupcake-pan cups (2½-by-1¼ inches) with paper liners.

3. Sift flour with baking powder and salt. Set aside.

4. In large bowl of electric mixer, at medium speed, cream butter with sugar until light and fluffy. Beat in eggs.

5. At low speed, beat in flour mixture alternately with milk, beginning and ending with flour mixture. Stir in vanilla, melted chocolate and walnuts.

6. Fill cupcake cups two-thirds full. Bake 20 minutes, or until top springs back when gently pressed with fingertip.

7. Turn out on wire rack.

8. Prepare frosting mix as package label directs.

9. Frost tops of cupcakes.

10. Make faces with candies.

Makes 24 cupcakes.

PINK PARTY CAKE

1 pkg (10 oz) frozen sliced
    strawberries, thawed
1 pkg (14½ oz) angel food cake
    mix

Strawberry Frosting:
2 egg whites
½ cup sugar
¼ teaspoon salt

Small pink and yellow gumdrops

1. Preheat oven to 375F. Drain strawberries, reserving juice.

2. Prepare cake mix as package label directs, using ⅓ cup juice from strawberries and 1 cup water.

3. Bake in 10-inch tube pan. Let cool completely.

4. Make Frosting: In top of double boiler, combine strawberries and remaining juice with egg whites, sugar and salt.

5. Place over boiling water (water in lower part of double boiler should not touch upper section); cook, beating constantly with portable electric mixer, until stiff peaks form when beater is slowly raised—5 to 7 minutes.

6. Remove from boiling water; cool slightly.

7. Spread frosting over top and side of cake. Decorate with gumdrops cut into flowers.

Makes 12 servings.

❧

PINK POSY CAKE

1. Bake cake as directed in Pink Party Cake, above. When cool, cover hole in center with a 4-inch-diameter circle of cardboard, cut from a paper plate.

2. Make Frosting as above; remove 1½ cups; set aside.

3. Spread remaining frosting over top and side of cake.

4. Using half of reserved frosting in decorating bag with number-4 plain tip, make diagonal lines, 2 inches apart, around side of cake. Then make diagonal lines in opposite direction, to make a diamond pattern.

5. Using rest of frosting in a decorating bag with number-199 open-star tube, make shell border around base and top edge of cake.

6. Arrange 3 paper doilies and real pink flowers or roses in center top of the cake.

Makes 12 servings.

ROCKET ICE-CREAM CAKE

Cake:
6 eggs
1/2 teaspoon cream of tartar
3/4 cup granulated sugar
1/3 cup unsweetened cocoa
1 teaspoon vanilla extract
  Confectioners' sugar
2 pints chocolate or chocolate-
  chip ice cream, slightly
  softened

Frosting:
1/2 cup softened butter or
  margarine
2 squares unsweetened
  chocolate, melted
2 tablespoons milk
1/2 teaspoon vanilla extract
1 cup confectioners' sugar

1. Make Cake: Separate eggs, placing yolks in small bowl of electric mixer and whites in large bowl. Let whites warm to room temperature—about 1 hour.

2. Preheat oven to 375F. Lightly grease bottom of a 15½-by-10½-by-1-inch jelly-roll pan; then line with waxed paper.

3. At high speed, beat egg whites with cream of tartar just until soft peaks form when beater is slowly raised. Gradually beat in ¼ cup granulated sugar; continue beating until stiff peaks form.

4. With same beater, at high speed, beat yolks with rest of granulated sugar until thick and lemon-colored—about 5 minutes. At low speed, beat in cocoa and 1 teaspoon vanilla.

5. With wire whisk or rubber scraper, using an under-and-over motion, gently fold yolk mixture into beaten egg whites just until combined.

6. Turn into prepared pan, spreading evenly. Bake 12 to 14 minutes, or just until surface springs back when gently pressed with fingertip.

7. Meanwhile, onto clean towel, sift confectioners' sugar in a 15-by-10-inch rectangle. Turn out cake onto sugar; gently peel off paper. With very sharp knife, trim edges.

8. Starting with long edge, roll up cake in the towel. Place, seam side down, on wire rack; let cool about 30 minutes.

9. Gently unroll cake. Spread with ice cream; roll up (cake tends to crack slightly). Wrap in foil or plastic film; freeze until firm —about 1 hour.

10. Meanwhile, make Frosting: In small bowl of electric mixer, at medium speed, beat butter until creamy. Add chocolate, milk, and ½ teaspoon vanilla; beat well.

11. Add confectioners' sugar; beat till smooth and well mixed.

12. Spread over cake. Decorate with nose cone and tail fins, made from construction paper. Serve at once, or return to freezer until party time.

Makes 10 servings.

PINK PISTACHIO ICE CREAM CAKE

2 quarts strawberry ice cream
1 quart pistachio ice cream
1 cup strawberry jam
2 cups heavy cream, whipped

½ cup chopped pistachio nuts
1 pint box strawberries, washed,
    hulled, and halved

1. Let ice cream soften slightly. Line 3 (8-inch) layer-cake pans with plastic wrap.

2. Press each quart ice cream firmly and evenly into a prepared layer-cake pan.

3. Freeze, covered, until very firm—several hours.

4. To assemble: Remove ice cream from pans; remove plastic wrap. Place a strawberry layer on serving plate; spread with half of jam. Add pistachio layer; spread with rest of jam. Top with remaining strawberry layer.

5. Frost top and side with the whipped cream. Sprinkle side with pistachio nuts. Freeze until very firm—about 3 hours. (For longer storing, wrap frozen cake in plastic film or foil.)

6. To serve: Decorate top of cake with strawberry halves.

Makes 12 to 15 servings.

HOLIDAY BAKED ALASKA

2 pints pistachio ice cream
1½ pints strawberry ice cream
    Chocolate Sauce or Cardinal
        Sauce, pages 122, 343

Meringue:
8 egg whites

½ teaspoon cream of tartar
¼ teaspoon salt
1 cup sugar

1 (8-inch) yellow cake layer

1. Refrigerate a 1½-quart bowl at least ½ hour. Remove pistachio ice cream from freezer, and place on shelf in refrigerator to soften slightly—about ½ hour if the ice cream is frozen very hard.

2. With large spoon, press pistachio ice cream firmly and evenly around side of chilled bowl. Place in freezer until firm—about ½ hour. Meanwhile, let strawberry ice cream soften in refrigerator.

3. Press strawberry ice cream into center of bowl, smoothing top. Cover with plastic wrap or foil. Place in freezer, and freeze until firm—several hours or overnight.

4. To unmold: With a small spatula, loosen ice cream from side of bowl. Invert onto cookie sheet; place a hot, damp dishcloth over bowl; shake gently to release. Immediately return to freezer until firm—at least 2 hours.

5. Meanwhile, make sauce.

6. About 1 hour before serving, let the egg whites warm to room temperature—about 45 minutes.

7. Preheat oven to 425F. Make Meringue: In large bowl, with electric mixer at high speed, beat egg whites with cream of tartar and salt until soft peaks form when beater is slowly raised.

8. Gradually beat in sugar, 2 tablespoons at a time. Continue beating until stiff peaks form when beater is raised.

9. Place sheet of foil on cookie sheet and grease lightly. Arrange the cake layer in center. With broad spatula, place ice cream on cake.

10. With small spatula, spread meringue over ice cream and cake, spreading it down onto foil all around to seal completely. Make swirls with spatula.

11. Bake, on lowest shelf of oven, 8 to 10 minutes, or until meringue is golden.

12. With small spatula dipped in warm water, carefully loosen meringue from foil; with broad spatula, remove Alaska to serving plate. Serve with Cardinal Sauce or Chocolate Sauce.

Makes 12 servings.

BANANA SPLIT

Small ripe bananas
Vanilla ice cream
Strawberry ice cream
Chocolate ice cream
Prepared fudge sauce
Strawberry Sauce (below)

Prepared creamy marshmallow topping
Whipped cream
¾ cup chopped walnuts
Whole strawberries, with hulls on

1. For each serving, peel 2 bananas; cut one in half lengthwise, and place one half on each side of oval dish. Cut other banana in quarters, and place at ends of dish.

2. Using large, number-6, ice-cream scoop, make 1 vanilla, 1 strawberry, and 1 chocolate ice-cream ball. Place vanilla and strawberry balls in center of dish; place chocolate ball on top.

3. Spoon 2 tablespoons fudge sauce over vanilla ice cream, 2 tablespoons Strawberry Sauce over strawberry ice cream, 2 tablespoons marshmallow topping over chocolate ice cream.

4. Decorate with whipped cream in pastry bag, using number-6 decorating tip. Sprinkle with walnuts; garnish with strawberries.

STRAWBERRY SAUCE

1 pkg (10 oz) frozen sliced
   strawberries
¼ cup sugar

1 tablespoon cornstarch
2 tablespoons strawberry
   preserves

1. Drain strawberries, reserving syrup. Add water to syrup to measure 1 cup. In small saucepan, combine sugar and cornstarch. Gradually add strawberry syrup, stirring until smooth.

2. Over low heat, slowly bring to boiling, stirring until mixture is thickened and translucent.

3. Remove from heat. Stir in strawberries and preserves.

4. Stir until preserves are melted. Refrigerate until cold. Makes 1⅓ cups.

ICE-CREAM-CONE CLOWNS

2 quarts strawberry ice cream
   Gumdrops

Semisweet chocolate pieces or
   seedless raisins
10 ice-cream cones

1. Using a large ice-cream scoop, make 10 ice-cream balls. Place in foil-lined shallow pan; return to freezer until firm.

2. Make faces on ice-cream balls, using whole red gumdrops for nose, slivered gumdrop for mouth, chocolate pieces for eyes. For hats, set a cone on top of each.

3. Return to freezer until serving time. Makes 10 clowns.

CHOCOLATE ICE-CREAM CONES

2 pkgs (6-oz size) semisweet   Decorations (see Note)
   chocolate pieces   3 pints assorted ice cream
12 ice-cream cones

1. Melt chocolate over hot, not boiling, water.

2. With small spatula, spread 1 tablespoon melted chocolate inside each cone. Swirl top edge of cone in chocolate; spread to make a ¾-inch-deep border.

3. Decorate or sprinkle with one or more decorations.

4. Top each cone with scoop of ice cream. Serve at once.

Makes 12 servings.

Note: Decorate cones with chocolate-covered peanuts; miniature marshmallows, halved crosswise; miniature nonpareils; chocolate sprinkles; colored sprinkles; chopped walnuts; colored sugar; flaked coconut; light or dark raisins.

MARSHMALLOW ICE-CREAM CONES

¼ lb large marshmallows   12 ice-cream cones
2 teaspoons milk   Decorations (see Note above)
                                 3 pints assorted ice cream

1. Over hot, not boiling, water, melt marshmallows slightly. Add milk.

2. Cook, stirring occasionally, until completely melted.

3. Swirl top edge of cone in mixture; spread with spatula to make a ¾-inch-deep border.

4. Decorate or sprinkle with one or more decorations.

5. Top each cone with scoop of ice cream. Serve at once.

Makes 12 servings.

FLOWERPOT SUNDAES

1 pint vanilla ice cream
1 pint pistachio ice cream
1 pint strawberry ice cream
  Marshmallows
  Round lollipops in various colors
  A can or tube of pink frosting
    with a squirter nozzle

Spearmint gumdrop leaves,
  split in half
Green sugar crystals
Multicolor tiny mints
Chocolate shot

1. With ice-cream scoop, fill six (8-oz size) paper cups with ½ pint ice cream each. Place, covered, in freezer.

2. To make lollipop flowers: Cut marshmallows with scissors around edge to make petals. Attach a marshmallow "flower" to one side of lollipop with a squirt of frosting.

3. Make rosette of frosting in center of marshmallow flower.

4. Attach spearmint leaves, one on each side of lollipop-stick stem, with a dab of frosting. Insert flowers in ice cream. Sprinkle ice cream with green sugar crystals, multicolor mints or chocolate shot.

5. Keep the sundaes in the freezer until ready to serve.

Note: The pink frosting, gumdrop leaves, green sugar crystals, and chocolate shot can be found in most supermarkets. The multicolor tiny mints can be found in most candy stores.

PEPPERMINT ICE-CREAM SUNDAE PIE

3 pints vanilla ice cream, slightly
    softened
¼ lb peppermint-stick candy,
    crushed
2 cups chocolate wafer crumbs

⅓ cup softened butter or
    margarine
  Chocolate Sauce, page 344
1 cup heavy cream, whipped
¼ cup chopped walnuts

1. Turn ice cream into a large bowl. With spoon, swirl crushed candy into ice cream just enough to give a marbled effect—do not overmix. Return ice cream to containers; freeze.

2. Combine wafer crumbs with butter; mix with fork until thoroughly combined.

3. Press crumb mixture evenly on bottom and side of a 9-inch pie plate. Refrigerate until well chilled—about 1 hour.

4. Meanwhile, make Fudge Sauce.

5. Fill pie shell with scoops of ice cream, mounding in center.

6. Pour ½ cup fudge sauce over the top. Store in freezer until serving. ·

7. Just before serving, garnish with mounds of whipped cream; sprinkle with nuts. Pass rest of fudge sauce, if desired.

Makes 8 servings.

Note: You may substitute any flavor ice cream for vanilla and omit peppermint candy.

STRAWBERRY PARFAITS

1 cup canned chocolate syrup
2 pints vanilla ice cream
¾ cup strawberry preserves
1 pint strawberry ice cream
¾ cup prepared marshmallow
    sauce

1 cup heavy cream
2 tablespoons confectioners'
    sugar
8 fresh strawberries, optional

1. Spoon 1 tablespoon chocolate syrup into bottom of each of 8 (8-oz) chilled parfait glasses (or any tall glasses).

2. Add to each, in order, 1 rounded tablespoon vanilla ice cream, 1 rounded tablespoon strawberry preserves, 1 small scoop (¼ cup) strawberry ice cream, and 1 tablespoon prepared marshmallow sauce.

3. Top each with 1 scoop vanilla ice cream, then drizzle each with 1 tablespoon chocolate syrup. Place in freezer.

4. Whip cream with confectioners' sugar. Decorate each parfait with whipped cream and a strawberry, if desired. Freeze until firm. If keeping more than 1 day, cover with plastic film.

5. To serve: If parfaits have been in freezer more than 24 hours, remove them from freezer 15 minutes before serving.

Makes 8 servings.

SUNDAES EN GÊLEÉ

1 pkg (3 oz) strawberry-flavored
   gelatine
1 cup boiling water

6 to 8 ice cubes
1 quart vanilla ice cream

1. Combine gelatin with boiling water in an 8-by-8-by-2-inch baking dish. Stir to dissolve gelatine completely.

2. Add ice cubes. Stir until ice cubes are half melted; then discard the ice cubes.

3. Refrigerate mixture until very firm—at least 1 hour. Cut into ½-inch cubes.

4. To serve, spoon gelatine cubes over ice cream.

Makes 8 servings.

Ice-Cream Drinks

❋

ICE-CREAM SODAS

CHOCOLATE-MINT SODA

In a large glass, combine ⅔ cup milk, 1 tablespoon canned chocolate syrup, few drops peppermint extract; stir well, with a long spoon. Add 2 scoops vanilla ice cream. Fill glass to top with ginger ale; stir well. Top with 2 tablespoons whipped cream or whipped topping. Streak with 1 teaspoon canned chocolate syrup.

STRAWBERRY-LIME SODA

Put 2 scoops lime sherbet and ¼ cup crushed strawberries (fresh or frozen) in a large glass. Fill to top with ginger ale; stir well, with a long spoon.

DOUBLE STRAWBERRY SODA

Put 2 scoops strawberry ice cream in a large glass. Spoon 1 tablespoon strawberry jam over ice cream. Fill to top with ginger ale; stir well, with a long spoon.

PINEAPPLE-LEMON SODA

Put 2 scoops lemon sherbet and ¼ cup drained pineapple chunks (canned) in a large glass. Fill to top with ginger ale; stir well, with a long spoon.

ORANGE-SHERBET FREEZE

Put 2 scoops orange sherbet in a large glass. Spoon on 2 teaspoons orange marmalade. Fill glass to top with ginger ale; stir well, with a long spoon. Top with 2 tablespoons drained canned mandarin-orange sections.

ROOT BEER FLOAT

Put 2 scoops ice cream (any flavor) in a large glass. Fill to the top with root beer; then stir well, with a long spoon.

FRESH STRAWBERRY SODA

½ cup strawberries, fresh or
    thawed frozen
1 cup milk

2 tablespoons sugar
½ cup vanilla ice cream
   Ginger ale

1. Put strawberries, milk, and sugar into blender container; cover, and blend on high speed 20 seconds.

2. Add ice cream; flick blender switch on and off several times, merely to mix. Half fill 2 tall, 14-ounce glasses. Fill to top with ginger ale.

Makes 2 sodas.

ICE-CREAM MILK SHAKES

Peanut Butter: In electric blender,* blend at high speed, for 1 minute, 1 cup milk and 2 tablespoons creamy-style peanut butter. Add 2 No. 16 (or medium) scoops vanilla ice cream; then blend 1 minute longer. This makes 2 cups.

* All milk shakes can be made using a portable electric mixer and 1-quart measure or medium bowl.

FLAVOR VARIATIONS

Strawberry: Substitute 2 tablespoons strawberry jam for peanut butter.

Raspberry: Substitute 2 tablespoons raspberry jam for peanut butter.

Pineapple: Substitute 3 tablespoons drained, canned crushed pineapple for peanut butter.

Chocolate: Substitute 1 tablespoon canned chocolate syrup for peanut butter.

Banana: Substitute ½ medium-size ripe banana, cut in small pieces, for peanut butter.

Gingersnap: Omit peanut butter. Break 6 gingersnaps into pieces. Add milk, and let soak a few minutes until soft. Add ice cream, and continue as directed above.

ORANGE-CHOCOLATE ICE-CREAM MOLD

1 quart chocolate ice cream,
   softened
1 pint orange sherbet

½ cup heavy cream, whipped
Chocolate curls, page 346
Orange peel, cut in thin strips

1. Chill well a 1-quart decorative mold.

2. Using back of wooden spoon or rubber scraper, press chocolate ice cream evenly over interior of mold to form a shell.

3. Freeze until firm—about 1 hour.

4. Meanwhile, let sherbet stand in refrigerator about 30 minutes to soften.

5. Fill mold with sherbet. Cover with foil; freeze several hours or overnight.

6. To unmold: Wipe outside of mold with hot, damp cloth; turn out onto chilled plate.

7. Serve at once, garnished with whipped cream, chocolate curls and orange peel.

Makes 8 servings.

HAWAIIAN PUNCH POPSICLES

1 can (6 oz) frozen Hawaiian
   Punch concentrate
1 pint vanilla ice cream

6 (7-oz size) cold-drink paper cups
6 popsicle sticks or wooden
   spoons

1. Combine punch concentrate with 2 punch cans of water; stir until mixed.

2. Place a scoop of ice cream, about ⅓ cup, in each paper cup.

3. Fill cups with punch to within an inch of top. Insert a stick into center of ice cream in each. Do not push ice cream into bottom of cup.

4. Freeze 3 hours, or until firm.

5. Slip cups off the frozen popsicles just before serving.
Makes 6.

✖✖

FROZEN-YOGURT-ON-A-STICK

2 cups yogurt
½ cup strawberry preserves

½ teaspoon vanilla extract
8 popsicle sticks

1. In blender, combine all ingredients; blend until smooth.
2. Pour into 8-by-8-by-2-inch baking pan, spreading evenly. Freeze until firm—several hours or overnight.
3. Remove from freezer; let stand 5 minutes to soften. Cut in half, then cut each half crosswise into 4 pieces. Insert a stick into each popsicle. Return to freezer about ½ hour (or until firm) before serving.

Makes 8 servings.

✖✖

JELLY-FILLED CRÊPES

1 cup unsifted all-purpose flour
¼ cup butter or margarine,
    melted and cooled; or ¼ cup
    salad oil
2 whole eggs
2 egg yolks

1½ cups milk
    Butter or margarine, melted
1 jar (12 oz) strawberry or
    raspberry preserves or
    currant jelly
    Confectioners' sugar

1. In medium bowl, combine flour, ¼ cup melted butter, the whole eggs, egg yolks and ½ cup milk; beat with rotary beater until smooth. Beat in the remaining milk until well blended.
2. Refrigerate, covered, at least 30 minutes.
3. Slowly heat an 8-inch skillet until a drop of water sizzles and rolls off. For each crêpe, brush skillet lightly with butter. Pour in about 2 tablespoons batter, rotating pan quickly, to spread batter completely over bottom of skillet.
4. Cook until lightly browned; then turn and brown other side. Turn out onto wire rack.
5. Spread each crêpe with 1 tablespoon preserves. Fold in half, then in half again, like a handkerchief. Sprinkle with confectioners' sugar.
6. Serve at once; or keep warm in a 300F oven while making the rest. Sprinkle again with confectioners' sugar before serving.

Makes 16 crêpes (8 servings).

ЕЗ

QUICK GLAZED DOUGHNUTS AND HOLES

1 pkg (8 oz) buttermilk
   refrigerator biscuits
Orange marmalade or honey

⅓ cup butter or margarine, melted
Cinnamon-sugar (see Note)

1. Preheat oven to 450F.

2. Flatten biscuits; cut out center from each (about ½ inch). Stretch each biscuit to form a 4-inch ring. Place on cookie sheet.

3. Bake 6 to 8 minutes, or until golden-brown.

4. Bake centers 4 to 6 minutes.

5. While still warm, brush doughnuts and "holes" with honey or marmalade thinned with water, or dip in melted butter; roll in cinnamon-sugar.

Makes 10 doughnuts and "holes."

Note: Mix ⅓ cup granulated sugar with 1 teaspoon ground cinnamon.

ЕЗ

CHOCOLATE FONDUE

2 pkg (6-oz size) semisweet
   chocolate pieces
1 can (13 oz) evaporated milk,
   undiluted
½ cup orange juice
1 tablespoon grated orange peel

For dipping in fondue:
   Pineapple chunks,
      marshmallows, squares of
      poundcake or angel food
      cake, banana slices, dates,
      pitted dried prunes, dried
      apricots

1. In a heavy saucepan, combine chocolate and evaporated milk. Cook, stirring constantly, over low heat until chocolate is melted. Stir in orange juice and peel; remove from heat. (This may be made ahead, and reheated, stirring, in top of double boiler just before serving.)

2. Serve warm in fondue pot; surround with cake and fruit for dipping on fondue forks or other long-handled forks.

Makes 8 to 10 servings.

ЕЗ

LITTLE PASTRIES

1 cup piecrust mix
2 tablespoons cold water
   Applesauce, or drained canned
     crushed pineapple, or preserves

Sugar
Jelly or jam
Confectioners' sugar

1. Preheat oven to 400F.

2. Mix piecrust mix with cold water as package label directs. Roll out to form a 12-inch circle, about 1/8 inch thick.

3. Cut as desired: For Turnovers, cut into circles, 2, 3 or 4 inches in diameter. Cover half of pastry circle with applesauce or crushed pineapple or preserves; use 1 tablespoon filling for 4-inch; 1/2 tablespoon for 3-inch; 1 teaspoon for 2-inch. Moisten edges of turnovers with water; fold other half of pastry over; pinch edge together to seal. Brush tops with water. Prick with fork. Bake on cookie sheet 20 minutes, or until golden-brown.

4. For Rounds and Jelly Tarts: Cut 2-inch circles. Brush with water; prick with fork. Bake pastries, at 425F, 8 minutes.

5. For tarts, cut out 1/2-inch rounds from centers of half the rounds. Brush, prick with fork, and bake as above. Cool. Spread half of 2-inch rounds with jelly or preserves; top with rounds with hole in center.

6. Sift confectioners' sugar lightly over tops of all pastries.

Makes 9 to 12 assorted pastries.

ЕЗ

CHOCOLATE CANDY PIE

20 regular-size marshmallows
1/2 cup milk
2 bars (1.05 oz size) milk
   chocolate with almonds

1 1/2 cups heavy cream
   9-inch prepared graham-
     cracker pie shell, page 10

1. In medium saucepan, combine marshmallows and milk. Cook over low heat, stirring occasionally, until marshmallows are melted.

2. Add chocolate bars, broken in several pieces, and continue cooking, stirring constantly, until chocolate is melted. Remove from heat; pour into 9-by-9-by-2-inch pan; place in freezer, to cool quickly —about 10 minutes.

3. Whip 1 cup cream; fold into chocolate mixture. Pour into pie shell.

4. Refrigerate pie until well chilled—at least 3 hours.

5. Whip rest of cream. Use to decorate around edge.

Makes 6 to 8 servings.

RAISIN-PEANUT POPCORN BALLS

5 cups freshly popped popcorn
1 cup raisins
1 cup salted peanuts
3/4 cup light-brown sugar, packed

2/3 cup granulated sugar
1/3 cup light corn syrup
1/2 teaspoon vanilla extract

1. In large bowl, combine popcorn, raisins and peanuts; toss to mix well.

2. In heavy saucepan, combine both kinds of sugar, 1/2 cup water and the corn syrup. Stir to mix well. Bring to boiling; boil, without stirring, to 250F on candy thermometer, or until a small amount in cold water forms a hard ball. Remove from heat; add vanilla.

3. Pour syrup over popcorn mixture. Mix well with wooden spoon. With buttered hands, quickly form into balls.

Makes 10 popcorn balls.

CEREAL POPCORN BALLS

Make recipe above, substituting 2 cups favorite prepared cereal, such as puffed wheat, puffed rice or wheat flakes, for peanuts and raisins.

PEANUT-BUTTER POPCORN BALLS

3 cups miniature marshmallows
2 tablespoons butter or margarine

1/2 cup chunk-style peanut butter
5 cups freshly popped popcorn

In large, heavy kettle over low heat, cook marshmallows, butter and peanut butter, stirring, until marshmallows are melted. Add popcorn; stir to mix well. With buttered hands, form into balls.

Makes 6 large popcorn balls.

CHRISTMAS POPCORN BALLS

6 tablespoons salad oil
½ cup unpopped popcorn
   (see Note)
1½ cups salted peanuts, coarsely
   chopped
¼ cup candied red cherries,
   quartered

¼ cup candied green cherries,
   quartered
1 cup light corn syrup
½ cup sugar
1 pkg (3 oz) strawberry-flavored
   or lime-flavored gelatine

1. To pop popcorn: Heat oil in a heavy, 4-quart saucepan over medium heat. To test temperature of pan, add 1 kernel of corn; cover pan and shake often. When kernel pops, add ½ cup popcorn in a single layer; cover; shake pan often. Continue until all corn in pan is popped. Turn into large bowl.

2. Add peanuts and candied cherries to popcorn; toss to combine.

3. In a 1-quart saucepan, combine corn syrup and sugar. Cook, stirring with a wooden spoon, over medium heat, until sugar is dissolved. Without stirring, bring mixture to a full, rolling boil. Remove from heat.

4. Add gelatine; stir until dissolved.

5. Pour syrup mixture over popcorn mixture; toss to coat well.

6. Drop mixture onto waxed paper, to make about 1½ dozen mounds. With lightly buttered hands, form popcorn mixture into balls. Place on waxed-paper-lined tray, to dry at room temperature.

Makes about 1½ dozen.

To store: When popcorn balls are thoroughly dry, wrap individually in plastic wrap or colored foil. Will keep several weeks at room temperature.

Note: Or use 1 bag (3½ ounces or about 12 cups) ready-to-eat popcorn.

APPLES-ON-A-STICK

2 *cups sugar*
2 *cups light corn syrup*
2 *bottles (1¾-oz size) red*
   cinnamon candies (⅓ cup)

½ *teaspoon cinnamon*
6 *medium-size red apples*
6 *wooden skewers*

1. In medium saucepan, combine sugar, corn syrup, and cinnamon candies with 1 cup cold water.

2. Over medium heat, stir constantly just until sugar and candies are dissolved. Do not boil.

3. Add cinnamon; stir to mix well.

4. Bring syrup to boiling; continue cooking, without stirring, to 300F on candy thermometer.

5. Meanwhile, wash apples and dry well. Remove stem from each; insert a skewer partway in stem end, far enough to hold apple firmly.

6. Remove syrup from heat.

7. Working quickly, dip each apple (holding by skewer) into syrup to coat completely. Place, skewer end up, on well-greased cookie sheets to let taffy harden. Let stand at room temperature until serving.

Makes 6.

Note: Use ripe, red eating apples, such as McIntosh or Delicious.

OLD-FASHIONED DESSERTS

Memories are made of warming, satisfying custards and cobblers. A generation ago an everyday dessert might have been a creamy tapioca, a shimmering caramel custard (now generally—and sadly—reserved for French menus), a frothy lemon snow or a crumbly shortcake.

Once your family samples any of these delightful dishes from the past, we know that they too will remember them for years to come.

CHOCOLATE BLANCMANGE

2¼ cups milk
3 squares unsweetened
   chocolate, cut up
3 tablespoons cornstarch

½ cup sugar
¼ teaspoon salt
1 teaspoon vanilla extract
  Whipped cream

1. In medium-size, heavy saucepan, slowly heat 2 cups milk with chocolate, stirring, until chocolate is melted.

2. In small bowl, combine cornstarch, sugar, salt and remaining milk; stir to mix well.

3. Gradually stir into hot chocolate mixture. Bring to boiling, stirring; boil 1 minute, stirring constantly.

4. Remove from heat; add vanilla.

5. Turn into 4 or 5 individual dessert dishes or parfait glasses. Place waxed paper directly on surface of each. Refrigerate until very well chilled—several hours. Serve topped with whipped cream.

Makes 4 or 5 servings.

TAPIOCA CREAM

2 cups milk
3 tablespoons quick-cooking
   tapioca
2 egg yolks, slightly beaten

¼ cup sugar
  Dash salt
½ teaspoon vanilla extract
2 egg whites

1. In top of double boiler, heat milk until bubbles form around edge. Stir in tapioca. Cook, covered, stirring occasionally, over hot water until tapioca is transparent—about 30 minutes.

2. Into egg yolks, beat sugar and salt. Stir in a little hot milk mixture; pour back into double boiler. Continue cooking over hot water until mixture is thick enough to coat a metal spoon. Remove from heat; stir in vanilla. Let cool slightly.

3. In medium bowl, beat egg whites until stiff. Fold tapioca mixture into egg whites just to combine slightly. Pour into serving dishes. Refrigerate until well chilled. Serve plain or with whipped cream or fruit.

Makes 6 servings.

PINEAPPLE TAPIOCA CREAM

Make Tapioca Cream, above. Fold in 1 can (8¾ oz) crushed pineapple, drained. Pour into serving dishes. Refrigerate.

BAKED CARAMEL CUSTARDS

½ cup sugar	Dash salt
2 cups milk	½ teaspoon vanilla extract
3 eggs	Nutmeg

1. In small, heavy skillet, over very low heat, melt ¼ cup sugar, stirring, until a light-golden syrup forms.

2. Pour into 5 (6-oz) custard cups, rotating to coat bottoms; cool.

3. Preheat oven to 350F. Heat milk just until bubbles form around edge of pan. In medium bowl, beat eggs slightly; beat in remaining ¼ cup sugar, salt and vanilla.

4. Stir in milk. Pour mixture into custard cups, dividing evenly. Sprinkle with nutmeg.

5. Place in shallow pan. Pour hot water to ½-inch level around custard cups.

6. Bake 35 minutes or until silver knife inserted ½ inch into center of custard comes out clean. Be careful not to overbake.

7. Refrigerate to chill well—several hours or overnight.

8. To serve: Run a sharp knife around edge of custard cup to loosen. Invert on serving plate; shake to release. Serve plain or with whipped cream, if desired.

Makes 5 servings.

PLAIN BAKED CUSTARDS

Omit caramelizing sugar. Make custards, beginning with step 3. Serve custards in cups; do not unmold.

✼

CARAMEL FLAN

¾ cup sugar

Custard:
  2 cups milk
  2 cups light cream
  6 eggs

½ cup sugar
½ teaspoon salt
  2 teaspoons vanilla extract

  Boiling water

1. Place ¾ cup sugar in large, heavy skillet. Cook over medium heat, until sugar melts and forms a light-brown syrup. Stir to blend.

2. Immediately pour syrup into heated, 8¼-inch-diameter-round, shallow baking dish. Holding dish with pot holders, quickly rotate, to cover bottom and sides completely. Set aside.

3. Preheat oven to 325F.

4. Make Custard: In medium saucepan, heat milk and cream just until bubbles form around edge of pan.

5. In large bowl, with rotary beater, beat eggs slightly. Add sugar, salt, and vanilla. Gradually stir in hot milk mixture. Pour into prepared dish.

6. Set dish in shallow pan; pour boiling water to ½-inch level around dish.

7. Make 35 to 40 minutes, or until silver knife inserted in center comes out clean. Let custard cool, then refrigerate—4 hours or overnight.

8. To serve: Run small spatula around edge of dish to loosen. Invert on shallow serving dish; shake gently to release. The caramel acts as sauce.

Makes 8 servings.

✼

SOFT CUSTARD (CUSTARD SAUCE)

1½ cups milk
  3 egg yolks

¼ cup sugar
½ teaspoon vanilla extract

1. In top of double boiler over direct heat, heat milk until tiny bubbles appear around edge of pot.

2. Beat yolks and sugar to mix well.

3. Very slowly pour hot milk into egg mixture, beating constantly.

4. Return mixture to double-boiler top; place over hot, not boiling, water. Water in lower part of double boiler should not touch upper part.

5. Cook, stirring constantly, until thin coating forms on metal spoon—8 to 10 minutes.

6. Pour custard immediately into bowl; place sheet of waxed paper directly on surface.

7. Set bowl in cold water, to cool. Stir in vanilla. Refrigerate. Serve over strawberries, sliced bananas, oranges.

Makes 1½ cups.

FLOATING ISLAND

Soft Custard, page 149   ¼ *cup confectioners' sugar*
3 egg whites

1. Make Soft Custard as directed. Pour cooled custard into individual serving dishes. Refrigerate to chill well.

2. Meanwhile, let egg whites warm to room temperature in small bowl of electric mixer.

3. Preheat oven to 350F.

4. Beat egg whites at high speed just until soft peaks form when beater is slowly raised. Add 1 tablespoon sugar; beat until incorporated; add second tablespoon of sugar; beat; add rest of sugar; continue beating until stiff peaks form when beater is slowly raised.

5. Drop heaping tablespoons of meringue on a layer of hot water in a shallow baking pan. Bake until golden brown—about 8 minutes. With a slotted spatula, remove meringues from water; drain on paper towels. Pile several on each custard. Refrigerate until serving.

Makes 4 servings.

23

FLOATING ISLAND À L'ORANGE

Custard:
1 pkg (3¼ oz) vanilla-pudding-
    and-pie-filling mix
2 tablespoons sugar
  Dash salt
2 egg yolks
3 cups milk
1 tablespoon grated orange peel

Meringue:
2 egg whites
⅛ teaspoon cream of tartar
  Dash salt
⅓ cup sugar
1 medium orange
1 tablespoon orange peel,
    in thin strips

1. Make Custard: In medium saucepan, combine pudding mix, 2 tablespoons sugar, dash salt, and the egg yolks. Gradually stir in milk; add grated orange peel.

2. Cook over medium heat, stirring constantly, until mixture comes to boiling. Pour into large, shallow serving dish; cover and refrigerate.

3. Meanwhile, make Meringue: Let egg whites warm to room temperature. Preheat oven to 350F. Invert an 8-inch layer-cake pan; lightly butter the bottom.

4. In small bowl, with electric mixer at high speed, beat egg whites with cream of tartar and salt until foamy. Gradually beat in sugar, 2 tablespoons at a time, beating well after each addition. Continue to beat until stiff peaks form when beater is slowly raised.

5. Spoon meringue onto pan, swirling in center. Bake 10 minutes, or until browned. Place pan on wire rack. With spatula, gently loosen meringue from pan.

6. Peel orange; slice crosswise.

7. Remove custard from refrigerator; slide meringue onto center of custard. Arrange orange slices, cut in half, around edge. Sprinkle with thin orange-peel strips.

8. Refrigerate until well chilled—at least 1 hour.
Makes 8 servings.

TRIFLE

Custard:
1 cup sugar
1 tablespoon cornstarch
1/2 teaspoon salt
4 cups milk (1 quart)
8 egg yolks
2 teaspoons vanilla extract
1 tablespoon sherry

2 Sponge Cake Layers, page 259 or 2 (8-inch) baker's sponge-cake layers
3/4 cup sherry
6 tablespoons raspberry preserves
6 tablespoons toasted chopped almonds
1/2 cup currant jelly
1/2 cup heavy cream, whipped
Whole toasted almonds

1. Make Custard: In a heavy, medium-size saucepan, combine sugar, cornstarch and salt. Gradually add milk; stir until smooth.

2. Cook over medium heat, stirring constantly with wire whisk or wooden spoon, until mixture is thickened and comes to boil. Simmer 1 minute. Remove from heat.

3. In medium bowl, beat egg yolks slightly. Gradually add a little hot mixture, beating well.

4. Stir into rest of hot mixture. Cook over low heat, stirring constantly, just until mixture thickens. Remove from heat; stir in vanilla and 1 tablespoon sherry.

5. Strain custard immediately into bowl. Refrigerate, covered, until it is well chilled—several hours or overnight.

6. Split sponge-cake layers in half crosswise, to make four layers in all. Brush each layer with sherry.

7. Spread three of the layers with 2 tablespoons preserves each; sprinkle each with 2 tablespoons chopped almonds. In attractive, deep serving bowl, stack prepared layers, jam side up, spreading each with about 1 cup chilled custard. Top with plain layer, then remaining custard.

8. Spoon currant jelly around edge. Decorate with whipped-cream rosettes, using a pastry bag with number-5 star tip, and whole almonds. Refrigerate until serving time.

Makes 8 to 10 servings.

ᗡᗡ

BAKED RICE CUSTARD

1/3 cup raw regular white rice	3 eggs
5 cups milk	3/4 cup sugar
1 teaspoon salt	1 1/2 teaspoons vanilla extract

1. In top of double boiler, combine rice, 4 cups milk and the salt. Cook over boiling water, covered and stirring occasionally, 1 hour, or until rice is tender.

2. Preheat oven to 350F. Grease a 2-quart casserole; place in baking pan.

3. In a large bowl, combine eggs, sugar, vanilla, and remaining milk; beat just until blended. Gradually stir in hot rice mixture.

4. Pour into prepared casserole. Pour hot water to 1-inch depth around casserole.

5. Bake, uncovered, 60 to 65 minutes, or until sharp knife inserted in custard 1 inch from edge of casserole comes out clean.

6. Remove from hot water to wire rack, and let cool. Then refrigerate until well chilled—at least 3 hours, or overnight.

Makes 8 servings.

ᗡᗡ

OLD-FASHIONED RICE PUDDING

1/2 cup raw regular white rice	2 tablespoons rose water
1 quart milk	(see Note)
1 cinnamon stick (about 3 inches)	1 teaspoon freshly grated nutmeg
1/2 cup butter or regular margarine	8 egg yolks
3/4 cup sugar	4 egg whites

1. In top of double boiler, combine rice, milk and cinnamon stick. Boil, covered, over hot water about 1 hour, or until rice is tender. Preheat oven to 350F.

2. To rice mixture, add butter, sugar, rose water and nutmeg; mix well. Let cool.

3. Lightly butter a 2-quart casserole. Beat egg yolks and whites just to mix well; stir into rice mixture until well combined.

4. Place casserole in pan filled with boiling water, 1 inch deep. Bake 45 to 50 minutes, or until custard is set and a sharp knife inserted 1 inch from edge of pudding comes out clean. Rice pudding may be served slightly warm or well chilled.

Makes 8 servings.

Note: Rose water may be purchased at a drugstore or gourmet shop. You may substitute 1 teaspoon vanilla extract for rose water.

❧

HEAVENLY RICE

1 cup raw regular white rice	1 cup miniature marshmallows
4 cups milk	1/2 cup heavy cream, whipped
1/2 cup sugar	1/2 teaspoon vanilla extract
1/8 teaspoon salt	5 pineapple slices, drained, cut in
1 can (8 1/4 oz) pineapple chunks,	half
drained	1/2 cup toasted coconut (see Note)

1. Day ahead: In top of double boiler, combine rice, milk, 1/4 cup sugar and the salt; mix well.

2. Place over hot, not boiling, water. Cook, covered, stirring occasionally, until rice is very soft and mixture is creamy—1 1/4 to 1 1/2 hours. (Add water as needed to bottom of double boiler.) Remove from heat.

3. Refrigerate until chilled—about 2 hours.

4. In large bowl, combine rice mixture, pineapple chunks and marshmallows; stir until well combined.

5. Refrigerate, covered, overnight.

6. To serve: Fold whipped cream and vanilla into rice mixture. Turn into chilled 2-quart serving bowl. Decorate with halved pineapple rings and toasted coconut.

7. Refrigerate an hour or so before serving.

Makes 8 to 10 servings.

Note: To toast coconut, preheat oven to 350F. Place coconut on cookie sheet. Toast, stirring occasionally, until light golden—about 5 minutes.

❧

STEAMED BREAD PUDDING

1 quart milk	1 tablespoon orange-flower water
8 slices white bread, crusts	(see Note)
removed	3/4 cup sugar
1/4 cup butter or margarine	1/2 teaspoon freshly ground
6 egg yolks	nutmeg
3 egg whites	1/2 teaspoon salt
	1/2 cup orange marmalade

1. Heat milk just until scalded.

2. In large bowl, break bread into cubes; add butter. Stir hot milk into bread and butter, stirring until butter is melted and bread is disintegrated. Let cool to lukewarm.

3. Lightly grease with butter a 1¾-to-2-quart straight-sided bowl or pudding mold.

4. In a small bowl, with rotary beater, beat egg yolks and whites with orange-flower water just until frothy. Stir in sugar, nutmeg, and salt.

5. Stir egg mixture into lukewarm-milk mixture just until combined. Pour into prepared mold.

6. Cover with lid or with foil tied tightly over top. Place on rack in a large kettle. Fill kettle with boiling water to within 1 inch of the top of bowl.

7. Bring to boiling; simmer, with kettle covered, 1½ hours, or until pudding is firm in center.

8. Let cool 30 minutes. Run a knife around edge to loosen. Invert on serving platter to unmold.

9. Spread top with marmalade. Serve at once, or serve cold. Makes 8 servings.

Note: Orange-flower water may be purchased at a drugstore or gourmet shop. You may substitute 1 teaspoon vanilla extract for the orange-flower water.

BAKED PEAR BREAD PUDDING

1 can (1 lb) pear halves, drained, cut into 1-inch cubes	4 cups milk
¼ cup raisins	⅔ cup granulated sugar
1 teaspoon cinnamon	¼ teaspoon salt
5 slices white bread, crusts removed	5 eggs
	1 teaspoon vanilla extract
¼ cup butter or margarine, softened	2 tablespoons currant jelly
	Confectioners' sugar

1. Preheat oven to 350F. Lightly butter an 8-by-8-by-2-inch baking dish.

2. Toss pears with raisins and cinnamon. Spread in bottom of prepared dish. Spread bread slices generously with butter. Cut each slice in half diagonally. Arrange overlapping in dish, buttered side up.

3. In saucepan, heat milk until bubbles form around edges of pan; remove from heat. Add granulated sugar and salt; stir to dissolve.

4. In large bowl, beat eggs. Gradually stir in hot milk mixture; stir in vanilla extract. Pour the mixture over bread.

5. Set dish in pan of hot water; bake 40 to 50 minutes, or until knife inserted comes out clean.

6. Remove pudding from water, and cool at least 10 minutes before serving. Decorate with jelly and confectioners' sugar. Serve warm or cold.

Makes 6 to 8 servings.

BAKED RAISIN BREAD PUDDING

Omit pears; use ½ cup raisins; bake as above.

BREAD AND BUTTER PUDDING

½ cup butter, softened	3½ cups milk
18 slices white bread, crusts removed	¼ cup sugar
	5 eggs, well beaten
¾ cup raisins	Nutmeg

1. Butter bread slices. Use a few buttered bread slices to cover bottom of 10-by-7-inch baking dish. Sprinkle with half of raisins.

2. Continue to layer buttered bread and raisins. The final layer should be of bread—no raisins.

3. Preheat oven to 350F. Heat milk slightly; add sugar; stir to dissolve. Stir into beaten eggs; beat until well combined, not frothy. Pour over bread. Press top layer down to fit snugly. Sprinkle with grated nutmeg.

4. Bake until nicely browned—about 1 hour. Serve slightly warm with whipped cream or light cream.

Makes 8 servings.

BREAD PUDDING WITH BRANDY SAUCE

10 slices day-old bread, broken in pieces	1 teaspoon vanilla extract
1 quart milk, heated	½ teaspoon nutmeg
1 cup light cream	1 teaspoon cinnamon
4 eggs	¼ cup butter or margarine, melted
1 cup sugar	½ cup seedless raisins
	Brandy Sauce (below)

1. Preheat oven to 350F.

2. In large bowl, combine bread, milk and cream.

3. In medium bowl, beat eggs slightly. Stir in sugar. Add to bread mixture.

4. Stir in vanilla, nutmeg, cinnamon, butter and raisins.

5. Pour into buttered shallow 2-quart baking dish, set in large shallow pan. Pour hot water into larger pan to depth of 1 inch.

6. Bake 1 hour, or until knife inserted in center comes out clean.

7. Serve warm, with Brandy Sauce.

Makes 8 servings.

BRANDY SAUCE

3 egg yolks
¾ cup sugar
1 teaspoon vanilla extract
1½ cups milk

1 tablespoon cornstarch
¼ cup water
3 tablespoons brandy

1. In small saucepan, beat egg yolks slightly. Add sugar, vanilla, and milk; blend well.

2. Cook over low heat, stirring until mixture boils.

3. In small bowl, blend cornstarch and water until smooth. Stir into hot mixture. Cook, stirring, until thickened.

4. Remove from heat and stir in brandy.

5. Serve slightly warm or chilled.

Makes about 2 cups.

BAKED APPLE CHARLOTTE

1 loaf (1 lb) sliced white bread,
    crusts removed
1 cup sugar
4 teaspoons ground cinnamon
6 green apples (2 lb)
¼ cup butter or margarine

4 cups grated fresh white-bread
    crumbs (about 12 slices,
    crusts removed)

Sauce (see Note):
1 cup apple jelly
2 tablespoons golden rum

1. Lightly butter inside of a 2-quart charlotte mold or a straight-sided Pyrex bowl. Cut 6 slices bread in half; use to line inside of mold, overlapping. Using a heart-shaped cookie cutter, cut 6 hearts from bread slices, to fit in bottom of mold.

2. Combine sugar and cinnamon.

3. Pare, core, and thinly slice apples—should measure 5½ cups.

4. Preheat oven to 350F.

5. In bottom of mold, layer 1⅓ cups apple slices; sprinkle with ¼ cup sugar-cinnamon mixture; dot with 1 tablespoon butter; top with 1 cup bread crumbs. Make three more layers.

6. Bake 1 hour and 15 or 20 minutes, or until apples are tender when tested with a wooden pick.

7. Let pudding cool on wire rack 10 minutes. If desired, brush with a little melted apple jelly. Meanwhile, make Sauce: In small saucepan, over low heat, melt jelly. Remove from heat; stir in rum.

8. To serve: Carefully loosen around edge of mold with spatula. Turn out on platter. Serve warm with sauce.

Makes 8 servings.

Note: Or use 1 pint softened vanilla ice cream as sauce.

QUEEN OF PUDDINGS

4 day-old white bread slices	2 cups milk
2 tablespoons butter or margarine, softened	½ cup sugar
Cinnamon	1 teaspoon vanilla extract
½ cup dark raisins	¾ cup strawberry or apricot
4 eggs, separated	preserves

1. Preheat oven to 350F. Lightly grease a 1½-quart flat baking dish.

2. Trim crusts from bread and discard. Spread bread with butter; sprinkle generously with cinnamon; then cut into quarters.

3. Place bread in prepared baking dish; sprinkle with raisins.

4. In medium bowl, with rotary beater, beat egg yolks with milk, ¼ cup sugar, and the vanilla just until well combined, not frothy. Pour over bread in baking dish.

5. Set baking dish in pan; add hot water to measure 1 inch. Bake 45 to 50 minutes, or until a sharp knife inserted 1 inch from edge comes out clean.

6. Meanwhile, make a meringue: In medium bowl, with rotary beater, beat egg whites until foamy. Add remaining ¼ cup sugar, 2 tablespoons at a time, beating well after each addition. Continue beating until stiff peaks form when beater is slowly raised.

7. Heat preserves in small saucepan.

8. Remove bread pudding from oven. Lift out of pan of water. Increase oven temperature to 400F.

9. Pour preserves over pudding evenly. Spread with meringue, bringing out to corners and to edges of dish all around.

10. Return pudding to oven; bake 6 to 8 minutes longer, or until meringue is lightly browned. Serve warm or chilled.

Makes 8 servings.

⁂

PRUNE WHIP

1 pkg (12 oz) pitted prunes
2 teaspoons lemon juice
2 egg whites
    Dash salt

¼ cup sugar
¼ cup heavy cream, whipped

    Whipped cream, or Custard
        Sauce, page 348

1. Cook prunes as package label directs. Drain prunes, reserving liquid. Remove ½ cup cooked prunes for later.

2. Purée remaining prunes in blender or food mill with ½ cup of cooking liquid. Add lemon juice. Let cool.

3. With mixer at high speed, beat egg whites with salt until frothy. Gradually beat in sugar; beat until stiff peaks form.

4. Add purée of prunes, ¼ cup at a time, beating well. Beat at high speed for 2 minutes.

5. Chop remaining prunes and fold into mixture along with ¼ cup cream, whipped. Turn into 6 or 8 sherbet dishes.

6. Refrigerate. Garnish each with a little whipped cream, if desired, or serve with Custard Sauce.

Makes 6 to 8 servings.

⁂

LEMON SNOW PUDDING

1 envelope unflavored gelatine
¾ cup sugar
⅛ teaspoon salt
1¼ cups boiling water

⅓ cup fresh lemon juice
2 egg whites

    Custard Sauce, page 348

1. In large bowl of electric mixer, combine gelatine with sugar and salt; mix thoroughly.

2. Add boiling water; stir to dissolve gelatine and sugar. Stir in lemon juice; mix thoroughly.

3. Refrigerate until mixture is consistency of unbeaten egg white—45 minutes or longer.

4. Add egg whites; beat, at high speed, until mixture forms stiff peaks when beater is raised—takes about 20 minutes.

5. Turn into a 2-quart mold. Refrigerate until chilled and firm enough to unmold—overnight.

6. To serve: Loosen edge of mold with sharp knife. Invert on serving platter; shake gently to release. If necessary, place a hot, damp dishcloth on bottom of mold; shake again to release.

7. Serve with Custard Sauce.

Makes 8 servings.

STRAWBERRY SNOW

3 egg whites (⅓ cup)
1 pkg (10 oz) frozen strawberries, thawed
1 envelope unflavored gelatine
½ cup sugar

1 tablespoon lemon juice
⅛ teaspoon salt
Red food color (optional)

Custard Sauce, page 348

1. In medium bowl, let egg whites stand at room temperature 1 hour.

2. Meanwhile, drain strawberries, reserving syrup. Sprinkle gelatine over syrup in small saucepan, to soften. Place over low heat, stirring until gelatine is dissolved.

3. Turn strawberries, ¼ cup sugar, the lemon juice, salt, few drops food color, ¼ cup water, and the gelatine into blender container. Cover; blend at low speed 1 minute.

4. Turn into large bowl. Set in pan of ice and water. Let stand, stirring occasionally, just until beginning to set—about 20 minutes.

5. With electric mixer at high speed, beat egg whites until soft peaks form when beater is slowly raised. Gradually beat in remaining sugar. Continue beating until stiff peaks form.

6. With same beater, at high speed, beat gelatine mixture until light. Fold in beaten egg white until well blended. Turn into 1-quart mold.

7. Refrigerate until firm—at least 3 hours.

8. To serve: Run a small spatula around edge of mold. Invert over serving platter; place a hot, damp dishcloth on bottom of mold; shake gently to release. Serve with Custard Sauce.

Makes 6 servings.

ß

ORANGE JELLY

1 tablespoon unflavored gelatine
½ cup sugar
¼ cup lemon juice

1¼ cups orange juice
Whipped cream

1. Sprinkle gelatine over ½ cup cold water in top of double boiler; let stand 5 minutes to soften. Stir over hot water to dissolve gelatine.

2. Add sugar; stir until dissolved.

3. Remove from hot water; stir in lemon juice and orange juice to mix well.

4. Pour into 4 or 5 sherbet dishes or custard cups. Refrigerate until firm, about 4 hours.

5. Serve right in sherbet dishes, or unmold if using custard cups. To Unmold: Run a knife around edge of mold. Invert on serving plates. Place a hot, damp dishcloth over bottom; shake to release. Repeat if necessary. Serve with whipped cream.

Makes 4 or 5 servings.

ß

COFFEE JELLY

1 tablespoon unflavored gelatine
½ cup sugar

1½ cups strong coffee
Whipped cream

Make as directed in Orange Jelly, above, substituting strong coffee for lemon and orange juices.

Makes 4 or 5 servings.

ß

SHERRY JELLY

2 envelopes unflavored gelatine
1 cup granulated sugar
1½ cups boiling water
½ cup orange juice
¼ cup lemon juice

1 cup sherry
1 cup heavy cream, whipped
2 tablespoons confectioners'
   sugar

1. Combine gelatine and granulated sugar in medium bowl, mixing well. Add boiling water, stirring until dissolved.

2. Add orange juice, lemon juice and sherry; mix well.

3. Pour into 8 (5-oz) molds or 1-quart mold. Refrigerate until firm—6 hours or overnight.

4. To serve: Run sharp knife around edge of molds to loosen. Invert over serving plates; shake gently to release. If necessary, place a hot, damp dishcloth over molds and shake again to release. Top with whipped cream combined with confectioners' sugar.

Makes 8 servings.

SPANISH CREAM

1 envelope unflavored gelatine	Dash salt
1⅔ cups milk	1 teaspoon vanilla extract
2 egg yolks	2 egg whites
¼ cup granulated sugar	

1. Sprinkle gelatine over ⅓ cup milk in small bowl; let stand 5 minutes to soften.

2. Heat 1⅓ cups milk in top of double boiler over medium heat just until bubbles form around edge.

3. Meanwhile, with rotary beater, beat egg yolks slightly; beat in sugar and salt until thick.

4. Stir in hot milk; return mixture to top of double boiler; cook, stirring, over hot water until mixture forms a coating on metal spoon. Add softened gelatine; stir until dissolved.

5. Add vanilla. Set top of double boiler in pan of ice water; stir occasionally until mixture is consistency of unbeaten egg whites.

6. Beat egg whites just until stiff peaks form. Beat custard until foamy; fold into egg whites to combine well.

7. Pour into 5 custard cups. Refrigerate until firm—several hours.

8. To serve, unmold, if desired. Serve plain or with strawberries or chocolate sauce or whipped cream.

Makes 5 servings.

CHARLOTTE RUSSE

1 envelope unflavored gelatine	About 12 ladyfingers, split
6 tablespoons sugar	1½ cups heavy cream
2 eggs, separated	Toasted whole almonds
¾ cup milk	(see Note)
About ½ cup dry sherry	½ cup heavy cream, whipped

1. In top of double boiler, combine gelatine and sugar; mix well.

2. Beat egg yolks slightly; beat in milk. Stir into gelatine mixture. Cook over simmering water, stirring constantly, until mixture coats a metal spoon. Remove from heat; stir in ⅓ cup sherry.

3. Pour into bowl; set bowl in a larger bowl, filled with ice.

4. Stir occasionally until custard begins to mound slightly—20 to 30 minutes.

5. Meanwhile, sprinkle cut sides of ladyfingers lightly with sherry—about 4 tablespoons in all.

6. Rinse a 7- or 8-cup charlotte mold or straight-side mold with cold water; drain well. Line side of mold with 18 split ladyfingers, split side inside.

7. Beat egg whites until stiff but not dry. Beat 1½ cups cream stiff. With rubber scraper, fold egg whites, then whipped cream, into chilled gelatine mixture, to combine thoroughly.

8. Pour half into prepared mold. Layer with remaining split ladyfingers. Cover with rest of gelatine mixture, filling mold.

9. Refrigerate until firm—about 4 hours.

10. To unmold: With small spatula, loosen around edge of mold. Invert mold over serving plate; hold a hot, damp dishcloth over mold; shake to release.

11. Garnish with toasted almonds and mounds of whipped cream, or decorate, using a pastry bag and a number-5 decorating tip.

Makes 10 servings.

Note: To toast almonds, preheat oven to 350F. Spread almonds in single layer on cookie sheet, until golden—about 7 minutes.

꙰

STRAWBERRY CHARLOTTE RUSSE

2 pint boxes fresh strawberries
    (see Note)
1 tablespoon lemon juice
¾ cup sugar

2 envelopes unflavored gelatine
8 ladyfingers, split
2 cups heavy cream
    Whipped cream (optional)

1. Wash strawberries gently in cold water. Drain; hull. Lightly grease a 9-inch springform pan.

2. In medium bowl, crush berries with potato masher. Press through sieve to make a purée. Purée should measure 2 cups.

3. In medium bowl, combine purée, lemon juice, and sugar; stir to dissolve sugar.

4. Sprinkle gelatine over ½ cup cold water in small bowl. Place over hot water; stir to dissolve.

5. Blend gelatine into strawberry mixture.

6. Place in bowl of ice cubes, stirring occasionally, until consistency of unbeaten egg white—about 15 minutes.

7. Press uncut sides of ladyfingers against inside of prepared pan, ¼ inch apart.

8. In large bowl, with rotary beater, beat 2 cups cream until stiff. Carefully fold gelatine mixture into cream.

9. Turn into prepared pan. Refrigerate until firm—8 hours, or overnight.

10. To serve: Run spatula around edge of mold; remove side of springform pan. Place on serving platter. Garnish with mounds of whipped cream and whole fresh strawberries, if desired.

Makes 8 servings.

Note: You may use 2 packages (10-ounce size) frozen strawberries, thawed, for fresh berries. (Do not crush berries or put through sieve.) Blend berries and juice in blender to make 2½ cups purée. Proceed as directed.

꙰

PINEAPPLE BAVARIAN CREAM

4 egg yolks
½ cup sugar
1 cup milk
1 can (8¼ oz) crushed pineapple

1 envelope unflavored gelatine
1 teaspoon vanilla extract
1 cup heavy cream
    Sweetened whipped cream
        (optional)

1. In small bowl of electric mixer, at high speed, beat egg yolks with sugar until very thick. Meanwhile, heat milk just until bubbles form around edge of pan. Gradually stir milk into yolk mixture.

2. Turn custard into heavy saucepan; cook, stirring, over medium heat until custard thickens and coats a metal spoon.

3. Meanwhile, drain pineapple, reserving liquid; sprinkle gelatine over ¼ cup reserved pineapple juice; let stand 5 minutes to soften.

4. Remove custard from heat. Add softened gelatine and vanilla; stir to dissolve gelatine; pour into a large bowl to cool.

5. Set in a larger bowl of ice water; stir occasionally until gelatine begins to thicken and is consistency of unbeaten egg whites.

6. Beat 1 cup cream until stiff; fold into gelatine mixture along with drained pineapple until combined.

7. Pour into a 6-cup fancy mold. Refrigerate until firm enough to unmold—several hours or overnight.

8. To unmold: Run a sharp knife around edge of mold to loosen. Invert over serving platter. Place a hot, damp dishcloth over the mold; shake to release. Repeat if necessary. Serve with whipped cream, if desired.

Makes 6 to 8 servings.

DANISH FRUIT PUDDING

2 pkg (10-oz size) frozen sliced strawberries, thawed
2 pkg (10-oz size) frozen raspberries, thawed

Sugar
¼ cup cornstarch
Whipped cream or light cream

1. Drain berries; reserve juice (2 cups). Turn berries into six to eight dessert dishes or a medium serving bowl.

2. In large saucepan, combine 2 tablespoons sugar and the cornstarch; mix well. Stir in reserved fruit juice and ½ cup cold water; mix well.

3. Cook over medium heat, stirring, until mixture is thickened and translucent (do not boil)—takes 10 minutes.

4. Pour over berries in individual dessert dishes or large serving bowl. Sprinkle surface of each lightly with sugar. Refrigerate several hours, or until well chilled.

5. To serve: Decorate top of each with a mound of whipped cream, or serve with light cream.

Makes 6 to 8 servings.

ALMOND JUNKET

1 envelope unflavored gelatine
1½ cups boiling water
 Sugar
½ cup milk
2 teaspoons almond extract

Garnish:
½ cup currant jelly
2 slices canned pineapple,
 drained
 Canned mandarin-orange
  sections, drained

1. In small bowl, sprinkle gelatine over ¼ cup cold water; let stand 5 minutes to soften.

2. In medium saucepan, combine boiling water with 3 tablespoons sugar; boil 2 minutes. Remove from heat; stir in milk.

3. Add softened gelatine and almond extract, stirring until gelatine is dissolved.

4. Pour into 13-by-9-by-2-inch pan, to make a layer about ¼ inch thick. Refrigerate until firm and well chilled—about 1 hour.

5. Make syrup: In small saucepan, combine ¼ cup sugar with ¼ cup water. Bring to boiling; reduce heat, and stir until sugar is dissolved. Add ½ cup water. Pour into glass serving bowl; refrigerate.

6. At serving time, cut junket into small cubes. Spoon cubes into syrup in serving bowl. Garnish with cubes of currant jelly, pineapple slices, and orange sections.

Makes 6 to 8 servings.

BAKED INDIAN PUDDING

⅓ cup yellow cornmeal
4 cups hot milk
¾ cup light or dark molasses
2 eggs, slightly beaten
2 tablespoons butter or
 margarine, melted

⅓ cup light-brown sugar, packed
1 teaspoon salt
¼ teaspoon cinnamon
¾ teaspoon ground ginger
½ cup cold milk
 Vanilla ice cream or light cream

1. In top of double boiler, slowly stir cornmeal into hot milk. Cook over boiling water, stirring constantly, 20 minutes.

2. Preheat oven to 300F. Grease 2-quart (8½-inch round) baking dish.

3. In small bowl, combine rest of ingredients, except cold milk

and ice cream; stir into cornmeal mixture; mix well. Turn into prepared dish; pour cold milk on top, without stirring.

4. Bake, uncovered, 2 hours, or just until set but quivery on top; do not overbake. Let stand 30 minutes before serving. Serve warm, with ice cream.

Makes 8 servings.

APPLE BROWN BETTY

2 cups grated soft bread crumbs	1½ lbs pared, sliced tart apples
⅔ cup light-brown sugar, packed	(about 4)
¼ teaspoon cinnamon	3 tablespoons butter or
½ teaspoon ground nutmeg	margarine, melted
1 teaspoon grated lemon peel	Light cream or ice cream
1½ tablespoons lemon juice	

1. Preheat oven to 375F. Lightly grease a 1-quart deep casserole. In bottom of dish, sprinkle one-third bread crumbs.

2. Combine sugar, cinnamon, nutmeg and lemon peel; add ¼ cup water and lemon juice.

3. Layer half the apples over bread crumbs; sprinkle with half the sugar-spice mixture.

4. Cover with one-third crumbs, then rest of apples and a layer of remaining sugar-spice mixture.

5. Combine rest of bread crumbs with melted butter; sprinkle crumbs over top. Bake until apples are tender, about 30 minutes.

6. Serve warm with light cream or ice cream.

Makes 6 servings.

APPLE CAKE SQUARES

2 cups unsifted all-purpose flour	4 cups finely diced pared raw
2 cups sugar	apples (about 1½ lb)
2 teaspoons baking soda	½ cup chopped walnuts
1 teaspoon cinnamon	½ cup softened butter or
½ teaspoon nutmeg	margarine
½ teaspoon salt	2 eggs

1. Preheat oven to 325F. Grease a 13-by-9-by-2-inch baking pan.

2. Into large bowl, sift flour with sugar, soda, cinnamon, nutmeg, salt.

3. Add apples, nuts, butter, eggs. Beat until just combined—it will be thick. Turn into prepared pan.

4. Bake 1 hour, or until top springs back when lightly pressed with fingertip. Cool in pan on wire rack.

5. Serve warm, cut into squares. Top with whipped cream or ice cream, if desired.

Makes 10 to 12 servings.

CHERRY CAKE-PUDDING

1 cup unsifted all-purpose flour
1 teaspoon baking powder
1/8 teaspoon salt
2 tablespoons butter or
   margarine
1 1/4 cups sugar

3/4 cup milk
1 can (1 lb) pitted sour red
   cherries packed in water
6 to 8 drops red food color
   (optional)

Vanilla ice cream

1. Preheat oven to 350F. Lightly butter a 10-by-6-inch baking dish.

2. Sift flour with baking powder and salt; set aside.

3. In medium bowl, with wooden spoon, blend butter with 1 cup sugar. Beat in flour mixture (in fourths) alternately with milk (in thirds), beginning and ending with flour mixture. Turn batter into prepared baking dish.

4. Drain cherries, reserving 1/2 cup liquid. In small saucepan, combine liquid, cherries, red food color, and remaining sugar; bring to boiling.

5. Pour hot cherry mixture over batter. Bake 30 to 35 minutes, or until it is golden-brown and top springs back when gently pressed with fingertip.

6. Serve warm, with ice cream.

Makes 6 to 8 servings.

DATE-WALNUT SQUARES WITH WHIPPED CREAM

3/4 cup finely chopped dates
2/3 cup chopped walnuts
3 tablespoons flour
1 teaspoon baking powder
2 eggs, separated

1 teaspoon vanilla extract
1/4 teaspoon salt
1/2 cup light-brown sugar,
   firmly packed
1/2 cup heavy cream, whipped

1. Preheat oven to 350F. Lightly grease an 8-by-8-by-2-inch baking pan.

2. Place dates and walnuts in a large bowl. Sift flour and baking powder over them. Toss dates and walnuts, to mix well.

3. Add slightly beaten egg yolks and the vanilla; mix well.

4. In medium bowl, beat egg whites and salt until soft peaks form when beater is slowly raised. Add sugar gradually, beating until stiff peaks form.

5. With rubber scraper, fold into date-walnut mixture just until combined.

6. Turn into prepared pan; bake 20 minutes. Let cool in pan 10 minutes. Cut into 9 squares. Serve warm, with whipped cream.

Makes 9 servings.

OLD-FASHIONED GINGERBREAD WITH LEMON SAUCE

1½ cups sifted all-purpose
    flour*
1½ teaspoons baking soda
¼ teaspoon salt
½ teaspoon ground cinnamon
½ teaspoon ground ginger

¼ teaspoon ground cloves
1 egg
1 cup light molasses
½ cup butter or margarine,
    melted
Lemon Sauce, below

* Sift before measuring.

1. Preheat oven to 375F. Lightly grease and flour an 8-by-8-by-2-inch baking pan.

2. Into medium bowl, sift flour with baking soda, salt and spices.

3. In large bowl, using portable electric mixer, beat egg with molasses, butter and ½ cup hot water until well combined.

4. Gradually beat in flour mixture, beating until smooth.

5. Turn into prepared pan; bake 25 minutes, or until cake tester inserted in center comes out clean.

6. Let gingerbread cool in pan 10 minutes. Cut into 9 squares; then turn out. Serve warm, with Lemon Sauce.

Makes 9 servings.

LEMON SAUCE

½ cup sugar
2 tablespoons cornstarch
¼ cup butter or margarine

2 teaspoons grated lemon peel
Dash salt
¼ cup lemon juice

1. In small saucepan, combine sugar and cornstarch. Add 1 cup water, stirring until smooth.

2. Bring to boiling, stirring. Reduce heat; simmer, stirring, until mixture is thickened and translucent—about 5 minutes.

3. Remove from heat. Stir in butter, lemon peel, salt and lemon juice. Cool slightly. Serve warm.

Makes 1¾ cups.

OLD-FASHIONED PINEAPPLE UPSIDE-DOWN CAKE

3 cans (8¼-oz size) sliced
   pineapple in heavy syrup
   (12 slices)
¼ cup butter or regular
   margarine
⅔ cup light-brown sugar, packed
⅓ cup pecan halves
1 cup unsifted all-purpose flour

¾ cup granulated sugar
1½ teaspoons baking powder
½ teaspoon salt
¼ cup shortening
½ cup milk
1 egg
1 cup heavy cream, chilled, or
   1 pint vanilla ice cream

1. Preheat oven to 350F. Drain pineapple slices, reserving 2 tablespoons of the syrup.

2. In a very heavy, or iron, 10-inch skillet with heat-resistant handle, melt butter over medium heat. (See Note.) Add brown sugar, stirring until sugar is melted. Remove from heat.

3. Arrange 8 pineapple slices on sugar mixture, with one slice in the center and overlapping the rest slightly around edge of pan. Fill centers with pecan halves. Halve three remaining pineapple slices and arrange around inside edge of skillet with pecans in their centers.

4. Into medium bowl, sift flour with granulated sugar, baking powder and salt. Add shortening and milk. With electric mixer at high speed, beat 2 minutes or until mixture is smooth.

5. Add egg and reserved 2 tablespoons pineapple syrup; beat 2 minutes longer.

6. Gently pour cake batter over pineapple in skillet, spreading evenly, being careful not to disarrange pineapple.

7. On rack in center of oven, bake 40 to 45 minutes, or until golden in color and surface of cake springs back when it's gently pressed with fingertip.

8. Let skillet stand on wire rack 5 minutes to cool just slightly. With rotary beater, beat cream until stiff.

9. With small spatula, loosen cake from edge of skillet all around. Place serving platter over the cake, and turn upside down, shake gently; lift off skillet.

10. Serve cake warm, with the whipped cream or ice cream.

Makes 8 servings.

Note: The pineapple upside-down cake was traditionally baked in an iron skillet. If your skillet does not have an iron or heatproof handle, wrap handle in foil before placing in the oven.

APPLE UPSIDE-DOWN CAKE

½ cup butter or margarine
⅔ cup granulated sugar
1¾ lb medium-size green apples,
    pared and sliced

Cake:
1 cup sifted* all-purpose flour
¾ cup granulated sugar

1½ teaspoons baking powder
½ teaspoon salt
¼ cup shortening
⅔ cup milk
1 egg

Whipped cream

* Sift before measuring.

1. Preheat oven to 350F.

2. In heavy, 10-inch skillet, melt butter over low heat. (See Note.) Add sugar, stirring until melted. Remove from heat.

3. Arrange apple slices overlapping on sugar mixture in skillet.

4. Make Cake: Into medium bowl, sift flour with granulated sugar, baking powder and salt. Add shortening and milk. With electric mixer at medium speed, beat 2 minutes.

5. Add egg; beat 2 minutes longer. Pour cake batter carefully over apples in skillet, spreading evenly.

6. Bake 40 to 45 minutes, or until cake springs back when gently pressed with fingertip.

7. Let stand on wire rack just 5 minutes. With small spatula, loosen cake from edge of skillet. Cover with serving plate; invert; shake gently; then lift off pan.

8. Serve cake warm. Top individual servings with whipped cream. Or top with small spoonfuls of vanilla ice cream, if desired.

Makes 8 servings.

Note: If skillet does not have an iron or heatproof handle, wrap handle in aluminum foil.

OLD-FASHIONED STRAWBERRY SHORTCAKE

Shortcake:
  2 cups sifted* all-purpose flour
 ¼ cup granulated sugar
  3 teaspoons baking powder
 ½ teaspoon salt
 ½ cup butter or regular margarine
  1 egg

* *Sift before measuring.*

Milk

Strawberry Topping:
  3 pint boxes fresh strawberries
 ¾ cup granulated sugar
  1 cup heavy cream
  2 tablespoons confectioners'
       sugar

1. Preheat oven to 425F. Lightly grease an 8-by-8-by-2-inch square baking pan or an 8-by-1½-inch round layer pan.

2. Sift flour with ¼ cup granulated sugar, the baking powder and salt into a large bowl.

3. Cut butter into chunks; add to flour mixture. With pastry blender, or two knives used scissors fashion, cut in butter until it is in very small particles, all coated with flour mixture. Mixture will resemble coarse cornmeal.

4. Break egg into a measuring cup. Add milk to measure ¾ cup. Mix with fork.

5. Make a well in center of mixture. Pour in milk all at once; mix quickly, with fork, just to moisten flour. Do not overmix; there will be lumps in the dough.

6. Turn into prepared pan, scraping out bowl with rubber scraper. With fingers (dipped in a little flour), lightly press out dough so that it fits corners of the pan and is even.

7. Bake 25 to 30 minutes, or until golden and cake tester inserted in center comes out clean.

8. Meanwhile, make Strawberry Topping: Wash strawberries in cold water; drain. Reserve several of the nicest berries for garnish.

9. Remove hulls from rest of berries; slice berries into a bowl. Add granulated sugar; mix well.

10. Loosen edges of the shortcake with a sharp knife; then turn out on a wire rack.

11. To serve: Beat cream with a rotary beater just until it is stiff. Gently stir in confectioners' sugar.

12. Using serrated-edge knife, carefully cut cake in half crosswise. Put bottom, cut side up, on serving plate. Spoon half of the sliced berries over the shortcake layer.

13. Set top of cake in place, cut side down. Spoon rest of sliced berries over top of cake. Mound whipped cream lightly in center. Garnish with the reserved whole strawberries. Serve at once.

Makes 9 servings.

❈

PEACH OR NECTARINE SHORTCAKES

2 cups packaged buttermilk-
    biscuit mix
¼ cup butter or regular
    margarine
    Granulated sugar
⅔ cup milk

1½ to 2 lb fresh peaches (see
    Note) or nectarines (3 cups,
    sliced)
½ cup heavy cream
2 tablespoons confectioners'
    sugar

1. Preheat oven to 400F.

2. In large bowl, combine biscuit mix, butter and 2 tablespoons granulated sugar. Cut in butter until mixture resembles coarse crumbs.

3. Stir in milk, mixing just until flour mixture is moistened.

4. Turn dough onto lightly floured pastry cloth or board. Knead gently ten times. Roll out to ¾-inch thickness. With floured 3-inch cutter, cut out 6 biscuits.

5. Place on ungreased cookie sheet; bake 15 minutes, or until golden.

6. Meanwhile, wash peaches; peel; slice into a large bowl. Sprinkle with ½ cup granulated sugar.

7. Whip cream with confectioners' sugar until stiff.

8. To serve each shortcake: Split biscuit. Spread with butter, if desired. Spoon ¼ cup peaches over bottom, then a spoonful of whipped cream. Replace top; spoon on ¼ cup peaches and top with whipped cream.

Makes 6 servings.

Note: Or use 2 packages (10-ounce size) thawed frozen sliced peaches, undrained. Do not add sugar.

BOSTON CREAM PIE

4 eggs
1 cup sugar
1 cup sifted* cake flour
3/4 teaspoon baking powder
1/4 teaspoon salt
Vanilla extract
1 teaspoon lemon juice

Custard Filling:
1 1/2 cups milk

* Sift before measuring.

1 pkg (3 1/4 oz) vanilla pudding-
   and-pie-filling mix
Vanilla extract

Glaze:
2 squares unsweetened
   chocolate
3 tablespoons butter or
   margarine
1 cup confectioners' sugar
Vanilla extract

1. In large bowl, let eggs warm to room temperature.

2. Preheat oven to 350F. At medium speed, beat eggs until thick and lemon-colored. Gradually beat in sugar, 1 tablespoon at a time, until very thick and light—about 5 minutes.

3. Meanwhile, sift flour with baking powder and salt. In measuring cup, combine 1/4 cup water, 1 teaspoon vanilla, and lemon juice. Blend flour mixture, one third at a time, into egg mixture alternately with water mixture. Beat 1 minute.

4. Turn into 2 ungreased, 9-inch layer pans, dividing evenly. Bake 25 minutes, until surface springs back when pressed with fingertips. Invert pans, setting rims on 2 other pans. Cool 1 hour.

5. Make Filling: Make pudding as label directs, reducing milk to 1 1/2 cups; add 1 teaspoon vanilla. Cool; refrigerate, with sheet of waxed paper placed directly on surface, several hours.

6. Make Glaze: In small saucepan, melt chocolate and butter over low heat. Remove from heat; add sugar and 3/4 teaspoon vanilla, mixing until smooth. Stir in 2 1/2 to 3 tablespoons hot water, one teaspoon at a time, until glaze is of pouring consistency.

7. To assemble: On cake plate, put cake layers together with filling; pour glaze over top, letting it run down sides. Refrigerate— about 1/2 hour.

Makes 8 servings.

ध

LEMON PUDDING CAKE

2 tablespoons butter or regular margarine
½ cup granulated sugar
2 eggs, separated
3 tablespoons flour

1¾ cups milk
¼ cup lemon juice
2 teaspoons grated lemon peel
Confectioners' sugar

1. Preheat oven to 350F.

2. In large bowl with electric mixer, beat butter with granulated sugar until well blended. Beat in egg yolks until blended.

3. At low speed, blend in flour; add milk, lemon juice and peel.

4. Beat egg whites until soft peaks form when beater is raised. Using a wire whisk or rubber scraper, fold egg whites into lemon mixture.

5. Turn mixture into a shallow, 8½-inch round baking dish. Set dish in pan; pour boiling water into pan to depth of 1 inch.

6. Bake 40 to 45 minutes, or until golden-brown and knife inserted in center comes out clean.

7. Let stand at least 15 minutes before serving. Sprinkle top lightly with confectioners' sugar. Serve warm, with whipped cream, if desired.

Makes 6 servings.

ध

CHOCOLATE ICEBOX CAKE

4 pkg (3-oz size) ladyfingers, split lengthwise
3 cups semisweet chocolate pieces

1 cup granulated sugar
1 teaspoon vanilla extract
8 eggs, separated
Confectioners' sugar

1. Line the side, then the bottom of a 9-inch springform pan with ladyfingers, split side in.

2. In medium saucepan, combine chocolate pieces, granulated sugar and ⅓ cup water. Over low heat, stir constantly until chocolate is melted. Remove from heat. Add vanilla; beat with wooden spoon until smooth. Set aside and let cool slightly.

3. In large bowl, with portable electric mixer at medium speed, beat egg yolks slightly. Gradually add chocolate mixture, beating constantly. Continue beating until thickened.

4. With clean beater, beat egg whites just until stiff peaks form when beater is slowly raised. With wire whisk or rubber scraper, using an under-and-over motion, gently fold beaten egg whites into chocolate mixture just until combined.

5. Spread a fourth of chocolate mixture over ladyfingers in springform pan. Cover mixture with a layer of ladyfingers. Repeat three times, ending with ladyfingers.

6. Refrigerate until firm—about 4 hours.

7. Gently remove side of pan; place cake (still on bottom of pan) on serving plate. Sprinkle cake liberally with confectioners' sugar.

Makes 12 servings.

PINEAPPLE ICEBOX DESSERT

3/4 cup crushed vanilla wafers
1/2 cup butter or margarine, softened
1 1/2 cups confectioners' sugar
1 egg, beaten

1 can (1 lb, 4 oz) crushed pineapple
2/3 cup pecans, coarsely chopped
1 cup heavy cream, whipped

Pineapple Sauce (below), optional

1. Day before serving: Lightly grease 8-inch, square cake pan. Pack half the crumbs in bottom of pan.

2. In medium bowl, with wooden spoon, cream butter and sugar until fluffy. Add egg, beating well.

3. Drain pineapple well, reserving syrup for Pineapple Sauce. Fold in pineapple and pecans. Fold in whipped cream just until well combined.

4. Turn into prepared pan, spreading evenly. Sprinkle with rest of crumbs.

5. Cover top of pan with foil or plastic film. Refrigerate 24 hours.

6. Cut in squares. Serve with sauce, if desired.

Makes 8 to 10 servings.

PINEAPPLE SAUCE

1/2 cup sugar
1 tablespoon cornstarch

1/4 teaspoon grated lemon peel
1 can (8 oz) crushed pineapple

1. In small saucepan, combine sugar and cornstarch; mix well.

2. Measure reserved pineapple syrup (above) and, if necessary, add water to make ¾ cup. Gradually add pineapple syrup, stirring until smooth. Add lemon peel and crushed pineapple.

3. Bring to boiling over medium heat, stirring; boil until mixture is thickened and translucent. Cover and refrigerate.

Makes about 1½ cups.

FRESH BERRY COBBLER

3 cups blueberries, blackberries
    or raspberries, washed
½ cup sugar
½ teaspoon lemon juice
2 tablespoons butter or
    margarine

1½ cups packaged biscuit mix
3 tablespoons butter or regular
    margarine, melted
1 egg, slightly beaten
½ cup milk
    Whipped cream or ice cream

1. Preheat oven to 400F. Grease well a 10-by-6½-by-2-inch baking dish.

2. Toss berries lightly with sugar and lemon juice. Place in baking dish. Dot with 2 tablespoons butter.

3. In medium bowl, combine biscuit mix, melted butter, egg and milk. Lightly mix with fork just until combined. Drop dough over fruit.

4. Bake 30 to 35 minutes, or until top is golden-brown. Serve warm with whipped cream or ice cream.

Makes 6 servings.

APPLE COBBLER

Filling:
5 cups sliced, peeled tart apples
    (about 1½ lb)
¾ cup sugar
2 tablespoons flour
1 tablespoon lemon juice
1 teaspoon vanilla extract
½ teaspoon cinnamon
¼ teaspoon salt
2 tablespoons butter or margarine

Batter:
½ cup unsifted all-purpose flour
½ cup sugar
½ teaspoon baking powder
¼ teaspoon salt
2 tablespoons butter or
    margarine, softened
1 egg, slightly beaten

Light cream or whipped cream

1. Make Filling: In medium bowl, combine apple, ¾ cup sugar, 2 tablespoons flour, the lemon juice, vanilla, cinnamon, ¼ teaspoon salt, and ¼ cup water. Turn into 8-by-8-by-2-inch baking dish. Dot with 2 tablespoons butter.

2. Preheat oven to 375F.

3. Make Batter: In medium bowl, combine all batter ingredients; beat with wooden spoon until smooth. Drop in 9 portions over filling, spacing evenly. Batter will spread during baking.

4. Bake 35 to 40 minutes, or until apple is tender and crust is golden. Serve warm, with cream.

Makes 9 servings.

PEACH OR NECTARINE COBBLER

Substitute 5 cups peeled, sliced ripe peaches or nectarines (3½ to 4 lb) for apples; proceed as above.

TRILBY CREAM

¾ lb marshmallows	2 cups heavy cream
¼ cup chopped preserved ginger in syrup	¼ cup confectioners' sugar
	1 teaspoon vanilla extract
2 tablespoons ginger syrup	18 red candied cherries
¼ cup orange juice	⅓ cup coarsely chopped walnuts

1. Cut or snip marshmallows into sixths. Place in medium bowl with chopped preserved ginger and the ginger syrup. Add orange juice; mix well.

2. Refrigerate, covered, until marshmallows are softened—about 30 minutes.

3. In large bowl, combine cream, sugar, and vanilla; beat with rotary beater until stiff. Fold in marshmallow mixture and 12 cherries, quartered. Turn into large crystal serving bowl.

4. Refrigerate, covered, 6 hours or overnight. At serving time, sprinkle top with walnuts and remaining whole cherries.

Makes 12 servings.

TRADITIONAL
FAVORITES

In many families, certain time-honored desserts are reserved for great occasions—the plum pudding at holiday time, a chocolate mousse for important dinners, or a golden floating island to mark a family gathering. Here we give you a selection; any one might play a memorable role in your own celebrations to come.

CARAMEL CUSTARD RING RENVERSÉE

Syrup:
½ cup granulated sugar

Custard:
5 eggs
½ cup granulated sugar
¼ teaspoon salt

1 teaspoon vanilla extract
3 cups milk

Fruit for Center:
½ pint fresh strawberries, washed
      and hulled (1 cup)
1 cup drained pineapple cubes
½ lb seedless green grapes

1. Preheat oven to 325F. Sprinkle ½ cup sugar evenly over bottom of a small, heavy skillet. Cook slowly over very low heat, stirring occasionally with a wooden spoon, just until sugar melts to a golden syrup. (If the sugar is cooked too long and at too high a temperature, it will be too dark and taste burned.)

2. Immediately pour syrup into bottom of 5-cup ring mold (8½ inches across and 2 inches deep). Tilt mold while syrup is still liquid, to coat bottom and side. (Caramel syrup will harden.) Let cool.

3. In large bowl, with wire whisk, beat eggs with sugar, salt and vanilla to mix well. Gradually add milk, beating until smooth, not frothy.

4. Place prepared ring mold in shallow baking pan. Remove 1 cup egg mixture; reserve. Pour rest of mixture into mold.

5. Place baking pan on middle rack in oven; pour reserved mixture into mold (this eliminates spilling). Pour hot water into pan 1 inch deep around mold. Bake 50 to 55 minutes, or until a silver knife inserted 1 inch from edge comes out clean.

6. Do not overbake; custard continues to bake after removal from oven. Remove mold from hot water to rack to cool completely; then refrigerate to chill—at least 1 hour. (Custard can be made day ahead.) The custard will settle slightly on cooling.

7. To unmold: Loosen edge with spatula. Place serving plate upside down on mold and reverse the two; shake gently to release; caramel will run down side.

8. Toss fruit together lightly; use to fill center of custard. Spoon some of caramel sauce over each serving.

Makes 6 to 8 servings.

CHOCOLATE MOUSSE

8 eggs
2 cups semisweet chocolate
     pieces
10 tablespoons sweet butter

¼ cup cognac or brandy
    Whipped cream
    Candied violets

1. One or two days before serving, separate eggs, turning whites into a medium bowl. Let whites warm to room temperature.

2. In top of double boiler, over hot, not boiling, water, melt chocolate and butter; stir to blend. Remove from hot water.

3. Using wooden spoon, beat in egg yolks, one at a time, beating well after each addition. Set aside to cool. Stir in cognac.

4. When the chocolate mixture has cooled, beat egg whites with rotary beater just until stiff peaks form when beater is slowly raised.

5. With rubber scraper or wire whisk, gently fold chocolate mixture into egg whites, using an under-and-over motion. Fold only enough to combine—there should be no white streaks.

6. Turn into an attractive, 6-cup serving dish. Refrigerate overnight.

7. To serve, decorate with whipped cream and candied violets. Makes 12 servings.

Note: For 6 servings, use 4 eggs, 1 pkg (6 oz) semisweet chocolate pieces, 5 tablespoons sweet butter and 2 tablespoons cognac or brandy. Make as directed above, using a 3-cup serving dish. Decorate as above.

CRÈME BRÛLÉE

3 cups heavy cream
6 egg yolks
⅓ cup granulated sugar

1 teaspoon vanilla extract
⅓ cup light-brown sugar, packed

1. Heat cream in heavy saucepan just until bubbles form around the edge of the pan.

2. In double-boiler top, with electric mixer, beat egg yolks with granulated sugar until thick and light yellow. Gradually stir in hot cream.

3. Place over hot, not boiling, water; cook, stirring constantly,

until mixture coats a metal spoon—about 15 minutes. Add vanilla.

4. Strain custard into a 1-quart, shallow baking dish. Refrigerate 8 hours or overnight.

5. Just before serving, carefully sift brown sugar over surface. Set dish in baking pan; surround with ice. Run under broiler just until sugar melts slightly and caramelizes—it will form a crust.

Makes 8 servings.

Note: For 4 servings, cut recipe in half; make as directed, cooking 10 minutes over hot water. Strain into 4 individual soufflé dishes or a 2- or 3-cup shallow baking dish.

POTS DE CRÈME

3 cups heavy cream
1/2 cup sugar
1 tablespoon vanilla extract

5 egg yolks
Chocolate curls, page 346

1. Preheat oven to 325F. Place 8 (5-oz) custard cups or 10 (3-oz) pot-de-crème cups in a baking pan.

2. In medium saucepan, combine cream and sugar; cook over medium heat, stirring occasionally, until sugar is dissolved and mixture is hot. Remove from heat; stir in vanilla.

3. In medium bowl, with wire whisk or rotary beater, beat egg yolks until blended—not frothy. Gradually add cream mixture, stirring constantly.

4. Strain, using fine strainer, into 4-cup measure. (If desired, first line strainer with cheesecloth.) Pour into cups.

5. Set baking pan on oven rack. Pour hot water to 1/2-inch level around cups.

6. Bake 25 to 30 minutes, or until mixture just begins to set around edges.

7. Immediately remove cups from water, and place on wire rack. Let cool 30 minutes; then refrigerate, each covered with plastic film, foil, or lid, till chilled—at least 4 hours.

8. To serve: Top with sweetened whipped cream, if desired. Then garnish with chocolate curls.

Makes 8 to 10 servings.

CHOCOLATE POT DE CRÈME

3 cups heavy cream
½ cup sugar
1½ squares unsweetened
    chocolate, broken

1 teaspoon vanilla extract
4 egg yolks
    Chocolate curls, page 346

Make and bake as in Pots de Crème, above, adding chocolate to cream and sugar in step 2. Cook, stirring, until chocolate is melted and mixture is hot.

GOLDEN FLOATING ISLAND

Custard Sauce:
 2 cups milk
 4 egg yolks
 ⅓ cup sugar
    Dash salt
 ¾ teaspoon vanilla extract

Meringue:
 4 egg whites (½ cup)
 ⅛ teaspoon cream of tartar

    Dash salt
 ½ cup sugar
    Boiling water

Caramel Syrup:
 ¼ cup sugar
 ¼ cup hot water

 8 large strawberries, washed,
    with hulls left on

1. Heat milk in top of metal double boiler, over direct heat, until tiny bubbles form around edge. In small bowl, using rotary beater, beat egg yolks, ⅓ cup sugar and dash salt. Slowly beat hot milk into egg mixture. Pour back into top of double boiler.

2. Place over gently simmering water. (Water in lower part of double boiler should not touch upper part.) Cook, stirring constantly, until a thin coating forms on metal spoon—8 to 10 minutes. Pour immediately into a medium bowl. Set bowl in cold water.

3. When cool, add vanilla. Place sheet of waxed paper directly on surface. Refrigerate several hours.

4. Meanwhile, in large electric mixer bowl, let whites warm to room temperature—about 1 hour. Lightly butter inside of a 5-cup mold. Preheat oven to 350F.

5. Make Meringue: At high speed, beat whites with cream of tartar and salt until foamy. Beat in ½ cup sugar, 2 tablespoons at a time; beat after each addition. Beat until stiff peaks form when beater is slowly raised. Spoon into mold. Press to remove air pockets.

6. Place in deep pan. Add boiling water, 1¾ inches deep. Bake,

uncovered, 25 minutes, or until knife inserted in center comes out clean. Cool on rack 5 minutes.

7. Spoon custard into serving dish. With spatula, loosen edge of mold. Unmold on custard.

8. Sprinkle 1/4 cup sugar over bottom of small, heavy skillet. With spoon, stir occasionally over low heat until sugar turns to a golden syrup. Slowly stir in hot water; stir to melt sugar. Spoon over meringue. Refrigerate 1 hour. Decorate with berries.

Makes 8 servings.

ZABAGLIONE

4 egg yolks
1/3 cup sugar
Dash salt
1/2 cup blended Marsala (see Note)
Fresh strawberries or raspberries (optional)

1. In top of double boiler, combine egg yolks, sugar, salt and Marsala. Blend well.

2. Cook over hot (not boiling) water; water in bottom should not touch top of double boiler.

3. While cooking, beat with portable electric mixer until mixture stands in stiff peaks when beater is raised—about 5 minutes. Serve warm in tall sherbet glasses, or serve cold with fruit.

Makes 4 servings.

Note: Blend 1/4 cup cream Marsala with 2 tablespoons sherry and 2 tablespoons almond Marsala (if not available, use cream Marsala); mix well.

CHOCOLATE BOMBE

1 pkg (3 oz) ladyfingers, split lengthwise
1/3 cup amber rum

Chocolate Filling:
8 squares (1-oz size) unsweetened chocolate, or 1 1/2 cups semisweet chocolate pieces
1 cup butter or regular margarine, softened
2 cups unsifted confectioners' sugar
8 egg yolks
2 teaspoons vanilla extract

Chocolate Glaze:
1/2 cup semisweet chocolate pieces
1 tablespoon butter or margarine

Corn syrup (optional)
Candied violets (optional)

1. Line a 1½-quart bowl with plastic film.

2. Brush cut sides of ladyfingers with rum. Arrange 6 ladyfinger halves, cut side up, in bottom of bowl; line side of bowl in same way. Reserve rest of ladyfingers.

3. Make Chocolate Filling: In top of double boiler, over hot, not boiling, water, melt 8 squares of chocolate. Remove from hot water.

4. In large bowl, combine 1 cup butter, the sugar and egg yolks. With portable electric mixer at high speed, beat mixture until smooth and fluffy.

5. At low speed, gradually beat in melted chocolate and the vanilla until well blended. Turn mixture into bowl lined with lady-fingers, spreading it smooth on top. Arrange remaining ladyfingers, cut side down, over top.

6. Refrigerate 4 hours or overnight.

7. At least 1 hour before serving: Run spatula around edge of bowl to loosen; invert on serving platter, and peel off plastic film.

8. Make Chocolate Glaze: In top of double boiler, over hot, not boiling, water, combine chocolate pieces and butter, stirring just until melted. Spread evenly over ladyfingers, covering completely to make a smooth glaze.

9. Refrigerate until firm—½ hour or until serving time. To serve: Brush surface lightly with corn syrup, if desired. Decorate with a few candied violets. To serve, cut in small wedges.

Makes 20 servings.

✄

PEARS VÉFOUR

8 medium-size firm Bartlett or
    Anjou pears (about 3 lb)
¼ cup lemon juice
1½ cups sugar
1 (-inch) piece vanilla bean, or
    ¼ teaspoon vanilla extract
    English Custard Sauce,
      page 349
2 tablespoons Grand Marnier

Pear Filling:
1 cup crushed almond
    macaroons
¼ cup Grand Marnier
1 cup heavy cream
    Candied violets
    Fresh mint leaves

1. Wash pears. Core each from blossom end, leaving pear whole. Remove stem ends; pare. Brush with lemon juice.

2. In a large skillet, combine sugar with vanilla bean or extract and 3 cups water; bring to boiling over medium heat, stirring until sugar is dissolved. Add pears. Reduce heat; simmer, covered, until

pears are tender but not soft—about 15 minutes. Remove vanilla bean if used.

3. Turn pears and syrup into large bowl. Refrigerate, covered, until chilled—about 3 hours.

4. Meanwhile, make Custard Sauce.

5. Turn into medium bowl; stir in 2 tablespoons Grand Marnier. Put sheet of waxed paper directly on surface of sauce in bowl. Refrigerate until well chilled and ready to use—at least 3 hours.

6. Make Pear Filling: Combine the crushed macaroons with 2 tablespoons Grand Marnier; mix well.

7. Carefully remove pears from syrup. Fill center of each with a slightly rounded tablespoonful of Pear Filling; brush pears with 2 tablespoons Grand Marnier. Refrigerate.

8. About 1 hour before serving, beat cream until stiff. Stir 1/2 cup whipped cream into chilled custard sauce. Spoon mixture into a large, chilled shallow serving bowl. Arrange 7 pears around edge of bowl and one in the center. Garnish pears with remaining whipped cream, using pastry bag with decorating tip, if desired. Refrigerate until serving time; then garnish with candied violets and mint.

Makes 8 servings.

❈

ENGLISH PLUM PUDDING

1 jar (8 oz) mixed candied fruit
1 jar (4 oz) candied citron
1 jar (4 oz) candied pineapple
1/4 lb suet
1/2 cup walnuts
1 1/2 cups raisins
1 cup currants
1 tablespoon cinnamon
1 1/2 teaspoons ground ginger
1/4 teaspoon nutmeg
1/2 teaspoon allspice
1/4 teaspoon salt

1 cup sugar
1/2 cup strawberry preserves
1 1/2 cups packaged dry bread
  crumbs
4 eggs
2 tablespoons milk
1/2 cup brandy
1/2 cup sherry

Hard Sauce, page 351 or
Pudding Sauce, page 352

1. Chop candied fruit, citron, pineapple, suet and walnuts fine. In large bowl, combine fruit, citron, pineapple, suet, walnuts, raisins, currants, spices, salt, sugar, preserves and bread crumbs.

2. In large bowl, with electric mixer, beat eggs until very thick. Beat in milk, brandy and sherry; blend well.

3. Add egg mixture to fruit mixture. With large spoon, mix well.

Turn batter into a well-greased 1 1/2-quart pudding mold or a 1 1/2-quart Pyrex bowl.

4. Wrap mold completely in several thicknesses of cheesecloth. Secure cheesecloth around top with string. Place mold on trivet in kettle.

5. Pour in boiling water to come halfway up side of mold. Cover kettle. Steam pudding 4 hours. (Water should boil gently; add water as needed.) Unmold and serve, or cool and store.

6. To store: Refrigerate pudding, still in mold wrapped in cheese-cloth, several weeks.

7. To serve: Steam pudding, still in mold and covered with cheesecloth, on trivet in kettle. Steam pudding 50 to 60 minutes, or until heated through. Remove cheesecloth; loosen edge of pudding from mold with spatula; turn out on serving tray.

8. To flame pudding: Pour several tablespoons brandy over hot pudding. Heat 1/4 cup brandy gently in a small heavy saucepan. When vapor rises, ignite; pour flaming over pudding; carefully carry to table. Serve with Hard Sauce or Pudding Sauce.

Makes 12 servings.

BABA AU RHUM

3/4 cup warm water (105 to 115F)
2 pkg active dry yeast
1/4 cup sugar
1 teaspoon salt
6 eggs
3 3/4 cups sifted* all-purpose flour
3/4 cup soft butter or margarine
1/2 cup finely chopped citron
1/4 cup currants or seedless
    raisins

Rum Syrup:
2 1/2 cups sugar
1 medium unpeeled orange,
    sliced crosswise
1/2 unpeeled lemon, sliced
    crosswise
1 to 1 1/2 cups light rum

Apricot Glaze:
1 cup apricot preserves
1 teaspoon grated lemon peel
2 teaspoons lemon juice

* Sift before measuring.

1. Lightly grease a 10-by-4-inch tube pan. If possible, check temperature of warm water with thermometer.

2. Sprinkle yeast over water in large bowl of electric mixer; stir until dissolved.

3. Add sugar, salt, eggs, and 2 1/4 cups flour. At medium speed, beat 4 minutes, or until smooth, scraping side of bowl and guiding

mixture into beater with rubber scraper.

4. Add butter; beat 2 minutes, or until very well blended.

5. At low speed, beat in rest of flour; beat until smooth—about 2 minutes.

6. Stir in citron and currants. Batter will be thick.

7. Turn batter into prepared pan, spreading evenly. Cover with towel.

8. Let rise in warm place (85F), free from drafts, 1 hour and 10 minutes, or until baba has risen to within ½ inch of top of pan.

9. Meanwhile, preheat oven to 400F. Gently place baba on oven rack (do not jar; baba may fall).

10. Bake 40 to 45 minutes, or until deep golden-brown and cake tester inserted in center comes out clean.

11. Meanwhile, make Rum Syrup: In medium saucepan, combine sugar with 2 cups water; bring to boiling, stirring, until sugar is dissolved. Boil, uncovered, 10 minutes.

12. Reduce heat. Add orange and lemon slices; simmer 10 minutes. Remove from heat; add rum.

13. With metal spatula, carefully loosen sides of baba from pan. Turn out of pan onto wire rack; let cool 15 minutes. Return baba to pan.

14. Set pan on large sheet of foil; gradually pour hot syrup, along with fruit slices, over baba. Continue pouring until all syrup is absorbed.

15. Let baba stand 2 hours or longer.

16. Meanwhile, make Apricot Glaze: In small saucepan, over low heat, melt apricot preserves. Stir in lemon peel and juice; strain. Refrigerate 30 minutes, or until ready to use.

17. To serve baba: Discard fruit slices. Invert baba onto round serving platter. Brush top and side with Apricot Glaze.

18. If desired, serve with whipped cream.

Makes 12 to 16 servings.

FRUIT
FOR DESSERT

Fresh fruits have found a new place on our tables. Thanks to modern marketing methods, fresh fruits have become less seasonal and more available and appealing—fresh strawberries can now be found in stores during most of the year, and even more exotic tropical fruits, such as mangoes, papayas and kiwi fruit are now fairly commonplace. And, thanks to the modern trend toward lighter and lower-in-colorie desserts, hostesses are serving fruits in more interesting ways. Following are some delectable cases in point, from a simple baked apple to sophisticated strawberries Sabayon.

Selection and Storage of Fresh Fruits

APPLES

Store small quantities in the refrigerator. Store larger quantities of firm, well-shaped apples in a cool, dry place.

To keep cut apples from turning brown, dip cut surface in lemon juice.

Some varieties of apples can be purchased throughout the country no matter what the time of year (although the apples you'll find November through June have probably been in cold storage).

The apples most available are *Delicious* apples, which are excellent for eating raw; *Golden Delicious*, which are not only good to munch but fine for general cooking; *McIntosh*, which require less cooking time than other varieties and are marvelous in applesauce and pies; *Rome Beauty*, which are best for baking—and wonderful for pies; *Winesap*, apples that are good to bite into and can be stored longer than most; *Cortland*, a good all-purpose apple for everything from munching to making into pies or sauce; and *Granny Smith*, imported from Australia in the spring and summer, an apple that cooks up well into everything.

BANANAS

Keep both ripe and unripe at room temperature, away from light. Use bananas flecked with brown for eating; the green-tipped, unripe ones for cooking.

BERRIES

Choose fruit that is bright, clean and fresh-looking. Do not wash berries until ready to use, and always wash before hulling. Drain well. Strawberries and raspberries are highly perishable and should be used soon after buying. If they must be stored for a brief time, empty them into a flat pan lined with paper towels and store, uncovered, in refrigerator.

Serve with confectioners' sugar or with fine granulated sugar.

CHERRIES

Store, uncovered, in refrigerator. Do not wash until ready to eat; any dampness hastens mildew. Cherries are very perishable and should be used soon after buying.

GRAPEFRUIT

The best grapefruit has a smooth, tight skin and should feel heavy in the hand (this indicates lots of juice). As the grapefruit season progresses, the fruit is noticeably sweeter (more sugar develops). This does not indicate degree of ripeness, since all grapefruit are tree-ripened. Store in refrigerator or a cool place.

To serve: Wash and cut in half crosswise with a long-bladed knife. Remove seeds. With grapefruit knife or sharp paring knife, cut around edges separating fruit from rind. Then cut between each segment and dividing membrane. Serve with or without sugar.

KIWI FRUIT

Kiwi Fruit, sometimes known as Chinese gooseberry, comes from New Zealand and has an unusual taste similar to watermelon and strawberry. It is ripe for eating when soft to the touch. To speed ripening, store at room temperature in a closed polyurethane bag. Chill before serving. To serve: cut in half, rub off hairs, and eat with a spoon.

LEMONS and LIMES

Select those heavy for their size, with waxy skin and moderate firmness. Keep in refrigerator. They last longer, whole or cut, when wrapped in foil or plastic wrap.

MANGOS

Mangos are a sweet and juicy tropical fruit, as commonplace in the tropics as apples are here. Mangos come in two shapes, elongated, or almost round. The inside of the fruit is a bright golden with a long, flat seed at the center. They are ready to eat when they yield to gentle pressure. The outside color—green, yellow, or tinged with red or yellow—doesn't matter. If still firm when purchased, there is no need to refrigerate. Mangos will ripen in a few days in your fruit bowl at room temperature, and then may be refrigerated.

To serve: Score the mango skin into four quarters; peel as a banana and eat out of hand. Or, lay the mango on a counter, and with a sharp knife halve-cut from end to end. Eat fruit out of the half with a spoon. Nice also in a fresh fruit cup or salad.

MELONS

Let melons ripen at room temperature. They are ripe when they are slightly soft to touch and have a faintly sweet odor. Then refrigerate to chill well. When storing cut melon in refrigerator, wrap well to keep flavor from permeating other foods.

To serve: Wash; cut with long-bladed knife into wedges; remove seeds. Serve with a wedge of lemon or lime.

NECTARINES

The nectarine is a variant of the peach, with a smooth skin; almost all come from California. They are ripened and stored in the same manner as peaches, below.

ORANGES

Buy oranges that are heavy for their size (indicating more juice), firm, and free from decay. Neither russeting nor green skin tone affects quality, since all oranges are tree-ripened. Should be stored in refrigerator or in a cool place.

To serve: To remove orange sections whole for salads or fruit cups, use seedless (navel) oranges or varieties with a minimum of seeds. Hold the fruit over a bowl so that no juice is lost in the process. Remove the rind by cutting round in a spiral from top to bottom. With a sharp knife loosen the sections by cutting on either side of the dividing membranes. Lift out the section; remove seeds.

Seedless oranges may be placed on a board and cut with a sharp knife into crosswise slices for dessert and for salads.

PAPAYA

A staple of the tropics, "tree melon" is as popular there as cantaloupe is here and served in the same manner, with salt or a wedge of lemon or lime. The mature green papaya will ripen in 4 or 5 days at about room temperature or slightly warmer. Store ripened fruit in refrigerator.

PEACHES

Peaches should be ripened at room temperature, away from light. When they yield to a slight pressure of thumb and forefinger, store in refrigerator. Do not wash before storing. If you prefer fruit that's not too cold, bring to room temperature for an hour or so before serving.

PEARS

Pears are never tree-ripened. They are best when picked at a right stage of maturity and allowed to ripen at room temperature, away from light. When fruit responds to a slight pressure around the stem end, it is usually ready to eat. Pears need a rather humid atmosphere to ripen properly, and if air is dry from artificial heat, it's not a bad idea to keep a cup of water in the bottom of the fruit bowl. To deter ripening, refrigerate; but bring to room temperature to serve.

PERSIMMONS

The large, orange-red persimmon grown in California is almost jellylike in consistency when it is ready to serve. Wash; remove the calyx and peel with a sharp knife; serve whole with a spoon, or cut from the pit in slices for salads or fruit cups.

PLUMS

Select only plump, fresh-looking, full-colored plums. If not ripe enough, ripen at room temperature away from light. Store in refrigerator. Wash just before serving.

PINEAPPLE

Pineapple from Hawaii, according to law, may be picked only when a certain degree of sugar concentration (ripeness) has been reached. Pineapples do not really ripen after picking.

To serve: Wash; remove the crown by cutting around it with a pointed knife. Place the pineapple on its side on a board and with a long-bladed knife, cut into ¾-inch rounds. Cut the rind from each round and remove the "eyes" with the point of the knife. Cut each round in half; remove the hard core; cut in thin wedges. Sprinkle with sugar and place in the refrigerator until the sugar is dissolved in the extracted juice.

BAKED APPLES

1/2 cup light corn syrup
1/2 cup sugar
1/4 cup orange marmalade
1/4 cup butter or margarine
 6 baking apples (about 3 lb),
    Rome Beauty

1/2 cup light-brown sugar,
   firmly packed
 3 tablespoons raisins
1/2 teaspoon cinnamon

1. Preheat oven to 375F. In small saucepan, combine corn syrup, 1/2 cup sugar, marmalade and butter.

2. Cook over medium heat, stirring until sugar is dissolved. Pour into 12-by-8-by-2-inch baking dish.

3. Wash and core apples; pare only at top, about 1 inch down. In small bowl, combine 1/2 cup brown sugar, raisins, and cinnamon. Fill centers of apples with raisin mixture. Place in syrup, pared side down. Bake, covered, 30 minutes.

4. Turn apples, pared side up. Baste with syrup.

5. Bake, uncovered, basting occasionally, 15 minutes longer, or until apples are tender. Place apples and syrup in serving dish.

Makes 6 servings.

BAKED APPLES SAINT JEAN

6 medium baking apples (2 lb)
2 tablespoons lemon juice
6 tablespoons sugar
6 tablespoons butter or
    margarine, melted

1/2 cup apricot preserves
1/2 cup coarsely crushed almond-
    macaroon crumbs or Grape
    Nuts
Calvados, applejack, or brandy

1. Preheat oven to 400F.

2. Pare and core apples; do not cut all the way through, so that bottoms are intact.

3. Brush apples with lemon juice; arrange in shallow baking dish. Fill each cavity with 1 tablespoon sugar; then spoon 1 tablespoon melted butter into each cavity. Pour any leftover lemon juice into bottom of dish.

4. Cover top of dish completely with foil. Bake 30 minutes, basting after 15 minutes with liquid in dish.

5. Remove apples from oven. With spatula, spread each with

apricot preserves; sprinkle each with crushed macaroons.

6. Return to oven for 5 minutes. Meanwhile, heat brandy. Pour over apples to serve.

Makes 6 servings.

MERINGUED APPLES

1 cup sugar
1/8 teaspoon salt
5 medium Golden Delicious or
   Rome Beauty apples (2 lb)
2 tablespoons orange juice
   or red wine

Meringue:
 3 egg whites
1/3 cup sugar
1/2 teaspoon vanilla extract
1/2 cup flaked coconut

1. In large saucepan, bring 1 cup water, 1 cup sugar and the salt to boiling. Meanwhile, pare, core and quarter apples. Add to hot syrup; bring back to boiling; reduce heat and cook gently, covered, 20 minutes, or until apple is just tender.

2. With slotted spoon, remove apple to a buttered, 1-quart shallow baking dish. Sprinkle apple with orange juice. Preheat oven to 325F.

3. Continue to cook syrup from apple, uncovered, until syrup is reduced to 1/2 cup; then pour over apple.

4. Make meringue: With portable mixer, beat egg whites in medium bowl until soft peaks form; gradually beat in sugar, beating until stiff peaks form when beater is slowly raised. Gently fold in vanilla and coconut.

5. Spread meringue over apple. Bake 20 minutes, or until meringue is golden. Serve warm or cold.

Makes 6 servings.

ROSY CINNAMON APPLES

1/2 cup sugar
 1 cup red cinnamon candies

6 medium-size tart apples (2 1/2
   lbs), such as Winesap
Light cream

1. In medium skillet, dissolve sugar and candies in 3 cups hot water, stirring; bring to boiling; simmer, uncovered, 5 minutes.

2. Pare and core apples; arrange on side in syrup.

3. Cook, uncovered, over medium heat 10 minutes. Turn apples; cook 10 to 15 minutes longer, covered, or until tender when pierced with cake tester.

4. Serve slightly warm or well-chilled in their syrup with cream. Makes 6 servings.

APPLESAUCE MERINGUE

3 egg whites
2 jars (15-oz size) applesauce
1/2 teaspoon cinnamon

6 tablespoons granulated sugar
2 tablespoons confectioners' sugar

1. Let egg whites warm to room temperature in large bowl of electric mixer—about an hour.

2. Preheat oven to 375F. Turn applesauce into a large baking dish (about 10-by-6-inches). Stir cinnamon into applesauce to mix well.

3. At high speed, beat egg whites until soft peaks form when the beater is slowly raised. Gradually beat in granulated sugar; beat just until stiff peaks form.

4. Spread meringue evenly over applesauce, then make swirls with the spatula. Sprinkle top evenly with confectioners' sugar.

5. Bake 12 to 15 minutes or until meringue is slightly golden and crusty. Serve warm.

Makes 6 servings.

COUNTRY APPLESAUCE

2 lb tart cooking apples

1/2 to 2/3 cup sugar, depending on tartness of apples

1. Wash, core, and pare apples; cut into quarters. Measure about 7 1/2 cups.

2. In medium saucepan, bring 1/2 cup water to boiling. Add apples; bring to boiling.

3. Reduce heat; simmer, covered, 20 to 25 minutes; stir occasionally. Add water, if needed.

4. Stir in sugar until well combined. Serve warm or cold.

Makes about 3 cups.

SPICED APPLESAUCE

Proceed as with Country Applesauce, but add 1 teaspoon lemon juice, ¼ teaspoon cinnamon, and ⅛ teaspoon nutmeg to apples with sugar.

ROSY APPLESAUCE

3 lb McIntosh apples, washed,   1 cup sugar
   quartered and cored

1. In a large saucepan, combine apples, with their skins, with ½ cup water. Bring to boiling; reduce heat and simmer, covered, until very tender—about 15 minutes.
2. Put apples and cooking liquid through food mill, or press through colander, to remove skins. Add sugar.
3. Heat applesauce to simmering, stirring to prevent sticking. Serve slightly warm or cool. Refrigerate, covered, to store.
   Makes 2 pints.

BANANAS FLAMBÉ

4 large bananas   ½ cup superfine sugar
½ cup sweet butter   ⅓ cup dark rum

1. Peel bananas, removing any strings; cut bananas in half lengthwise, then cut crosswise on the diagonal, to make 1½-inch pieces.
2. In large skillet, melt butter; add sugar; heat, stirring, until golden.
3. Add bananas; sauté, turning occasionally, until tender—about 5 minutes.
4. Ignite rum; add flaming to bananas.
5. Serve at once, over vanilla ice cream, if desired.
   Makes 6 servings.

CANTALOUPE BALLS À L'ORANGE

¼ cup slightly thawed frozen
    orange-juice concentrate,
    undiluted
2 tablespoons light corn syrup

1 tablespoon kirsch
4 cups ripe cantaloupe balls
6 fresh mint sprigs

1. In medium bowl, combine orange-juice concentrate, corn syrup and kirsch; mix well.

2. Add melon balls; toss lightly to combine.

3. Refrigerate, covered, until well chilled—about 2 hours.

4. To serve: Spoon into six dessert dishes or 1 large compote. Garnish with mint.

Makes 6 servings.

CHILLED CANTALOUPE SOUP

1 (3 lb) ripe cantaloupe
½ cup dry sherry

¼ cup sugar
1 tablespoon lime juice

1. Cut melon in half; scoop out seeds. Scoop out cantaloupe meat.

2. In blender, combine cantaloupe and rest of ingredients. Blend until smooth—several times if necessary. Refrigerate, covered, until very cold.

Makes 4 cups; 5 servings.

BAKED FRUIT FLAMBÉ

½ cup orange marmalade
2 teaspoons grated lemon peel
¼ cup lemon juice
1½ cups light-brown sugar,
    firmly packed
1½ teaspoons cinnamon
1 can (1 lb) peach halves,
    drained

1 can (1 lb, 1 oz) pear halves,
    drained
1 jar (9½ oz) pineapple sticks,
    drained
2 bananas, peeled and quartered
½ cup white rum

1. Preheat oven to 400F. In small saucepan, combine marmalade, lemon peel, and lemon juice; mix well. Bring just to simmering over low heat. Set aside.

2. Meanwhile, in medium bowl, combine brown sugar and cinnamon; mix well.

3. Dry fruit (except the banana quarters) well on paper towels. Dip all pieces of fruit in marmalade mixture, then in sugar mixture, coating completely.

4. Arrange the fruit in a 13½-by-9-by-2-inch baking dish; bake 15 minutes.

5. Just before serving, slowly heat rum in small saucepan. Ignite; pour flaming rum over fruit. Nice served over ice cream.

Makes 8 servings.

CHINESE FRUIT BOWL

1 ripe pineapple (3 lb)
1 pint strawberries, washed and
    hulled
1 can (11 oz) litchi nuts, drained
1 can (11 oz) mandarin-orange
    sections, drained
½ cup preserved whole kumquats

2 bananas, sliced on the diagonal
½ cup syrup from preserved
    kumquats
¾ cup white rum
2 tablespoons chopped candied
    ginger (optional)

1. With a long-bladed, sharp knife, cut pineapple into quarters, right through frond. Remove pineapple, in one piece, from shells. Remove core. Slice pineapple into wedges, ¼ inch thick. (Makes about 4 cups.)

2. In large bowl, gently toss pineapple wedges with remaining ingredients. Refrigerate, covered, until well chilled—2 hours or longer.

Makes 12 to 14 servings.

FRESH FRUIT WITH GRAND MARNIER

1 large grapefruit
2 large oranges
1 large unpared apple, sliced and
    cut in 1-inch pieces
1 large unpared pear, sliced and
    cut in 1-inch pieces

1 cup grapes, halved and seeded
1 pint strawberries, hulled
1 tablespoon sugar
¼ cup Grand Marnier

1. With sharp paring knife, remove rind and membrane from grapefruit and oranges. Remove sections from the fruit and cut in half, catching juice and sections in a large bowl. Squeeze any juice in membrane into bowl.

2. Add remaining fruits; sprinkle with sugar. Pour Grand Marnier over all; toss lightly to mix well.

3. Refrigerate, covered, until well chilled—several hours. Makes 12 servings.

FRESH FRUITS ON ICE

2 pint boxes fresh strawberries
1 pint box fresh raspberries
1 pint box fresh blueberries

½ to ¾ cup granulated sugar
1½ cups orange juice
Crushed ice

1. Wash all the berries; drain. Hull strawberries.

2. In a deep, glass serving bowl, place a layer of strawberries. Sprinkle strawberries generously with some of sugar.

3. Continue layering the remaining berries, sprinkling each layer generously with sugar.

4. Pour 1½ cups of orange juice over berries. Let stand at room temperature 1 hour.

5. Just before serving, cover berries with a thin layer of crushed ice.

Makes 8 servings.

GRILLED GRAPEFRUIT WITH KIRSCH

4 grapefruit, halved
1 cup sugar

1 cup kirsch

1. Cut out centers and remove seeds from each grapefruit half. Cut around each section with grapefruit knife, to loosen.

2. Sprinkle each half with 2 tablespoons sugar, then with 2 tablespoons kirsch.

3. Broil, 4 inches from heat, about 5 minutes, or until bubbly and brown. Garnish with mint sprigs, if desired.

Makes 8 servings.

MELON DELIGHT WITH MINT SAUCE

Mint Sauce:
1 bunch fresh mint
¼ cup sugar
1 jar (10 oz) mint jelly

Fruit:
1 large fresh fully ripe pineapple
1 pt fresh strawberries
1 large honeydew melon

1. Make Sauce: Wash mint. Reserve 6 to 8 sprigs for garnish; remove stems from remainder. With scissors, snip mint leaves very fine—you'll have about ½ cup.

2. Combine snipped mint and sugar in a small bowl, and let stand 1 hour.

3. Melt jelly in top of double boiler, over boiling water. Blend in mint-sugar mixture and ¼ cup water.

4. Cover; let cool; then refrigerate until chilled.

5. Prepare Fruit: Cut off top of washed pineapple. Remove rind by cutting down pineapple in wide slices. Remove eyes by cutting V-shape wedges full length of pineapple, following diagonal pattern of eyes. Lift out wedges, and discard. Cut pineapple crosswise into ½-inch slices; remove core. Cut slices into chunks (you'll have about 4 cups).

6. Wash and hull strawberries; halve, if large. Combine with pineapple chunks.

7. Cut melon into 6 to 8 wedges. Scrape out seeds.

8. Heap each wedge with about 1 cup pineapple-strawberry mixture. Spoon about 2 tablespoons mint sauce over each portion. Garnish with sprig of mint.

Makes 6 to 8 servings.

ORANGES ORIENTALE

8 large navel or Temple oranges
1½ cups sugar
1½ cups light corn syrup

Red food color (optional)
¼ cup lemon juice
¼ cup Cointreau

1. With sharp paring knife, remove peel from 4 oranges in 1½-inch-long strips. Remove any white membrane from strips; cut each into ⅛-inch-wide pieces. (Or, if desired, remove peel with a coarse grater.) Makes about 1 cup.

2. Peel remaining oranges; remove any white membrane from all oranges. Place oranges, whole or cut in half, in large bowl; set aside.

3. In small saucepan, combine prepared peel with 2 cups cold water. Bring to boiling, covered. Remove from heat; drain. Reserve peel.

4. In large saucepan, combine sugar and corn syrup with a few drops red food color and 1½ cups water; bring to boiling, over high heat, stirring until sugar is dissolved. Cook, uncovered and over medium heat, 10 minutes. Add reserved peel.

5. Continue cooking 30 minutes longer, or until syrup is slightly thickened. Remove from heat; stir in lemon juice and Cointreau.

6. Pour hot syrup over oranges in bowl. Refrigerate, covered, at least 8 hours; turn oranges occasionally.

7. Serve chilled oranges topped with some of the syrup and candied peel. Decorate, if desired, with candied violets. Serve with dessert forks and fruit knives.

Makes 8 servings.

AMBROSIA

4 large navel oranges
1 pkg (12 oz) frozen pineapple
    chunks, thawed
2 tablespoons Cointreau or
    orange juice

4 medium bananas
4 tablespoons confectioners' sugar
1 can (3½ oz) flaked coconut

1. Peel oranges; remove white membrane. Cut oranges crosswise into ⅛-inch-thick slices.

2. Drain pineapple, saving syrup. Combine syrup and Cointreau; set aside.

3. Peel bananas. Cut on the diagonal into ⅛-inch-thick slices.

4. In attractive serving bowl, layer half the orange slices; sprinkle with 2 tablespoons confectioners' sugar. Layer half the banana slices and half the pineapple; sprinkle with half the coconut.

5. Repeat layers of fruit and sugar. Pour syrup mixture over fruit. Sprinkle with remaining coconut.

6. Refrigerate several hours, or until well chilled.

Makes 10 servings.

꽃

PEACHES ROYALE

2 cans (1-lb, 1-oz size) peach
     halves, drained; or 6 pared,
     large fresh peach halves
1 pint strawberries, washed
1/3 cup brandy

Strawberry Chantilly:
1/2 cup heavy cream
1/2 cup confectioners' sugar
1 cup strawberries, washed,
     hulled, and crushed (see
     Note)

1. In attractive serving dish, arrange peach halves and whole strawberries. Pour brandy over fruit. Refrigerate, covered, at least 2 hours.

2. Meanwhile, make Strawberry Chantilly: In medium bowl, combine heavy cream, confectioners' sugar, and the crushed strawberries. Refrigerate, covered, along with beater, 2 hours.

3. Beat just until stiff. Serve as sauce along with fruit.

Makes 6 servings.

Note: You may substitute 1 package (10 ounces) frozen sliced strawberries, thawed and drained.

꽃

BAKED FRESH PEACHES

6 fresh ripe peaches (about 2 lb)
1/2 cup honey

3 tablespoons lemon juice
Heavy cream

1. Preheat oven to 350F. Wash peaches; peel. Cut in halves; remove pits.

2. Arrange peach halves in 2-quart casserole.

3. Combine honey and lemon juice with 1 cup water. Pour over peaches.

4. Bake, covered, 30 minutes, or until tender.

5. Serve warm or cold, with cream poured over.

Makes 6 servings.

꽃

POACHED FRESH PEACHES

1/4 cup apricot preserves
1 teaspoon grated orange peel
3 tablespoons sugar

4 ripe, fresh peaches (about 1 1/2
     lb), peeled, halved and pitted
1/4 cup sherry

1. In medium saucepan, combine preserves, orange peel and sugar with ½ cup water.

2. Cook, stirring, over low heat until mixture is syrupy and falls in heavy drops from side of spoon—about 5 minutes.

3. Add peach halves to syrup. Simmer, uncovered, about 10 minutes, or until peaches are tender.

4. Add ¼ cup sherry. Refrigerate, covered, several hours, or until well chilled.

5. Serve peaches with syrup spooned over them.

Makes 4 servings.

APRICOT-GLAZED POACHED PEARS

2 lb ripe Anjou pears (6 to 8)
4 cups sugar

1 teaspoon vanilla extract
1 jar (12 oz) apricot preserves

1. With vegetable peeler, pare pears, leaving them whole, with stems on.

2. In a 3½-quart saucepan, combine sugar and 2 cups water. Heat, stirring until sugar is dissolved. Bring to boiling; boil, uncovered, 10 minutes.

3. Add vanilla. Add pears; simmer, uncovered, over low heat 40 minutes, or just until pears are tender and slightly transparent. Remove pears with slotted spoon; drain on paper towels.

4. In small saucepan, heat preserves, stirring, until melted. Boil 1 minute. Press through sieve. Brush over pears, coating well. Arrange in serving dish; refrigerate several hours.

Makes 6 to 8 servings.

FRESH PEARS IN PORT

1 cup sugar
4 fresh pears, pared, halved and
    cored

½ cup white or tawny port

1. In 4-quart saucepan, combine sugar and 3 cups water; heat until sugar dissolves.

2. Add pears; cover; simmer gently until tender—about 30 minutes.

3. Carefully place pears, with about 1 cup syrup, in bowl. Add port; refrigerate, covered, overnight.

4. Serve pears with syrup.

Makes 8 servings.

※

PEARS SABAYON

1 cup granulated sugar
4 fresh ripe pears, pared, halved,
   and cored

Sauce:
 4 egg yolks
 1 cup confectioners' sugar
 ¼ cup sherry
 ¾ cup heavy cream

1. In 4-quart saucepan, combine granulated sugar and 3 cups water; heat until sugar dissolves.

2. Add pears; cover; simmer gently until tender—about 30 minutes. Remove from heat.

3. Carefully place pears, with about 1 cup syrup, in bowl; refrigerate several hours.

4. Make Sauce: In top of double boiler, with rotary beater or wire whisk, beat egg yolks, confectioners' sugar, and sherry until light.

5. Place over hot, not boiling, water; water should not touch bottom of double-boiler top. Cook, stirring constantly, 8 to 10 minutes.

6. Refrigerate several hours. Mixture thickens on standing.

7. In medium bowl, beat cream until soft peaks form when beater is raised. Carefully fold in chilled sauce.

8. Drain pears. Serve topped with sauce.

Makes 8 servings.

STRAWBERRIES OR RASPBERRIES SABAYON

2 pint boxes strawberries or red
   raspberries, washed and
   drained; or 3 pkgs (10-oz size)
   frozen strawberries or

raspberries, thawed and
   drained
Sabayon Sauce, above

Place berries in serving bowl or dessert dishes. Stir sauce; pour over fruit.

Makes 6 servings.

FRESH PINEAPPLE IN SHELL

1. With long knife, cut each chilled pineapple into quarters, right through frond. Remove core. Then, with knife, cut between shell and fruit, separating fruit from shell in one piece.

2. Leaving fruit in place, slice in half; then cut crosswise eight times to make wedges. Keep refrigerated until serving. Serve fruit right in shell.

Each pineapple makes 4 servings.

FRESH PINEAPPLE FLAMBÉ

1 large pineapple (about 4 lb)	1/2 cup dark rum
2 tablespoons butter or margarine	1 sugar cube
1/2 cup light-brown sugar, packed	Lemon extract

1. Preheat oven to 350F.

2. Slice top from pineapple about 1 1/2 inches below frond. Set top aside.

3. With grapefruit knife or other sharp knife, remove meat from pineapple shell, leaving shell intact. Discard core of pineapple; cut meat into 1/2-inch chunks.

4. Place pineapple shell in shallow pan; heat in oven about 10 minutes.

5. In medium skillet, melt butter; add brown sugar and rum; stir to combine. Add pineapple chunks; over low heat, stir until heated through—about 10 minutes.

6. To serve: Place warm pineapple shell on serving platter. Spoon in pineapple chunks and sauce, mounding high. Place top of pineapple on serving dish next to pineapple.

7. Soak sugar cube in lemon extract; place on top of pineapple chunks. Ignite with match. Serve flaming. (This dessert is nice served over ice cream, too.)

Makes 6 to 8 servings.

ᘔᘖ

PINEAPPLE LUAU

4- to 5-lb ripe pineapple   Confectioners' sugar
  Golden rum

1. Cut 1½-inch slice from top, including frond, and bottom of pineapple. Set slices aside.

2. With long, narrow, sharp knife, remove pineapple from shell in one piece, leaving shell intact.

3. Cut pineapple lengthwise into 12 spears. Remove core. Roll each spear in rum, then in sugar.

4. Replace spears in shell.

5. Replace bottom and top of pineapple. Stand in shallow dish.

6. Refrigerate until chilled—at least 2 hours.

7. Serve in the shell. Guests help themselves to pineapple spears.

Makes 6 servings.

ᘔᘖ

FRESH FRUIT IN PINEAPPLE SHELL

1 medium-size fresh, ripe   1 cup fresh strawberries
    pineapple   1 cup seedless green grapes,
¼ cup Cointreau   halved
2 tablespoons confectioners'
    sugar

1. With a long-bladed knife, cut the pineapple, right through the frond, into quarters. With scissors, snip off the tips of the frond, if desired.

2. Remove pineapple, in one piece, from shells. Refrigerate the shells.

3. Cut core from pineapple and discard. Cut pineapple into chunks; place chunks in a large bowl. Add the Cointreau and the confectioners' sugar; mix gently.

4. Refrigerate pineapple, covered, 3 hours, or until ready to serve.

5. Meanwhile, wash the strawberries; drain. Reserve a few berries for garnish. Hull remaining berries, and slice. Refrigerate all the berries until ready to use. Also wash and refrigerate the green grapes.

6. Just before serving, toss sliced strawberries and halved green grapes with the pineapple chunks. Spoon fruit into chilled pineapple shells. Garnish with reserved whole strawberries.

Makes 4 servings.

❇

POACHED FRESH PLUMS

1 lb fresh Italian plums   2 thin slices lemon
½ cup sugar

1. Wash plums. Cut in half; remove pits.

2. In a medium saucepan, combine sugar and 1½ cups water. Bring to boiling; boil 5 to 6 minutes.

3. Add plums and lemon; return to boiling. Reduce heat and simmer about 4 minutes.

4. Cool; refrigerate, covered, until well chilled.

Makes 4 to 6 servings.

❇

COLD PLUM SOUP

2 cans (17-oz size) purple plums   ⅓ cup lime juice
⅛ teaspoon ground cinnamon   ⅔ cup light rum
   Dash ground cloves

1. Drain plums, reserving syrup. Remove pits from plums.

2. Combine plums, reserved syrup, and remaining ingredients. Blend in blender, about one third at a time.

3. Refrigerate, covered, until well chilled (see Note)—4 hours or overnight.

4. Serve in chilled glasses or individual dishes set in ice. Garnish with a dab of whipped cream sprinkled with cinnamon, if desired.

Makes 5 cups; 6 servings.

Note: Place in freezer an hour or two to chill more quickly, if desired.

PRUNES IN PORT, WITH CREAM

1½ cups port
1 pkg (16 oz) dried prunes
1 cup granulated sugar
2 teaspoons vanilla extract

1 cup heavy cream
1 tablespoon confectioners'
　sugar
¼ cup canned flaked coconut

1. Pour port over prunes in large bowl; refrigerate, covered, overnight.

2. Next day, combine prunes in wine with sugar and 1 cup water in medium saucepan; bring to boiling, covered.

3. Reduce heat, and simmer 30 minutes.

4. Remove from heat; stir in 1 teaspoon vanilla.

5. Turn into serving dish; refrigerate until well chilled—about 2 hours.

6. Just before serving, whip cream just until stiff. Fold in confectioners' sugar and rest of vanilla.

7. Garnish prunes with whipped cream. Then sprinkle with flaked coconut.

Makes 8 servings.

STEWED RHUBARB

1 cup sugar
4 cups cut rhubarb, in 1-inch
　pieces (about 1¾ lb)

1 teaspoon grated lemon peel
　(optional)

1. Combine sugar with ½ cup water in medium saucepan. Over medium heat, stir until sugar is dissolved and syrup comes to boiling.

2. Reduce heat. Add rhubarb and lemon peel; simmer, covered, 10 minutes, or until tender, not mushy.

3. Remove from heat. Let stand, covered, on wire rack until cool.

Makes 4 to 6 servings.

✣

BAKED SPICED RHUBARB

4 cups rhubarb, cut in 1-inch
    pieces (about 2 lb); or 2 pkgs
    (1-lb size) frozen rhubarb in
    syrup

1 cup sugar
1-inch cinnamon stick
4 whole cloves

1. Preheat oven to 400F.

2. Place rhubarb in a 2-quart casserole. Sprinkle with sugar; add cinnamon and cloves. If using frozen rhubarb, place frozen fruit in a 10-by-8-by-2-inch baking dish. Sprinkle with only ¼ cup sugar; add spices.

3. Bake, covered, 10 minutes. Stir gently to dissolve sugar, and baste fruit with syrup. Bake 15 minutes longer, or until rhubarb is tender but not mushy.

4. Let stand, covered, on wire rack until cool.

Makes 4 to 6 servings.

✣

STRAWBERRIES À LA BLUE FOX

30 fresh jumbo strawberries

Sherry Cream:
 2 egg yolks
 2 tablespoons granulated sugar

2 tablespoons sherry, port or
    marsala
Confectioners' sugar
1 cup heavy cream

1. Wash strawberries in cold water; drain well; hull. From point, slit each berry into quarters, but not through bottom. Refrigerate.

2. Make sherry cream: In top of double boiler, with portable electric mixer at medium speed, beat egg yolks with granulated sugar and sherry until well combined.

3. Place over boiling water; beat at medium speed until mixture is thick and forms soft peaks when beater is slowly raised—about 5 minutes. Remove from heat.

4. Immediately set top of double boiler in bowl of ice; continue beating until mixture is cool—about 2 minutes. Let stand in ice in refrigerator 30 minutes longer.

5. Meanwhile, in medium bowl, combine ¼ cup confectioners' sugar and the cream. Refrigerate along with electric-beater blades, 30 minutes.

6. Add chilled cooked mixture to chilled cream mixture; beat until stiff.

7. Fill each strawberry with cream mixture—using pastry bag with decorating tip, if desired—bringing mixture to a peak at top. Refrigerate.

8. To serve: Sprinkle filled berries lightly with confectioners' sugar. Arrange, standing up, on mound of crushed ice, if desired.

Makes 8 to 10 servings.

FRESH STRAWBERRIES À LA COLONY

2 pint boxes strawberries	1/2 pint vanilla ice cream
1/2 cup sugar	1/2 cup heavy cream
1/3 cup Cointreau or Grand Marnier	1/4 teaspoon almond extract

1. Gently wash berries in cold water. Drain on paper towels; hull. Turn into large serving bowl; sprinkle with sugar, Cointreau; toss gently. Refrigerate 1 hour, stirring occasionally.

2. Let ice cream soften in refrigerator about 1 hour.

3. Beat heavy cream just until stiff. Fold in almond extract.

4. Gently fold whipped cream and softened ice cream into strawberry mixture. Serve at once.

Makes 8 servings.

FONDANT-DIPPED STRAWBERRIES

2 pint boxes large strawberries	3 tablespoons lemon juice
2 1/2 cups confectioners' sugar	2 tablespoons light corn syrup

1. Wash strawberries gently; drain well on paper towels. Leave hulls and stems on.

2. In top of double boiler, combine sugar, lemon juice, and corn syrup. Cook, stirring, over hot water until mixture is smooth and shiny and thin enough to coat strawberries. Remove from heat; keep warm over hot water.

3. Holding each strawberry by the stem, dip into fondant, covering berry. Place dipped berries, hull end down, 2 inches apart, on wire racks placed on cookie sheets.

4. Let strawberries dry on racks at least 1 hour before serving.

(Strawberries can be dipped in the morning for serving later in the day, but do not hold overnight.)

Makes about 30.

※

STRAWBERRIES WITH MINT

2 pint boxes fresh strawberries
2 tablespoons chopped fresh mint
   leaves

1 teaspoon grated orange peel
½ cup orange juice
½ cup confectioners' sugar

1. Gently wash strawberries in cold water; drain; hull.

2. In medium bowl, lightly toss strawberries with mint, orange peel, and orange juice.

3. Turn into serving bowl; sprinkle with confectioners' sugar. Refrigerate at least 1 hour before serving.

4. If desired, top individual servings with sweetened whipped cream.

Makes 6 servings.

※

STRAWBERRIES AU NATUREL

2 pint boxes fresh strawberries
⅔ cup plus 6 tablespoons dairy
   sour cream

⅓ cup plus 2 tablespoons light-
   brown sugar, firmly packed

1. Gently wash strawberries in cold water; drain well.

2. Hull berries; slice into large bowl.

3. Add ⅔ cup sour cream and ⅓ cup sugar; mix gently.

4. Divide into 6 serving dishes.

5. Top each with 1 tablespoon sour cream and 1 teaspoon sugar.

6. Chill 1 hour before serving.

Makes 6 servings.

※

STRAWBERRIES IN PORT

2 pint boxes fresh strawberries
½ cup sugar

1 cup red or white port wine

1. Gently wash strawberries in cold water; drain; and hull.

2. In medium bowl, gently toss strawberries with sugar. Add wine.

3. Refrigerate at least 2 hours, stirring occasionally.

4. If desired, top individual servings with sweetened whipped cream.

Makes 6 servings.

STRAWBERRIES WITH RASPBERRY SAUCE

2 pint boxes fresh strawberries   *1 pkg (10 oz) frozen raspberries, partially thawed*

1. Gently wash strawberries in cold water; drain; hull.

2. Mound in shallow serving dish. Refrigerate.

3. Make Raspberry Sauce: Press raspberries through sieve, or blend in electric blender, covered, about 1 minute.

4. To serve, spoon sauce over strawberries.

Makes 6 servings.

STRAWBERRIES ROMANOFF

2 pint boxes fresh strawberries   *1 teaspoon almond extract*
1 cup confectioners' sugar   *2 tablespoons Cointreau or orange*
1 cup heavy cream   *juice*

1. Gently wash strawberries in cold water; drain; hull.

2. In medium bowl, sprinkle sugar over berries; toss gently.

3. Refrigerate 1 hour, stirring occasionally.

4. In chilled bowl, with rotary beater, whip cream until stiff. Add almond extract and Cointreau.

5. Fold into strawberries. Serve at once.

Makes 8 servings.

STRAWBERRIES AND PINEAPPLE WITH SOUR CREAM

1 can (13½ oz) pineapple
    chunks, drained
1½ cups fresh strawberry halves
¾ cup dairy sour cream

¼ cup maple or maple-flavored
    syrup
Light-brown sugar

1. Divide pineapple and strawberries evenly into 6 dessert dishes.

2. In small bowl, combine sour cream with maple syrup until well blended. Spoon over fruit.

3. Refrigerate until well chilled—at least 1 hour.

4. Just before serving, sprinkle brown sugar over each.

Makes 6 servings.

WATERMELON CHA-CHA-CHA

1 large ripe watermelon

1 cup light rum

1. Cut a plug in center of melon (plug should be about 2½ inches square and about 3 inches deep).

2. Pour rum into hole. Trim pink flesh from plug, leaving rind about ½ inch thick; replace the plug in the watermelon.

3. Place melon in refrigerator, plug side up, and chill 6 to 8 hours, or until flavor permeates melon.

4. Cut in wedges and serve.

Makes 16 servings.

WATERMELON FRUIT BASKET

1 long (13-inch) ripe watermelon
    (about 10 lb), washed
1 pint strawberries, washed
    and hulled
2 cups pineapple chunks (1 small
    [2 lb] pineapple)

3 cups honeydew-melon balls (1
    melon)
1 cantaloupe, cut in half, peeled
    and cut into slices
1 lb green grapes, washed and
    separated into clusters
    Kirsch (optional)

1. Make handle: On top of watermelon, insert wooden picks to outline a handle, 1½ inches wide.

2. On each side of the handle 6 inches from bottom of watermelon, insert wooden picks to form 2 scallops.

3. With sharp knife, cut around scallops and handle. Remove the two pieces from each side of the handle.

4. Cut watermelon meat from under handle. With melon-ball cutter, scoop out 3 cups watermelon balls from inside of watermelon; discard seeds.

5. With sharp knife; cut around inside of watermelon so shell is about ¾ inch thick.

6. Fill basket with fruit. Wrap with plastic film to hold fruit in place. Refrigerate until well chilled.

7. At serving time, remove wrap. Sprinkle with kirsch.
Makes 10 servings.

RUMTOPF (RUM POT)

1 can (1 lb, 14 oz) whole peeled
   apricots, drained
1 can (1 lb, 13½ oz) sliced
   pineapple, drained
1 can (1 lb, 14 oz) peach halves,
   drained

2 cans (1 lb, 14-oz size) Bartlett
   pears, drained
1 container (16 oz) frozen whole
   strawberries, thawed and
   drained
2 cups sugar
⅘ quart light rum

1. Cut apricots in half; remove pits. Cut pineapple slices into 1-inch pieces. Cut peach and pear halves in half.

2. In large container, layer fruits, with strawberries on top. Add sugar and rum. Stir to mix. Cover with plastic film.

3. Let stand in cool, dark place, about 1 week, then store in refrigerator, covered, to mellow.

4. Store a month or two. Serve, well chilled, as a deluxe fruit compote or as a sauce over ice cream or sherbet.
Makes 3½ quarts.

Fruit and Cheese

Europeans' favorite dessert, fruit with cheese, is fast becoming ours as well. It's a perfect ending for many meals.

The fruit must be nicely chilled, at its peak of ripeness, served with fruit knives. A fruit bowl arrangement might be: crisp, chilled apples, ripe pears, strawberries, peaches or nectarines, and grapes.

The cheese should be at room temperature, unless it is a fresh soft cheese, which should be slightly chilled. The soft, ripened type should be very "ripe," almost running.

On your cheese board, serve a selection of cheeses to give variety in flavor and texture. A combination might be: a creamy Gervais, Brie (everyone's favorite), a mild Bonbel, and the stronger Stilton, all served with plain crackers, French bread and sweet butter. (See the guide below for more suggestions.)

Wines might be a continuation of the white or red wine served at dinner or a port wine. Nuts in the shell are a nice addition.

Guide to Dessert Cheeses

Bel Paese (Ital., U.S.)—Creamy, delicate cheese, faintly tart. Serve on cheese tray or with red wine, crackers and fruit for dessert.

Bonbel (Fr.)—Delicate cheese, good with crackers and white wine.

Boursault (Fr.)—Very soft, rich and perishable dessert cheese. Add crackers, fruit, white wine.

Boursin (Fr.)—Similar to Boursault. Get plain (not garlic) for dessert.

Brick (U.S.)—Find out how old it is before you buy. When young, it's mild, good after dinner with white wine.

Brie (Fr.)—The ultimate luxury cheese. Mild and delectably runny when just ripe (perfect for dessert with wine). Gets a bit stronger and more golden in color as it matures. Always buy a slice off a whole brie or, if it's a large party, buy the whole thing.

Caerphilly (Brit.)—From the Cheddar family, has a buttermilk flavor and a firm texture. Serve this mild dessert cheese with white wine.

Camembert (Fr.)—Rich, runny cheese. Serve like Brie. Buy whole round (in small, circular box).

Cheddar (Brit., Can., U.S.—Vt., N.Y., Wisc., Tillamook, Oreg.)— Classic tangy cheese; colors range from white to orange. Good for any purpose; cooks well. Serve with apple pie, or with beer or ale. Try aged Cheddar with red wine, sherry or port.

Cheshire (Brit.)—Relative of Cheddar, mild buttermilk flavor. Serve before or after dinner, with beer, ale or white wine.

Colby (U.S.)—Mild cheese in the Cheddar family. Lacy texture.

Crema Danica (Den.)—Very soft, creamy, delicate dessert cheese. Leave out to soften.

Danish Blue (Den.)—Buttery, rich, blue-veined cheese, perfect before or after dinner, or in a salad.

Edam (Neth.)—Mild, semisoft cheese, though a bit tangier than Gouda. Good after dinner. Generally red rind, ball shape.

Emmenthaler (Switz.)—Classic "Swiss cheese" with large eyes. Sweet, nutty flavor that's delicious with red wine and fruit after dinner.

Gervais (Fr.)—Rich double-cream cheese. Good for desserts and with any wine.

Gorgonzola (Ital.)—Very creamy, green-veined cheese. Serve before or after dinner with full-bodied red wine.

Gouda (Neth.)—Serve like Edam. Nutlike flavor. Usually comes in yellow wheels.

Gourmandise (Fr.)—Very creamy, sweet dessert cheese flavored with kirsch or walnuts.

Gruyère (Switz., Fr.)—Tangier, slightly saltier than Emmenthaler. Not to be confused with processed-cheese triangles sold as Gruyère in the U.S. Serve with white wine or beer.

La Grappe, Grappion, Tome au Marc (Fr.)—Different names for that creamy, soft, white cheese covered with grape seeds. Serve for dessert with wine.

Monterey Jack (U.S.)—Semisoft, mild cheese, made partly from skim milk. Good with fruit and wine for dessert.

Petit-Suisse (Fr.)—Very perishable and rich triple-cream cheese. Sumptuous dessert with sugar and strawberries.

Pont-l'Evêque (Fr.)—Very soft, very strong cheese. Leave out to ripen, serve with full-bodied red wine.

Port-Salut (Fr., Den., U.S.)—Creamy aromatic cheese. Gets more aromatic with age, and so be warned. Danish version is always strong. Serve mild with white wine, stronger with red.

Roquefort (Fr.)—Sharp and pungent, blue-veined sheep's-milk cheese. Good before and after a meal and crumbled in salad. Like all blue cheeses, best with robust red wine or port.

Stilton (Brit.)—The great English blue-veined cheese, made from rich milk and cream. Serve with crackers and port.

CAKES AND FROSTINGS

Cake making is an exacting art requiring precision and skill. Success in cake baking is not a matter of luck but is a combination of a well-tested recipe, good ingredients, skill in mixing and the proper equipment.

Notes on Cake Baking

1. Follow the recipe exactly with no substitutions or changes. Always use standard measuring utensils and cake pans.

2. These cake recipes were tested using sifted all-purpose or cake flour, unless stated otherwise. This means that the flour must be sifted before measuring. To measure flour: Lightly heap the cup or spoon to overflowing; then level off excess with a straightedge knife or spatula.

3. We always use double-acting baking powder.

4. When a recipe calls for shortening, use one of the soft emulsifier types, such as Crisco.

5. Do not use shortening in recipes that specifically call for butter or margarine.

6. Our cake recipes were tested using large eggs.

7. Make sure all ingredients are at room temperature.

8. Eggs are easier to separate when they are cold from the refrigerator.

9. Egg whites to be used in cakes, meringues, etc., should be allowed to stand at room temperature about one hour to warm up after taking them from the refrigerator. They will give much greater volume when beaten.

10. Use pans of the size recommended in the recipe. To measure pans: For diameter, width, or length, measure across the top of pan with ruler, from one inside edge to the other. For depth, measure inside of side wall.

11. To ensure even and delicate browning of cakes, use metal cake pans with a bright, shiny finish. If using oven-glass cake dishes, decrease oven temperature 25 degrees to prevent overbrowning.

12. If baking a single cake, place on rack in center of oven. If baking two layers, place both on same rack in center of oven, being careful pans do not touch sides of oven or each other. If baking three layers, adjust oven racks to divide oven into thirds; do not place one pan directly over another.

13. Do not open oven door to test cake until minimum baking time has elapsed.

14. Be sure batter is divided evenly between pans. Do not fill pans more than two thirds full.

OVEN TEMPERATURE

The accuracy of the oven is very important for successful cake baking. A too-hot oven produces a dry texture, shrinkage and dark color. An oven that is not hot enough causes cakes to fall or to be doughy and sticky.

To test your oven, place a mercury-type thermometer (Taylor is a good brand) on center oven rack. Set temperature. Heat 15 minutes with door closed; take reading; check again after 10 minutes. Take reading through window in oven door. If there is none, open and close door very quickly.

If the oven is off the selected temperature by more than 25° up or down, the thermostat should be calibrated by a serviceman. Otherwise you may compensate by setting temperature slightly lower or higher as needed.

Always keep a good thermometer in the oven during baking and roasting to avoid any catastrophe.

TO PREPARE PANS

If recipe says to grease and flour pans, use shortening or butter, sprinkle with flour, shake to coat evenly, and discard excess.

To line bottom with waxed paper: Place pan on paper; draw around bottom to fit exactly; cut out.

TEST FOR DONENESS

1. Cake will begin to shrink slightly from side of pan.

2. For a delicate cake, the surface will spring back when gently pressed with fingertip.

3. For a pound-type cake, a wire cake tester or wooden pick inserted near center will come out clean.

4. Be careful not to overbake or cake will be dry.

TO REMOVE CAKES FROM PANS

Layer Cakes: Carefully run a knife or metal spatula around edge of cake to loosen from pan; invert on wire rack; remove pan. Then place another wire rack on top of cake; invert again, so cake cools right side up.

Tube Cakes: Using an up-and-down motion, run a knife or metal spatula carefully around edge of cake and around tube to loosen cake from pan. If tube pan does not have a lift-out bottom, hit pan sharply on table; then invert pan and turn out cake.

TO CUT CAKES

Angel Food, Chiffon, and Sponge Cakes: Use a knife with serrated edge. Cut cake gently, back and forth, with a sawing motion.

Frosted Layer Cakes: Use a knife with a thin, sharp edge. Rinse knife in hot water after making each cut.

TO FREEZE CAKES

Kinds to Freeze: All types of unfrosted cake may be frozen.

Frosted Cakes: Cakes frosted with butter or fudge frostings may be frozen successfully. (Do not freeze cakes with whipped-cream or fluffy frostings.) Freeze cakes, unwrapped, until frosting is firm, then wrap in freezer wrap; label, and freeze. If possible, place wrapped cake in a box when freezing to prevent crushing.

Unfrosted Cakes: Wrap completely cooled cakes in freezer wrap; label, and freeze. When freezing layer cakes, wrap each layer separately. If possible, place wrapped cake in a box when freezing to prevent crushing.

Length of Storage: Unfrosted cakes may be stored in freezer 2 to 3 months. Frosted cakes may be stored only 1 to 2 months.

TO THAW CAKES

Unfrosted Layers: Let stand, still wrapped, at room temperature about 1 hour. Let larger cakes stand, still wrapped, about 2 hours.

Frosted Cakes: Remove freezer wrap. Let stand at room temperature until thawed—about 2 hours.

TO STORE CAKES

Cover loosely with moisture-proof wrap, or place under a "cake saver" or large, inverted bowl, or in a lightly covered cake tin. Store cakes with whipped cream or cream fillings in refrigerator.

Cakes are divided into two groups:
1. Those containing fat, known as butter cakes.
2. Those without fat, or sponge-type cakes.

Butter Cakes

ONE-BOWL OR QUICK BUTTER CAKES

One-bowl cakes are those in which the ingredients are mixed in one bowl according to a strict formula. They are not mixed by the conventional method. They are a good choice for the novice cake baker since, other than a mix they are the easiest type of cake to make. They are at their best when freshly baked; they do not keep as well as the other types of cakes.

✿

APPLESAUCE CAKE SQUARES

2½ cups sifted* all-purpose flour
1¾ cups sugar
¼ teaspoon baking powder
1½ teaspoons baking soda
1½ teaspoons salt
1 teaspoon cinnamon
½ teaspoon cloves

½ teaspoon each allspice, nutmeg
½ cup shortening
1 can (15 oz) applesauce (1¾ cups)
3 eggs (⅔ cup)
1 cup seedless raisins, chopped
1 cup finely chopped walnuts

* Sift flour before measuring.

1. Preheat oven to 350F. Grease well and flour a 13-by-9-by-2-inch baking pan.

2. Sift flour, sugar, baking powder, baking soda, salt and spices into large bowl of electric mixer. Add shortening and applesauce; beat 1 minute at low speed just to combine.

3. At medium speed, beat 2 minutes, constantly guiding batter into beaters with rubber scraper.

4. Add eggs; beat 2 minutes.

5. Combine raisins and walnuts; fold into batter with rubber scraper.

6. Turn batter into prepared pan; bake 45 minutes, or until cake tester inserted in center comes out clean.

7. Let cake cool completely in pan on wire rack. Frost as desired. Makes 16 servings.

ยว

APPLESAUCE-DATE CAKE

2 cups unsifted all-purpose flour
2 teaspoons baking soda
1 teaspoon cinnamon
½ teaspoon allspice
½ teaspoon nutmeg
¼ teaspoon cloves
¼ teaspoon salt
2 eggs

1 cup light-brown sugar,
    firmly packed
½ cup butter or regular margarine,
    softened
2 cups hot applesauce
1 cup chopped dates
¾ cup coarsely chopped walnuts
    Cream Cheese Frosting,
    page 288

1. Preheat oven to 350F. Grease well and flour a 9-by-9-by-2-inch baking pan.

2. Into large bowl of electric mixer, sift flour with baking soda, cinnamon, allspice, nutmeg, cloves, and salt. Then add the eggs, brown sugar, soft butter, and 1 cup hot applesauce; at low speed, beat just until the ingredients are combined.

3. At medium speed, beat 2 minutes longer, occasionally scraping the side of the bowl and guiding mixture into the beater with a rubber scraper.

4. Add remaining applesauce, dates, and walnuts; beat 1 minute. Pour batter into prepared pan.

5. Bake 50 minutes, or until cake tester inserted in center comes out clean. Let cool in pan 10 minutes. Remove from pan, and let cool on wire rack.

6. Frost top of cooled cake with Cream Cheese Frosting. Cut into 9 squares.

Makes 9 servings.

ยว

CRANBERRY OR BLUEBERRY TEA CAKE

1 cup fresh cranberries (see
    Note), cut in half
¾ cup sugar
1 egg
1½ cups sifted* cake flour
2 teaspoons baking powder

½ teaspoon ground cinnamon
¾ teaspoon salt
⅓ cup milk
3 tablespoons butter or
    margarine, melted
1 teaspoon vanilla extract

* Sift before measuring.

1. Preheat oven to 400F. Grease well a shallow, 1½-quart (10-by-6-by-1½-inch) baking dish. In small bowl, combine cranberries with 2 tablespoons sugar.

2. In medium bowl, with wooden spoon, beat egg. Gradually beat in ½ cup sugar; beat until well combined.

3. Sift together flour, baking powder, cinnamon and salt. Add to egg mixture alternately with milk. Beat well after each addition.

4. Add butter and vanilla. Beat thoroughly. Fold in cranberries.

5. Pour batter into prepared pan. Sprinkle top with 2 tablespoons sugar. Bake 25 minutes, or until top springs back when lightly touched with fingertip. Serve warm.

Makes 8 servings.

Note: You may substitute whole blueberries for cranberries.

McCALL'S BEST GOLD CAKE

2½ cups sifted* cake flour
1½ cups sugar
1 teaspoon salt
3 teaspoons baking powder
½ cup shortening
1¼ cups milk

5 egg yolks (½ cup)
1 teaspoon vanilla extract, or 2 teaspoons grated lemon peel, or 1 tablespoon grated orange peel

* Sift before measuring.

1. Preheat oven to 350F. Grease well and flour three 8-by-1½-inch layer-cake pans, or two 9-by-1½-inch layer-cake pans, or a 13-by-9-by-2-inch baking pan.

2. Into large bowl of electric mixer, sift flour with sugar, salt, and baking powder.

3. Add shortening and ¾ cup milk. At medium speed, beat 2 minutes, occasionally scraping side of bowl and guiding mixture into beaters with rubber scraper.

4. Add egg yolks, vanilla, and remaining milk; beat 2 minutes longer.

5. Pour batter into prepared pans; bake layers 30 to 35 minutes; oblong 35 to 40 minutes; or until surface springs back when gently pressed with fingertip.

6. Cool in pans 10 minutes. Remove from pans; cool thoroughly on wire racks. Fill and frost as desired.

FAVORITE ONE-EGG CAKE

2 cups sifted* cake flour
1 cup sugar
2½ teaspoons baking powder
1 teaspoon salt

⅓ cup shortening
1 cup milk
1 egg
1 teaspoon vanilla extract

* Sift before measuring.

1. Preheat oven to 350F. Grease well and flour two 8-by-1½-inch layer-cake pans, or a 9-by-9-by-1¾-inch baking pan.

2. Into large bowl of electric mixer, sift flour with sugar, baking powder, and salt.

3. Add shortening and milk. At medium speed, beat 2 minutes, occasionally scraping side of bowl and guiding mixture into beaters with rubber scraper.

4. Add egg and vanilla; beat 2 minutes longer.

5. Pour batter into prepared pans; bake layers 25 to 30 minutes; square 30 to 35 minutes; or until surface springs back when gently pressed with fingertip.

6. Cool in pans 10 minutes. Remove from pans; cool thoroughly on wire racks. Fill and frost as desired.

SILVERY WHITE CAKE

4 egg whites
2¼ cups sifted* cake flour
1½ cups sugar
3½ teaspoons baking powder
1 teaspoon salt

½ cup shortening
1 cup milk
1½ teaspoons vanilla extract, or 1
    teaspoon vanilla extract plus
    ¼ teaspoon almond extract

* Sift before measuring.

1. In small bowl, let egg whites warm to room temperature—about 1 hour.

2. Meanwhile, preheat oven to 350F. Grease well and flour two 8-by-1½-inch layer-cake pans, or two 9-by-1½-inch layer-cake pans, or a 13-by-9-by-2-inch baking pan; or line bottoms of pans with waxed paper and grease.

3. Into large bowl of electric mixer, sift flour with sugar, baking powder, and salt.

4. Add shortening, ¾ cup milk, and vanilla. At low speed, beat only until ingredients are combined.

5. At medium speed, beat 2 minutes, occasionally scraping side of bowl and guiding mixture into beaters with rubber scraper.

6. Add unbeaten egg whites and rest of milk; beat 2 minutes longer.

7. Pour batter into prepared pans; bake layers 30 to 35 minutes; oblong 35 to 40 minutes; or until surface springs back when gently pressed with fingertip.

8. Cool in pans 10 minutes. Remove from pans; cool thoroughly on wire racks. Fill and frost as desired.

❧

SOUR CREAM FUDGE CAKE

2 squares unsweetened chocolate	1 teaspoon salt
2 cups sifted* cake flour	½ cup shortening
1½ cups sugar	1 cup sour cream
1 teaspoon baking soda	2 eggs
	1 teaspoon vanilla extract

* Sift before measuring.

1. Preheat oven to 350F. Grease well and flour two 8-by-1½-inch layer-cake pans, or a 13-by-9-by-2-inch baking pan.

2. Melt chocolate over hot, not boiling, water; let cool.

3. Into large bowl of electric mixer, sift flour with sugar, soda, and salt.

4. Add shortening and sour cream. At medium speed, beat 2 minutes, occasionally scraping side of bowl and guiding mixture into beaters with rubber scraper.

5. Add eggs, vanilla, chocolate, and ¼ cup hot water; beat 2 minutes longer.

6. Pour batter into prepared pans; bake layers 30 to 35 minutes; oblong 35 to 40 minutes; or until surface springs back when gently pressed with fingertip.

7. Cool in pans 10 minutes. Remove from pans; cool thoroughly on wire racks. Fill and frost as desired.

SCOTCH CHOCOLATE CAKE SQUARES

2 cups sifted* all-purpose flour
2 cups granulated sugar
½ teaspoon salt
½ cup regular margarine
½ cup shortening
¼ cup unsweetened cocoa
2 eggs, slightly beaten
½ cup buttermilk
1 teaspoon baking soda

* Sift before measuring.

1 teaspoon cinnamon
1 teaspoon vanilla extract

Icing:
½ cup regular margarine
¼ cup unsweetened cocoa
6 tablespoons milk
1 pkg (1 lb) confectioners' sugar
1 teaspoon vanilla extract
2 cups flaked coconut
1 cup chopped pecans

1. Preheat oven to 350F. Into large bowl, sift flour with granulated sugar and salt; set aside. Grease a 13-by-9-by-2-inch baking pan.

2. In small saucepan, combine ½ cup margarine, the shortening, ¼ cup cocoa, and 1 cup water; bring to boiling. Pour over flour mixture.

3. Add eggs, buttermilk, soda, cinnamon, and 1 teaspoon vanilla; with portable electric mixer, beat just until smooth. Immediately pour into prepared pan.

4. Bake 40 to 45 minutes, or until surface springs back when gently pressed with fingertip.

5. Meanwhile, make Icing: In medium saucepan, combine margarine, cocoa, and milk; bring just to boiling. Remove from heat.

6. Add sugar and vanilla; with spoon, beat until smooth. Stir in coconut and nuts. Spread over hot cake as it is removed from oven. Cool in pan on wire rack. Cut into squares.

Makes 15 servings.

CONVENTIONAL BUTTER CAKES

"Butter" cakes with a high fat content are made by the "creaming" or conventional method of mixing: The fat is creamed with the sugar until very light and fluffy, then eggs are beaten in one by one and well beaten. The flour mixture is added alternately with the milk, often by hand, to avoid overbeating. Sometimes, for a lighter, more delicate cake, the eggs may be separated. Then the egg yolks are beaten into the creamed fat-and-sugar mixture until very light. The egg whites are beaten until stiff and gently folded into the batter by hand at the very last, after the flour and milk.

AMBROSIA CAKE

3 cups sifted* cake flour
2½ teaspoons baking powder
½ teaspoon salt
1 cup butter or regular
    margarine, softened
2 cups sugar
4 eggs

1 teaspoon vanilla extract
1 cup milk

Orange Filling (page 301)

White Mountain Frosting
    (page 298)

½ cup shredded coconut

* Sift before measuring.

1. Preheat oven to 350F. Grease well and flour three (9-by-1½-inch) round layer-cake pans.

2. Sift flour with baking powder and ½ teaspoon salt. In large bowl of electric mixer, at high speed, beat butter and 2 cups sugar until light. Add 4 eggs, one at a time, beating well after each addition. Add 1 teaspoon vanilla. Continue beating, occasionally scraping side of bowl with rubber scraper, until light and fluffy—about 2 minutes.

3. At low speed, beat in flour mixture (in fourths) alternately with milk (in thirds), beginning and ending with flour mixture. Beat just until smooth—about 1 minute.

4. Pour batter into prepared pans; bake 20 to 25 minutes, or until surface springs back when gently pressed with fingertip. Cool in pans on wire racks 10 minutes. Remove from pans; cool thoroughly on wire racks.

5. Make orange filling. Cool completely before spreading between cake layers.

6. Make frosting.

7. Spread frosting on top and side of cake. Sprinkle with coconut. Makes 12 servings.

BANANA-DATE CAKE

2¾ cups sifted* all-purpose flour
2 teaspoons baking powder
½ teaspoon baking soda
¼ teaspoon salt
½ cup butter or regular margarine, softened
1½ cups granulated sugar
2 eggs

2 teaspoons vanilla extract
1 cup mashed ripe banana
½ cup buttermilk
½ cup finely chopped dates
¼ cup chopped walnuts or pecans
Confectioners' sugar

* Sift before measuring.

1. Preheat oven to 350F. Grease well a 9-by-5-by-3-inch loaf pan. Sift flour with baking powder, soda and salt.

2. In large bowl, with electric mixer at high speed, beat butter, granulated sugar, eggs and vanilla, occasionally scraping side of bowl with scraper, until light and fluffy—about 3 minutes.

3. In small bowl, combine banana and buttermilk. At low speed, beat in flour mixture (in fourths) alternately with banana mixture (in thirds), beginning and ending with flour mixture; beat until smooth—about 1 minute.

4. Stir in dates and walnuts. Pour batter into prepared pan; bake 1 hour and 10 to 15 minutes, or until cake tester inserted in center comes out clean. Cool in pan on wire rack 15 minutes. Then turn out on rack; cool completely. Dust top with confectioners' sugar. Serve in slices.

Makes 1 loaf, 10 servings.

ยง

MAYOR'S CHOCOLATE CAKE
(Helen Exum)

¾ cup shortening
2 cups granulated sugar
Dash salt
1 teaspoon vanilla extract
5 eggs
1 teaspoon baking soda
1 cup buttermilk
2 cups sifted* all-purpose flour

3 squares unsweetened
chocolate, melted

Fruit Filling (page 300)
Mayor's Chocolate Icing
(page 287)

* Sift before measuring.

1. Preheat oven to 325F. Lightly grease a 15½-by-10½-by-1-inch jelly-roll pan. Line pan with waxed paper; grease paper.

2. In large bowl of electric mixer, at medium speed, beat shortening until fluffy; gradually beat in sugar; beat until very light and fluffy. Add salt and vanilla.

3. Beat in eggs, one at a time, beating well after each addition.

4. Add soda to buttermilk, and stir until foamy. At low speed, add flour and buttermilk alternately to batter, beginning and ending with flour.

5. Stir in chocolate to combine well. Pour into prepared pan, spreading evenly. Bake 35 minutes, just until surface springs back when gently pressed with fingertip.

6. Turn cake onto a wire rack; remove paper; let cool.

7. To serve: Cut cake in half crosswise to make two layers. Spread between with Fruit Filling; frost top and sides with Chocolate Icing.

Makes 16 servings.

MEXICAN CHOCOLATE CAKE
(Ann Criswell)

½ cup regular margarine
½ cup salad oil
2 squares unsweetened chocolate
2 cups unsifted all-purpose flour
1 teaspoon baking soda
2 cups granulated sugar
½ cup sour milk (place 1½
   teaspoons vinegar in a 1-cup

measure; fill with milk to
   measure ½ cup
2 eggs, beaten
1 teaspoon cinnamon
1 teaspoon vanilla extract

Mexican Chocolate Frosting,
   (page 290)

1. Preheat oven to 350F. Lightly grease a 15½-by-10½-inch jelly-roll pan.

2. Combine margarine, oil, chocolate and 1 cup water in a saucepan and heat until chocolate is melted.

3. Combine flour, baking soda, sugar, milk, eggs, cinnamon and vanilla in large bowl; then combine with chocolate mixture. Pour batter into prepared pan; bake 20 to 25 minutes, or until surface springs back when gently pressed with fingertip.

4. Five minutes before cake is done, make Frosting. Frost cake while still warm. Cut into squares.

Makes 10 to 12 servings.

THE PERFECT CHOCOLATE CAKE

1 cup unsifted unsweetened
   cocoa
2 cups boiling water
2¾ cups sifted* all-purpose flour
2 teaspoons baking soda
½ teaspoon salt
½ teaspoon baking powder

* Sift before measuring.

1 cup butter or regular
   margarine, softened
2½ cups granulated sugar
4 eggs
1½ teaspoons vanilla extract

Chocolate Frosting (page 286)

Whipped Cream Filling (page
   299)

1. Make cake: In medium bowl, combine cocoa with boiling water, mixing with wire whisk until smooth. Let cool completely.

2. Sift flour with soda, salt and baking powder. Preheat oven to 350F. Grease well and lightly flour three 9-by-1½-inch layer-cake pans.

3. In large bowl of electric mixer, at high speed, beat 1 cup butter, the granulated sugar, eggs and 1½ teaspoons vanilla, scraping bowl occasionally with rubber scraper, until light—about 5 minutes. At low speed, beat in flour mixture (in fourths), alternately with cocoa mixture (in thirds), beginning and ending with flour mixture. Do not overbeat. Divide evenly into prepared pans; smooth tops.

4. Bake 25 to 30 minutes, or until surface springs back when gently pressed with fingertip. Cool in pans 10 minutes. Carefully loosen sides with spatula; remove from pans; cool on wire racks.

5. Make frosting.

6. Make filling.

7. Place a cake layer on serving plate, top side down; spread with half of filling. Place second layer top side down; spread with rest of filling. Place third layer, top side up, on top.

8. With spatula, frost side first, covering whipped cream; use rest of frosting on top, swirling decoratively. Refrigerate at least 1 hour before serving.

9. To cut, use a sharp, thin-bladed knife; slice with a sawing motion.

Serves 10 to 12.

PICNIC CHOCOLATE CAKE

Preheat oven to 350F. Grease well and lightly flour a 13-by-9-by-2-inch pan. Make cake as above. Bake 45 minutes. Cool; frost as above; do not fill.

Makes 12 servings.

CLOVE CAKE

3 cups sifted* all-purpose flour
1 tablespoon ground cloves
1 tablespoon ground cinnamon
1 teaspoon baking powder
½ teaspoon baking soda
⅛ teaspoon salt
1 cup seedless raisins
1 cup shortening, butter, or
    regular margarine, softened

2¼ cups sugar
5 eggs
1 cup buttermilk or sour milk**

    Caramel Frosting (page 295)

** To sour milk: Put 1 tablespoon
    lemon juice or vinegar into
    measuring cup. Add milk to make
    1 cup.

* Sift before measuring.

1. Preheat oven to 350F. Lightly grease 10-by-4-inch tube pan.

2. Sift 2¾ cups flour with the cloves, cinnamon, baking powder, soda, and salt; set aside. Toss raisins with remaining flour.

3. In large bowl of electric mixer, at medium speed, beat shortening until creamy. Gradually add sugar, beating until mixture is light and fluffy—about 5 minutes.

4. In small bowl, beat eggs until very light and fluffy. Blend into sugar mixture at medium speed, using rubber scraper to clean side of bowl.

5. At low speed, alternately blend flour mixture (in thirds), and milk (in halves), into sugar-egg mixture, beginning and ending with flour mixture. Beat only until blended. Stir in floured raisins.

6. Pour batter into tube pan; bake 60 to 65 minutes, or until cake tester inserted in the center of the cake comes out clean.

7. Cool in pan on wire rack 20 minutes. Gently loosen with a spatula; turn out of pan onto rack. Cool completely—about 1 hour.

8. Frost with Caramel Frosting.

Makes 16 servings.

DEVIL'S-FOOD CAKE

3 squares unsweetened
    chocolate
2¼ cups sifted* cake flour
2 teaspoons baking soda
½ teaspoon salt
½ cup butter or regular
    margarine, softened
2½ cups light-brown sugar, firmly
    packed
3 eggs

* Sift before measuring.

2 teaspoons vanilla extract
½ cup sour milk** or buttermilk
1 cup boiling water

    Quick Fudge Frosting (page
    289)

** To sour milk: Place 1½
    teaspoons lemon juice or
    vinegar in measuring cup. Add
    milk to measure ½ cup. Let
    stand a few minutes before
    using.

1. Melt chocolate over hot, not boiling, water. Let cool.

2. Preheat oven to 350F. Grease well and flour two 9-by-1½-inch layer-cake pans; or three 8-by-1½-inch layer-cake pans.

3. Sift flour with soda and salt; set aside.

4. In large bowl of electric mixer, at high speed, beat butter, sugar, eggs, and vanilla until light and fluffy—about 5 minutes—occasionally scraping side of bowl with rubber scraper.

5. At low speed, beat in chocolate.

6. Beat in flour mixture (in fourths), alternately with milk (in thirds), beginning and ending with flour mixture. Beat just until smooth—about 1 minute.

7. Beat in water just until mixture is smooth. Batter will be thin.

8. Pour batter into prepared pans; bake 30 to 35 minutes, or until surface springs back when gently pressed with fingertip.

9. Cool in pans 10 minutes. Remove from pans; cool thoroughly on wire racks. Fill and frost with Quick Fudge Frosting, or as desired.

FUDGE CAKE

4 squares (1-oz size)
  unsweetened chocolate
½ cup hot water
1¾ cups granulated sugar
  Cake flour
1 teaspoon baking soda
1 teaspoon salt

½ cup butter or regular
  margarine, softened
3 eggs
⅔ cup milk
1 teaspoon vanilla extract

Chocolate Butter-Cream
  Frosting (page 286)

1. Cut 2 waxed-paper circles to fit bottoms of 2 (9-by-1½-inch) round layer-cake pans. Lightly grease bottoms and sides of pans; place waxed paper in pans.

2. In top of double boiler, combine chocolate and hot water. Place over hot, not boiling, water, stirring constantly, until chocolate is melted—mixture will be thick.

3. Add ½ cup sugar; cook, stirring, until sugar is dissolved—about 2 minutes. Remove from hot water; let cool while preparing batter.

4. Preheat oven to 350F. Sift flour onto sheet of waxed paper. Measure 2 cups. Sift measured flour with soda and salt. Set aside.

5. In large bowl of electric mixer, at medium speed, beat butter until light. Gradually add rest of sugar; beat until very light and fluffy—at least 5 minutes. Stop beater several times, and scrape down side of bowl with rubber spatula.

6. Add eggs, one at a time, beating well after each addition and scraping down side of bowl.

7. At low speed, add flour mixture (in fourths), alternately with milk (in thirds), beginning and ending with flour mixture. Beat after each addition just until blended.

8. Add chocolate mixture and vanilla; beat at low speed just until well blended—do not overbeat. Turn into pans, dividing evenly.

9. Bake 25 to 30 minutes, or until top of cake springs back when gently pressed in center with fingertip.

10. Let cool in pans on wire rack 10 minutes. With small spatula, loosen edges. Place cake rack over one layer; invert; remove pan. Peel off waxed paper. Repeat with second layer. Let cool completely.

11. Just before frosting cake, make Chocolate Butter-Cream Frosting.

Makes 8 to 10 servings.

LANE CAKE
(Jo Ellen O'Hara)

Four Cake Layers:
  8 egg whites
3¼ cups sifted* cake flour
3½ teaspoons baking powder
  ¾ teaspoon salt

* *Sift before measuring.*

1 *cup lightly salted butter,*
  softened
2 *cups sugar*
1 *teaspoon vanilla extract*
1 *cup milk*

Lane Cake Filling (page 300)
  White Mountain Frosting
    (page 298)

1. Make cake layers: In large bowl of electric mixer, let egg whites warm to room temperature—about 1 hour.

2. Lightly grease four 9-inch layer-cake pans; line bottoms of pans with rounds of waxed paper; grease lightly.

3. Sift flour with baking powder and salt. Preheat oven to 375F.

4. At medium speed, in large bowl, beat butter until light and fluffy. Gradually beat in sugar until very light and fluffy. Add vanilla.

5. At low speed, beat in flour mixture (in fourths) alternately with milk (in thirds), beginning and ending with flour mixture; blend until smooth.

6. Beat egg whites, at high speed, until stiff peaks form when beater is slowly raised.

7. Gently fold egg whites into batter using a wire whisk or rubber scraper. Turn into prepared pans, dividing batter evenly.

8. Bake layers 18 to 20 minutes or just until surface springs back when gently pressed with fingertip.

9. Cool on wire rack 10 minutes before removing from pans. Cool layers completely.

10. Make filling.

11. Spread filling between cooled layers and on top of cake.

12. Make frosting. Frost side with White Mountain Frosting.

MACAROON CAKE

6 eggs
1 cup shortening
1/2 cup regular margarine
3 cups sugar
1/2 teaspoon almond extract
1/2 teaspoon coconut extract

3 cups sifted* cake flour
1 cup milk
2 cans (3 1/2-oz size) flaked
    coconut or 2 cups grated
    fresh coconut

* Sift before measuring.

1. Separate eggs, placing whites in a large bowl, yolks in another large bowl. Let whites warm to room temperature—about 1 hour.

2. Preheat oven to 300F. Grease a 10-inch tube pan.

3. With electric mixer at high speed, beat egg yolks with shortening and margarine until well blended. Gradually add sugar, beating until light and fluffy. Add extracts; beat until blended.

4. At low speed, beat in flour (in fourths), alternately with milk (in thirds), beginning and ending with flour.

5. Add coconut; beat until well blended.

6. Beat egg whites just until stiff peaks form. With wire whisk or rubber scraper, gently fold whites into batter until well combined. Turn into prepared pan.

7. Bake 2 hours, or until a cake tester inserted near center comes out clean.

8. Cool in pan on wire rack 15 minutes. Remove from pan; cool thoroughly on wire rack. Sift confectioners' sugar over top, if desired.

Makes 12 to 16 servings.

OATMEAL PRALINE CAKE

1½ cups boiling water
 1 cup raw quick-cooking
    rolled oats
1½ cups unsifted all-purpose flour
 1 teaspoon baking soda
 1 teaspoon cinnamon
 1 teaspoon nutmeg
 ½ cup butter or regular
    margarine
 1 cup granulated sugar
 1 cup light-brown sugar, firmly
    packed

 2 eggs
 1 teaspoon vanilla extract

Topping:
 3 tablespoons butter or regular
    margarine
 ¾ cup light-brown sugar,
    firmly packed
 ¾ cup shredded coconut
 ½ cup coarsely chopped walnuts
 1 egg
 3 tablespoons milk

1. Pour boiling water over rolled oats in small bowl; stir with a fork, to mix well. Let stand 40 minutes to cool.

2. Preheat oven to 350F. Grease and flour a 9-by-9-by-2-inch baking pan.

3. Sift together flour, soda, cinnamon, and nutmeg. Set aside.

4. In large bowl, with electric mixer at medium speed, beat ½ cup butter until creamy. Add granulated sugar and 1 cup brown sugar, a little at a time, beating until light and fluffy.

5. Add 2 eggs, one at a time, beating after each addition; then beat until light and fluffy. Beat in vanilla.

6. Add rolled-oat mixture, mixing until well combined.

7. At low speed, beat in flour mixture, until completely mixed.

8. Turn batter into prepared pan. Bake 50 minutes, or until top springs back when gently pressed with fingertip.

9. Meanwhile, make Topping: In small bowl, combine all topping ingredients. Spread over hot cake.

10. Return cake to oven. Bake 10 minutes longer, or until topping is golden.

11. Cool in pan on wire rack. Cut into squares.

Makes 12 servings.

MERINGUE CAKE

4 egg whites
⅔ cup unsifted all-purpose flour
1½ teaspoons baking powder
5 tablespoons butter or regular
    margarine, softened
Granulated sugar
4 egg yolks

5 tablespoons milk
1 cup walnuts, finely chopped

Filling:
2 cups heavy cream
¼ cup confectioners' sugar
10 walnut halves
Cocoa

1. In large bowl of electric mixer, let egg whites warm to room temperature—about 1 hour. Grease and flour two 9-by-1½-inch round layer-cake pans.

2. Preheat oven to 300F. Sift together flour and baking powder.

3. In small bowl of electric mixer, beat butter and ⅔ cup granulated sugar until light and fluffy. Add egg yolks, one at a time, beating well after each addition.

4. At low speed, add flour mixture alternately with milk, beginning and ending with flour mixture.

5. Turn into prepared pans. Sprinkle chopped walnuts on top. Wash and dry beaters.

6. With electric mixer at high speed, beat egg whites until foamy. Gradually beat in 1¼ cups granulated sugar, 2 tablespoons at a time. Continue beating until stiff peaks form when beater is slowly raised.

7. Spread half of the meringue over batter in each pan.

8. Bake 40 minutes, or until meringue is pale golden and cake is done.

9. Remove to rack; cool layers in pan 60 minutes.

10. Meanwhile, make filling: In large bowl of electric mixer, beat together heavy cream and confectioners' sugar until stiff; refrigerate.

11. With spatula, carefully loosen layers from pans.

12. Place one layer on serving plate, meringue side up. Spread with half of whipped cream.

13. Place remaining layer on top, meringue side up. Garnish top with remaining whipped cream and walnut halves. Sift cocoa over the top.

14. Refrigerate about 4 hours.

Makes 8 to 10 servings.

BEST SPICE CAKE

2½ cups sifted* cake flour
1 teaspoon baking powder
1 teaspoon baking soda
1 teaspoon salt
1 teaspoon cinnamon
½ teaspoon ground cloves
⅛ teaspoon pepper

* Sift before measuring.

½ cup butter or regular
    margarine, softened
½ cup light-brown sugar,
    firmly packed
1 cup granulated sugar
2 eggs
1 teaspoon vanilla extract
1¼ cups buttermilk

1. Preheat oven to 350F. Grease well and flour two 8-by-1½-inch layer-cake pans, or a 13-by-9-by-2-inch baking pan.

2. Sift flour with baking powder, soda, salt, cinnamon, cloves, and pepper.

3. In large bowl of electric mixer, at high speed, beat butter, sugars, eggs, and vanilla until light and fluffy—about 5 minutes—occasionally scraping side of bowl with rubber scraper.

4. At low speed, beat in flour mixture (in fourths), alternately with buttermilk (in thirds), beginning and ending with flour mixture. Beat just until smooth—about 1 minute.

5. Pour batter into prepared pans; bake layers 30 to 35 minutes; bake oblong 40 to 45 minutes; or until surface springs back when gently pressed with fingertip.

6. Cool in pans 10 minutes. Remove from pans; cool thoroughly on wire racks. Fill and frost as desired.

WALNUT RAISIN SPICE CAKE

Butter or margarine
1½ cups seedless raisins
1½ cups walnuts
1½ teaspoons baking soda
1½ cups boiling water
2¼ cups sifted* all-purpose flour
1½ teaspoons cinnamon
¼ teaspoon salt

* Sift before measuring.

¾ cup butter or regular
    margarine, softened
1½ cups sugar
2 eggs
2 egg yolks
1½ teaspoons lemon juice
1½ teaspoons vanilla extract

Cream Cheese Frosting
(page 288)

1. Preheat oven to 350F. Grease and flour lightly 3 (8-by-1½-inch) layer-cake pans.

2. Finely chop raisins and 1 cup walnuts; place in a medium bowl. Add baking soda, then stir in boiling water. Let cool ½ hour.

3. Sift flour with cinnamon and salt.

4. In large bowl, with electric mixer at medium speed, beat butter until creamy. Add sugar, a little at a time, beating until light and fluffy. Stop beater once or twice; scrape down side of bowl with rubber spatula.

5. Add eggs and egg yolks, one at a time. Beat after each addition and scrape side of bowl with rubber spatula. Beat until light and fluffy. Add lemon juice and vanilla.

6. With wooden spoon, beat in flour mixture, in fourths, alternately with nut mixture, in thirds; begin and end with flour.

7. Pour batter into prepared pans. Place in oven, leaving space between pans. Bake 25 to 30 minutes, or until top springs back when lightly pressed with fingertip and cake pulls away from edge.

8. Cool on wire rack 5 minutes. With small spatula, loosen edge. Turn out on wire rack; turn top up; let cool completely, about 1 hour.

9. Make Frosting.

10. Using 1½ cups frosting put layers together. Use rest of frosting to cover top and side of cake.

11. With metal spatula, make decorative swirls in frosting; coarsely chop ½ cup walnuts; sprinkle around top. Refrigerate until serving.

Makes 16 servings.

POUND CAKES

In the old days, a pound cake was literally a "pound cake"—it took a pound of butter, a pound of eggs, a pound of sugar, a pound of flour, and considerable culinary skill to make one. Consequently, pound cake was a special treat, to be saved for special occasions. A perfect pound cake is still a special treat, but the old rule of thumb has given way to a more scientific blend of ingredients, and a perfect cake depends more on a good recipe than great culinary skill.

Included here are some of our best pound cake recipes.

RICH POUND CAKE

9 egg whites (1¼ cups)	9 egg yolks
3 cups sifted* all-purpose flour	2 cups butter or regular
1 teaspoon baking powder	margarine, softened
½ teaspoon salt	2 teaspoons vanilla extract
2 cups sugar	Confectioners' sugar

* Sift before measuring.

1. In large bowl of electric mixer, let egg whites warm to room temperature—about 1 hour.

2. Preheat oven to 350F. Grease and flour a 10-inch tube pan. Sift flour, baking powder, and salt.

3. With electric mixer at high speed, beat egg whites until foamy. Gradually beat in 1 cup sugar, ¼ cup at a time, beating after each addition. Continue beating until soft peaks form when beater is slowly raised. Turn into a medium bowl.

4. In same bowl, at high speed, beat yolks with remaining sugar, butter and vanilla for 5 minutes. At low speed, beat in flour mixture just until smooth.

5. At low speed, gradually beat in egg-white mixture, just until blended, scraping bowl and guiding batter into beater with a rubber scraper.

6. Turn into prepared pan; bake 65 minutes, or until a cake tester inserted in center comes out clean. Cool on rack 15 minutes. Remove from pan; cool completely. Sprinkle top lightly with confectioners' sugar. Slice thinly.

Makes 30 slices.

SOUR CREAM POUND CAKE

3 cups granulated sugar
1 cup regular margarine
6 eggs, separated
3 cups sifted* all-purpose flour
1/4 teaspoon baking soda

* Sift before measuring.

1 cup sour cream
1 teaspoon vanilla extract
1 teaspoon almond extract
2 teaspoons butter flavoring
   (optional)
1 teaspoon lemon extract

1. Preheat oven to 350F. Grease and flour a 10-inch tube pan.

2. In large bowl of electric mixer, at medium speed, cream sugar and margarine until very creamy. Add egg yolks, one at a time, beating well after each addition. Sift flour three times.

3. Add baking soda to sour cream; stir well.

4. Into sugar mixture, beat in flour, at low speed, alternately with sour cream mixture, beginning and ending with flour. Blend well. Add extracts.

5. Beat egg whites until stiff peaks form when beater is slowly raised. Using a wire whisk gently fold into flour mixture until well-combined. Turn into prepared pan. Bake about 1 1/4 to 1 1/2 hours, or until cake tester inserted in center comes out clean.

6. Let cool completely in pan on wire rack.

Makes 12 servings.

EASY LEMON POUND CAKE

1 pkg (8 oz) soft cream cheese
4 eggs
1 pkg (1 lb, 2 1/2 oz) yellow cake
   mix

3/4 cup milk
2 tablespoons grated lemon peel

1. Preheat oven to 350F. Grease well and flour a 9-inch tube pan.

2. In large bowl of electric mixer, at medium speed, beat cheese until light and fluffy. Scrape beaters with rubber scraper.

3. Add eggs, one at a time, beating well after each addition.

4. At low speed, beat in cake mix (in 3 additions) alternately with milk (in 2 additions), beginning and ending with cake mix; beat just until well combined. Blend in lemon peel.

5. Turn into prepared pan; bake 55 minutes, or until cake tester inserted in center comes out clean.

6. Let cake stand in pan on wire rack 15 minutes; then turn out onto wire rack; cool completely. If desired, sprinkle with confectioners' sugar.

Makes 12 servings.

Note: This cake is better if made the day before. Store, wrapped in foil, in refrigerator.

WALNUT-BOURBON POUND CAKE

2 cups finely chopped walnuts
½ cup bourbon
3½ cups sifted* all-purpose flour
1½ teaspoons baking powder
½ teaspoon salt
½ teaspoon nutmeg
½ teaspoon cinnamon
¼ teaspoon ground cloves

* Sift before measuring.

8 eggs
2 cups butter or regular
    margarine, softened
2 cups sugar
1 teaspoon vanilla extract

½ cup bourbon
    Coffee Glaze, page 293
    Mixed nuts

1. Preheat oven to 350F. Grease well and flour a 10-inch tube pan.

2. In small bowl, combine walnuts and ½ cup bourbon; mix well. Let stand.

3. Sift together flour, baking powder, salt, and spices. Set aside.

4. In large bowl, with electric mixer, beat the eggs until they are thick and light.

5. In another large bowl, with same mixer at medium speed, beat butter with sugar until light; beat in vanilla.

6. Add beaten eggs, beating at low speed, then at high speed until mixture is thick and fluffy.

7. At low speed, gradually beat in flour mixture just until combined. Stir in bourbon-walnut mixture.

8. Turn batter into prepared pan; spread with rubber scraper so that batter is slightly higher at side and against tube. Place a 12-inch square of brown paper over pan.

9. Bake 1 hour and 10 minutes (remove paper after 30 minutes),

or until cake tester inserted in center comes out clean.

10. Cool in pan on wire rack 15 minutes. Turn out of pan; cool completely on wire rack.

11. Soak 18-inch square of cheesecloth in ½ cup bourbon. Wrap cake completely in cheesecloth, then in foil. Store several days in an airtight container.

12. Just before serving, glaze with Coffee Glaze, and decorate with nuts. Slice thinly.

Makes 1 large pound cake.

PETITS FOURS

2 pkg (1-lb, 1-oz size) pound-cake
     mix
4 eggs
     Apricot Glaze, page 292

Fondant Frosting, page 296
Pink and green cake-decorating
     tubes

1. Preheat oven to 350F. Lightly grease and flour a 15½-by-10½-by-1-inch jelly-roll pan.

2. Prepare both packages of pound-cake mix as package label directs, using 4 eggs and liquid called for.

3. Turn into prepared pan. Bake 30 to 35 minutes, or until top springs back when pressed with fingertip.

4. Cool 10 minutes in pan. Turn out on wire rack; let cool completely.

5. Meanwhile, make Apricot Glaze and Fondant Frosting.

6. Using a 2-inch cookie cutter, cut out shapes from cooled cake. (You'll have 32 or 33.)

7. To glaze cakes: Place on fork, one at a time. Hold over bowl of glaze, and spoon glaze over cake, completely covering top and side.

8. Place cakes, uncoated side down and 2 inches apart, on wire racks placed on cookie sheets. Let stand until glaze is set—at least 1 hour.

9. To frost: Place glazed cakes on fork, one at a time. Spoon frosting over cake, to run over top and down side evenly. Frost half of cakes white and half pink.

10. Let cakes dry completely on wire racks—about 1 hour. Repeat frosting if necessary. Let dry.

11. To decorate: Make little posies and leave with decorating

tubes, or drizzle any remaining frosting over tops. Refrigerate several hours. Let stand at room temperature 1 hour before serving.

Makes 32 or 33.

FRUIT CAKES

Fruit cakes, because of the high proportion of fruit they contain, belong in a class by themselves. Technically they belong to the "butter" cakes. But they must be baked at a much lower temperature and for a longer period. Since they age better than any other type of cake, recipes for large cakes are preferred to smaller ones.

BEST OF ALL FRUIT CAKES

1 lb golden raisins
1/2 lb seeded raisins
1/4 lb currants
1/2 cup dark rum or brandy
1 lb candied pineapple
1/2 lb candied red cherries
1/4 lb candied citron
1/8 lb candied lemon peel
1/8 lb candied orange peel
2 cups unsifted all-purpose flour
1/2 teaspoon mace
1/2 teaspoon cinnamon
1/2 teaspoon baking soda
1/4 lb almonds, shelled, blanched, and coarsely chopped

1/4 lb walnuts or pecans, shelled and coarsely chopped
1/2 cup butter or regular margarine, softened
1 cup granulated sugar
1 cup brown sugar, packed
5 eggs, slightly beaten
1 tablespoon milk
1 teaspoon almond extract

Rum or brandy

1 can (8 oz) almond paste
Frosting Glaze (page 293)
Angelica
Candied red cherries

1. In large bowl, combine raisins and currants. Add 1/2 cup rum; toss to combine. Let stand, covered, overnight.

2. Next day, line a 10-inch tube pan: On heavy brown paper, draw an 18-inch circle, and cut out. Set pan in center of circle; draw around base of pan and tube. With pencil lines outside, fold paper into eighths; snip off tip. Unfold circle; cut along folds to second circle. Grease both the tube pan and unpenciled side of paper well. Fit paper, greased side up, into pan.

3. Prepare fruits: With sharp knife, cut pineapple in thin wedges; cut 1/2 pound cherries in half; cut citron and lemon and orange peels into very thin strips. Add to raisins and currants; mix well.

4. On sheet of waxed paper, sift 1½ cups flour with spices and baking soda. Set aside. Preheat oven to 275F.

5. Combine remaining ½ cup flour with nuts and fruits; toss lightly.

6. In large bowl of electric mixer, at medium speed, beat butter until light. Gradually beat in granulated sugar, then brown sugar, beating until very light and fluffy.

7. Beat in eggs, milk, and almond extract until thoroughly combined.

8. At low speed, beat in flour mixture, mixing just until combined. Turn batter into fruit and nuts. Mix well with hands.

9. Turn into prepared pan, pressing batter down in pan evenly all around.

10. Bake 3 hours and 15 minutes, or until a cake tester inserted near center comes out dry.

11. Let cake stand in pan on wire rack 30 minutes to cool slightly. Turn out of pan; gently remove paper. Let cool completely.

12. To store: Wrap cake in cheesecloth soaked in rum or brandy. Place in a cake tin with a tight-fitting cover. Add a few pieces of raw, unpeeled apple. (As cheesecloth dries out, resoak in rum or brandy.) Store in a cool place several weeks.

13. To decorate cake for serving: Roll almond paste between 2 sheets of waxed paper into an 8-inch circle. Remove top sheet of paper. Invert paste onto cake; remove paper. With sharp knife, trim edge of paste; then press knife to cake. Spread paste with Frosting Glaze, letting it run down side of cake. Cut angelica into thin slices. Cut cherries in half. Decorate.

Makes a 5-pound fruit cake.

EASY CHRISTMAS CHERRY CAKE

1 cup butter, softened	4 cups unsifted all-purpose flour
2 cups sugar	1 pkg (15 oz) light raisins
1 teaspoon almond extract	1 jar (8 oz) candied cherries
8 eggs	1 jar (8 oz) chopped candied citron

1. Preheat oven to 300F. Grease a 10-inch tube pan. Line bottom and side with brown paper; grease paper.

2. In large bowl, with electric mixer at medium speed, beat butter with sugar and almond extract until light and fluffy.

3. Add eggs, one at a time, beating well after each addition.

4. At low speed, gradually beat in flour.

5. Add raisins, cherries, and citron; with spoon, mix until well combined. Turn into prepared pan.

6. Bake about 2 hours and 25 minutes, or until cake tester inserted near center comes out clean.

7. Let cool in pan on wire rack 30 minutes. Turn out of pan; let cool completely on rack.

Makes a 5-pound cake.

DUNDEE CAKE

2 cups sifted* all-purpose flour	1/2 cup light raisins
1 teaspoon baking powder	1/4 cup candied cherries, halved
1/2 teaspoon salt	3/4 cup butter or regular margarine,
1/8 teaspoon nutmeg	softened
1 cup dried currants	2/3 cup sugar
3/4 cup diced mixed candied fruits	3 eggs
and peels	3 tablespoons sliced blanched
3/4 cup seeded dark raisins	almonds

* Sift before measuring.

1. Preheat oven to 325F. Grease well a 9-inch tube pan.

2. Reserve 2 tablespoons flour. Sift remaining flour with baking powder, salt, and nutmeg. Set aside.

3. In medium bowl, combine currants, candied fruits and peels, raisins, cherries, and reserved flour; mix well. Set aside.

4. In large bowl, with electric mixer at medium speed, beat butter with sugar until light and fluffy. Add eggs, one at a time, beating well after each addition.

5. At low speed, gradually add flour mixture, beating until well combined.

6. Stir fruit mixture into batter until combined. Turn into prepared pan; smooth top with spatula. Sprinkle with almonds; gently press into top.

7. Bake 60 to 65 minutes, or until cake tester inserted in center comes out clean. Let cool in pan on wire rack 15 minutes. Remove from pan; let cool completely.

Makes a 9-inch tube cake.

SYLVIA'S BLACK FRUIT CAKE

Fruit Mixture:
- *1/4 cup diced candied citron*
- *1/4 cup diced candied lemon peel*
- *1/4 cup diced candied orange peel*
- *1/3 cup coarsely chopped figs*
- *1/2 cup coarsely chopped dates*
- *1 pkg (11 oz) currants*
- *1 pkg (15 oz) seedless dark raisins*
- *1 1/4 cups seeded dark raisins, separated*
- *1/2 cup blanched almonds, coarsely chopped*
- *1/4 cup light rum*

Cake Batter:
- *3 cups sifted* all-purpose flour*
- *1/2 teaspoon salt*
- *1/2 teaspoon cinnamon*
- *1/2 teaspoon allspice*
- *1/2 teaspoon nutmeg*
- *6 tablespoons butter or regular margarine, softened*
- *1 cup light-brown sugar, firmly packed*
- *2 eggs*
- *3/4 cup light molasses*
- *1/2 teaspoon baking soda*
- *3/4 cup cold coffee*
- *1/4 cup light rum*

Rum
Fruit Cake Glaze (page 294)

** Sift before measuring.*

1. Prepare Fruit Mixture: In large kettle, combine candied fruits, figs, dates, currants, raisins, almonds, and 1/4 cup rum; using hands, mix well. Let stand at room temperature, covered, overnight.

2. Next day, line a 9-inch tube pan: On heavy brown paper, draw a 16 1/2-inch circle, and cut out. Set pan in center of circle; draw around base of pan and tube. With pencil lines outside, fold paper into eighths; snip off tip. Unfold circle; cut along folds to second circle. Grease both the tube pan and the paper well; fit paper, greased side up, into pan.

3. Preheat oven to 275F. Make Cake Batter: Sift flour with salt and spices; set aside.

4. In large bowl of electric mixer, at high speed, beat butter with sugar and eggs until smooth and fluffy—about 5 minutes.

5. Combine molasses and baking soda. At low speed, gradually beat into egg mixture, beating until well combined. Then beat in flour mixture (in fourths), alternately with coffee mixed with 1/4 cup rum (in thirds), beginning and ending with flour mixture; beat just until combined.

6. Add batter to fruit mixture; with hands mix until well combined. Turn into prepared pan, pressing down well with rubber scraper, to make top smooth and even.

7. Bake 3 to 3 1/2 hours, or until cake tester inserted in center

comes out clean. Let cool in pan on wire rack 30 minutes. (Cake will have cracks on top.)

8. Turn out of pan; peel off paper. Let cool completely on wire rack.

9. Wrap cooled cake in cheesecloth that has been soaked in ⅓ cup rum. Then wrap very tightly in plastic film or foil. Store in refrigerator or in an airtight tin container. Resoak cheesecloth with rum as it dries out—about once a week. Store cake 5 to 6 weeks to develop flavor.

10. To serve: Brush with Fruit Cake Glaze. If desired, before glazing decorate with wedges of candied pineapple and halved candied cherries.

Makes a 5¾-pound tube cake.

WHITE FRUIT CAKE

Fruit Mixture:
  4 cans (4½-oz size) blanched
      almonds, coarsely chopped
  2 pkg (10-oz size) light raisins
  1 jar (8 oz) diced candied citron
  1 jar (8 oz) candied red cherries,
      halved
  1 jar (4 oz) candied pineapple
      slices, cut into strips
  ¼ cup brandy

Cake Batter:
1½ cups butter or regular

      margarine, softened
  2 cups sugar
  1 teaspoon almond extract
  6 eggs
  4 cups unsifted all-purpose flour
  ¾ cup milk

    Brandy
  1 can (8 oz) almond paste
  Frosting Glaze (page 293)
    Angelica
    Candied citron
    Candied cherries

1. Prepare Fruit Mixture: In large kettle, combine almonds, raisins, diced citron, 1 jar cherries, the pineapple, and ¼ cup brandy; mix well. Let stand at room temperature, covered, overnight.

2. Next day, line a 10-inch tube pan: On heavy brown paper, draw a 16½-inch circle, and cut out. Set pan in center of circle; draw around base of pan and tube. With pencil lines outside, fold paper into eighths; snip off tip. Unfold circle; cut along folds to circle drawn around base of pan. Grease both tube pan and paper well; fit paper, greased side up, into pan.

3. Preheat oven to 275F.

4. Make Cake Batter: In large bowl, with electric mixer at high speed, beat butter, sugar, and almond extract until smooth and

fluffy. Add eggs, one at a time, beating after each addition until light and fluffy.

5. At low speed, beat in flour (in fourths) alternately with milk (in thirds), beginning and ending with flour.

6. Add batter to fruit mixture; mix until well combined. Turn the batter into the prepared pan, packing lightly.

7. Bake 3¼ hours, or until cake tester inserted in cake comes out clean. Let cool completely in pan on wire rack. Turn out of pan; peel off paper.

8. Wrap cooled cake in cheesecloth that has been soaked in ⅓ cup brandy. Then wrap very tightly in plastic film or foil. Store in refrigerator. Resoak cheesecloth with brandy as it dries out—about once a week. Store cake 5 to 6 weeks, to develop flavor.

9. To decorate before serving: Roll almond paste between 2 sheets of waxed paper into an 8-inch circle. Remove top sheet of paper. Invert paste onto top of cake; remove paper. With sharp knife, trim edge of paste; then press paste to cake. Spread paste with Frosting Glaze, letting it run down side of cake. Cut angelica to make stems for flowers. Cut candied citron and cherries for the leaves and petals. Decorate cake.

Makes a 7-pound tube cake.

Sponge-type Cakes

These include sponge and angel cakes. They contain no fat or baking powder; they owe their lightness and leavening to a high proportion of stiffly beaten egg whites. Chiffon cakes are modified sponge cakes, which do contain baking powder and some fat in the form of oil. One word of caution: make certain the oil is very fresh for use in chiffon cakes or the cake may have an off-flavor, even rancid, taste. Jelly rolls are made from a sponge-cake batter baked in a jelly-roll pan. They are rolled up while still warm and pliable.

❊

McCALL'S BEST SPONGE CAKE

4 eggs	1 cup sugar
1 cup sifted* cake flour	1 teaspoon vanilla extract
¾ teaspoon baking powder	1 teaspoon lemon juice
¼ teaspoon salt	½ cup red-currant jelly
¼ teaspoon cream of tartar	Confectioners' sugar

* Sift before measuring.

1. Separate eggs, whites in large bowl, yolks in small bowl. Let whites warm to room temperature—1 hour.

2. Preheat oven to 350F.

3. Sift flour, baking powder, salt.

4. Add cream of tartar to egg whites. With electric mixer at medium speed, beat whites until foamy. Gradually beat in ½ cup sugar, a tablespoonful at a time. Continue beating until stiff, glossy peaks form when beater is raised.

5. With same beater, beat egg yolks until thick and lemon-colored. Gradually beat in remaining sugar, a tablespoonful at a time. Beat until thick and light—2 minutes.

6. In measuring cup, combine ¼ cup water, vanilla, lemon juice.

7. At low speed, blend flour mixture, one third at a time, into egg-yolk mixture alternately with water mixture. Beat 1 minute.

8. With wire whisk or rubber scraper, fold into egg-white mixture.

9. Pour batter into 2 ungreased 8-inch layer-cake pans.

10. Bake 25 to 30 minutes, or just until surface springs back when lightly pressed with fingertip.

11. Invert pans, setting rims on 2 other pans. Cool 1½ hours.

12. Loosen around edge. Tap inverted pan on counter top, to loosen.

13. Spread one layer, crust side down, with currant jelly. Top with other layer, crust side up. Sprinkle top with confectioners' sugar put through a sieve, if desired.

Makes 8 to 10 servings.

ORANGE SPONGE CAKE

6 egg whites
1¾ cups sifted* all-purpose flour
½ teaspoon salt
1½ cups sugar

6 egg yolks
6 tablespoons fresh orange juice
1 tablespoon grated orange peel

* Sift before measuring.

1. In large bowl of electric mixer, let egg whites warm to room temperature—about 1 hour.

2. Meanwhile, preheat oven to 350F.

3. Sift flour with salt.

4. With electric mixer at medium speed, beat egg whites until foamy. Gradually beat in ½ cup sugar, beating after each addition.

5. Continue beating until soft peaks form when beater is slowly raised.

6. In small bowl of electric mixer, at high speed and with the same beater, beat egg yolks until thick and lemon-colored.

7. Gradually beat in remaining sugar; continue beating until mixture is smooth and well blended.

8. At low speed, blend in flour mixture, guiding mixture into beater with rubber scraper.

9. Add orange juice and orange peel, beating just until combined—about 1 minute.

10. With wire whisk or rubber scraper, using an under-and-over motion, gently fold egg-yolk mixture into egg whites just until blended.

11. Pour batter into an ungreased 10-inch tube pan; bake 35 to 40 minutes, or until center of cake springs back when it is gently pressed with fingertip.

12. Invert pan over neck of bottle; let cake cool completely—about 1 hour.

13. With spatula, carefully loosen cake from pan; remove. Serve plain or sprinkled with confectioners' sugar, or frost as desired.

Makes 12 servings.

STRAWBERRY CREAM CAKE

6 egg whites
1¾ cups sifted* all-purpose flour
½ teaspoon salt
1½ cups granulated sugar
6 egg yolks
¼ cup fresh lemon juice
1 tablespoon grated lemon peel

2 pints strawberries, washed
    and hulled
2 cups heavy cream, chilled
½ cup confectioners' sugar
½ teaspoon vanilla extract
¼ cup currant jelly, melted

* Sift before measuring.

1. In large electric-mixer bowl, let egg whites warm to room temperature—1 hour. Sift flour with salt.

2. With mixer at high speed, beat egg whites until foamy. Beat in ¾ cup of the granulated sugar, 2 tablespoons at a time, beating after each addition. Beat until soft peaks form when beater is slowly raised. Preheat oven to 350F.

3. In small mixer bowl, at high speed and with the same beater, beat yolks until very thick and lemon-colored. Gradually beat in remaining granulated sugar; beat 2 minutes, until very thick.

4. Add lemon juice, 2 tablespoons water and the lemon peel, beating just to combine—1 minute. With wire whisk, fold in flour mixture just to combine.

5. With wire whisk, with an under-and-over motion, gently fold egg-yolk mixture into egg whites just to blend; do not overmix; cake will be heavy.

6. Pour batter into an ungreased 10-by-4-inch tube pan; bake 40 minutes, or until top springs back when gently pressed with fingertip. Note: cake will not come to top of pan. Invert pan over neck of bottle; let cake cool completely—1 hour.

7. With spatula, carefully loosen cake from pan; remove cake.

8. Divide cake into thirds with toothpicks. With these as guide, split cake into three layers, using a long-bladed serrated knife. Place bottom layer, cut side up, on plate.

9. Slice 1 pint berries. In medium bowl, beat cream with confectioners' sugar; add vanilla.

10. Spread bottom layer with ¾ cup cream and half of sliced berries. Repeat with second layer. Top with last layer, cut side down. Frost top and side with rest of whipped cream; toss 1 pint berries with jelly. Arrange on the cake. Refrigerate 1 hour.

Serves 12.

ANGEL FOOD CAKES

McCALL'S BEST ANGEL FOOD CAKE

1¾ cups egg whites (12 to 14)	½ teaspoon salt
1¼ cups sifted* cake flour	1½ teaspoons cream of tartar
1¾ cups sugar	1 teaspoon vanilla extract
* Sift before measuring.	½ teaspoon almond extract

1. In large bowl, let egg whites warm to room temperature—about 1 hour.

2. Meanwhile, preheat oven to 375F.

3. Sift flour with ¾ cup sugar; resift 3 times; set aside.

4. With portable electric mixer, at high speed, beat egg whites with salt and cream of tartar until soft peaks form when beater is slowly raised.

5. Gradually beat in remaining sugar, ¼ cup at a time, beating well after each addition. Continue beating until stiff peaks form when beater is slowly raised.

6. With rubber scraper or wire whisk, gently fold extracts into egg whites until combined.

7. Sift flour mixture, one fourth at a time, over egg whites. With wire whisk or rubber scraper, using an under-and-over motion, gently fold in each addition with 15 strokes, rotating bowl a quarter of a turn after each addition.

8. Then fold an additional 10 strokes; flour mixture should be blended into egg whites.

9. With rubber scraper, gently push batter into ungreased 10-inch tube pan. With spatula or knife, cut through batter twice.

10. With rubber scraper, gently spread batter in pan until it is smooth on top and touches side of pan.

11. Bake, on lower oven rack, 35 to 40 minutes, or until cake tester inserted in center comes out clean.

12. Invert pan over neck of bottle; let cake cool completely—about 2 hours.

13. With spatula, carefully loosen cake from pan; remove. Serve plain, or frost as desired.

Makes 16 servings.

ЕЗ

McCALL'S BEST DAFFODIL CAKE

White Batter:
1¾ cups egg whites (12 to 14)
1¼ cups sifted* cake flour
1½ cups sugar
½ teaspoon salt

* Sift before measuring.

1½ teaspoons cream of tartar
1½ teaspoons vanilla extract

Yellow Batter:
5 egg yolks
2 tablespoons cake flour
2 tablespoons sugar
2 tablespoons grated lemon peel

1. In large bowl, let egg whites warm to room temperature—about 1 hour.

2. Meanwhile, preheat oven to 375F.

3. Make White Batter: Sift flour with ½ cup sugar, resift 3 times. Set aside.

4. With electric mixer, at high speed, beat egg whites with salt and cream of tartar until soft peaks form when beater is slowly raised.

5. Gradually beat in 1 cup sugar, ¼ cup at a time, beating well after each addition. Continue beating until stiff peaks form when beater is slowly raised.

6. With rubber scraper or wire whisk, gently fold vanilla into egg whites until well combined.

7. Sift flour mixture, one fourth at a time, over egg whites. With wire whisk or rubber scraper, using an under-and-over motion, gently fold in each addition with 15 strokes, rotating bowl a quarter of a turn after each addition.

8. Then fold an additional 10 strokes; flour mixture should be completely blended into egg whites. Put one third batter into medium bowl.

9. Make Yellow Batter: In small bowl, combine egg yolks with cake flour and sugar. With portable electric mixer, at high speed, beat until thick and lemon-colored. Stir in lemon peel.

10. With rubber scraper or wire whisk, using an under-and-over

motion, gently fold egg-yolk mixture into one third batter, with 15 strokes.

11. For marbled effect, spoon batters alternately into an un-greased 10-inch tube pan, ending with white batter on top. With spatula or knife, cut through batter twice.

12. With rubber scraper, gently spread batter in pan until it is smooth on top and touches side of pan.

13. Bake, on lower oven rack, 35 to 40 minutes, or until cake tester inserted in center comes out clean.

14. Invert pan over neck of bottle; let cake cool completely—about 2 hours.

15. With spatula, carefully loosen cake from pan; remove. Serve plain, sprinkled with confectioners' sugar.

Makes 10 to 12 servings.

JELLY-ROLL CAKE

4 eggs
3/4 cup sifted* cake flour
1 teaspoon baking powder
1/2 teaspoon salt

3/4 cup granulated sugar
Confectioners' sugar
1 cup raspberry preserves

* Sift before measuring.

1. In small bowl of electric mixer, let eggs warm to room tem-perature—about 1 hour.

2. Preheat oven to 400F. Lightly grease bottom of 15½-by-10½-by-1-inch jelly-roll pan; then line bottom of pan with waxed paper.

3. Sift flour with baking powder and salt; set aside.

4. At high speed, beat eggs until very thick and lemon-colored. Beat in granulated sugar, 2 tablespoons at a time; continue beating 5 minutes longer, or until very thick.

5. With rubber scraper, gently fold in flour mixture just until combined.

6. Turn into prepared pan, spreading evenly. Bake 9 minutes, or just until surface springs back when gently pressed with fingertip.

7. Meanwhile, on a clean tea towel, sift confectioners' sugar, forming a 15-by-10-inch rectangle.

8. Invert cake on sugar; gently peel off waxed paper.

9. Starting with narrow end, roll up cake (towel and all); place, seam side down, on wire rack to cool—20 minutes.

10. Gently unroll cake; remove towel. Spread with raspberry preserves; roll up again.

11. Place, seam side down, on serving plate; let stand, covered, at least 1 hour before serving.

12. To serve, sift confectioners' sugar over top; slice on diagonal. Serve with a bowl of chilled sweetened whipped cream, if desired.

Makes 8 to 10 servings.

CHOCOLATE ROLL

6 egg whites
3/4 cup granulated sugar
6 egg yolks
1/3 cup unsweetened cocoa
1 1/2 teaspoons vanilla extract
Dash salt

Confectioners' sugar

Filling:
2 cups heavy cream, chilled
1/3 cup confectioners' sugar
1 teaspoon vanilla extract

1 bar (8 oz) milk chocolate

1. In large bowl of electric mixer, let egg whites warm to room temperature—1 hour. Grease bottom of a 15 1/2-by-10 1/2-by-1-inch jelly-roll pan; line with waxed paper; grease lightly.

2. Preheat oven to 375F.

3. At high speed, beat egg whites just until soft peaks form when beater is slowly raised.

4. Add 1/4 cup granulated sugar, 2 tablespoons at a time, beating until stiff peaks form when beater is slowly raised. With same beaters, beat yolks at high speed, adding remaining 1/2 cup granulated sugar, 2 tablespoons at a time. Beat until mixture is very thick—about 4 minutes.

5. At low speed, beat in cocoa, 1 1/2 teaspoons vanilla and the salt just until smooth. With wire whisk or rubber scraper, using an under-and-over motion, gently fold cocoa mixture into beaten egg whites just until blended.

6. Spread evenly in pan. Bake 15 minutes, or until surface springs back when gently pressed with fingertip. Sift confectioners' sugar in 15-by-10-inch rectangle onto towel. Turn cake out on sugar; lift off pan; peel paper off cake.

7. Roll up, jelly-roll fashion, starting with short side, towel and all. Cool completely on rack, seam side down—at least 1/2 hour.

8. Meanwhile, make filling: Combine heavy cream and 1/3 cup

confectioners' sugar in medium bowl. Beat with electric mixer until thick; add vanilla; mix well. Refrigerate.

9. Unroll cake; spread with three fourths of the filling, 1 inch from edge. Reroll. Place, seam side down, on serving plate. Spread remaining filling evenly over the top. Refrigerate for 1 hour before serving.

10. Make chocolate curls: Place chocolate bar, still wrapped, in a warm spot just until soft, not melting. With a vegetable peeler, pressing lightly, pare along bar in a long, thin stroke to form a curl. Make enough to cover top and sides of roll; refrigerate.

11. To serve: Arrange chocolate curls over entire roll. Sprinkle lightly with confectioners' sugar.

Makes 8 to 10 servings.

CHOCOLATE CHIFFON CAKE

1 cup egg whites (7 or 8)	1½ teaspoons baking soda
½ cup unsifted unsweetened cocoa	1 teaspoon salt
	½ cup salad oil
¾ cup boiling water	7 egg yolks
1¾ cups sifted* cake flour	2 teaspoons vanilla extract
1¾ cups granulated sugar	½ teaspoon cream of tartar

* Sift before measuring.

1. In large bowl of electric mixer, let egg whites warm to room temperature—about 1 hour.

2. Preheat oven to 325F.

3. Place cocoa in small bowl; add boiling water, stirring until smooth. Let mixture cool about 20 minutes.

4. Into a second large bowl, sift flour with granulated sugar, soda and salt. Make a well in center; pour in salad oil, egg yolks, vanilla and cooled cocoa mixture. With spoon or electric mixer, beat just until smooth.

5. Sprinkle cream of tartar over egg whites. With mixer at high speed, beat until very stiff peaks form when beater is slowly raised. Do not underbeat.

6. Pour batter over egg whites; with rubber scraper or wire whisk, gently fold in just until blended. Turn batter into ungreased 10-inch tube pan.

7. Bake 60 minutes, or until cake springs back when gently pressed with fingertip.

8. Invert pan over neck of bottle; let cake cool completely—about 1½ hours. With spatula, carefully loosen cake from pan; remove.

Makes 10-inch tube cake.

❧

COCONUT CHIFFON CAKE

1 cup egg whites (6 or 7)	6 egg yolks
2 cups sifted* cake flour	2 tablespoons coconut extract
1⅓ cups sugar	1 teaspoon vanilla extract
2½ teaspoons baking powder	½ teaspoon cream of tartar
1 teaspoon salt	1 can (3½ oz) flaked coconut
½ cup salad oil	

* Sift before measuring.

1. Let egg whites warm to room temperature in large bowl of electric mixer—about 1 hour. Meanwhile, preheat oven to 325F.

2. Sift flour with sugar, baking powder and salt into another large bowl. Make well in center.

3. Add, in order, oil, egg yolks, ⅔ cup water and the coconut and vanilla extracts; beat with spoon until smooth.

4. Beat egg whites at high speed with cream of tartar until stiff peaks form when beater is slowly raised.

5. With whisk or rubber scraper, using an under-and-over motion, gently fold egg-yolk mixture and flaked coconut into egg whites just to blend.

6. Pour into an ungreased 10-inch tube pan; bake 50 to 60 minutes, or until cake springs back when gently pressed with fingertip.

7. Invert cake over neck of bottle; let cool completely—about 1½ hours.

8. Carefully loosen cake from pan; remove. Serve plain or sprinkle lightly with confectioners' sugar.

Makes 16 servings.

APRICOT RUM CAKE

Chiffon Cake:
- 1 cup egg whites
- 2 cups sifted* all-purpose flour
- 1½ cups sugar
- 3 teaspoons baking powder
- 1 teaspoon salt
- ½ cup salad oil
- 5 egg yolks
- 3 tablespoons grated orange peel
- 1 teaspoon vanilla extract
- ½ teaspoon cream of tartar

Rum Syrup:
- 1½ cups sugar

* Sift flour before measuring.

- 1 unpeeled medium orange, sliced
- ½ unpeeled lemon, sliced
- 1 cup light or amber rum

Apricot Glaze:
- ½ cup apricot preserves
- ½ tablespoon lemon or orange juice

- 1 can (1 lb, 14 oz) whole peeled apricots, drained, pitted
- 1 can (1 lb, 1 oz) whole Kadota figs, drained
- ¼ cup pecans or walnuts
- 1 cup heavy cream, whipped

1. Make chiffon cake: Let egg whites warm to room temperature in large bowl of electric mixer—about 1 hour.

2. Preheat oven to 325F. Sift flour with 1½ cups sugar, the baking powder and salt into another large bowl. Make well in center.

3. Add, in order, oil, egg yolks, ¾ cup water, the orange peel and vanilla; beat with spoon until smooth.

4. In large bowl of electric mixer, at high speed, beat egg whites with cream of tartar until stiff peaks form when beater is slowly raised.

5. Pour egg-yolk mixture gradually over egg whites; with rubber scraper or wire whisk, using an under-and-over motion, gently fold into egg whites just until blended.

6. Turn into ungreased 10-inch tube pan; bake 55 minutes.

7. Increase temperature to 350F; bake 10 minutes longer, or until cake tester inserted in center comes out clean.

8. Invert pan over neck of bottle; let cake cool completely—1½ hours.

9. Meanwhile, make rum syrup: In medium saucepan, combine sugar with 1½ cups water; bring to boiling, stirring until sugar is dissolved. Add orange and lemon slices. Boil, uncovered, 10 minutes, or until syrup measures 1 cup. Remove from heat. Add rum.

10. With cake tester, make holes, 1 inch apart, in top of cake in pan. Pour warm syrup over cake, ¼ cup at a time. Let stand at

room temperature 1 hour, or until all syrup is absorbed.

11. Make apricot glaze: In small saucepan, melt preserves over low heat. Stir in lemon juice; strain.

12. Carefully loosen cake from pan; invert onto wire rack; then turn, top side up, onto serving plate. Brush glaze over top and side of cake. Refrigerate.

13. To serve: If desired, garnish cake with apricots, figs, nuts and green leaves. Cut cake into wedges. Pass whipped cream, to spoon over cake.

Makes 12 servings.

❧

CHOCOLATE-MOUSSE DESSERT CAKE

Chocolate Chiffon Cake, page 266

Chocolate Cream:
3 cups heavy cream

1½ cups sifted confectioners' sugar
¾ cup unsweetened cocoa
2 teaspoons vanilla extract
¼ teaspoon salt
1 teaspoon unflavored gelatine

1. Make and cool cake as directed.

2. Make Chocolate Cream: Pour cream into large bowl; refrigerate until very cold—about 30 minutes.

3. Add sugar, cocoa, vanilla, and salt; beat until stiff enough to hold its shape. Refrigerate.

4. Sprinkle gelatine over 2 tablespoons cold water, to soften. Heat over hot water, stirring until dissolved; let cool.

5. Prepare cake for filling: Cut 1-inch slice, crosswise, from top of cake; set aside. With sharp knife, outline a cavity in cake, being careful to leave 1-inch-thick walls around center hole and side. With spoon, carefully remove cake from this area, being sure to leave 1-inch-thick base. Reserve 1¼ cups crumbled cake.

6. Measure 2½ cups chocolate cream into small bowl; fold in cooled gelatine. Use to fill cavity in cake. Replace top.

7. Mix ½ cup chocolate cream with reserved crumbled cake. Use to fill center hole of cake.

8. Frost top and side of cake with remaining chocolate cream. Refrigerate until well chilled.

Makes 12 servings.

🎄

APPLE CAKE

3 cups sifted* all-purpose flour
1½ teaspoons baking soda
½ teaspoon salt
3 cups finely chopped, pared
    tart apple
½ cup chopped walnuts or
    pecans

1 teaspoon grated lemon peel
2 cups sugar
1½ cups salad oil (see Note)
2 eggs
    Cream Cheese Frosting, page
    288
1 cup chopped walnuts

* Sift before measuring.

1. Preheat oven to 350F. Grease well and flour three 9-by-1½-inch round layer-cake pans. Sift flour with baking soda and salt. In small bowl, combine chopped apple, ½ cup chopped nuts and the lemon peel.

2. In large mixing bowl, combine sugar, salad oil and eggs; beat well with wooden spoon. Add sifted dry ingredients, mixing until smooth.

3. Add apple mixture; stir until well combined. Spread evenly into prepared pans. Bake 30 to 40 minutes, or until surface springs back when pressed lightly with fingertip.

4. Cool in pans 10 minutes. Remove from pans; cool thoroughly on wire racks.

5. Meanwhile, make Cream Cheese Frosting.

6. Fill and frost cake. Press remaining 1 cup nuts on side. Refrigerate until serving time.

Makes 10 to 12 servings.

Note: Use fresh oil.

🎄

CARROT WHIPPED-CREAM CAKE

3 cups sifted* all-purpose flour
2 teaspoons baking powder
1 teaspoon baking soda
2 teaspoons ground cinnamon
1 teaspoon salt
2 cups granulated sugar
1½ cups salad oil (see Note)

* Sift before measuring.

4 eggs
3 cups grated carrot (1 lb)

Whipped Cream Frosting:
  2 cups heavy cream, chilled
  ½ cup unsifted confectioners'
    sugar
  1 teaspoon vanilla extract
    Pecan or walnut halves

1. Preheat oven to 350F. Sift flour with baking powder, soda, cinnamon and salt. Grease well and flour three 9-by-1½-inch round layer-cake pans.

2. In large mixing bowl, with electric mixer at medium speed, beat granulated sugar, salad oil and eggs until well blended—about 2 minutes. Add carrot; mix well.

3. At low speed, gradually add flour mixture, beating just until well combined. Batter will be thin. Pour batter into prepared pans, dividing evenly. Bake 30 to 35 minutes, or until surface springs back when gently pressed with fingertip.

4. Cool in pans 10 minutes. Carefully loosen sides with spatula; remove from pan. Cool completely on racks.

5. Make whipped-cream frosting: In medium bowl, whip cream with confectioners' sugar and vanilla until stiff. Refrigerate if not using at once.

6. To frost: Put layers together with whipped-cream frosting, ¾ cup for each layer. Frost side and top. (If desired, decorate edge and bottom using a pastry bag with number-6 star tip.) Arrange pecan halves on top. Refrigerate 1 hour before serving.

Makes 10 to 12 servings.

Note: Use fresh oil.

PUMPKIN SPICE CAKE

1 cup seedless raisins
½ cup muscat raisins
1 cup walnuts
2 cups sifted* all-purpose flour
2 teaspoons baking soda
½ teaspoon salt
2 teaspoons ground cloves

* Sift flour before measuring.

2 teaspoons ground cinnamon
1 teaspoon ground ginger
4 eggs
2 cups sugar
1 cup salad oil (see Note)
1 can (1 lb) pumpkin
Cream Cheese Frosting, page 288

1. Preheat oven to 350F. Grease well a 13-by-9-by-2-inch baking pan. Coarsely chop raisins and walnuts.

2. Sift flour with baking soda, salt, cloves, cinnamon and ginger into large bowl. Add raisins and walnuts; toss lightly to combine.

3. In large bowl of electric mixer, at high speed, beat eggs until thick and yellow. Gradually beat in sugar until thick and light. At low speed, beat in oil and pumpkin, to blend well. Gradually stir in flour mixture until well blended.

4. Turn into prepared pan. Bake 50 minutes, or until surface

springs back when gently pressed with fingertip.

5. Let cool completely in pan placed on wire rack.

6. To serve, loosen edge with spatula. Invert on cake plate. Frost with Cream Cheese Frosting. Cut into squares.

Makes 12 servings.

Note: This cake improves in flavor if it is stored a day or two in refrigerator. Use fresh oil.

TORTES

The classic torte is a light, airy "sponge-type" cake of many layers. These are made without flour, or with very little flour. Sometimes, bread crumbs, ground nuts or grated chocolate takes the place of flour. The high proportion of beaten egg whites gives lightness and volume. The layers are usually put together with a rich, cream filling or sometimes with whipped cream to give flavor and richness.

The layers may be made ahead and frozen, then thawed and filled for serving.

Our collection runs from the fairly traditional to the frankly untraditional. All are great; we leave the choice to you.

※

BLACK FOREST CHERRY CAKE

6 eggs, at room temperature
1 cup granulated sugar
1 teaspoon vanilla extract
1/2 cup sifted* flour
1/2 cup unsweetened cocoa
2/3 cup sweet butter or regular
    margarine, melted

* Sift flour before measuring.

Syrup:
1/3 cup granulated sugar
  3 tablespoons kirsch or Cointreau

Glazed Cherries

Filling:
  3 cups heavy cream
1/2 cup confectioners' sugar

Whole candied cherries
1 (8 oz) milk-chocolate bar

1. Preheat oven to 350F. Grease well and flour three (8-by-1½-inch) layer-cake pans.

2. In large bowl of electric mixer, at high speed, beat eggs until light and fluffy. Beat in 1 cup granulated sugar gradually; continue beating until very thick—about 10 minutes. Add vanilla.

3. Sift flour with cocoa. Then fold into egg mixture in fourths, using a wire whisk or rubber scraper. Also fold in butter, in fourths, just until combined. Gently turn into prepared pans. Bake 15 minutes, or until surface springs back when gently pressed with finger.

4. Let layers cool in pans on wire rack 5 minutes. Then loosen

edges with metal spatula; turn out on wire rack to cool completely.

5. Meanwhile, make syrup: In small saucepan, combine ⅓ cup granulated sugar with ½ cup water. Stir over medium heat, to dissolve sugar. Then bring to boiling; boil, uncovered, 5 minutes. Set aside to cool; add kirsch.

6. Also, make Glazed Cherries.

7. To assemble: Place layers on cookie sheets. Make several holes with toothpicks; spoon syrup over cake layers.

8. Make filling: Beat cream with confectioners' sugar until stiff. Invert one cake layer on cake plate for bottom. Spread glazed cherries over bottom layer. Then spread with 1 cup whipped cream.

9. Place second layer on top; spread with 1 cup whipped cream. Place third layer on top. Spread top and side with remaining whipped cream, making 12 whipped-cream rosettes around top edge. You may use a spoon or put some of whipped cream through a pastry tube with a number-5 tip. Refrigerate.

10. Make chocolate curls: Let chocolate bar soften slightly. Using vegetable parer, scrape across chocolate to make curls; refrigerate.

11. To serve: Place chocolate curls around side of cake, covering completely. Place cherry on each rosette.

Makes 12 servings.

GLAZED CHERRIES

1 cup canned pitted Bing cherries, drained	1 tablespoon cornstarch
2 tablespoons kirsch or Cointreau	⅔ cup cherry juice

1. In small bowl, combine cherries and kirsch; let stand about 1 hour.

2. Meanwhile, in small saucepan, combine cornstarch and ⅓ cup cherry juice; stir to dissolve cornstarch. Stir in remaining juice.

3. Bring to boiling, stirring; reduce heat and simmer 5 minutes, or until thickened and translucent. Let cool completely.

4. Add cherries in kirsch to cooled cornstarch mixture; mix well. Use to fill Black Forest Cherry Cake.

DATE-NUT TORTE

1/3 cup sifted* all-purpose flour
1/2 teaspoon baking powder
1/4 teaspoon salt
1 cup chopped pitted dates
3/4 cup chopped pecans or walnuts

1 teaspoon grated lemon peel
3 egg yolks
3/4 cup sugar
3 egg whites
Whipped cream

* Sift before measuring.

1. Preheat oven to 325F. Lightly grease an 8-by-8-by-2-inch baking pan.

2. On sheet of waxed paper, sift flour with baking powder and salt. Add dates, pecans, and lemon peel; toss well. Set aside.

3. In medium bowl, with portable electric mixer or rotary beater, beat egg yolks with 1/4 cup sugar until very thick and light. With rubber scraper, fold in flour mixture just until combined.

4. In large bowl of electric mixer, at high speed, beat egg whites just until soft peaks form when beater is slowly raised.

5. Add remaining sugar, 2 tablespoons at a time, beating well after each addition. Continue beating until stiff peaks form when beater is raised.

6. With rubber scraper, fold flour mixture into egg whites until well combined. Turn into prepared pan.

7. Bake 50 minutes, or until surface springs back when gently pressed with fingertip.

8. Let cool in pan on wire rack.

9. To serve: Cut into rectangles. Top with whipped cream.
Makes 8 servings.

EASTER TORTE

4 egg whites
1 1/4 cups sifted* all-purpose flour
1/4 teaspoon salt
1 cup granulated sugar
4 egg yolks
2 tablespoons fresh lemon juice
2 teaspoons grated lemon peel

* Sift before measuring.

1 pkg (3 oz) vanilla-pudding-and-
pie-filling mix
1 3/4 cups milk
1/2 teaspoon almond extract
2 cups heavy cream
1 1/4 cups confectioners' sugar
1 1/2 cans (8-oz size) almond paste
1 to 2 drops green food color

1. In large bowl of electric mixer, let egg whites warm to room temperature—about 1 hour.

2. Meanwhile, preheat oven to 350F. Sift flour with salt.

3. With electric mixer at high speed beat egg whites until foamy. Gradually beat in ½ cup granulated sugar, beating after each addition. Continue beating until soft peaks form when beater is slowly raised.

4. In small bowl of electric mixer, at high speed and with the same beater, beat egg yolks until thick and lemon-colored. Gradually beat in remaining granulated sugar; continue beating until mixture is smooth and well blended.

5. Add lemon juice, 2 tablespoons water and the lemon peel, beating just until combined—about 1 minute.

6. With wire whisk, gently fold flour mixture into yolk mixture to combine.

7. With wire whisk or rubber scraper and using an under-and-over motion, gently fold yolk mixture into egg-white mixture just until blended.

8. Pour the batter into two ungreased round, 8-by-1½-inch layer-cake pans; bake 25 minutes, or until the surface springs back when it is gently pressed with fingertip.

9. Invert cake layers by hanging pan between two other pans. Cool completely—about 1 hour. With spatula, carefully loosen cake; remove.

10. Prepare pie filling as package directs, using 1¾ cups milk and adding ½ teaspoon almond extract. Chill.

11. Beat cream with ¼ cup confectioners' sugar until stiff; refrigerate. Slice cake layers in half horizontally, to make four layers.

12. To assemble: Place a layer, cut side up, on cake plate. Spread with half of filling. Repeat with whipped cream on next layer. Repeat with remaining layers, ending with top layer, cut side down. Mound the remaining whipped cream on top, spreading to edge.

13. On wooden board, knead 1 cup confectioners' sugar into the almond paste until smooth. Add food color; continue kneading to blend in color.

14. Roll out almond paste, between two sheets of waxed paper, to a 14-inch round. Carefully place almond paste on top of torte. Tuck ends under cake. Sprinkle top with confectioners' sugar. Chill 4 hours. If desired, decorate top with chickens made from yellow-tinted almond paste.

Makes 10 servings.

🖸

HAZELNUT TORTE

Torte Layers:
7 eggs
1/4 teaspoon salt
1 cup granulated sugar
1 teaspoon vanilla extract
1 1/4 cups ground hazelnuts
1 1/4 cups ground pecans
1/4 cup packaged dry bread
  crumbs
1 teaspoon baking powder
1/2 teaspoon salt

Filling:
1 cup heavy cream, chilled
1/2 cup confectioners' sugar
1 teaspoon vanilla extract

Chocolate Frosting:
4 squares unsweetened
  chocolate

1/4 cup butter or regular
  margarine
3 cups sifted confectioners'
  sugar
1/2 cup hot water
1 teaspoon vanilla extract

1 cup raspberry preserves
1/2 cup whole hazelnuts

Coffee Frosting:
2 teaspoons instant coffee
2 tablespoons hot water
1/4 cup butter or regular
  margarine, softened
1 3/4 cups sifted confectioners'
  sugar

1. Separate eggs, putting whites into large bowl of electric mixer, yolks in smaller one. Let whites warm to room temperature—about 1 hour.

2. Preheat oven to 375F. Line bottom of three (8-inch) round layer-cake pans with circles of waxed paper.

3. With mixer at high speed, beat whites with 1/4 teaspoon salt until soft peaks form when beater is slowly raised. Gradually beat in 1/2 cup granulated sugar, 2 tablespoons at a time, beating until stiff peaks form.

4. With same beater, beat yolks until thick and light. Gradually beat in rest of granulated sugar, beating until thick—3 minutes; beat in 1 teaspoon vanilla.

5. Combine ground nuts, crumbs, baking powder and 1/2 teaspoon salt; turn into yolk mixture; mix well. With an under-and-over motion, fold into the egg whites just to combine.

6. Pour into prepared pans, dividing evenly; smooth surfaces. Bake 25 minutes, or until surface springs back when gently pressed with fingertip. To cool, hang each pan upside down between two other pans—1 hour.

7. Make filling: In medium bowl, combine cream, 1/2 cup confectioners' sugar and 1 teaspoon vanilla. Beat until stiff; refrigerate.

8. Make chocolate frosting: In top of double boiler, over hot water, melt chocolate and ¼ cup butter. Remove from water; add 3 cups confectioners' sugar, the hot water and vanilla; mix until smooth. Set in larger bowl of ice cubes to chill. Stir until thickened.

9. Loosen sides of layers from pans with spatula. Turn out of pans; peel off paper. On plate, assemble layers, spreading each layer first with half of raspberry preserves, then with half of filling.

10. Frost torte with chocolate frosting; refrigerate 1 hour.

11. Slice hazelnuts, reserving 6 whole ones for top. Make coffee frosting: In medium bowl, dissolve coffee in hot water. Add butter and confectioners' sugar; mix until smooth.

12. Place coffee frosting in pastry bag with number-4 star tip. Decorate making ruching around bottom of cake and three even triangles on top. Arrange sliced hazelnuts inside the three triangles. Place whole hazelnuts in center.

13. For easier cutting, refrigerate 2 hours before serving.
Make 12 servings.

LEMON-COCONUT CREAM TORTE

1 pkg (14½ oz) angel food cake
   mix
1 pkg (3⅜ oz) lemon pudding-
   and-pie-filling mix
2 tablespoons lemon juice

1 tablespoon grated lemon peel
2½ cups heavy cream
2 cans (3½-oz size) flaked
   coconut

1. Day before serving: Prepare angel food cake mix, and bake in 10-inch tube pan as package label directs. Let pan hang over neck of bottle at least 2 hours, until cake is completely cool.

2. Meanwhile, prepare pie-filling mix as package label directs for pie, reducing water to 2 cups. Remove from heat. Stir in lemon juice and peel. Pour into medium bowl. Refrigerate, covered, at least 1 hour, until completely cool.

3. Split cooled cake into 5 even layers. Whip 1 cup heavy cream. Fold into lemon filling, along with half the coconut.

4. Assemble cake layers on serving plate, using about 1¼ cups lemon mixture between each 2 layers. Refrigerate, covered, overnight.

5. Several hours before serving, whip remaining 1½ cups cream. Use to frost top and side of cake. Sprinkle evenly with remaining coconut. Refrigerate until serving time.

Makes 16 servings.

LINZER TORTE

1½ cups sifted* all-purpose flour	2 teaspoons grated lemon peel
½ teaspoon ground cinnamon	1 cup sweet butter, softened
Dash ground cloves	2 uncooked egg yolks
½ cup granulated sugar	1½ cups raspberry jam
1 cup ground unblanched	1 egg yolk, slightly beaten
almonds	1 tablespoon cream
2 hard-cooked egg yolks, sieved	Confectioners' sugar

* Sift flour before measuring.

1. Into large bowl of electric mixer, sift flour with cinnamon and cloves. Add granulated sugar, almonds, sieved yolks and lemon peel; mix well.

2. At medium speed, beat in butter and 2 egg yolks; beat until smooth. Form dough into ball; refrigerate several hours, or until it can be rolled out.

3. Lightly grease a 9-inch springform pan. Press about three fourths of dough evenly on bottom and side of pan. Spread jam over bottom to make an even layer.

4. On a lightly floured surface or pastry cloth, with a stockinet-covered rolling pin, roll remaining dough to form a rectangle 9 by 6 inches.

5. Cut 6 strips, 1 inch wide and 9 inches long. Lay 3 strips across the pan, spacing evenly. Lay remaining 3 strips diagonally across first strips, spacing evenly to form diamonds.

6. With fingers, press edge of pastry all around to form a rim.

7. Combine egg yolk with cream; mix with fork. Use to brush lightly over lattice and rim of torte. Refrigerate about 1 hour, or until ready to bake.

8. Preheat oven to 350F. Bake torte 45 to 50 minutes, or until lightly browned. Let cool slightly on wire rack. Then remove outer edge of pan. Let cool completely before serving. Sprinkle with confectioners' sugar. Serve right on bottom of pan.

Makes 8 servings.

Plate   I.   Strawberry Cream Cake

Plate   II. Clockwise from left: Hazelnut Torte, McCall's Best Spice Cake with Seafoam Frosting, Raspberry Cream Torte, Petits Fours, Chocolate Chiffon Cake with Coffee Butter Frosting, Old-Fashioned Gingerbread with Lemon Sauce, Charlotte Russe, and Macaroon Cake

Plate   III. Clockwise from left: Old-Fashioned Strawberry Shortcake, Danish Fruit Pudding, Baked Apple Charlotte, Floating Island à l'Orange, Oranges Orientale, Strawberry Ice Cream Cake Roll, Pontchartrain Ice Cream Pie, Pears Véfour, and Strawberry Snow with Custard Sauce

Plate   IV. Clockwise from top: Gâteau St. Honoré, Brandy Apple Pie, Black Bottom Pie, Glazed Pear Cream Pie, a dish of Glazed Fruit Tarts, Pecan Tartlets, and Lemon-Curd Tarts, and Rhubarb Chiffon Pie

Plate   V.   Chocolate Mousse

IV

PECAN TORTE

4 eggs
¼ teaspoon cream of tartar
6 tablespoons butter or
   margarine, softened
1½ cups light-brown sugar, packed
1 teaspoon vanilla extract

3½ cups finely ground pecans
1 cup heavy cream
2 tablespoons confectioners'
   sugar
½ cup chopped pecans

1. Preheat oven to 350F. Grease well 2 (8-by-1½-inch) cake pans. Line bottoms with waxed paper; lightly grease paper.

2. Separate eggs, putting whites into large bowl of electric mixer and yolks into small bowl.

3. Add cream of tartar to whites, and with mixer at high speed; beat just until stiff peaks form when beater is slowly raised. With same beater, beat yolks at high speed, until thick and lemon colored. Remove beaten yolks to a small bowl.

4. In small bowl of electric mixer, beat butter and brown sugar until well blended. Stir in beaten egg yolks, vanilla, and ground pecans.

5. With rubber scraper, using an under-and-over motion, gently fold yolk mixture into whites until well combined.

6. Pour into prepared pans. Bake 40 minutes, or just until surface springs back when gently pressed with fingertip.

7. Cool in pans on wire rack, 10 minutes. Remove from pans; peel off waxed paper; and cool layers completely.

8. To serve: In bowl, whip cream and confectioners' sugar until stiff. Place one cake layer on serving plate, bottom side up. Spread with some of cream. Arrange second layer, right side up, over cream. Spread top with some of cream.

9. Spoon remaining cream into cake decorating bag with star tip and decorate edge of cake. Sprinkle center with chopped pecans. Refrigerate until ready to serve.

Makes 8 to 10 servings.

RASPBERRY CREAM TORTE

4 egg whites
1¼ cups sifted* all-purpose flour
¼ teaspoon salt
1 cup granulated sugar
4 egg yolks
2 tablespoons fresh lemon juice
2 teaspoons grated lemon peel

2 cups heavy cream
¼ cup confectioners' sugar
1 jar (12 oz) raspberry or
   strawberry preserves
½ cup coarsely chopped
   pistachio nuts

* Sift before measuring.

1. In large bowl of electric mixer, let egg whites warm to room temperature—about 1 hour.

2. Meanwhile, preheat oven to 350F.

3. Sift flour with salt.

4. With electric mixer at high speed, beat egg whites until foamy. Gradually beat in ½ cup granulated sugar, beating after each addition.

5. Continue beating until soft peaks form when beater is slowly raised.

6. In small bowl of electric mixer, at high speed and with the same beater, beat egg yolks until thick and lemon-colored.

7. Gradually beat in remaining granulated sugar; continue beating until mixture is smooth and well blended.

8. At low speed, blend in flour mixture, guiding it into beater with rubber scraper.

9. Add lemon juice, 2 tablespoons water and the lemon peel, beating just until combined—about 1 minute.

10. With wire whisk or rubber scraper and using an under-and-over motion, gently fold egg-yolk mixture into egg-white mixture just until blended.

11. Pour batter into two ungreased, 8-by-1½-inch layer-cake pans; bake 25 minutes, or until surface springs back when gently pressed with fingertip.

12. Invert cake layers by hanging pan between two other pans. Cool completely—about 1 hour. With spatula, carefully loosen cake from pan; remove.

13. Beat cream with confectioners' sugar until stiff; refrigerate. Slice layers in half horizontally, to make four layers.

14. To assemble: Place a layer, cut side up, on cake plate. Spread with ⅓ cup raspberry preserves and ½ cup whipped cream.

Repeat with remaining layers, ending with top layer cut side down.

15. Frost top and side: With whipped cream in pastry bag with number-6 decorating tip, make ruching around top edge of cake. Sprinkle with nuts. For easier cutting, refrigerate 1 hour.

Makes 8 to 10 servings.

Frostings and Fillings

Uncooked frostings (also known as "butter" frostings) are the easiest to make. The butter is softened, then confectioners' sugar is gradually added and beaten with an electric mixer until completely smooth.

Cooked frostings are more difficult; they often require the use of a candy thermometer. There are two types: 1) boiled frosting, in which a sugar syrup is cooked to a certain degree and beaten into stiffly beaten egg whites; 2) the fudge-type frosting, in which the sugar mixture is cooked to a certain degree, then beaten until it becomes thick enough to spread.

❊

HOW TO FROST A LAYER CAKE

1. Be sure both cake and frosting are cool.

2. Brush off all loose crumbs with a pastry brush; trim off any ragged edges with kitchen scissors.

3. Select a cake plate or tray that will set off the cake to the best advantage. It should be flat and at least 2 to 3 inches larger in diameter than the cake.

4. Cut 4 strips of waxed paper, each 10 by 3 inches. Place strips, overlapping, around edge of cake plate. Invert a cake layer in the center of the cake plate. If there is a difference in thickness of the layers, use the thicker or thickest for the bottom.

5. Using a flexible metal spatula, spread top of bottom layer smoothly with frosting or filling, almost to the outer edge.

6. Place the next layer, right side up, on first layer. Repeat with other layers. If layers have a tendency to slide, anchor them with wooden picks or wooden skewers until the filling has set, before frosting side and top of cake.

7. Spread side of cake with a thin coating of frosting, to set crumbs. Then spread frosting from top edge down over the side, making sure cake is completely covered. If frosting is fluffy or creamy type, swirl as you spread.

8. Pile the remaining frosting on top, and spread it lightly to the edge, swirling it as you spread.

9. If you wish to sprinkle the top and side with grated chocolate, coconut, or finely chopped nuts, this should be done while the frosting is still moist.

10. When cake frosting is set, carefully pull out waxed-paper strips.

Uncooked Frostings

CHOCOLATE BUTTER CREAM FROSTING

4 squares (1-oz size)
   unsweetened chocolate
½ cup butter or regular
   margarine

1 egg
2⅔ cups confectioners' sugar
1 teaspoon vanilla extract
⅛ teaspoon salt

1. Fill large bowl half full of ice cubes; add ½ cup cold water.

2. In top of double boiler, combine chocolate and butter. Place over hot, not boiling, water, stirring occasionally, until chocolate is melted. Remove from hot water.

3. Quickly stir in egg. Add sugar, ⅓ cup water, the vanilla, and salt; stir until well blended.

4. Place pan in prepared ice water. With portable electric mixer at high speed, beat until of spreading consistency—about 5 minutes.

Makes enough to fill and frost a 9-inch layer cake.

CHOCOLATE FROSTING

(For Perfect Chocolate Cake)
1 pkg (6 oz) semisweet
   chocolate pieces
½ cup light cream

1 cup butter or regular
   margarine
2½ cups unsifted confectioners'
   sugar

1. Make frosting: In medium saucepan, combine chocolate pieces, cream and butter; stir over medium heat until smooth. Remove from heat.

2. With wire whisk, blend in 2½ cups confectioners' sugar. In bowl set over ice, beat until it holds shape.

Makes enough to frost top and side of 2 or 3 (9-inch) layers.

MAYOR'S CHOCOLATE ICING

1 pkg (6 oz) semisweet chocolate
   pieces
¼ cup butter
½ cup sour cream

1 teaspoon vanilla extract
¼ teaspoon salt
3 cups confectioners' sugar

1. Melt chocolate and butter over hot water; remove.

2. Blend in sour cream, vanilla and salt. Gradually beat in sugar to make frosting a spreading consistency.

Makes enough to frost 2 (9-inch) layers.

CHOCOLATE SOUR CREAM FROSTING

1 pkg (6 oz) semisweet chocolate
   pieces

½ cup dairy sour cream
Dash salt

1. Melt chocolate pieces in top of double boiler, over hot water. Remove top of double boiler from hot water.

2. Add sour cream and salt. With portable electric mixer at medium speed, or rotary beater, beat frosting until creamy and of spreading consistency.

Makes enough to frost top and side of an 8-inch or 9-inch two-layer cake; or top of a 13-by-9-by-2-inch cake; or top and side of a 10-inch tube cake.

Note: To make enough frosting to fill and frost an 8-inch or 9-inch two-layer cake, use 1½ pkg (6-oz size) semisweet-chocolate pieces and ¾ cup dairy sour cream.

COCOA CREAM FROSTING

⅓ cup light cream or evaporated
   milk, undiluted
¼ cup butter or regular margarine,
   softened
¼ teaspoon salt

½ cup sifted unsweetened cocoa
1 teaspoon vanilla extract, or
   ½ teaspoon rum extract
3 cups sifted confectioners' sugar

1. In small saucepan, heat cream until bubbles form around edge of pan. Let cool slightly.

2. In medium bowl, combine butter, salt, cocoa, vanilla, 1/4 cup hot cream, and 1 1/2 cups sugar.

3. With portable electric mixer at medium speed, or wooden spoon, beat mixture until smooth.

4. Gradually add remaining sugar, beating until smooth and fluffy. If frosting seems too thick to spread, gradually beat in a little more hot cream.

Makes enough to fill and frost an 8-inch or 9-inch two-layer cake.

Note: If frosting is too thin, set in bowl of ice water. Beat until thick enough to spread.

CREAM CHEESE FROSTING I

1 pkg (8 oz) cream cheese,
  softened
2/3 cup butter or regular
  margarine, softened

3 teaspoons vanilla extract
1 1/2 lbs confectioners' sugar

1. In large bowl, with electric mixer, at medium speed, beat cheese with butter and vanilla until creamy.

2. Add confectioners' sugar; beat until light and fluffy.

Makes enough to fill and frost 3 (8-inch) layers.

CREAM CHEESE FROSTING II

1/2 pkg (8-oz size) cream cheese,
  softened
1/3 cup butter or regular
  margarine, softened

1 1/2 teaspoons vanilla extract
3/4 lb confectioners' sugar

1. In large bowl, with electric mixer, at medium speed, beat cheese with butter and vanilla until creamy.

2. Add confectioners' sugar; beat until light and fluffy.

Makes enough to fill and frost 2 (9-inch) layers or frost a 13-by-9-inch layer.

※

COFFEE BUTTER FROSTING

1/3 cup butter or regular
    margarine, softened
3 1/2 cups sifted confectioners'
    sugar

1 tablespoon instant coffee
3 tablespoons hot milk
1 teaspoon vanilla or rum
    extract, or brandy flavoring

1. In medium bowl, combine butter, sugar, coffee, and 2 table-spoons hot milk and the vanilla.

2. With portable electric mixer at medium speed, or wooden spoon, beat mixture until smooth and fluffy.

3. If frosting seems too thick to spread, gradually beat in a little more hot milk.

Makes enough to fill and frost an 8-inch or 9-inch two-layer cake.

※

QUICK FUDGE FROSTING

2 squares unsweetened chocolate
1/4 cup butter or regular margarine,
    softened
3 cups sifted confectioners' sugar
1/8 teaspoon salt

1/4 cup hot light cream or
    evaporated milk, undiluted
1 teaspoon vanilla extract, or 1/2
    teaspoon rum extract

1. Melt chocolate over hot water. Remove from heat; let cool.

2. In medium bowl, combine butter, sugar, salt, and 3 table-spoons hot cream. With wooden spoon, or portable electric mixer at medium speed, beat until mixture is smooth.

3. Add chocolate; continue beating until frosting is thick enough to spread. Add vanilla.

4. If frosting seems too thick, gradually beat in a little more hot cream.

Makes enough to fill and frost an 8-inch or 9-inch two-layer cake.

※

MARZIPAN FROSTING

2 cans (4 1/2-oz size) blanched
    whole almonds
2 cups sifted confectioners' sugar

1 egg white
1/2 teaspoon almond extract

1. In electric blender, at high speed, grind almonds, half a can at a time. Turn into large bowl.

2. Add sugar; stir to combine well.

3. In small bowl, combine egg white with 2 teaspoons water and the almond extract.

4. Pour into almond mixture; stir.

5. Turn out onto wooden board sprinkled with confectioners' sugar. With hands, knead until smooth.

6. To frost cake: With rolling pin, roll out marzipan on board, sprinkled with confectioners' sugar, to size of top of cake.

7. Turn cake upside down on marzipan, fitting top evenly. With spatula, press marzipan to cake around edge.

8. Turn cake up again, marzipan on top. Smooth marzipan with metal spatula. Brush off excess sugar.

9. Then glaze with Frosting Glaze.

Makes enough to frost top of fruitcake made from basic recipe.

Note: Or use 2 (8-oz) cans almond paste for frosting. Roll out, and fit on top of cake, as above.

MEXICAN CHOCOLATE FROSTING

½ cup regular margarine
2 squares unsweetened
  chocolate

6 tablespoons milk
1 pkg (1 lb) confectioners' sugar
1 teaspoon vanilla extract
½ cup chopped pecans

1. Combine margarine, chocolate and milk in a saucepan and heat until bubbles form around the edge. Remove from heat.

2. Add confectioners' sugar, vanilla and pecans; beat. Ice cake while still warm. (Frosting is not stiff.)

MOCHA FROSTING

4 squares (1-oz size)
  unsweetened chocolate
¼ cup butter or regular
  margarine

3 cups unsifted confectioners'
  sugar
½ cup hot, strong, brewed coffee
  (see Note)
1½ teaspoons vanilla extract

1. Melt chocolate and butter in top of double boiler, over hot, not boiling water.

2. Remove; add confectioners' sugar, hot coffee and vanilla. Beat until smooth.

3. Turn into a bowl; place in a larger bowl of ice cubes; chill until of spreading consistency—20 minutes.

Makes enough to frost top and sides of loaf cake.

Note: Use 2 level teaspoons regular instant coffee in ½ cup hot water.

ঞ্চ

ORANGE FROSTING

2 tablespoons butter or regular margarine, softened
2 egg yolks

1 tablespoon grated orange peel
4 cups sifted confectioners' sugar
2 to 3 tablespoons orange juice

1. In small bowl of electric mixer, combine butter, egg yolks, orange peel, sugar, and 2 tablespoons orange juice.

2. With mixer at medium speed, beat until frosting is smooth and easy to spread. If frosting seems too thick to spread, gradually beat in a little more orange juice.

Makes enough to frost top and side of a 10-inch tube cake.

ORANGE GLAZE

Prepare half recipe, adding enough orange so glaze can be poured over top of a 10-inch tube cake and run unevenly down sides.

ঞ্চ

PEANUT-BUTTER FROSTING

2 tablespoons butter or regular margarine, softened
½ cup creamy or chunk-style peanut butter

3 cups sifted confectioners' sugar
1 teaspoon vanilla extract
¼ to ⅓ cup milk or light cream

1. In small bowl, combine butter, peanut butter, sugar, vanilla, and ¼ cup milk.

2. With portable electric mixer at medium speed, or wooden spoon, beat frosting until creamy and of spreading consistency. If

frosting seems too thick to spread, gradually beat in a little more milk.

Makes enough to fill and frost an 8-inch or 9-inch two-layer cake.

🞉

APRICOT GLAZE

1½ cups apricot preserves   ½ cup sugar

1. In medium saucepan, combine preserves, sugar, and ½ cup water; bring to boiling, over medium heat. Boil, stirring, 5 minutes.
2. Remove from heat. Press through sieve into a bowl.
Makes 1½ cups.

🞉

CHOCOLATE GLAZE

2 tablespoons butter or margarine   1 cup sifted confectioners' sugar
1 square unsweetened chocolate   2 tablespoons boiling water

1. Melt butter and chocolate over hot water. Remove from heat; let cool.
2. In small bowl, combine chocolate mixture with remaining ingredients.
3. With rotary beater, beat just until mixture is smooth and well combined. (Glaze seems thin, but will thicken on standing.)
Makes about ½ cup.

🞉

FUDGE GLAZE

2 squares unsweetened   1½ cups sugar
   chocolate   ½ cup milk
4 tablespoons butter or   1 teaspoon corn syrup
   shortening   1 teaspoon vanilla extract
½ teaspoon salt   1 cup chopped nuts

Grate chocolate. Combine all ingredients except vanilla and nuts. Bring to a boil, and cook 2 minutes. Remove from heat; cool; then beat. Add vanilla and nuts and spread over Chocolate Pound Cake. It will be a thin, fudgelike glaze.

COFFEE GLAZE

2 tablespoons milk
1 teaspoon instant coffee
2 tablespoons butter or regular
  margarine

1¼ cups unsifted confectioners'
  sugar
¼ teaspoon vanilla extract

1. In small saucepan, heat milk with instant coffee and butter, stirring until coffee is dissolved. Remove from heat.

2. Gradually stir into sugar in small bowl; beat until smooth and well combined. Add vanilla. Let cool slightly—about 5 minutes. Glaze will thicken on standing.

3. Use to glaze Walnut-Bourbon Pound Cake, covering top completely and letting some of glaze run down the side.

Makes about ⅔ cup.

LEMON GLAZE

1 tablespoon butter or regular
  margarine
1 pkg (1 lb) confectioners' sugar

⅓ cup lemon juice
1 teaspoon grated lemon peel

In medium bowl, with wooden spoon, beat butter, sugar, lemon juice and peel until smooth. Then drizzle over cake, letting it run down sides.

Makes ¾ cup.

FROSTING GLAZE

1½ cups confectioners' sugar
2 tablespoons light cream

¼ teaspoon almond extract

1. In small bowl, combine sugar, cream and almond extract; beat with portable electric mixer until smooth.

2. Spread over cake, letting frosting run down side.

✣

FRUIT CAKE GLAZE

⅓ cup light corn syrup   *1 tablespoon lemon juice*

1. In small saucepan, combine corn syrup, lemon juice and 1 tablespoon water; stir.

2. Bring to boiling; reduce heat; simmer, stirring, 5 minutes, or until reduced to ⅓ cup. Cool completely before using.

Makes ⅓ cup.

Cooked Frostings

CARAMEL FROSTING

½ cup butter or regular margarine
1 cup light-brown sugar,
   firmly packed
⅓ cup light cream or evaporated
   milk, undiluted

2 cups unsifted confectioners'
   sugar
1 teaspoon vanilla extract

1. Melt butter in small saucepan, over low heat. Remove from heat.

2. Add brown sugar, stirring until smooth. Over low heat, bring to boiling, stirring; boil, stirring, 1 minute. Remove from heat.

3. Add cream; over low heat, return just to boiling. Remove from heat; let cool to 110F on candy thermometer, or until bottom of saucepan feels lukewarm.

4. With portable electric mixer at medium speed, or wooden spoon, beat in 2 cups confectioners' sugar until frosting is thick. If frosting seems too thin to spread, gradually beat in a little more confectioners' sugar. Add vanilla.

5. Set in bowl of ice water; beat until frosting is thick enough to spread and barely holds its shape.

Makes enough to frost top and side of an 8-inch or 9-inch two-layer cake; or top of a 13-by-9-by-2-inch cake.

COFFEE CARAMEL FROSTING

¾ cup butter or regular
   margarine
1½ cups light-brown sugar, packed
½ cup light cream or evaporated
   milk, undiluted

3 cups unsifted confectioners'
   sugar
1½ teaspoons vanilla extract
1 tablespoon instant coffee

1. Melt butter in small saucepan over low heat. Remove from heat.

2. Add brown sugar, stirring until smooth. Over low heat, bring to boiling, stirring; boil, stirring, 1 minute. Remove from heat.

3. Add cream; over low heat, return just to boiling. Remove from heat; let cool to 110F on candy thermometer, or until bottom of pan feels lukewarm.

4. With portable electric mixer at medium speed, or with wooden spoon, beat in confectioners' sugar until frosting is thick. (If it seems too thin to spread, gradually beat in a little more confectioners' sugar.) Add vanilla and coffee.

5. Set in bowl of ice water; beat until frosting is thick enough to spread.

Makes enough to fill and frost top and side of an 8-inch or 9-inch two-layer cake.

FONDANT FROSTING

2¾ cups granulated sugar
    Dash salt
¼ teaspoon cream of tartar

3 to 3½ cups sifted
    confectioners' sugar
½ teaspoon almond extract
    Food color (optional)

1. In medium saucepan, combine granulated sugar, salt, and cream of tartar with 1½ cups water. Over low heat, cook, stirring, until sugar is dissolved.

2. Over medium heat, cook without stirring, to 226F on candy thermometer.

3. Transfer to top of double boiler; let cool to lukewarm (110F on candy thermometer).

4. With wooden spoon, gradually beat in just enough confectioners' sugar to make frosting thick enough to coat spoon but thin enough to pour. Add almond extract. Remove half of frosting (about 1½ cups) to small bowl. If desired, add a few drops food color, to tint a delicate color.

5. Keep white frosting over hot, not boiling, water, to keep thin enough to pour. If frosting is too thin, add a little more confectioners' sugar; if too thick, thin with a little warm water. After using white frosting, heat tinted frosting, and use in same way.

Makes 3 cups.

SEVEN-MINUTE FROSTING

2 egg whites (¼ cup)
1½ cups granulated sugar
1 tablespoon light corn syrup, or

¼ teaspoon cream of tartar
1 teaspoon vanilla extract

1. In top of double boiler, combine egg whites, sugar, corn syrup, and ⅓ cup water.

2. With portable electric mixer or rotary beater, beat about 1 minute to combine ingredients.

3. Cook over rapidly boiling water (water in bottom should not touch top of double boiler), beating constantly, about 7 minutes, or until stiff peaks form when beater is slowly raised.

4. Remove from boiling water. Add vanilla; continue beating until frosting is thick enough to spread—about 2 minutes.

Makes enough to fill and frost an 8-inch or 9-inch two-layer cake; or to frost a 13-by-9-by-2-inch cake.

COFFEE SPICE

Beat in 2 teaspoons instant coffee, 1 teaspoon cinnamon, and ½ teaspoon nutmeg along with vanilla.

SEAFOAM FROSTING

Substitute 1½ cups light-brown sugar, firmly packed, for 1½ cups of the granulated sugar.

PEPPERMINT

Omit vanilla. Add ½ teaspoon peppermint extract. Fold in ¼ cup finely crushed peppermint candy.

COCONUT

Reduce vanilla to ½ teaspoon, and add ½ teaspoon coconut flavoring. Sprinkle top and side of cake with 1 can (3½ oz) flaked coconut.

FOUR-MINUTE FROSTING

Make Seven-Minute Frosting, halving each ingredient and beating over boiling water only 4 minutes. Makes enough to frost 12 cupcakes; or top of an 8-inch or 9-inch square cake.

WHITE MOUNTAIN FROSTING

½ cup egg whites (at room
   temperature)
1½ cups sugar

½ teaspoon cream of tartar
½ teaspoon vanilla extract

1. In small bowl of electric mixer, let egg whites warm to room temperature.

2. In medium saucepan, combine sugar and cream of tartar with ½ cup water. Cook, stirring, over medium heat until sugar is dissolved and syrup is clear. Continue cooking over medium heat, without stirring, to 240F on candy thermometer, or until a little spins a thin thread 6 to 8 inches long when dropped from tip of spoon.

3. Meanwhile, with mixer at medium speed, beat egg whites until soft peaks form when beater is slowly raised.

4. With mixer at high speed, slowly pour hot syrup in a thin stream over egg whites, beating constantly. Add vanilla; continue beating until stiff peaks form when beater is slowly raised and frosting is thick enough to spread. Spread frosting on cake.

Makes enough to fill and frost 2 (9-inch) layers or to frost side of Lane Cake.

BROILED COCONUT TOPPING

¼ cup soft butter or regular
   margarine
¼ cup light cream or evaporated
   milk, undiluted

½ cup light-brown sugar,
   firmly packed
1 cup flaked or shredded coconut

1. In small bowl, combine all ingredients; mix well.

2. Spread evenly over top of hot 8-inch or 9-inch square cake.

3. Run under broiler, 4 inches from heat, 2 to 3 minutes, or until topping is bubbly and golden. Cool cake in pan on wire rack; serve slightly warm.

✸

WHIPPED CREAM FILLING
(for Perfect Chocolate Cake)

1 cup heavy cream, chilled
¼ cup unsifted confectioners'
   sugar

1 teaspoon vanilla extract

Whip cream with confectioners' sugar and vanilla; refrigerate until using.

Makes about 2 cups.

✸

CHOCOLATE WHIPPED CREAM FILLING AND FROSTING

2 cups heavy cream
1 cup sifted confectioners' sugar

½ cup sifted unsweetened cocoa
⅛ teaspoon salt

1. Combine all ingredients in medium bowl. Refrigerate, covered, 30 minutes.

2. With portable electric mixer at high speed, or rotary beater, beat mixture until stiff. Refrigerate until ready to use.

Makes enough to fill and frost an angel-food or chiffon cake split crosswise into 3 layers; or to spoon over individual slices of an angel-food or chiffon cake.

MOCHA WHIPPED CREAM FILLING AND FROSTING

Combine 2 tablespoons instant coffee with rest of ingredients.

✸

CHOCOLATE CUSTARD FILLING

1 pkg (6 oz) semisweet chocolate
   pieces
½ cup soft butter or regular
   margarine

⅔ cup sifted confectioners' sugar
2 egg yolks
1 teaspoon vanilla extract
2 egg whites

1. Melt chocolate in top of double boiler, over hot water. Remove from heat; let cool.

2. In small bowl of electric mixer, at medium speed, beat butter until light. Add sugar gradually, beating until very light and fluffy.

3. Add egg yolks, one at a time, beating after each addition.

4. Gradually beat in chocolate. Add vanilla.

5. With rotary beater, beat egg whites just until stiff peaks form. With rubber scraper, using an under-and-over motion, fold egg whites into chocolate mixture just until blended.

Makes 2 cups.

FRUIT FILLING FOR MAYOR'S CHOCOLATE CAKE

3/4 cup evaporated milk
3/4 cup sugar
1/4 cup pitted chopped dates
1/4 cup seeded chopped raisins

1/4 cup chopped figs (or more dates)
1 teaspoon vanilla extract
1/2 cup nuts, chopped

1. Combine milk with 1/4 cup water in top of double boiler. Add sugar; cook over hot water; stir until sugar is dissolved.

2. Add fruit; cook until thick. Cool. Add vanilla and chopped nuts.

Makes about 1 1/2 cups.

LANE CAKE FILLING

3/4 cup butter
1 3/4 cups sugar
1/2 teaspoon salt
12 egg yolks
1/2 cup bourbon whisky
1 1/2 cups seedless raisins, soaked

in hot water 5 minutes and drained
1 1/2 cups shredded fresh coconut
1 1/2 cups candied cherries, quartered
1 1/2 cups coarsely chopped pecans

1. Beat butter in top of double boiler, using portable electric mixer. Add sugar, salt and egg yolks, beating well. Cook over simmering water until slightly thickened.

2. Remove from heat; add bourbon; beat one minute. Add fruits and nuts; cool.

░░

LEMON FILLING

4 egg yolks
½ cup sugar
¼ cup lemon juice

2 teaspoons grated lemon peel
1 tablespoon heavy cream

1. In top of double boiler, with rotary beater, beat egg yolks with sugar until smooth.

2. Stir in lemon juice and peel; cook over boiling water, stirring, 5 to 8 minutes, or until mixture thickens.

3. Remove from heat. Stir in cream; cool.

Makes 1 cup, or filling for an 8-inch two-layer cake.

░░

ORANGE FILLING

¾ cup sugar
2½ tablespoons cornstarch
⅛ teaspoon salt
½ cup orange juice

2 tablespoons grated orange
   peel
2 tablespoons lemon juice
2 tablespoons butter or regular
   margarine

1. In small saucepan, combine sugar with cornstarch and salt.

2. Gradually stir in orange juice and ½ cup water; over medium heat, bring to boiling, stirring. Boil 1 minute. Remove from heat.

3. Stir in remaining ingredients. Cool well.

Makes 1½ cups.

░░

VANILLA CREAM FILLING

½ cup sugar
¼ cup cornstarch
¼ teaspoon salt

2 cups milk
4 egg yolks, slightly beaten
1 teaspoon vanilla extract

1. In medium saucepan, combine sugar with cornstarch and salt.

2. Gradually add milk; over medium heat, bring to boiling, stirring. Remove from heat.

3. Add half of hot mixture to egg yolks; mix well. Gradually return to saucepan, stirring.

4. Over medium heat, bring to boiling, stirring. Remove from heat. Add vanilla. Cool completely before using to fill cake.
Makes 2 cups.

COCONUT CREAM FILLING

Add ½ cup flaked coconut and ½ teaspoon almond extract along with vanilla.

CHOCOLATE CREAM FILLING

Increase sugar to ¾ cup. Combine ¼ cup sifted unsweetened cocoa with sugar, cornstarch, and salt.
Makes 2 cups.

FROZEN DESSERTS AND ICE CREAM

Here you'll find dozens of delightful ways to glamorize America's favorite dessert—ice cream.

We've come a long way from the old-fashioned family freezer on the back porch, but we guarantee our modern versions are every bit as good. And the sherbets with the true taste of fresh fruit are out of this world!

Frozen Desserts

BISCUIT TORTONI

3 egg whites
¾ cup sugar
Dash salt
¼ cup whole blanched almonds

Almond extract
1½ cups heavy cream
¾ teaspoon vanilla extract
12 candied cherries

1. In small bowl of electric mixer, let egg whites warm to room temperature—about 1 hour.

2. Combine ¼ cup water with the sugar in a 1-quart saucepan; cook over low heat, stirring, until sugar is dissolved.

3. Bring to boiling over medium heat; boil, uncovered and without stirring, to 236F on candy thermometer, or until syrup spins a 2-inch thread when dropped from a spoon.

4. Meanwhile, at high speed, beat egg whites with salt just until stiff peaks form when beater is slowly raised.

5. Pour hot syrup in thin stream over egg whites, beating constantly until mixture forms very stiff peaks when beater is raised. Refrigerate, covered, 30 minutes.

6. Meanwhile, preheat oven to 350F. Place almonds in shallow pan, and bake just until toasted—8 to 10 minutes. Finely grind almonds in a blender.

7. Turn into a small bowl. Blend in 1½ teaspoons almond extract. Set aside.

8. In medium bowl, beat cream with ¼ teaspoon almond extract and the vanilla until stiff. With wire whisk or rubber scraper, fold into egg-white mixture until thoroughly combined.

9. Spoon into 12 paper-lined 2½-inch muffin-pan cups. Sprinkle with almond mixture; top with a cherry.

10. Cover with foil; freeze until firm—several hours or overnight. Serve right from freezer.

Makes 12 servings.

COFFEE TORTONI

2 egg whites, at room
   temperature
2 tablespoons instant coffee
1/4 teaspoon salt
1/4 cup granulated sugar
2 cups heavy cream

1/2 cup confectioners' sugar
2 teaspoons vanilla extract
2 teaspoons almond extract
1/2 cup coarsely chopped toasted
   almonds

1. In medium bowl, with portable electric mixer, beat egg whites until foamy. Beat in coffee and salt; beat in granulated sugar, a little at a time. Beat until stiff peaks form when beater is slowly raised.

2. Also, beat cream in medium bowl (use clean beaters) with confectioners' sugar just until stiff.

3. With wire whisk or rubber scraper, gently fold whipped cream into egg whites, along with vanilla and almond extracts.

4. Use to fill ten paper tortoni cups; sprinkle top of each with chopped toasted almonds. Freeze until firm—overnight. Let stand 5 minutes at room temperature before serving. (If storing in freezer longer, freezer-wrap.)

Makes 10 servings.

FROZEN MAPLE MOUSSE

1 1/4 cups maple or maple-flavored
   syrup
2 egg yolks

1/8 teaspoon salt
2 cups heavy cream
   Whipped cream (optional)

1. In the top of a double boiler, over direct heat, heat the maple syrup just until it is bubbly around the edge of the pan.

2. In small bowl, with electric mixer or rotary beater, beat egg yolks with salt until light-colored. Gradually beat in all the syrup. Return mixture to top of double boiler.

3. Cook over simmering water, stirring constantly, until mixture is slightly thickened and forms a coating on a metal spoon—10 to 15 minutes.

4. Set top of double boiler in ice water; beat mixture until thick and fluffy and well chilled—5 minutes.

5. In large, chilled bowl, beat 2 cups heavy cream just until stiff. Fold in syrup mixture. Pour into two ice-cube trays.

6. Freeze until firm about 1 inch from edge. Turn into large bowl; beat with wire whisk until smooth. Turn into 6-cup mold, preferably one with a tube.

7. Freeze, covered with plastic film, until firm—8 hours or overnight.

8. To serve: unmold onto chilled serving plate. Garnish with whipped cream, if desired.

Makes 8 servings.

FROZEN CHOCOLATE CREAM

1/4 cup sugar
1 pkg (6 oz) semisweet
   chocolate pieces

3 egg yolks
1 1/2 cups heavy cream
   Whipped cream

1. Combine sugar and 1/2 cup water in small saucepan; boil 3 minutes.

2. Place chocolate pieces in blender container. Pour in hot syrup.

3. Blend at high speed, covered, 6 seconds.

4. Add egg yolks; blend at high speed 5 seconds, or until smooth.

5. Add cream; blend at high speed 10 seconds.

6. Pour into 6 (6-oz) soufflé dishes or small parfait glasses, set on tray, and cover with foil.

7. Freeze 2 to 3 hours, or until firm.

8. To serve: Remove from freezer and place in refrigerator 20 to 30 minutes to soften slightly. Garnish with whipped cream.

Makes 6 servings.

FROZEN LEMON CREAM

1 1/2 cups heavy cream
4 eggs, separated
1 cup sugar
1/2 cup lemon juice

1 1/2 tablespoons grated lemon peel
   Sweetened whipped cream
   Coconut

1. Whip cream; set aside.

2. In medium bowl, with portable electric mixer at high speed, beat egg whites until soft peaks form when beater is slowly raised.

Gradually beat in sugar, 2 tablespoons at a time; continue beating until stiff peaks form.

3. With same beater, at medium speed, beat egg yolks until thick and light. Beat in lemon juice and peel until well combined.

4. Fold egg yolk mixture and whipped cream into egg whites. Turn ½ cup lemon mixture into each of 12 small dessert dishes.

5. Freeze until firm—about 2 hours.

6. Wrap desserts individually in foil or plastic film. Seal, label, and return to freezer.

7. To serve: Remove as many desserts as needed from freezer; unwrap. Let thaw in refrigerator, about 30 minutes.

8. Place each dish on a green leaf on a small plate. Garnish each with sweetened whipped cream and coconut.

Makes 12 servings.

GOLDEN PARFAITS

¾ cup sugar
3 egg yolks
Dash salt

2 cups heavy cream
2 teaspoons vanilla extract

1. In medium saucepan, combine sugar with ⅓ cup water. Over low heat, cook, stirring, until sugar is dissolved.

2. Over medium heat, bring to boiling, stirring. Reduce heat and boil gently, without stirring, to 230F on candy thermometer, or until a little mixture spins a thread when dropped from spoon.

3. Meanwhile, in medium bowl, with portable electric mixer at medium speed, beat egg yolks and salt until light.

4. Gradually beat hot syrup, in a thin stream, into egg yolks. Continue beating until mixture begins to cool. Let cool completely.

5. Beat cream until stiff. Add vanilla.

6. With rubber scraper, gently fold whipped cream into egg-yolk mixture.

7. Spoon into 6 to 8 parfait glasses or a serving bowl. Cover with foil; freeze until firm.

Makes 6 to 8 servings.

COFFEE PARFAITS

3/4 cup sugar
4 egg yolks
2 cups heavy cream
2 teaspoons vanilla extract
2 tablespoons instant coffee
1 square unsweetened chocolate, grated
Whipped cream

1. Combine sugar and 1/3 cup water in small saucepan.
2. Cook, stirring, over low heat until sugar is dissolved.
3. Bring to boiling; boil, uncovered, without stirring, to 230F on a candy thermometer.
4. Meanwhile, with portable electric mixer at low speed, beat egg yolks until thick and light. Pour sugar syrup in thin stream over egg yolks, beating constantly. Refrigerate 30 minutes.
5. In medium bowl, beat cream with vanilla and coffee just until stiff. Fold into egg-yolk mixture along with chocolate until well combined.
6. Spoon into 6 parfait glasses. Cover top of each glass with foil; freeze until firm.
7. To serve: Remove foil; garnish top of each parfait with whipped cream. If desired, sprinkle with candy coffee beans or grated chocolate.

Makes 6 servings.

STRAWBERRY PARFAITS

1 1/2 pint boxes fresh strawberries
12 large marshmallows
1 cup sugar
1 teaspoon lemon juice
2 cups heavy cream
1 tablespoon vanilla extract

1. Gently wash berries in cold water. Drain; hull. Measure 2 cups; refrigerate rest.
2. In medium saucepan, combine 2 cups berries, the marshmallows, 3/4 cup sugar, and the lemon juice. Over low heat, simmer 10 minutes, stirring occasionally. Do not scorch.
3. Remove from heat. Press through a sieve; cool.
4. In large bowl, beat cream until stiff. Stir in vanilla. Blend in strawberry purée. Pour into 2 ice-cube trays.

5. Freeze until mushy; stir thoroughly. Freeze until mushy; stir again. Freeze until firm.

6. To serve: Slice reserved strawberries; toss with remaining sugar. Divide frozen strawberry cream into 6 parfait glasses. Top with sliced berries.

Makes 6 servings.

FLOATING HEART RITZ

¾ cup sugar
3 egg yolks
   Dash salt
1 cup crumbled almond
   macaroons
4 ladyfingers, split
2 tablespoons Grand Marnier

1½ cups heavy cream
2 teaspoons vanilla extract
½ teaspoon almond extract
   Raspberry Sauce, page 343
½ cup heavy cream
   Chocolate curls, page 346

1. Line a 7-inch (6- to 7-cup) heart-shape mold with foil.

2. In small saucepan, combine sugar with ⅓ cup water; bring to boiling over medium heat, stirring until sugar is dissolved. Boil gently, without stirring, to 230F on candy thermometer, or until a little of sugar mixture spins a thread when dropped from spoon.

3. Meanwhile, in medium bowl, with portable electric mixer at medium speed, beat egg yolks and salt until light. Gradually beat in hot syrup, in a thin stream; continue beating until mixture begins to cool—about 2 minutes. Stir in macaroons. Refrigerate 30 minutes.

4. Meanwhile, sprinkle ladyfingers with Grand Marnier; set aside. Combine 1½ cups cream with extracts; beat until stiff.

5. With rubber scraper, fold whipped cream into macaroon mixture. Turn half of mixture into prepared mold; cover with ladyfingers; pour in remaining mixture. Freeze until firm—about 4 hours. Meanwhile, make Raspberry Sauce.

6. At serving time: Beat ½ cup cream until stiff. Unmold frozen heart onto chilled shallow serving dish; remove foil. Spoon Raspberry Sauce around base. Decorate top with whipped cream, using pastry bag with decorating tip, if desired. Garnish with chocolate curls.

Makes 8 to 10 servings.

Ice Cream and Sherbet

BASIC VANILLA ICE CREAM
(Crank-freezer type)

1 1/2 cups half-and-half or top milk
3/4 cup sugar
1/4 teaspoon salt
4 egg yolks
1 1/2 to 2 tablespoons vanilla extract
2 cups heavy cream

1. In top of double boiler, heat milk until film forms on surface. Do not boil. Stir in sugar and salt.

2. In medium bowl, beat egg yolks slightly. Gradually beat in small amounts of hot milk mixture until most of it is used.

3. Return to top of double boiler; cook, over boiling water, stirring, until as smooth and thick as mayonnaise—takes about 15 to 20 minutes.

4. Cool custard thoroughly. Stir in vanilla to taste and the heavy cream. Cover, and chill thoroughly.

5. To freeze: Pour custard into freezer container; insert dasher, and close container tightly. Pack freezer with ice and coarse salt in 8-to-1 proportion. Crank until dasher is difficult to turn. (If you use an electric freezer, follow manufacturer's instructions.)

6. Remove dasher (be careful that no salt water gets into ice cream). Replace top, and repack with ice and salt in 8-to-1 proportion. Mellow at least 2 hours.

Makes 1 quart; 6 servings.

PEPPERMINT ICE CREAM

Crush coarsely about 1/2 lb peppermint-stripe candy (you'll need 1 1/4 cups crushed candy). Prepare Basic Vanilla Ice Cream. When ice cream is frozen to semihardness, remove dasher. With a long wooden spoon, stir in candy. Pack down ice cream; replace cover, and mellow as in basic recipe.

PEACH ICE CREAM

Prepare Basic Vanilla Ice Cream; reduce vanilla to 1 tablespoon; add ½ teaspoon almond extract. Peel and purée 2 large ripe peaches; peel and coarsely chop 1 large peach. (Peaches should measure 2 cups.)

When ice cream is frozen to semihardness, remove dasher. With a long wooden spoon, stir in peaches. Pack down ice cream; replace cover, and mellow as in basic recipe.

STRAWBERRY ICE CREAM

2 cups light cream	¾ cup heavy cream
1 egg	1½ teaspoons vanilla extract
1 cup sugar	⅛ teaspoon salt
2 pint boxes strawberries	

1. In medium saucepan, heat 1 cup light cream until bubbles form around edge of pan.

2. In medium bowl, beat egg with ½ cup sugar until well blended. Gradually stir in hot cream. Return to saucepan, and cook over low heat, stirring constantly, until slightly thickened—15 to 20 minutes. Remove from heat; cool.

3. Meanwhile, wash and hull strawberries. Slice into a large bowl. Add remaining sugar. With potato masher, mash berries, to make a purée.

4. To cooled egg mixture, add remaining light cream, the heavy cream, vanilla, salt.

5. To freeze in 1-quart crank-type freezer: Pour custard mixture into freezer container; insert dasher, and close container tightly. Pack freezer with ice and coarse salt, in 4-to-1 proportion. Crank for 10 minutes. Open container; add crushed strawberries; then crank until dasher is difficult to turn. (If using an electric freezer, follow manufacturer's instructions.)

6. Serve ice cream immediately, or spoon into freezer containers, and place in freezer.

Makes 1 quart.

✿

CHOCOLATE-CINNAMON ICE CREAM

1 vanilla bean	¼ teaspoon salt
4 cups light cream	7 squares (1-oz size) semisweet
4 egg yolks	chocolate
1 cup sugar	2 tablespoons cinnamon
1 tablespoon cornstarch	1½ cups heavy cream

1. Split vanilla bean; with tip of knife, scrape seeds into light cream in a medium saucepan. Heat until bubbles appear around edge of pan.

2. In medium bowl, beat egg yolks with sugar, cornstarch, and salt until well combined. Gradually stir in hot cream. Return to saucepan; cook over medium heat, stirring constantly, until mixture is thickened and just comes to boiling.

3. Add chocolate and cinnamon. Remove from heat; stir until chocolate is melted. Set aside until cool.

4. Stir in heavy cream.

5. To freeze in 1-quart crank-type freezer:* Pour half of chocolate mixture into freezer container; insert dasher, and close container tightly. Pack freezer with ice and coarse salt in 4-to-1 proportion. Crank for 15 minutes, or until dasher is difficult to turn.

6. Serve immediately, or spoon into freezer containers; and place in freezer. Freeze other half. Serve with chocolate sauce.

Makes about 2 quarts.

* If using an electric freezer, follow manufacturer's directions.

MOCHA ICE CREAM

Add 2 tablespoons instant coffee along with chocolate; omit cinnamon.

✿

BLENDER STRAWBERRY ICE CREAM

1 tablespoon grated lemon peel	⅔ cup sweetened condensed milk
1 tablespoon lemon juice	1 cup heavy cream, whipped
1 pkg (10 oz) frozen strawberries, thawed	

1. Combine lemon peel, juice, and strawberries in blender. Blend, covered and at high speed, 20 seconds, or until smooth.

2. Reduce speed to low; remove cover; pour condensed milk in steady stream into strawberry mixture.

3. Fold strawberry mixture into whipped cream, using rubber scraper or wire whisk.

4. Pour mixture into ice-cube tray; cover with waxed paper. Freeze 2 to 3 hours, or until firm.

Makes 1 quart, 6 servings.

PEACH ICE CREAM

2 lb fresh ripe peaches
3 tablespoons lemon juice
1½ cups granulated sugar
2 eggs, separated

2 tablespoons confectioners'
sugar
1 cup heavy cream

1. Set refrigerator control at coldest temperature.

2. Reserve 2 peaches for garnish. Peel remaining peaches; halve, and remove pits. Place peach halves in mixing bowl with lemon juice; crush with potato masher.

3. Stir in granulated sugar.

4. In medium bowl, with rotary beater, beat egg whites with confectioners' sugar until soft peaks form.

5. In small bowl, beat egg yolks well.

6. Fold yolks gently into whites, using wire whisk or rubber scraper.

7. Whip cream until it holds soft peaks; fold gently into egg mixture.

8. Fold in peaches. Pour into 1-quart ice-cube tray or 8-inch square pan.

9. Freeze until firm around edges.

10. Transfer to bowl; beat with rotary beater until smooth and creamy. Return to tray.

11. Freeze until firm.

12. To serve: Peel and slice reserved peaches. Use to garnish servings.

Makes 1 quart, 6 servings.

COCONUT ICE CREAM

1 quart vanilla ice cream   1 cup canned flaked coconut
1 cup canned cream of coconut

1. Let ice cream soften slightly in refrigerator. Blend in blender with cream of coconut and flaked coconut until well combined but not melted.

2. Turn into ice-cube tray or a 1-quart fancy mold (see Note); freeze several hours before serving. (Freezer-wrap if storing a day or longer.) Nice with strawberry or chocolate sauce.

Makes 8 servings.

Note: If using a fancy mold, line first with large piece of foil, leaving an overhang; pack in the ice cream; freeze. To unmold: Firmly grasp foil and lift out ice cream; remove foil.

ЕЗ

CHOCOLATE SHERBET

¾ cup unsweetened cocoa   3½ cups milk
2 cups sugar   ½ teaspoon vanilla extract

1. In large saucepan, combine cocoa and sugar; stir to mix well. Gradually stir in milk.

2. Cook, stirring over low heat until sugar is melted and mixture is smooth; cook over low heat 5 minutes longer.

3. Remove from heat; stir in vanilla.

4. Turn into two ice-cube trays. Freeze until firm about 1-inch in from edge.

5. Turn into large bowl of electric mixer; beat just until smooth. Return to ice-cube trays; freeze again until firm (see Note). Let soften slightly; mound in serving dishes.

Makes a pint.

Note: If storing in freezer more than a day, freeze-wrap trays of sherbet.

✂

FIG SORBET

2 cans (17-oz size) Kadota figs   ⅓ cup light rum
½ cup honey or light corn syrup

    1. Drain figs, reserving syrup.

    2. Put figs in blender, one half at a time. Blend at high speed to form a purée. Combine with ¼ cup reserved syrup, the honey, and rum. (Or make a purée of figs by pressing through food mill; combine with rest of ingredients and ¼ cup reserved syrup.)

    3. Turn into refrigerator ice-cube trays; freeze until frozen 1 inch from edge—about 3 hours. Turn into large bowl of electric mixer; beat just until mushy, not melted.

    4. Turn into serving dishes, piling high. Store in freezer until serving. Garnish with canned figs, if desired.

    Makes 4 to 6 servings.

✂

HONEYDEW-MELON ICE

2 cups sugar   ¼ cup orange juice
1 large ripe honeydew melon   ⅓ cup lemon juice
  (4½ lb)

    1. Day ahead: In medium saucepan, combine sugar with 1½ cups water. Stir over low heat to dissolve sugar.

    2. Bring to boiling; boil gently, uncovered and without stirring, to 230F on candy thermometer, or until it spins a 2-inch thread from tip of spoon—about 45 minutes.

    3. Meanwhile, cut melon in half zigzag fashion. Discard seeds. Scoop out pulp but save a half shell. Blend pulp in blender or press through food mill. (There should be 4½ to 5 cups purée.)

    4. In large bowl, combine puréed melon with sugar syrup; mix well. Cool 15 minutes.

    5. Stir in orange and lemon juices. Turn into a 13-by-9-by-2-inch pan; place in freezer until frozen around edge—3 hours.

    6. Turn into a chilled large bowl; with electric beater at high speed, beat just until mushy, not melted.

    7. Return to pan; refreeze—several hours or overnight.

    8. To serve: Mound reserved half honeydew-melon shell with

small scoops of ice (these may be prepared ahead and stored in freezer until ready to use). Garnish with mint leaves, if desired. Let stand about 5 minutes at room temperature before serving.

Makes 8 servings.

ध

LIME SHERBET

1 envelope unflavored gelatine	2 cups light cream
2 cups milk	1/2 cup lime juice
1 1/3 cups sugar	1/4 cup lemon juice
1/2 teaspoon salt	2 tablespoons grated lemon peel

1. In small heavy saucepan, sprinkle gelatine over 1/2 cup milk to soften.

2. In medium bowl combine remaining milk, sugar, salt, and cream. Stir until sugar is dissolved. Stir in lime juice, lemon juice, and peel.

3. Heat gelatine mixture over low heat, stirring constantly until gelatine is dissolved. Remove from heat; slowly stir into mixture in bowl.

4. Turn into ice-cube tray; freeze until frozen 1 inch in from edge.

5. Turn into chilled bowl; with electric mixer or rotary beater beat mixture quickly until smooth but not melted. Return to ice-cube tray.

6. Freeze several hours or until firm.

7. To serve: Spoon into sherbet glasses.

Makes 6 servings.

ध

ORANGE SHERBET IN ORANGE SHELLS

2 tablespoons grated orange peel	2 cups light cream
7 large oranges	1/4 cup Cointreau
1/2 cup honey or light corn syrup	Fresh mint sprigs
2/3 cup sweet orange marmalade	

1. Grate peel from one orange. Cut tops from 6 oranges, cutting about one third of the way down. Squeeze juice from tops and bottoms of 7 oranges. Scrape any pulp from tops and bottoms of 6 oranges; reserve for serving. Juice should measure 2 cups.

2. In blender container, combine grated orange peel and juice,

honey, marmalade, cream and Cointreau. Blend ½ minute at high speed. Pour into 13-by-9-by-2-inch baking pan; freeze until firm 1 inch from edge all around—about 3 hours.

3. Blend again in blender ½ minute—until soft but not melted. Turn back into baking pan, or mound in reserved orange-shell bottoms. Freeze until firm—several hours or overnight. (Flavor improves overnight.)

4. Serve in orange shells, filling bottoms and putting tops in place. Decorate each with a mint sprig inserted through hole in top.

Makes 6 servings.

RASPBERRY SHERBET MOLD

3 pkg (10-oz size) quick-thaw
    frozen raspberries
¾ cup currant jelly
½ cup crème de cassis

1 cup fresh pineapple wedges
½ lb seedless green grapes,
    washed

1. Thaw frozen raspberries as label directs.

2. Combine raspberries with their juice, the jelly and crème de cassis in electric blender. Blend at medium speed ½ minute, to make a purée.

3. Turn into ice-cube trays; freeze until firm ½ inch from edge all around—about 3 hours.

4. Blend again in blender until soft and mushy but not melted. Turn into a 5-cup ring mold (plain or decorative). Freeze until firm, preferably overnight.

5. To unmold: Invert mold on serving platter. Cover with dish cloth dipped in hot water. Shake mold to release sherbet. Fill center of the mold with the fresh pineapple and green grapes.

Makes 8 servings.

CRÈME DE MENTHE SHERBET RING WITH STRAWBERRIES

3 pints lemon sherbet
⅓ cup green crème de menthe

1 quart fresh strawberries
    Confectioners' sugar

1. Let sherbet stand in refrigerator 30 minutes, to soften slightly.

2. Turn sherbet into large bowl; beat, with portable electric mixer, just until smooth but not melted.

3. Quickly stir in crème de menthe until well combined.

4. Turn mixture into a 5½-cup ring mold; freeze until firm—several hours or overnight.

5. Meanwhile, wash strawberries; drain. Do not hull. Refrigerate until ready to use.

6. To serve: Invert ring mold over round, chilled serving platter. Place hot, damp cloth over mold; shake to release sherbet.

7. Fill center of ring with strawberries. Dust berries lightly with sugar. Serve at once.

Makes 8 servings.

Ice-Cream Sundaes and Flambés

✳

BRANDIED APRICOTS FLAMBÉ

1 can (1 lb, 14 oz) whole apricots
6 tablespoons brandy
½ cup apricot preserves

1 teaspoon lemon juice
1 quart vanilla ice cream

1. Drain apricots, reserving ½ cup syrup. Remove pits from apricots.

2. Pour 2 tablespoons brandy over apricots; refrigerate, covered, 1 hour.

3. In medium saucepan, combine reserved syrup, preserves, and lemon juice; heat to boiling. Add apricots; turn into chafing dish, if desired.

4. In small saucepan, heat remaining brandy just until bubbles form around edge of pan. Ignite with match; pour over hot apricots.

5. Serve flaming apricots and syrup over ice cream.

Makes 6 servings.

✳

BRANDY ALEXANDER FRAPPÉS

1 quart vanilla ice cream
½ cup brandy
½ cup crème de cacao

Square of chocolate for
    chocolate curls, page 346

1. Refrigerate 8 sherbet glasses several hours to chill well.

2. Remove ice cream from freezer to refrigerator, to let soften —about ½ hour before using.

3. Just before serving, combine ice cream, brandy, and crème de cacao in blender. Blend at high speed until smooth.

4. Turn into chilled sherbet glasses. Decorate each with a chocolate curl.

Makes 8 servings.

❧

BANANAS FOSTER

1/4 cup butter or margarine
1/2 cup light-brown sugar,
    firmly packed
4 ripe bananas, peeled and split
    lengthwise

1/8 teaspoon cinnamon
1/2 cup white rum
1/4 cup banana liqueur (crème de
    banana)

1. Melt butter and brown sugar in flat chafing dish or attractive skillet. Add bananas in a single layer, and sauté, turning once, until tender—about 5 minutes.

2. Sprinkle with cinnamon; pour in rum and banana liqueur. Ignite with match; remove from heat, and baste bananas until the flame burns out.

3. Serve at once, with vanilla ice cream or sweetened whipped cream.

Makes 4 servings.

❧

CHERRIES JUBILEE

1 can (1 lb, 14 oz) pitted dark
    sweet cherries in extra-heavy
    syrup
1 cup brandy

1/4 cup sugar
1/4 cup currant jelly

1 quart vanilla ice cream

1. Drain cherries, reserving 1/2 cup syrup. Turn cherries into a small bowl.

2. In small saucepan, combine reserved syrup, 1/2 cup brandy, and the sugar. Bring to boiling; reduce heat, and simmer, uncovered, until mixture thickens slightly and is reduced to 1/2 cup. Pour over cherries. Let stand several hours.

3. Just before serving, in small saucepan, heat cherries in syrup until hot. Add currant jelly; stir until melted. Stir in 6 tablespoons brandy. Pour mixture into a small silver bowl.

4. Pour remaining 2 tablespoons brandy into ladle; heat over low heat just until vapor rises. Ignite with a match, and lower ladle

of flaming brandy into cherries. When flame fades, ladle cherry mixture over individual servings of ice cream.

Makes 8 servings.

CARAMEL-WALNUT SUNDAES

Caramel Sauce:
1 cup sugar
1 cup heavy cream
1 quart vanilla ice cream

18 vanilla wafers
3/4 cup walnut halves
1/2 cup heavy cream, whipped

1. Make Caramel Sauce: Combine sugar and 1/4 cup water in small, heavy skillet.

2. Heat, stirring constantly, just until sugar dissolves. Then cook over very low heat (mixture should just barely bubble), uncovered, 30 to 40 minutes, or until a light-amber color. Do not stir. Syrup should not be dark.

3. Remove from heat. Let cool slightly—about 5 minutes. Slowly add 1 cup cream, stirring constantly until syrup is smooth. Let cool.

4. To make sundaes: Place a scoop of ice cream in each of 6 chilled sherbet glasses.

5. Cut wafers in half, and press 6 halves into each scoop of ice cream. Place walnut halves between wafers.

6. Spoon 1 or 2 tablespoons caramel sauce over each sundae.

7. Decorate each with whipped cream, and top with a walnut half. Pass remaining sauce.

Makes 6 servings.

DOUBLE-CHOCOLATE-ALMOND ICE CREAM

2 pints chocolate ice cream
1/4 cup chocolate syrup
2 tablespoons crème de cacao
   (optional)

1/2 cup toasted unblanched whole
   almonds*

1. If ice cream is very hard, place in refrigerator 30 minutes, or until slightly softened.

2. In chilled large bowl, combine ice cream, syrup, and crème de cacao.

3. With electric mixer or wooden spoon, quickly mix until combined. Mix in almonds.

4. Spoon into 1-quart mold, or return to cartons. Freeze, covered, until firm—at least 4 hours.

5. To serve: Unmold onto serving plate. Decorate with whipped cream, if you wish.

Makes 6 to 8 servings.

* To toast almonds: Place in single layer in baking pan. Bake, in 350F oven, 10 to 12 minutes, or until skins start to crack.

COFFEE SUNDAES

1/2 cup light corn syrup
1/4 cup light cream
1/2 cup sugar
4 1/2 teaspoons instant coffee
1/4 teaspoon salt

2 tablespoons butter or margarine
1/2 teaspoon vanilla extract

1 pint vanilla or coffee ice cream

1. In small saucepan, combine corn syrup, cream, sugar, coffee, and salt.

2. Cook, over medium heat, stirring constantly, until mixture is well combined.

3. Over high heat, stirring constantly, bring mixture to boiling; boil 2 minutes.

4. Remove from heat. Stir in butter and vanilla.

5. To serve: Spoon sauce, warm or at room temperature, over ice cream. Garnish with whipped cream, candy coffee beans, and walnuts, if desired.

Makes 4 servings.

COUPE ELIZABETH

1 can (1 lb, 1 oz) Bing cherries
1 tablespoon cornstarch
1/2 cup Cherry Heering

1 1/2 quarts vanilla ice cream
Whipped cream
Cinnamon

1. Drain cherries; measure 1 cup juice. In small bowl, dissolve cornstarch in ½ cup juice. Combine with rest of juice in medium saucepan.

2. Bring to boiling, stirring; reduce heat and simmer until thickened and translucent—about 5 minutes. Let stand until cool.

3. Meanwhile, in small bowl, combine cherries and Cherry Heering; let stand about 1 hour.

4. Add cherries and liquid to thickened juice; mix well.

5. Make scoops of ice cream; pour cherry sauce over ice cream in serving dishes. Top with ruffle of whipped cream (put cream through a pastry bag with a number-6 decorating tip). Sprinkle cream lightly with cinnamon. Serve at once.

Makes 6 servings.

STRAWBERRY-COOKIE-SHELL SUNDAES

1 pint fresh strawberries*
½ cup granulated sugar

Cookie Shells:
 1 egg
⅓ cup sifted** confectioners'
    sugar

* Or use 1 pkg frozen sliced
  strawberries, thawed. Omit
  sugar.

** Sift before measuring.

2 tablespoons brown sugar
¼ teaspoon vanilla extract
¼ cup sifted** all-purpose flour
    Dash salt
2 tablespoons melted butter or
    margarine
2 tablespoons chopped pecans

 1 quart vanilla ice cream
½ cup chopped pecans

1. Wash strawberries; slice. Add granulated sugar. Refrigerate.

2. Preheat oven to 300F. Grease and flour 2 cookie sheets.

3. Make Cookie Shells: In medium bowl, with electric mixer, beat egg until soft peaks form when beater is raised. Gradually stir in confectioners' sugar and brown sugar, folding until sugars dissolve. Add vanilla.

4. Stir in flour and salt, mixing well. Gradually blend in butter and 2 tablespoons pecans.

5. Spoon about 2 tablespoons batter onto prepared cookie sheet. Spread thin, to make 5-inch round. Make 2 more rounds on cookie sheet and 3 rounds on other cookie sheet.

6. Bake, one sheet at a time, 15 minutes. Remove hot cookies from sheet with broad spatula. Mold each cookie, bottom down, over outside of 6-oz custard cup, to form shell. Cool.

7. To serve: Fill shells with ice cream. Spoon strawberries over ice cream. Top with chopped nuts.

Makes 6 servings.

⬥⬥

PEARS DE MENTHE

2 quarts vanilla ice cream
1/4 cup green crème de menthe

1 can (1 lb, 14 oz) pear halves,
  very well chilled
1 can (8 oz) chocolate syrup

1. Let ice cream stand at room temperature to soften. Turn into a large bowl.

2. With rubber scraper, swirl crème de menthe into soft ice cream just enough to make streaks; do not overmix. Turn ice cream into three or four ice-cube trays; refreeze until firm—about 4 hours.

3. To serve: Drain pear halves; arrange on glass serving dish. Mound a scoop of ice cream in center of each pear. Pour syrup over ice cream.

Makes 8 servings.

⬥⬥

PINEAPPLE FLAMBÉ SUNDAES

1 large, fully ripe pineapple (5 to
  6 lb)
8 (2 inch) coconut macaroons,
  crushed

1 jar (12 oz) apricot preserves
1 teaspoon grated lemon peel
1/2 cup brandy
1 1/2 quarts vanilla ice cream

1. Preheat oven to 400F. Cut off top of washed pineapple with serrated grapefruit knife; cut around inside of shell to loosen fruit, being careful not to pierce shell. Remove fruit from the shell in large pieces.

2. Discard core; cut pineapple into 1/2-inch chunks. (Pineapple should measure 4 cups.)

3. Toss pineapple chunks with macaroons; spoon into pineapple shell.

4. In small saucepan, combine apricot preserves with lemon peel; bring to boiling, stirring. Pour this over the pineapple-macaroon mixture in shell.

5. Wrap pineapple completely in foil. Stand in shallow pan; bake about 30 minutes, or until the pineapple mixture is hot.

6. Remove pineapple to serving platter. Slowly heat brandy in small saucepan; ignite. Pour, flaming, over pineapple mixture in shell.

7. Serve ice cream with hot pineapple spooned over.

Makes 8 to 10 servings.

PINEAPPLE-PEACH FLAMBÉ SUNDAES

Make Baked Pineapple Flambé as directed above, substituting 2 cups sliced, peeled peaches for 2 cups of the pineapple chunks.

PONTCHARTRAIN ICE-CREAM PIE

10-inch baked pie shell
1 quart strawberry or favorite
   flavor ice cream
1 quart chocolate or favorite
   flavor ice cream

5 egg whites
1/2 teaspoon vanilla extract
1/2 cup sugar

Chocolate Sauce, page 344

1. Prepare and bake pie shell; cool thoroughly.

2. Let ice cream soften slightly. Spoon in alternate layers into baked pie shell. Wrap and freeze until very firm—several hours, or overnight, if possible.

3. To serve: In large bowl of electric mixer let egg whites warm to room temperature—about 1 hour. At high speed beat egg whites and vanilla extract just until soft peaks form when beater is slowly raised.

4. Add sugar, 2 tablespoons at a time, beating well after each addition. Continue beating until meringue is shiny and stiff peaks form.

5. Spread meringue over pie, covering ice cream and edge of crust completely. Make swirls on top.

6. Broil, 5 to 6 inches from heat, until meringue is lightly browned—about 3 minutes.

7. Serve at once. Pass Chocolate Sauce.

Makes 8 servings.

Note: If ice-cream pie is frozen very hard, take from freezer about 20 to 30 minutes before putting meringue on and baking.

TRADER VIC'S ICE CREAM

1/4 cup chopped preserved kumquats	6 large scoops vanilla ice cream —about 1 quart
1/4 cup kumquat syrup	1/2 cup flaked coconut
1/2 cup brandy	

1. Mix chopped kumquats and syrup in shallow pan. Pour in brandy. Heat until bubbles appear around edge of pan; remove from heat and ignite with a match.

2. Spoon over ice cream in individual dishes; sprinkle generously with coconut. Serve at once.

Makes 6 servings.

Ice-Cream Fantasies

�

BAR-LE-DUC ICE-CREAM MOLDS

4 pints soft vanilla ice cream   4 jars (3-oz size) Bar-le-Duc

1. Pack 12 (4-oz) molds with ice cream.
2. Freeze until firm—about 2 hours.
3. Carefully scoop out about 1 tablespoon ice cream from center of each mold. Fill hollow with 1 tablespoon Bar-le-Duc. Replace scooped-out ice cream. Freeze until firm.
4. Remove 6 molds from freezer. To unmold: Dip each in hot water for 5 seconds; invert onto sheet of heavy-duty foil; unmold. Return to freezer until ready to serve. Repeat with remaining molds.
5. To serve: Transfer ice cream to individual plates. Top with remaining Bar-le-Duc. Serve at once.

Makes 12 servings.

✦

HOLIDAY ICE-CREAM BOMBE

2 pints pistachio or vanilla   ½ cup glacé cherries, chopped
  ice cream   1 cup crushed Italian macaroons
2 pints strawberry ice cream   2 tablespoons Cointreau or
1 pint chocolate ice cream   orange juice
1 cup heavy cream

1. Line a 2½-quart mixing bowl with plastic wrap. Place in freezer to chill well.
2. Place ice creams in refrigerator to soften slightly.
3. Line the bowl with the pistachio ice cream, pressing with spoon to form an inner shell in bowl. Freeze about ½ hour.
4. Spoon strawberry ice cream over pistachio forming an even layer. Freeze again.

5. Make a final layer of chocolate ice cream, leaving a hollow in center. Freeze again.

6. Beat cream until stiff; fold in cherries, macaroon crumbs and Cointreau. Freeze cream mixture about ½ hour.

7. Fill hollow in bombe with partially frozen cream filling. Cover top with foil; freeze until firm—6 hours or overnight.

8. To serve: Loosen around edge with spatula. Lift out, holding onto plastic film. Turn rounded side up on tray; remove film. Let stand 10 minutes to soften slightly. Smooth top with spatula. Serve with a sauce if desired.

Makes 10 to 12 servings.

ICE-CREAM MERINGUE TORTE

Meringue Layers:
 8 egg whites (1 cup)
 1 teaspoon cream of tartar
 ¼ teaspoon salt
1½ cups sugar

1½ quarts chocolate ice cream

Glaze:
 1 cup semisweet chocolate

1 tablespoon butter or regular margarine
2 tablespoons light corn syrup
2 tablespoons milk
20 whole hazelnuts or unblanched almonds
¼ cup finely chopped hazelnuts or unblanched almonds

1. Make meringue layers: In large bowl of electric mixer, let egg whites warm to room temperature—1 hour. Preheat oven to 250F.

2. Line two large cookie sheets with brown paper. Using 8-inch round cake pan as guide, draw four circles on paper. Grease paper well.

3. At high speed, beat egg whites with cream of tartar and salt just until soft peaks form when beater is slowly raised.

4. Gradually beat in sugar, 2 tablespoons at a time, beating well after each addition. Continue beating until egg whites are shiny and form stiff peaks when beater is slowly raised—about 5 minutes.

5. Spread one fourth of meringue evenly over each circle on brown paper. Bake 1 hour, or until crisp. Turn off oven; cool in oven 2 hours or overnight.

6. Several hours before serving, remove ice cream from freezer to soften slightly—10 minutes.

7. To assemble torte: Place one meringue layer on serving plate.

Spread with one pint softened ice cream. Repeat with remaining meringue layers and ice cream, ending with meringue. Freeze about 2 hours.

8. Make glaze: In top of double boiler, over hot, not boiling, water, melt chocolate pieces and butter. Remove from heat. Stir in corn syrup and milk, mixing until smooth. Dip the whole nuts into glaze with fork; let glaze harden—about 10 minutes.

9. Pour remaining glaze over top layer of torte, letting the glaze drip down side. Sprinkle chopped nuts over top. Arrange chocolate-coated nuts around the edge of top. Return to freezer until serving time—30 minutes.

Makes 12 servings.

Note: If desired, brush each meringue layer with 1 tablespoon golden rum before spreading with ice cream. May be made several days ahead and stored, well wrapped, in freezer.

SEASHELLS AND STARS

1. Line baking shells or shell-shape molds or small star-shape molds with foil. Pack ice cream or sherbet of desired flavor into mold, pressing firmly. Freeze until very firm—several hours or overnight.

2. To unmold: Grasp foil; pull out ice cream; invert on serving plate; peel off foil. Return to freezer if not serving at once.

3. For starfish: After unmolding star, make ridges on points with a knife or spatula.

4. If storing in freezer for more than a day or two, freezer-wrap in foil.

CHOCOLATE-GLAZED STRAWBERRY ICE-CREAM MOLD

2 quarts strawberry, cherry-
  vanilla, or cherry-Burgundy
  ice cream, slightly softened

Chocolate Glaze:
  4 squares semisweet chocolate
  ¼ cup butter or margarine
  1 teaspoon vanilla extract

1. Chill a 2-quart decorative mold.

2. Using back of spoon or rubber scraper, pack ice cream into mold.

3. Freeze, covered with foil, until firm—about 5 hours or overnight.

4. To unmold: Loosen edge with sharp knife. Invert mold on round of foil or serving platter. Place hot, damp cloth around mold, to melt ice cream slightly; then shake out ice cream.

5. Store in freezer until ready to glaze. (Freezer-wrap if stored longer than several hours.)

6. About an hour before serving, make Chocolate Glaze: In small saucepan, over low heat, heat chocolate only until partially melted. Remove from heat.

7. Add butter; stir until chocolate is completely melted and mixture is smooth. Add vanilla, mixing well.

8. Let stand at room temperature until cooled—about 15 minutes. Glaze should be of pouring consistency but not too warm.

9. Spoon glaze over top of mold, letting it run unevenly down side. Return to freezer until serving time.

Makes 8 to 10 servings.

PISTACHIO ICE-CREAM SURPRISE

4 pints pistachio ice cream
  Chocolate Sauce, page 344
½ cup coarsely chopped
  pistachios

1 cup heavy cream
¼ cup confectioners' sugar
½ teaspoon vanilla extract

1. Line side and bottom of 9-inch tube pan with foil. Press 3 pints ice cream firmly and evenly into pan. Then, with back of spoon, make a 1-inch-deep and 1-inch-wide trench in ice cream ½ inch from outside edge. Freeze until firm—about 2 hours.

2. Meanwhile, make Chocolate Sauce. Let cool to room temperature. Spoon ½ cup sauce into trench in firm ice cream; return to freezer for 1 hour. Refrigerate remaining sauce.

3. Spoon remaining ice cream evenly over sauce in trench, covering completely. Freeze, covered, until very firm—at least overnight.

4. To assemble: With spatula, loosen around edge of pan and center tube. Invert onto serving platter; peel off foil. Press pistachio nuts around side. Place in freezer.

5. Whip cream with confectioners' sugar and vanilla. Place in

pastry bag with number-6 star tip; decorate top of ice-cream ring. Freeze until firm. If keeping more than one day, wrap with plastic film.

6. To serve: Cut ring into wedges. Pass remaining chocolate sauce, reheated in double boiler.

Makes 10 to 12 servings.

ICE-CREAM-SUNDAE PIE

3 pints vanilla ice cream	⅓ cup soft butter or margarine
3 tablespoons green crème de	Chocolate Sauce, page 344
menthe*	1 cup heavy cream, whipped
2 cups chocolate-wafer crumbs	¼ cup chopped walnuts

1. Let ice cream soften slightly.

2. Turn ice cream into a large bowl. Pour crème de menthe over it, and, with spoon, swirl into ice cream just enough to give a marbled effect—do not overmix. Return ice cream to container; freeze until firm.

3. Meanwhile, combine wafer crumbs with butter; mix with fork until thoroughly combined.

4. Press crumb mixture evenly on bottom and side of a 9-inch pie plate. Refrigerate until well chilled—about 1 hour.

5. Make Fudge Sauce.

6. Fill cookie shell with scoops of ice cream, mounding in center.

7. Pour ½ cup fudge sauce over the top. Keep the pie in the freezer until serving.

8. Just before serving, garnish with mounds of whipped cream; sprinkle with nuts. Pass rest of fudge sauce, if desired.

Makes 8 servings.

* Or use ¼ pound peppermint-stick candy, crushed.

ENGLISH-TOFFEE GLACÉ PIE

Pastry Shell:
½ *pkg (11-oz size) piecrust mix*
¼ *cup brown sugar, packed*
¾ *cup chopped walnuts*
 1 *square unsweetened chocolate,
    grated*
 1 *teaspoon vanilla extract*

Filling:
 1 *quart chocolate or chocolate-
    fudge ice cream*

 1 *quart English-toffee, Jamoca-
    almond-fudge or coffee
    ice cream*

Coffee Whipped Cream:
 1 *cup heavy cream*
 2 *teaspoons instant coffee*
 2 *tablespoons confectioners'
    sugar*

Chocolate Curls, page 346

1. Make pastry shell: Preheat oven to 375F. In medium bowl, combine piecrust mix, brown sugar, nuts and grated chocolate; mix well with fork. Add 2 tablespoons water and the vanilla; blend well. With moistened hands, press mixture firmly to bottom and side of a well-buttered 9-inch pie plate. Bake 20 minutes. Cool. Freeze at least 1 hour before filling.

2. To fill shell: Let ice cream stand in refrigerator to soften slightly. Quickly fill bottom of pie shell with chocolate ice cream; then top with English-toffee ice cream, spreading evenly. (Do not let ice cream melt.) Freeze at least 2 hours.

3. Make the coffee whipped cream: With rotary beater, whip cream with instant coffee and confectioners' sugar just until stiff. Use to cover top of pie, making swirls, or press through a pastry bag with a number-6 rosette tip.

4. Decorate with chocolate curls.

5. Store in freezer until serving. To serve, let pie stand at room temperature 5 to 10 minutes for easier cutting.

Makes 8 to 10 servings.

❈

MINCEMEAT GLACÉ

1 cup prepared mincemeat   1 quart soft vanilla ice cream
¼ cup slivered toasted almonds

1. Drain mincemeat well; mix with almonds.

2. With spatula or back of large spoon, press ¼ ice cream into bottom of 5-cup mold. Then press ¾ of mincemeat mixture irregularly to side of mold. Pack in rest of ice cream, filling in any crevices with remaining mincemeat mixture.

3. Place mold in freezer; freeze overnight, or until ice cream is firm.

4. To unmold, loosen edge with sharp knife. Invert mold on round of aluminum foil or serving platter. Place hot, damp cloth around mold, to melt ice cream slightly; then shake out ice cream. Store in freezer until serving time. (Freezer-wrap if to be stored longer than several hours.)

Makes 8 servings.

Ice Cream and Cake Desserts

❖

STRAWBERRY ICE-CREAM-CAKE ROLL

Cake:
4 eggs
¾ cup sifted* cake flour
1 teaspoon baking powder
¼ teaspoon salt
¾ cup granulated sugar

* Sift flour before measuring.

1 teaspoon vanilla extract
Confectioners' sugar

1½ pints strawberry ice cream
½ pint orange or raspberry
   sherbet
2 cups heavy cream
5 or 6 large fresh strawberries
   with hulls in

    1. Make cake: In large bowl of electric mixer, let eggs warm to room temperature—about 1 hour.

    2. Preheat oven to 400F. Lightly grease bottom of 15½-by-10½-by-1-inch jelly-roll pan; line with waxed paper.

    3. Sift flour, baking powder and salt.

    4. At high speed, beat eggs until thick and lemon-colored. Gradually beat in granulated sugar, 2 tablespoons at a time; continue beating until they are thick and light—about 5 minutes.

    5. At low speed, blend in sifted ingredients and vanilla until combined.

    6. Turn into prepared pan; spread evenly. Bake 10 to 13 minutes, or until surface springs back when gently pressed with fingertip.

    7. Meanwhile, sift confectioners' sugar onto a clean towel in a 15-by-10-inch rectangle.

    8. With sharp knife, loosen sides of cake from pan. Turn out cake onto sugar; gently peel off waxed paper. Trim crisp edges from cake.

    9. Starting with short edge, roll cake in towel; place seam side down on wire rack until cool.

    10. Refrigerate 1 hour to chill well. Then gently unroll cake; remove towel. Let strawberry ice cream and the sherbet soften slightly in refrigerator.

11. Spread cake evenly with ice cream; then spread ice cream with sherbet; roll up cake. Place seam side down on platter; cover loosely with foil. Freeze until firm—at least 2 hours.

12. To serve: Arrange ice-cream-cake roll on serving platter. With rotary beater, whip cream until stiff. Use half of cream to frost cake roll all over, smoothing to make it even. Put remaining whipped cream in pastry bag with a number-6 rosette tip; decorate. Garnish with strawberries. Nice served with strawberry sauce.

Makes 8 to 10 servings.

NESSELRODE ICE-CREAM CAKE

3 pkg (4-oz size) ladyfingers (about 36)
½ cup light rum
½ cup apricot preserves
½ pint pistachio ice cream
¼ cup chopped candied fruit
8 candied red cherries, halved

½ pint strawberry ice cream
½ pint chocolate ice cream
1 cup heavy cream, well chilled
¼ cup confectioners' sugar
1 teaspoon vanilla extract
8 candied red cherries

1. Lightly grease with butter or margarine a round, 1½-quart baking dish, about 6½ inches in diameter and 4 inches deep.

2. Line bottom and side with split ladyfingers, cut sides inside. Brush ladyfingers lightly with some of rum.

3. Combine 1 tablespoon rum with apricot preserves; mix well; spread over ladyfingers on bottom layer.

4. Cover with more split ladyfingers; brush with rum. Then make a layer of pistachio ice cream; cover with split ladyfingers; sprinkle with rum.

5. Spoon candied fruit and halved cherries over top; sprinkle with a little rum. Make a layer of strawberry ice cream; cover with split ladyfingers; sprinkle with rum.

6. Make a layer of chocolate ice cream; cover with a last layer of split ladyfingers. Cover with plastic film.

7. Freeze in freezer 3 hours or longer.

8. At serving time, with rotary beater, whip cream just until stiff. Gradually beat in confectioners' sugar; add vanilla; beat until stiff enough to hold its shape.

9. To unmold cake: Run a spatula around edge of dish to loosen. Invert on serving platter. Put a hot damp cloth over dish; gently shake out dish. Repeat if necessary.

10. Press whipped cream through pastry bag with decorative tip, making swirls on top and side. Decorate top with cherries. Return to freezer until serving.

Makes 12 servings.

❇

NEAPOLITAN ICE-CREAM CAKE

2 pkg (3-oz size) lady fingers (about 24), unsplit
½ cup light rum
½ pint pistachio ice cream, slightly softened

1 pint strawberry ice cream, slightly softened
Chocolate syrup or Deluxe Chocolate Sauce (page 345)

1. Sprinkle ladyfingers lightly with the rum. Line a mold about 6 inches in diameter and 5 inches deep with some of the ladyfingers.

2. Fill bottom with pistachio ice cream; cover with a layer of ladyfingers; add strawberry ice cream; top with remaining ladyfingers.

3. Place in freezer 30 minutes or until serving.

4. To serve: Unmold cake on platter; pass syrup.

Makes 6 to 8 servings.

❇

STRAWBERRY ICE-CREAM TORTE

8-inch chocolate- or yellow-cake layer (see Note)
1 quart strawberry ice cream

2 tablespoons strawberry preserves
Confectioners' sugar
Chocolate syrup

1. Split cake layer in half crosswise.

2. Line an 8-inch layer-cake pan with plastic film. Pack with ice cream; freeze until very firm.

3. Shortly before serving, place a cake layer, split side up, on cake plate. Unmold ice-cream layer on top, removing plastic film. Spread with preserves. Top with remaining cake layer.

4. Place paper doily with cutout pattern on top. Sift confectioners' sugar over top; carefully remove doily. Serve torte with chocolate syrup.

Makes 12 servings.

Note: Made from packaged mix or favorite recipe. Freeze other layer.

DESSERT SAUCES

There is hardly a dessert that isn't better for a light, delectable sauce to serve over it.

Think of a chilled custard sauce to pour over fresh strawberries, or a cinnamony ice-cream sauce to melt over a hot apple dumpling; and then there's Sabayon sauce to serve with poached pears, even better with a hot chocolate soufflé. Here, we give you our favorite recipes—lots of them.

APRICOT SAUCE

1 jar (12 oz) apricot preserves   ½ tablespoon kirsch
2 tablespoons lemon juice

Melt preserves in small saucepan with lemon juice; strain. Add kirsch.

Makes 1 cup.

LEMON SAUCE

½ cup butter or margarine   ½ cup lemon juice
1 cup sugar   1 teaspoon grated lemon peel
3 eggs

1. Melt butter in top of double boiler, over hot, not boiling, water. Stir in sugar.

2. In medium bowl, with rotary beater, beat eggs with lemon juice until foamy. Add lemon peel. Stir into butter-sugar mixture.

3. Cook, stirring, until mixture thickens slightly and forms a coating on back of spoon.

4. Serve warm, over thin slices of cake.

Makes about 2 cups.

Note: Sauce may be stored in the refrigerator for several days, and then served cold or reheated slightly in the top of a double boiler, over hot water.

PINEAPPLE SAUCE

½ cup sugar   ¼ teaspoon grated lemon peel
1 tablespoon cornstarch   1 can (8¾ oz) crushed pineapple
1 can (6 oz) pineapple juice

1. In small saucepan, combine sugar and cornstarch; mix well.

2. Gradually add pineapple juice, stirring until smooth. Add lemon peel and crushed pineapple.

3. Over medium heat, bring to boiling, stirring, and boil until mixture is thickened and translucent.

4. Refrigerate until cold.

Makes about 1½ cups.

STRAWBERRY SAUCE

1 pkg (10 oz) frozen sliced
    strawberries, thawed
¼ cup sugar

1 tablespoon cornstarch
2 tablespoons strawberry
    preserves

1. Drain strawberries, reserving syrup. Add water to syrup to measure 1 cup.

2. In small saucepan, combine sugar and cornstarch. Gradually add strawberry syrup, stirring until smooth.

3. Over low heat, slowly bring to boiling, stirring, until mixture is thickened and translucent.

4. Remove from heat. Stir in strawberries and strawberry preserves.

5. Stir until preserves are melted. Refrigerate until cold.

Makes 1⅓ cups.

DELUXE STRAWBERRY SAUCE

2 pkg (10-oz size) frozen
    strawberries, thawed

1 tablespoon cornstarch
½ cup currant jelly

1. Drain strawberries, reserving liquid. Add enough water to liquid to make 2 cups.

2. In small saucepan, blend liquid with cornstarch. Bring to boiling over medium heat, stirring constantly; boil 5 minutes. Stir in jelly until melted. Remove from heat. Add strawberries. Refrigerate, covered, until cold.

Makes about 3 cups.

23

RASPBERRY SAUCE

2 pkg (10-oz size) frozen   2 tablespoons cornstarch
    raspberries, thawed   ½ cup currant jelly

1. Drain raspberries, reserving liquid. Add enough water to liquid to make 2 cups.

2. In small saucepan, blend liquid with cornstarch. Bring to boiling over medium heat, stirring constantly; boil 5 minutes. Stir in jelly until melted. Remove from heat; add raspberries. Refrigerate, covered, until cold.

Makes 2 cups.

23

CARDINAL SAUCE

1 pkg (10 oz) frozen strawberries,   2 teaspoons cornstarch
    thawed   1 teaspoon lemon juice
1 pkg (10 oz) frozen raspberries,   ½ cup red-currant jelly
    thawed

1. Turn strawberries and raspberries into a sieve held over a medium saucepan. Let drain. Set berries aside.

2. Combine cornstarch and lemon juice with berry liquid in saucepan.

3. Bring to boiling, stirring; boil gently 1 minute. Add currant jelly; stir until melted.

4. Remove jelly mixture from heat. Stir in berries. Refrigerate, covered, until well chilled—at least 2 hours.

Makes about 2¾ cups.

23

BUTTERSCOTCH SAUCE

⅓ cup butter or margarine   2 tablespoons light corn syrup
1 cup light-brown sugar, firmly   ⅓ cup heavy cream
    packed

Melt butter in saucepan over low heat. Stir in brown sugar, corn syrup, and cream; cook to boiling point. Then remove from heat, and cool slightly. Serve warm or cold.

Makes 1¼ cups.

❄

TOASTED-ALMOND CARAMEL SAUCE

½ cup whole blanched almonds
1 cup sugar

2 tablespoons corn syrup
1 cup heavy cream

1. Preheat oven to 325F. Place the almonds in 8-by-8-by-2-inch baking pan.
2. Bake until lightly browned—about 20 minutes. Let cool.
3. Combine sugar, corn syrup, and ¼ cup water in small, heavy skillet.
4. Heat, stirring constantly, just until sugar dissolves. Then cook, over very low heat, 45 minutes, or until a light-amber color. Syrup should not be dark.
5. Remove from heat. Let cool slightly—about 5 minutes. Slowly add cream, stirring constantly until syrup is smooth. Let cool.
6. Stir in nuts. Serve on ice cream.

Makes 1⅓ cups.

❄

CHOCOLATE SAUCE

½ cup sugar
¼ cup unsweetened cocoa
½ cup light cream
⅓ cup light corn syrup
¼ cup butter or margarine

2 squares unsweetened
    chocolate
Dash salt
1½ teaspoons vanilla extract

1. In small saucepan, combine sugar and cocoa; mix well. Add cream, corn syrup, butter, chocolate, and salt.
2. Cook over medium heat, stirring constantly, until sauce is smooth and comes to boiling. Remove from heat; stir in vanilla.

Makes 1½ cups.

DELUXE CHOCOLATE SAUCE

1/4 cup sugar
1/3 cup light cream
1 pkg (4 oz) sweet cooking
chocolate

1 square (1 oz) unsweetened
chocolate

1. In top of double boiler, combine sugar and 2 tablespoons cream; cook, over boiling water, until sugar is dissolved.

2. Cut up both kinds of chocolate. Remove double boiler from heat, but leave top over bottom. Add chocolate to cream mixture, stirring until melted.

3. With spoon, beat in remaining cream. Serve warm.

Makes 6 servings (about 1 cup).

QUICK CHOCOLATE SAUCE

1 pkg (6 oz) semisweet chocolate
pieces

2/3 cup evaporated milk, undiluted

1. Combine chocolate pieces and milk in medium saucepan. Stir constantly, over low heat, just until chocolate is melted.

2. Serve warm, over ice cream, pudding or cake.

Makes about 1 cup.

CHOCOLATE SAUCE BRAZILIAN
(A dark chocolate sauce for ice cream)

5 squares (1-oz size) semisweet
chocolate
1 square (1 oz) unsweetened
chocolate
1 tablespoon butter or margarine
1/2 cup sugar

1/3 cup light corn syrup
1/4 cup light cream
1 tablespoon instant-coffee
powder
1/4 cup dark rum

1. In top of double boiler, over hot water, melt chocolate, butter and sugar. Stir in corn syrup and cream. Beat until smooth. Add instant coffee; stir until dissolved.

2. In small, heavy saucepan, slowly heat rum just until vapor

rises. Ignite with match. Pour into chocolate mixture, stirring with wire whisk until smooth. Serve hot.

Makes 1½ cups.

Note: Refrigerate leftover sauce; heat over hot water before serving.

CHOCOLATE CURLS

Let a 1-oz square semisweet or unsweetened chocolate stand in paper wrapper in warm place about 15 minutes, just to soften slightly. For large curls, unwrap chocolate, and carefully draw vegetable parer across broad, flat surface of square. For smaller curls, draw paper across side of square. Lift curls with a wooden pick, to avoid breaking.

BRANDIED-DATE-AND-WALNUT SAUCE

2 cups light-brown sugar, packed   1 cup walnut halves
¼ cup brandy   ¼ cup brandy
1 pkg (8 oz) pitted dates

1. In medium saucepan, combine brown sugar with 1 cup water. Cook, stirring occasionally, over medium heat 20 minutes.

2. Add ¼ cup brandy, the dates, and walnut halves. Let cool.

3. To store: Turn into glass jar or plastic refrigerator container. Store, tightly covered, in refrigerator several weeks. Sauce improves in flavor as it mellows.

4. To serve: Heat sauce over low heat. Turn into serving dish. Heat ¼ cup brandy in small saucepan just until vapor starts to rise; ignite. At the table, pour flaming brandy over sauce. While sauce is still flaming, serve over ice cream.

Makes 3 cups.

MARSHMALLOW SAUCE

1 cup prepared creamy   ½ teaspoon vanilla extract
   marshmallow topping

In small bowl, with fork, beat marshmallow topping, 2½ teaspoons water, and the vanilla until smooth.

Makes 1 cup.

❇

RUM SAUCE

⅓ cup granulated sugar
⅓ cup light-brown sugar, firmly
    packed

1 lemon wedge
1 orange wedge
¼ cup dark rum

1. In small saucepan, combine sugars with 1 cup water; cook, stirring, over low heat until sugars are dissolved.

2. Bring to boiling. Add lemon and orange wedges; reduce heat, and simmer, uncovered, 30 minutes.

3. Discard lemon and orange wedges. Add rum just before serving. Serve warm over mincemeat pie or ice cream.

Makes ¾ cup.

❇

BRANDY SAUCE

4 egg yolks
½ cup sugar

⅓ cup brandy
½ cup heavy cream

1. In top of double boiler, beat egg yolks with sugar until very thick and light. Stir in brandy; cook, stirring, over hot, not boiling, water until thickened.

2. Refrigerate until well chilled.

3. Just before serving, pour cream into small bowl; beat until stiff. Fold into brandy mixture until well combined. Nice over steamed pudding.

Makes 1½ cups.

❇

FLUFFY BRANDY SAUCE

1 egg white
    Dash salt
1 cup sifted* confectioners'
    sugar

1 egg yolk
½ cup heavy cream, whipped
3 tablespoons brandy

* Sift before measuring.

1. In small bowl of electric mixer, at high speed, beat egg white with salt just until foamy.

2. Add ½ cup sugar, a few tablespoons at a time, beating well

after each addition. Continue beating just until egg white forms soft peaks when beater is raised.

3. Beat egg yolk in small bowl (with same beater) until thick and lemon-colored. Gradually add remaining sugar, beating until very thick and light.

4. At low speed, beat into egg-white mixture along with whipped cream and brandy, beating only until combined.

Note: Sauce may be made several hours ahead of time and refrigerated. Before serving, beat with fork, to fluff.

Makes 1½ cups.

CUSTARD SAUCE

1½ cups milk
3 egg yolks
¼ cup sugar

Dash salt
½ teaspoon vanilla extract

1. Heat milk in top of double boiler over direct heat until tiny bubbles appear around edge of pan.

2. Beat yolks, sugar and salt, to mix well.

3. Very slowly pour hot milk into egg mixture, beating constantly.

4. Return mixture to double-boiler top; place over hot, not boiling, water (water in lower part of double boiler should not touch upper part).

5. Cook, stirring constantly, until thin coating forms on metal spoon—8 to 10 minutes.

6. Immediately pour custard into a bowl; place sheet of waxed paper directly on surface.

7. Set bowl in cold water, to cool. Stir in vanilla. Refrigerate until very cold—several hours or overnight.

Makes 1½ cups.

✂

ENGLISH CUSTARD SAUCE

1/3 cup sugar
1 tablespoon cornstarch
2 cups milk
2 tablespoons butter or
    margarine

6 egg yolks
1 1/2 teaspoons vanilla extract
1/2 cup heavy cream

1. In medium saucepan, combine sugar and cornstarch. Gradually add milk; stir until smooth. Then add the butter.

2. Cook over medium heat, stirring constantly, until mixture is thickened and comes to boil. Boil 1 minute. Remove from heat.

3. In medium bowl, slightly beat egg yolks. Gradually add a little hot mixture, beating well.

4. Stir into rest of hot mixture; cook over medium heat, stirring constantly, just until mixture boils. Remove from heat; stir in vanilla.

5. Strain custard immediately into bowl. Refrigerate, covered, until cool. Stir in heavy cream. Return to refrigerator until well chilled.

Makes about 2 1/2 cups.

✂

SABAYON SAUCE

6 egg yolks
1/4 cup sugar

1/3 cup Grand Marnier
1/2 cup heavy cream, whipped

1. In top of double boiler, with electric mixer at medium speed, beat egg yolks until thick. Gradually beat in sugar; beat until mixture is light and soft peaks form when beater is slowly raised.

2. Place double-boiler top over simmering water (water in bottom should not touch base of top). Slowly beat in Grand Marnier; continue beating until mixture is fluffy and mounds—takes about 5 minutes.

3. Remove double-boiler top from hot water; set in ice water. Beat the custard mixture until cool. Gently fold in whipped cream.

4. Refrigerate sauce, covered, until serving. Stir well before serving.

Makes about 2 cups.

✣

IRISH-WHISKY SAUCE

¼ cup soft butter or regular
    margarine
2 cups light-brown sugar, firmly
    packed

1 egg
1 cup light cream
   Dash nutmeg
¼ cup Irish whisky

1. In top of double boiler, with electric mixer at medium speed, beat butter with sugar until light and creamy.
2. Beat in egg, cream, and nutmeg; beat until mixture is fluffy.
3. Cook, stirring occasionally, over hot, not boiling, water until mixture is thickened.
4. Remove from heat. Gradually stir in whisky.
5. Serve warm or cold, with pudding.
Makes 2½ cups.

✣

HOT VANILLA SAUCE

½ cup butter or margarine
1 cup sugar

½ cup light cream
1 teaspoon vanilla extract

1. Melt butter in medium saucepan.
2. Remove from heat. Add remaining ingredients, mixing well. Simmer, stirring, over low heat, about 5 minutes, or until sugar is dissolved and sauce is heated.
3. Serve hot, over steamed pudding.
Makes about 1½ cups.

✣

CHANTILLY CREAM

1 cup heavy cream

2 tablespoons confectioners' sugar

1. In small bowl, mix cream and sugar. Refrigerate till well chilled.
2. Beat just until stiff with rotary beater. Refrigerate until serving.
Makes 2 cups.

ꔪ

BRANDY HARD SAUCE

¼ cup soft butter or margarine   2 tablespoons brandy, light rum
1½ cups sifted* confectioners'   or sherry
    sugar

* Sift before measuring.

    1. In medium bowl, with portable electric mixer, beat butter until it is light.
    2. Add sugar gradually, beating until sauce is smooth and fluffy. Beat in rum.
    3. Refrigerate, covered, until ready to use.
    4. Let stand at room temperature, to soften slightly, before serving.
    Makes about 1 cup.

ꔪ

FRENCH HARD SAUCE

½ cup soft butter   1 egg yolk
1½ cups sifted* confectioners'   2 tablespoons cognac
    sugar

* Sift before measuring.

    Beat butter until fluffy. Gradually blend in sugar. Beat in egg yolk and cognac until light.
    Makes 1⅓ cups.

ꔪ

VANILLA HARD SAUCE

⅓ cup soft butter or margarine   1 cup unsifted confectioners'
1 teaspoon vanilla extract   sugar

    1. In small bowl of electric mixer, at high speed, cream butter until light.
    2. Add vanilla and sugar; beat until fluffy and smooth.
    Makes about ¾ cup.

PUDDING SAUCE

1 pkg (3 oz) cream cheese,
   softened
1 egg
1 cup confectioners' sugar
2 tablespoons butter or margarine,
   softened

1 teaspoon lemon juice
   Pinch salt
1 cup heavy cream, whipped
   About 2 tablespoons golden rum,
     or ½ to 1 tablespoon rum
     extract

1. Day before: In medium bowl, with spoon, beat cheese until light. Add egg, sugar, butter, lemon juice and salt; beat well.

2. Fold in whipped cream and rum just until combined.

3. Refrigerate, covered, overnight.

Makes 3 cups.

CINNAMON ICE-CREAM SAUCE

1 teaspoon cinnamon
1 tablespoon sugar

1½ pints soft vanilla ice cream

Combine cinnamon and sugar. Stir into ice cream until well blended and smooth. Serve immediately.

Makes 2 cups.

STERLING SAUCE

½ cup soft butter or margarine
⅔ cup light-brown sugar, firmly
   packed

1 tablespoon heavy cream
2 tablespoons dry sherry

1. In medium bowl, with portable electric mixer, beat butter with sugar until light and fluffy.

2. Gradually beat in cream and sherry.

3. Serve with thin slices of fruit cake or over steamed pudding.

Makes about 1 cup.

DESSERT CRÊPES AND BLINTZES

Crêpes, as you know, are very thin, delicate pancakes. We serve them for dessert with wonderful fillings and flame them with divine sauces. A plus for any hostess: Make the crêpes several hours ahead, then finish them off just in time for serving.

CREPÊS SUZETTE

Crêpes:
1 cup unsifted all-purpose flour
¼ cup butter or margarine,
    melted and cooled, or ¼ cup
    salad oil
2 eggs
2 egg yolks
1½ cups milk

Orange Butter:
¾ cup sweet butter
½ cup sugar
⅓ cup Grand Marnier
¼ cup grated orange peel

Orange Sauce:
½ cup sweet butter
¾ cup sugar
2 tablespoons shredded
    orange peel
⅔ cup orange juice
2 oranges, peeled and sectioned
½ cup Grand Marnier

    Butter or margarine
3 tablespoons Grand Marnier

   1. Make Crêpes: In medium bowl, combine flour, melted butter, eggs, egg yolks, and ½ cup milk; beat with rotary beater until smooth. Beat in the remaining milk until mixture is well blended.

   2. Refrigerate, covered, 1 hour or more.

   3. Meanwhile, make Orange Butter: In small bowl, with electric mixer, cream ¾ cup sweet butter with ½ cup sugar until light and fluffy. Add ⅓ cup Grand Marnier and ¼ cup orange peel; beat until well blended. Set aside.

   4. Make Orange Sauce: In large skillet, melt sweet butter. Stir in sugar, orange peel, and orange juice; cook over low heat, stirring occasionally, until peel is translucent—about 20 minutes. Add orange sections and ½ cup Grand Marnier. Keep warm.

   5. To cook crêpes: Slowly heat an 8-inch skillet until a drop of water sizzles and rolls off. For each crêpe, brush skillet lightly with butter. Pour in about 2 tablespoons batter, rotating pan quickly, to spread batter completely over bottom of skillet.

   6. Cook until lightly browned; then turn, and brown other side. Turn out onto wire rack.

   7. Spread each crêpe with Orange Butter, dividing evenly. Fold each in half, then in half again. When all are folded, place in Orange Sauce in chafing dish or skillet; cook over low heat until heated through.

   8. To serve: Gently heat 3 tablespoons Grand Marnier in small

saucepan just until vapor rises. Ignite with match, and pour over crêpes. Serve flaming.

Makes 6 to 8 servings.

23

CRÊPES SOUFFLÉS

Crêpes:
2 eggs
1 cup sifted* all-purpose flour
1 cup milk
1 tablespoon vanilla extract
1 teaspoon soft butter or
   margarine

Sauce:
3 egg yolks
1/2 cup granulated sugar
1/2 cup milk

1/4 cup light cream
1/4 teaspoon mace
1/4 cup golden rum

Soufflé Filling:
3 egg whites
1 cup confectioners' sugar
1/2 teaspoon grated orange peel
1/4 teaspoon vanilla extract
1/8 teaspoon almond extract
1/8 teaspoon yellow food color
   (optional)

* Sift before measuring.

1. Make Crêpes: In medium bowl, beat 2 eggs well. Add flour, 1 cup milk, 1 tablespoon vanilla, and the butter. Stir until smooth. Let stand at least 1/2 hour. (Best to refrigerate several hours, if possible.)

2. For each crêpe, lightly grease hot 7-inch skillet. Pour in about 2 tablespoons batter, rotating pan quickly to spread batter completely over bottom of pan.

3. Cook over medium heat until lightly brown on each side— about 2 minutes per side. Place crêpes on a plate as they are removed from skillet.

4. Make Sauce: Place egg yolks in top of double boiler; gradually stir in granulated sugar, milk, cream, and mace. Cook over simmering water, stirring constantly, until thickened—about 10 minutes. Remove from water; stir in rum. Keep warm.

5. Make Soufflé Filling: Beat egg whites in small bowl, with electric mixer at low speed, 3 minutes. Gradually beat in confectioners' sugar; continue beating about 10 minutes, until stiff peaks form when beater is slowly raised.

6. Add orange peel, extracts, and yellow food color; beat until well blended.

7. Preheat oven to 450F.

8. Spoon about 2 rounded tablespoons filling on center of each crêpe; fold in half, keeping filling inside. Place in shallow pan.

9. Bake, uncovered, 5 minutes, or until very hot and puffed. Spoon a little sauce over crêpes. Pass remaining sauce.

Makes 12 crêpes; 6 servings.

❧

STRAWBERRY DESSERT CRÊPES

Crêpes:
3 eggs
1 cup unsifted all-purpose flour
⅛ teaspoon salt
1 cup milk
2 tablespoons butter or
    margarine, melted

Strawberry Filling:
3 pints fresh strawberries,
    washed, hulled, sliced and
    tossed with ½ cup light-
    brown sugar, packed
2 cups sour cream or
    whipped cream
    Confectioners' sugar
    Whole strawberries

1. Make crêpes: In medium bowl, beat eggs well with fork until they are frothy.

2. Add flour and salt, beating until smooth. Gradually beat in milk and ¼ cup water; continue beating until smooth. Refrigerate, covered, until ready to use—at least 30 minutes.

3. To cook crêpes: Slowly heat an 8-inch skillet with sloping sides, or a crêpe pan, until a drop of water sizzles and rolls off.

4. For each crêpe, brush pan lightly with butter. Pour in about ⅓ cup batter, rotating pan quickly to spread batter completely over the bottom of the skillet.

5. Cook until lightly browned on bottom—about 30 seconds; turn and brown lightly on other side. Turn out onto serving plate (or keep warm in oven while making rest of crêpes).

6. Fill each crêpe with ½ cup strawberries. Top with 3 tablespoons sour cream. Fold crêpe over. Sprinkle with confectioners' sugar. Garnish with more cream and strawberries. Serve at once.

Makes 8 servings.

Note: Crêpes may be made ahead and reheated slightly in skillet before filling.

BANANA CRÊPES WITH APRICOT SAUCE

1 jar (12 oz) apricot preserves
8 medium-size ripe bananas
¼ cup lemon juice
    Butter or margarine

8 Crêpes, below
2 tablespoons light-brown sugar
⅓ to ½ cup golden rum

1. Melt preserves with ¼ cup water in small saucepan, stirring occasionally, over medium heat—10 minutes.

2. Peel bananas; remove tips at stem end. Brush with lemon juice. In 2 tablespoons hot butter in medium skillet, gently sauté bananas, turning gently, until tender—about 5 minutes. Do not break bananas.

3. Spread one side of each crêpe with 1 tablespoon sauce; top with a banana; fold crêpe around banana.

4. In chafing dish or skillet, heat 2 tablespoons butter with the brown sugar until melted. Add crêpes; cook gently about 5 minutes; add remaining apricot sauce and golden rum; cook 5 minutes longer. Serve warm with some of sauce spooned over crêpes.

Makes 8 servings.

CRÊPES

½ cup unsifted all-purpose flour
2 tablespoons butter or
    margarine, melted and
    cooled, or 2 tablespoons
    salad oil

1 whole egg
1 egg yolk
¾ cup milk

1. In small bowl, combine flour, melted butter, egg, egg yolk and ¼ cup milk. Beat with rotary beater until smooth. Beat in the remaining milk until the mixture is well blended. Refrigerate, covered, at least 30 minutes.

2. Slowly heat a 7-inch skillet until a drop of water sizzles and rolls off. For each crêpe, brush skillet lightly with butter. Pour in about 3 tablespoons batter, rotating pan quickly to spread batter completely over bottom.

3. Cook until lightly browned; then turn and brown other side. Turn out onto wire rack. (Stack crêpes with a piece of waxed paper between each two if not using for several hours.)

Makes 8 crêpes.

BLINTZES

Apple, Blueberry, Cheese or
   Cherry Filling, below

Blintzes:
3 eggs
3 tablespoons salad oil
1½ cups milk

1 cup unsifted all-purpose flour
½ teaspoon salt
About ⅓ cup butter or regular
   margarine, melted

Confectioners' sugar
1 cup sour cream

1. Make one of Fillings.

2. Make Blintzes: In medium bowl, beat eggs, salad oil, and milk until well mixed. Add flour and salt; beat until smooth.

3. Refrigerate, covered, 30 minutes. Batter should be consistency of heavy cream.

4. For each blintz: Melt ½ teaspoon butter in a 10-inch skillet. Pour in 3 tablespoons batter, rotating pan quickly, to spread batter evenly. Cook over medium heat until lightly browned on underside; then remove from pan. Stack blintzes, browned side up, as you take them from skillet.

5. Place about 3 tablespoons of filling on browned surface of each blintz. Fold two opposite sides over filling; then overlap ends, covering filling completely.

6. Melt rest of butter in large skillet. Add 3 or 4 blintzes, seam side down; sauté until golden-brown on underside; turn, and sauté other side. Keep blintzes warm in a low oven while cooking rest.

7. Sprinkle with confectioners' sugar. Serve hot, with sour cream. Makes 10.

APPLE FILLING

2 lb tart cooking apples, pared,
   cored, and sliced
1 cup sugar

1 teaspoon cinnamon
⅛ teaspoon nutmeg

1. In medium saucepan, combine apple, sugar, cinnamon, and nutmeg. Cook over low heat, stirring occasionally, 15 minutes, or until apple is very tender.

2. Let cool, covered, about ½ hour.
Makes 2 cups.

BLUEBERRY FILLING

1 can (1 lb, 4 oz) blueberry-pie   ⅛ teaspoon nutmeg
   filling

Combine pie filling and nutmeg in small bowl. Mix well.
Makes 2 cups.

CHEESE FILLING

1 pkg (8 oz) cream cheese,   1 egg yolk
   softened   2 tablespoons sugar
2 cups (1 lb) creamed cottage   ¼ teaspoon vanilla extract
   cheese

1. In medium bowl, combine cheeses, egg yolk, sugar, and
vanilla; beat with electric mixer until smooth.
2. Refrigerate, covered, until ready to use.
Makes about 2½ cups.

CHERRY FILLING

1 can (1 lb, 4 oz) cherry-pie filling   ⅛ teaspoon cinnamon

Combine pie filling and cinnamon in small bowl. Mix well.
Makes 2 cups.

MERINGUES

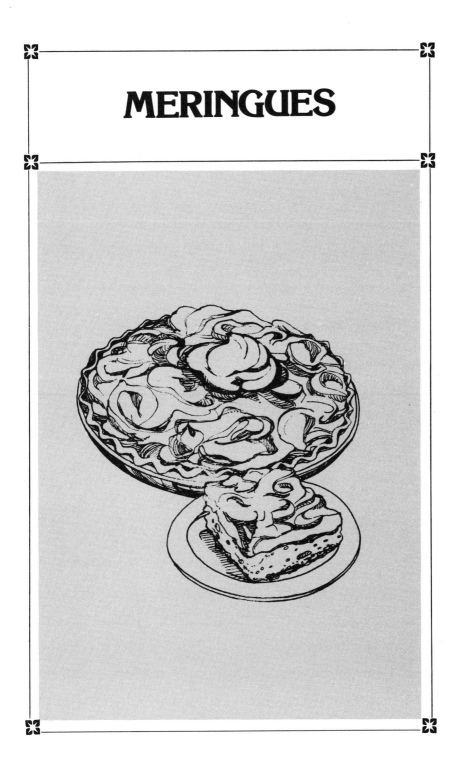

They look so fragile and difficult to make; yet anyone can make these elegant meringue desserts. Just follow our directions and we'll tell you the prettiest way to fill your delicate meringue shells.

BAKED MERINGUE SHELL

3 egg whites	1/4 teaspoon salt
1/4 teaspoon cream of tartar	3/4 cup sugar

1. Lightly butter bottom and side of a 9-inch pie plate.

2. In large bowl of electric mixer, let egg whites warm to room temperature—1 hour.

3. At high speed, beat egg whites with cream of tartar and salt just until very soft peaks form when beater is slowly raised.

4. Gradually beat in sugar, 2 tablespoons at a time, beating well after each addition. Continue beating until very stiff peaks form. Meringue should be shiny and moist.

5. Preheat oven to 275F. Spread two thirds of meringue on bottom of prepared pie plate. Use rest to cover side and mound around rim.

6. Bake 1 hour. Let cool in pan on wire rack.

7. To serve: Fill as directed, or nice with strawberry ice cream and strawberry sauce.

Makes 6 to 8 servings.

INDIVIDUAL MERINGUE SHELLS

1. Make meringue mixture as directed in Baked Meringue Shell.

2. On heavy brown wrapping paper, placed on large cookie sheets, spoon heaping tablespoons of meringue to form 8 mounds, 3 inches apart.

3. With back of spoon, shape the center of each mound into a shell.

4. Bake 60 minutes. Turn off heat; let stand in oven until cool. Use in place of Meringue Shell.

5. To store meringues: Wrap cooled meringues in waxed paper. Store in cool, dry place. Do not place in air-tight container.

Makes 8.

⛝

MERINGUE SHELL À LA MODE

Baked Meringue Shell, page 363
1 pint vanilla or strawberry
   ice cream
1 cup strawberries, washed
   and hulled

1 cup fresh blueberries, washed
2 cups fresh pineapple, cut
   into wedges

1. Make Meringue Shell, following steps 1 through 4.

2. Preheat oven to 275F. Spread three fourths of meringue on bottom and side of prepared pie plate. With rest of meringue in pastry bag, using a number-5 decorating tip, pipe a 1-inch-wide border around rim.

3. Bake 50 minutes. Let cool in pan on wire rack.

4. To serve: Fill shell with ice cream; mound strawberries in center. Arrange blueberries and pineapple around strawberries.

Makes 8 to 10 servings.

⛝

HEAVENLY LEMON PIE

Lemon Filling:
 4 egg yolks
½ cup granulated sugar
 1 tablespoon grated lemon peel
¼ cup lemon juice
½ cup heavy cream

9-inch Baked Meringue Shell,
   page 363

½ cup heavy cream, whipped
2 tablespoons confectioners'
   sugar

1. Make Lemon Filling: In top of double boiler, with rotary beater, beat egg yolks with granulated sugar until thick and light.

2. Stir in lemon peel and juice.

3. Cook, over hot, not boiling, water, stirring until thickened and smooth—10 minutes.

4. Remove from heat. Let cool completely, stirring occasionally. (To hasten cooling, place top of double boiler in bowl of ice cubes.)

5. With rotary beater, beat cream in small bowl just until stiff. With rubber scraper, using an under-and-over motion, gently fold into cooled lemon mixture just until smooth.

6. Turn into meringue shell, spreading evenly. Cover top loosely with foil; refrigerate overnight.

7. Just before serving, combine whipped cream with confectioners' sugar. Swirl over top.

Makes 8 servings.

INDIVIDUAL LEMON PIES

Use Lemon Filling in 8 Individual Meringue Shells. Refrigerate, lightly covered, overnight. To serve, garnish with whipped cream.

Makes 8 servings.

✖

ROYAL MERINGUE DESSERT

6 egg whites (1 cup)
1/2 teaspoon cream of tartar
1/2 teaspoon salt
1 1/2 cups granulated sugar
1/4 cup chopped pecans

Assorted fruits: 2 large navel oranges, sectioned; 3/4 cup

drained canned pineapple chunks; 3/4 cup seedless green grapes; 1 banana, sliced and dipped in orange juice
2 cups heavy cream
1/2 cup confectioners' sugar

1. In a large bowl, let the egg whites warm to room temperature —about 1 hour.

2. With electric mixer at high speed, beat egg whites with cream of tartar and salt until soft peaks form when beater is slowly raised. Gradually beat in granulated sugar, 2 tablespoons at a time, until very stiff peaks form. Mixture should be moist and shiny.

3. Preheat oven to 275F. Lightly butter and flour two large cookie sheets. Drop meringue by tablespoonfuls, using rubber scraper to push meringue from spoon, to form mounds, 1 inch apart. There should be 40 to 50. Sprinkle each with a little of the chopped pecans. Bake about 1 hour, or until crisp and very light golden color. Cool on wire rack.

4. Drain fruit; save juice for another time.

5. Beat cream with confectioners' sugar until stiff. Fold in three fourths of drained fruit.

6. Arrange some of meringues on round serving platter to form a 9-inch round layer. Spoon some of whipped-cream mixture on center of meringues, mounding. Arrange more meringues around and on top of whipped-cream mixture.

7. Continue to make a pyramid with meringues and whipped-cream mixture (you will need about 40 meringues in all). Fill in

spaces between meringues with more fruit. Decorate side with rest of fruit.

8. Place one meringue on top. Sprinkle with chocolate curls or shaved chocolate, if desired.

9. Refrigerate to chill well—4 hours or overnight.

Makes 10 to 12 servings.

Note: Meringues may be baked several days ahead, if desired, and stored in a cool, dry place until ready to assemble dessert.

MERINGUE TORTE

6 egg whites	1 cup heavy cream, whipped
1/4 teaspoon salt	Whole strawberries, fresh
1/2 teaspoon cream of tartar	or frozen
1 1/2 cups sugar	Canned pineapple slices,
1 teaspoon vanilla extract	drained
1/4 cup light rum	

1. Day before serving or early in morning: In large bowl of electric mixer, let egg whites warm to room temperature, 1 hour. Lightly butter bottom, not sides, of 9-inch tube pan.

2. Preheat oven to 450F.

3. To egg whites, add salt and cream of tartar, and beat until frothy. At high speed, beat in sugar, 2 tablespoons at a time, beating well after each addition. Add vanilla, and beat until stiff peaks form when beaters are slowly raised. Turn into tube pan, spreading evenly.

4. Place on middle rack of oven. Immediately turn off heat. Let stand in oven, several hours or overnight.

5. Loosen edges with spatula. Turn out torte on serving plate. Sprinkle surface with rum. Refrigerate until well chilled—at least 4 hours.

6. To serve: Frost top and sides with whipped cream. Decorate top with sliced strawberries; garnish with fruit.

Makes 10 servings.

SOUFFLÉS,
HOT AND COLD

Here we lift the curtain on the greatest-tasting soufflés we know, a magical way to end a meal. Just remember, the guests should wait for the soufflé and not the other way round. Serve it straight from the oven, the very moment it's ready, or risk a disaster.

A "true" soufflé is essentially a flavored sauce mixture, carefully combined with stiffly beaten egg whites which provide the leavening and lightness. When prepared exactly, the soufflé will be high and light, yet firm enough to "spoon," with a slight softness in the center.

The apricot and prune soufflés in this chapter do not fit the definition of a "true" soufflé.

The cold soufflés and gelatine desserts are quite different. They make refreshing summer desserts, spectacular for a buffet table.

CHOCOLATE SOUFFLÉ

8 egg whites
4 tablespoons butter or regular
    margarine, softened
2 tablespoons granulated sugar
1/2 cup all-purpose flour
3/4 cup Dutch-process
    unsweetened cocoa
1 cup granulated sugar

1/4 teaspoon salt
2 cups milk
6 egg yolks
1 teaspoon vanilla extract
1/4 teaspoon cream of tartar
1 cup heavy cream, chilled
1/4 cup confectioners' sugar

1. In large bowl of electric mixer, let egg whites warm to room temperature—1 hour.

2. With 1 tablespoon butter, grease 2-quart soufflé dish. Fold 26-inch piece waxed paper lengthwise in thirds. Grease with 1 tablespoon butter. Form 2-inch collar around dish; tie. Sprinkle dish and paper with 2 tablespoons sugar.

3. In medium-size heavy saucepan, with wire whisk, mix flour, cocoa, 3/4 cup granulated sugar, and the salt. Gradually blend in milk. Cook, stirring, over medium heat, until mixture comes to boil (large bubbles break on surface).

4. Beat yolks with a wire whisk. Beat in some of cocoa mixture. Gradually stir yolk mixture into rest of mixture in saucepan. Add 2 tablespoons butter and the vanilla, stirring until they are combined. Set aside to cool slightly. Meanwhile, preheat oven to 350F.

5. Add cream of tartar to egg whites. With electric mixer at high speed, beat just until soft peaks form when beater is slowly raised; scrape side of bowl several times with rubber scraper so that egg whites are beaten throughout.

6. Add 1/4 cup granulated sugar, 2 tablespoons at a time, beating well after each addition. Beat just until stiff peaks form when beater is raised. Whites will be shiny and satiny.

7. Turn a third of cocoa mixture over top of egg whites. Using a wire whisk or rubber scraper, gently fold mixture into whites, using under-and-over motion, just until combined. Fold in rest of cocoa mixture a half at a time. Caution: Overfolding reduces the volume.

8. Using a rubber scraper, gently turn soufflé mixture, without stirring, into prepared dish set in a large baking pan. Smooth top

with a metal spatula. Place pan and dish in oven on bottom rack.

9. Pour hot water into pan to measure 1 inch. Bake 1¼ hours. With rotary beater, beat cream with confectioners' sugar until stiff. Chill. To serve, remove collar. Break the top of the soufflé with fork. Serve with whipped cream and chocolate sauce, if desired.

Makes 8 servings.

LEMON SOUFFLÉ
(Do ahead)

6 egg whites
4 egg yolks
   Butter or margarine
   Granulated sugar
¼ cup all-purpose flour
⅓ cup granulated sugar
⅛ teaspoon salt

½ cup milk
4 tablespoons lemon juice
2 tablespoons grated lemon peel
2 tablespoons butter or margarine
¼ teaspoon cream of tartar
1 tablespoon confectioners' sugar
   Chantilly Cream, page 350

1. Place whites in large bowl of electric mixer, yolks in a small bowl. Let whites warm to room temperature—about 1 hour. Butter 1½-quart straight-side soufflé dish (7½-inch diameter). Sprinkle evenly with granulated sugar—about 1 tablespoon.

2. Fold a 26-inch-long piece of waxed paper lengthwise into thirds. Lightly butter one side, and sprinkle with granulated sugar. Wrap around soufflé dish, sugared side against dish, to form a collar extending 2 inches above top; tie with string.

3. In medium saucepan, combine flour, ⅓ cup granulated sugar, the salt, ½ cup water, and the milk; stir until smooth. Cook over medium heat, stirring constantly, until mixture is thickened and just comes to a boil. Remove from heat.

4. With wire whisk or wooden spoon, beat egg yolks; beat in a little cooked mixture. Gradually stir into rest of mixture in saucepan. Cook, stirring constantly, until mixture just begins to bubble. Remove from heat.

5. Add lemon juice and peel and 2 tablespoons butter; beat until well blended. Cool about 10 minutes.

6. Add cream of tartar to egg whites. With electric beater at high speed, beat until stiff peaks form when beater is slowly raised. Fold one third into lemon mixture until well combined. Carefully fold in remaining whites just until combined; do not overmix.

7. Turn into prepared dish. Refrigerate until baking time—no longer than 4 hours. (See note.)

8. About 1 hour before serving, preheat oven to 350F. Bake soufflé about 35 minutes, or until it is nicely browned and quivers only slightly when dish is shaken gently. Remove waxed paper; sprinkle top with confectioners' sugar. Serve at once, with Chantilly Cream.

Makes 6 to 8 servings.

Note: If desired, soufflé may be baked at once, without refrigerating, about 30 minutes.

ORANGE SOUFFLÉ SURPRISE
(Do ahead)

8 egg whites	½ teaspoon vanilla extract
Butter or margarine	¾ cup sifted all-purpose flour
Sugar	1 cup milk
4 ladyfingers, split	2 tablespoons grated orange
1¼ cups orange juice	peel
6 egg yolks	Chantilly Cream, page 350
¾ cup sugar	

1. In large bowl of electric mixer, let egg whites warm to room temperature—about 1 hour.

2. Lightly butter bottom and side of a 1½-quart straight-side soufflé dish (7½-inch diameter). Sprinkle evenly with 2 tablespoons sugar.

3. Fold 26-inch-long piece of waxed paper lengthwise into thirds. Lightly butter one side; then sprinkle evenly with sugar.

4. With string, tie collar (sugar side inside) around soufflé dish, to form a 2-inch rim above top.

5. Place ladyfingers in single layer in shallow dish. Sprinkle with ¼ cup orange juice; set aside.

6. In medium bowl, beat yolks at high speed until thick. Add ¼ cup sugar; beat until very thick and lemon-colored—about 3 minutes.

7. Beat in remaining orange juice and the vanilla to combine well. Add flour, blending thoroughly.

8. In large saucepan, heat milk with ¼ cup sugar, stirring to dissolve sugar, until bubbles form around edge of pan.

9. Stir hot milk mixture into egg-yolk mixture; pour back into saucepan. Cook, over medium heat, stirring constantly, till it thickens and begins to boil—about 10 minutes.

10. Turn mixture into large bowl. Add orange peel; let cool.

11. Meanwhile, at high speed, beat egg whites until foamy. Gradually beat in ¼ cup sugar. Continue beating until stiff peaks form when beater is slowly raised.

12. Gently fold egg whites into yolk mixture just until well combined.

13. Turn half of mixture into prepared dish. Arrange ladyfingers on top. Pour on the rest of the mixture. Refrigerate until baking time —no longer than 4 hours (see Note).

14. About 1 hour before serving, preheat oven to 375F. Bake soufflé, set in pan of hot water, 45 to 50 minutes, or until golden-brown. It should shake slightly in center.

15. Meanwhile, make Chantilly Cream.

16. Serve soufflé at once. The surprise is soft part in center. Serve as a sauce, with Chantilly Cream.

Makes 8 servings.

Note: If desired, soufflé may be baked at once, without refrigerating, 45 to 50 minutes, as directed above, in preheated oven, 375F.

❖

APRICOT SOUFFLÉ

8 egg whites, unbeaten	⅛ teaspoon salt
2½ cups dried apricots	1 cup cold heavy cream
¼ teaspoon almond extract	2 tablespoons confectioners'
Butter	sugar
Granulated sugar	⅛ teaspoon almond extract
¼ teaspoon cream of tartar	

1. In large bowl of electric mixer, let egg whites warm to room temperature—about 1 hour.

2. Meanwhile, in 3½ cups water, simmer apricots, covered, about ½ hour, or until very tender. Then press apricots, with cooking liquid, through sieve or food mill, or mix in electric blender, to make purée.

3. To 2 cups apricot purée add ¼ teaspoon almond extract; then refrigerate.

4. About 1 hour before dessert time, preheat oven to 325F.

5. Lightly butter 2-quart casserole; then sprinkle with a little granulated sugar.

6. Beat egg whites until foamy throughout; add cream of tartar and salt; continue beating to form soft peaks. Gradually add ½ cup

granulated sugar, 2 tablespoons at a time, beating after each addition until whites form stiff peaks.

7. Gently fold apricot purée into whites until thoroughly combined; turn into prepared casserole; set in pan of hot water. Bake 45 minutes.

8. At dessert time, whip the heavy cream until stiff; add confectioners' sugar and almond extract.

9. Serve soufflé at once with the whipped cream.

Makes 8 servings.

✼

PRUNE SOUFFLÉ

5 egg whites
1½ cups dried prunes
2 tablespoons butter or
    margarine
2 tablespoons plus ½ cup sugar
¼ teaspoon cream of tartar

¼ teaspoon salt
2 teaspoons grated lemon peel,
    or 1 tablespoon grated
    orange peel
½ cup finely chopped walnuts

1. In large bowl of electric mixer, let egg whites warm to room temperature—about 1 hour.

2. In medium saucepan, combine prunes with just enough water to cover; over medium heat, bring to boiling. Remove from heat; let stand, covered, 10 minutes.

3. Drain prunes, reserving liquid; remove pits. Press prunes and liquid through food mill, or blend in blender to make purée. Measure 1½ cups prune purée; set aside.

4. Preheat oven to 350F. Butter bottom and side of 2-quart casserole; then sprinkle with 2 tablespoons sugar, coating completely.

5. At high speed, beat egg whites with cream of tartar and salt just until soft peaks form when beater is slowly raised.

6. Gradually add ½ cup sugar (2 tablespoons at a time), beating well after each addition. Continue beating until stiff peaks form.

7. Combine prune purée with lemon peel and walnuts, mixing well.

8. With rubber scraper, using an under-and-over motion, gently fold prune mixture into egg whites just until combined.

9. Turn into prepared casserole; set in pan containing 1 inch hot water.

10. Bake 35 to 40 minutes, or until lightly browned. Serve warm, with whipped cream, if desired.

Makes 6 servings.

COLD COFFEE SOUFFLÉ

8 egg whites
2 envelopes unflavored gelatine
8 egg yolks
¼ teaspoon salt
1¾ cups sugar

2 tablespoons instant coffee
4 teaspoons vanilla extract
¼ teaspoon cream of tartar
2 cups heavy cream

1. In large bowl of electric mixer, let egg whites warm to room temperature—1 hour.

2. Make a paper collar for a 1-quart, straight-side soufflé dish: Tear off sheet of waxed paper 26 inches long; fold lengthwise in thirds. With string, tie collar around top of dish, to form a rim 2 inches above dish. Refrigerate until needed.

3. Sprinkle gelatine over ½ cup cold water in top of double boiler; let stand 5 minutes to soften.

4. In small bowl, combine egg yolks, salt, ¾ cup sugar and the coffee; beat with rotary beater until smooth and light.

5. Add to gelatine mixture; cook over boiling water, stirring, until gelatine dissolves—about 5 minutes. Add vanilla. Remove double-boiler top from water.

6. Refrigerate about 25 minutes, or until bottom feels just warm to the hand and mixture just starts to thicken. Or to hasten cooling, place in bowl of ice cubes, stirring occasionally.

7. With mixer at high speed, beat egg whites with cream of tartar just until soft peaks form when beater is slowly raised.

8. Gradually beat in remaining sugar, 1 tablespoon at a time, beating well after each addition; continue beating until stiff peaks form when beater is slowly raised.

9. Beat cream until stiff enough to hold its shape.

10. Turn whipped cream and gelatine mixture into egg whites. With wire whisk or rubber scraper, using an under-and-over motion, fold together just until combined. Turn into prepared soufflé dish.

11. Refrigerate until firm—several hours or overnight. Remove paper collar before serving. If desired, decorate with whipped cream and coffee candies.

Makes 10 servings.

✽

ESPONJOSA (COLD CARAMEL SOUFFLÉ)

12 egg whites (1⅔ cups)   English Custard Sauce, page
 2 pkg (1-lb size) superfine   349
     granulated sugar

1. In large bowl of electric mixer, let egg whites warm to room temperature—about 1 hour.

2. Meanwhile, place 1½ cups sugar in a heavy, medium skillet. To caramelize, cook over high heat, stirring, until sugar is completely melted and begins to boil—syrup should be a medium brown.

3. Hold a 3-quart oven-glassware casserole with pot holder, and pour in hot syrup all at once. Tilt and rotate casserole until bottom and side are thoroughly coated. Set on wire rack, and let cool.

4. Beat egg whites, at high speed, until very stiff—about 8 minutes.

5. While continuing to beat, gradually pour in 1 package sugar, in a continuous stream—takes about 3 minutes. Scrape side of bowl with rubber scraper. Beat 15 minutes.

6. Meanwhile (about 5 minutes before beating time is up), place ¾ cup sugar in heavy, medium skillet, and caramelize as in step 2. Remove from heat, and immediately place skillet in pan of cold water for 20 to 30 seconds, or until syrup is thick; stir constantly.

7. With beater at medium speed, gradually pour syrup into beaten egg-white mixture. Scrape side of bowl with rubber scraper. Return to high speed, and beat 12 minutes longer.

8. Preheat oven to 250F.

9. Turn egg-white mixture into prepared casserole, spreading evenly. Set in large baking pan; pour boiling water to 1-inch depth around casserole.

10. Bake 1 hour, or until meringue seems firm when gently shaken and rises about 1 inch above casserole.

11. Meanwhile, make English Custard Sauce.

12. Remove casserole from water; place on wire rack to cool. Refrigerate until very well chilled—6 hours or overnight.

13. To unmold: Run a small spatula around edge of meringue, to loosen. Hold casserole in pan of very hot water at least 1 minute. Invert onto serving dish.

14. Spoon caramel over meringue, and serve with custard sauce. Makes 16 servings.

COLD LEMON-AND-LIME SOUFFLÉ

3 egg whites
1 tablespoon butter or margarine
2 envelopes unflavored gelatine
1½ cups boiling water
1¾ cups sugar

½ teaspoon salt
2 teaspoons grated lemon peel
1 cup lemon juice
½ cup lime juice
1 cup heavy cream

1. In large bowl of electric mixer, let egg whites warm to room temperature—1 hour.

2. With butter, lightly grease bottom and side of 1½-quart, straight-side soufflé dish.

3. Sprinkle gelatine over 1 cup cold water in large bowl; let stand 5 minutes, to soften.

4. Stir in boiling water, 1½ cups sugar, and the salt; stir until gelatine and sugar are dissolved. Stir in lemon peel, lemon and lime juices.

5. Refrigerate until consistency of unbeaten egg white.

6. Then beat cream until stiff enough to hold its shape.

7. With mixer at high speed, beat egg whites just until soft peaks form when beater is slowly raised.

8. Gradually beat in remaining sugar (2 tablespoons at a time), beating well after each addition; continue beating until stiff peaks form when beater is slowly raised.

9. Turn whipped cream and gelatine mixture into egg whites. With wire whisk or rubber scraper, using an under-and-over motion, gently fold together. Turn into soufflé dish.

10. Refrigerate four hours, or overnight.

11. Just before serving, decorate, if desired, with rosettes of whipped cream.

Makes 6 to 8 servings.

COLD RASPBERRY SOUFFLÉ

4 egg whites
1 cup raspberries
1 envelope unflavored gelatine
4 egg yolks

¾ cup sugar
Dash salt
1 cup heavy cream

1. Put egg whites in large bowl, and let warm to room temperature.

2. To remove seeds from raspberries, press through food mill or sieve (or blend in electric blender, covered, about 1 minute; strain to remove seeds). Measure raspberry purée; add water to make 1 cup.

3. Sprinkle gelatine over ¼ cup cold water, and let soften. Meanwhile, in top of double boiler, combine egg yolks with ½ cup sugar; cook, stirring, over hot, not boiling, water until thickened—about 10 minutes. Add softened gelatine, stirring until dissolved; then let the mixture cool for 15 minutes.

4. Stir raspberry purée into cooled gelatine mixture. Beat egg whites with salt until they form very soft peaks when beater is raised. Gradually add remaining ¼ cup sugar, beating well after each addition; continue beating until whites are shiny and form stiff peaks when beater is raised.

5. Beat cream just until stiff; pile on top of meringue. Using spoon, rubber scraper, or wire whisk, gently fold raspberry-gelatine mixture into meringue and whipped cream until well combined.

6. Turn into 2-quart soufflé dish or bowl; refrigerate 2 hours, or until firm and spongy. If desired, decorate top of soufflé with whipped cream and a few raspberries.

Makes 6 to 8 servings.

COLD STRAWBERRY SOUFFLÉ

4 egg whites
2 pkg (10-oz size) frozen
    strawberries, thawed
1 envelope unflavored gelatine
4 egg yolks

1 tablespoon lemon juice
⅛ teaspoon salt
½ teaspoon vanilla extract
⅓ cup sugar
1 cup heavy cream

1. Make a collar for a 1-quart, straight-side soufflé dish: Cut a strip of foil 6 inches wide and long enough to go around edge of soufflé dish. Fold foil twice. Place band of foil tightly around dish, so it extends above dish to form a 1½-inch-deep collar. Fasten securely with string.

2. Let egg whites stand, in large bowl of electric mixer, at room temperature—about 1 hour.

3. Meanwhile, drain strawberries, reserving ½ cup syrup. Set aside a few large strawberries for garnish.

4. Sprinkle gelatine over reserved strawberry syrup in top of double boiler. Let stand 5 minutes to soften.

5. In small bowl, beat egg yolks with 3 tablespoons water. Stir into gelatine mixture.

6. Cook, stirring, over boiling water, until gelatine is dissolved and mixture is slightly thickened.

7. Remove from hot water. Stir in lemon juice, salt and vanilla to mix well. Refrigerate until mixture is cooled—about 20 minutes.

8. Press strawberries (except those reserved for garnish) through sieve to make a purée; this should measure about 1⅓ cups. Stir into gelatine mixture.

9. Beat egg whites, at high speed, just until soft peaks form when beater is slowly raised. Gradually beat in sugar; beat until stiff peaks form.

10. With rotary beater, beat cream until stiff.

11. Using rubber scraper or wire whisk, with an under-and-over motion, fold gelatine mixture and whipped cream into egg whites until well combined.

12. Turn evenly into prepared soufflé dish. Refrigerate until firm —about 4 hours.

13. To serve: Gently remove collar from soufflé. Garnish edge with reserved strawberries and more whipped cream, if desired.

Makes 8 servings.

DESSERT FRITTERS AND BEIGNETS

Here, we give you hot fruit fritters to end a meal. Our sweet batter blends nicely with any fruit, as you will see. Try the Banana Fritters with a caramel sauce and the Hot Peach Fritters with chilled almond cream.

The very light French fritters—Beignets Soufflés—are truly delicious. Start with pâte à chou (cream puff dough), and fry in hot fat until puffed and golden. Serve at once with a dusting of powdered sugar or with apricot sauce and whipped cream for a truly spectacular dessert.

BASIC SWEET BATTER FOR DESSERT FRITTERS

1 cup sifted* all-purpose flour
1 tablespoon sugar
1 teaspoon baking powder
1 teaspoon salt

2 eggs
½ cup milk
1 teaspoon salad oil
½ teaspoon vanilla extract
1 teaspoon grated lemon peel

* Sift before measuring.

Sift flour with sugar, baking powder, and salt. In small bowl, with rotary beater, beat remaining ingredients until mixed. Gradually add flour mixture, beating until smooth.

Makes 1½ cups.

APPLE-RING FRITTERS

1. Make Basic Sweet Batter, adding ¼ teaspoon cinnamon to dry ingredients. Peel and core 4 or 5 large apples; slice into ½-inch rings.

2. Meanwhile, in deep skillet or deep-fat fryer, slowly heat salad oil or shortening (at least 2 inches) to 375F on deep-frying thermometer.

3. Roll apple rings in flour: shake off excess. Then, with fingers, dip in batter, coating evenly. Deep-fry a few at a time, turning once, 3 to 4 minutes, or until golden-brown on both sides. Drain on paper towels. Serve hot, sprinkled with confectioners' sugar or cinnamon sugar.

Makes about 16 fritters, or 4 or 5 servings.

※

APRICOT FRITTERS

1. Make half of Basic Sweet Batter. On paper towels, drain very well 1 can (1 pound, 13 ounces) unpeeled apricot halves.

2. Meanwhile, in deep skillet or deep-fat fryer, slowly heat salad oil or shortening (at least 2 inches) to 375F on deep-frying thermometer.

3. Roll apricot halves in flour; shake off excess. Then, with fingers, dip in batter, coating evenly. Deep-fry a few at a time, turning once, 3 to 4 minutes, or until golden-brown on both sides. Serve hot, sprinkled with confectioners' sugar, with Almond Cream (page 383).

Makes 20 fritters, or 5 or 6 servings.

※

BANANA FRITTERS

1. Make Basic Sweet Batter. Peel 3 large, not overly ripe, bananas; slice on diagonal into ½-inch chunks. Sprinkle lightly with lemon juice (1 tablespoon in all) and nutmeg (½ teaspoon in all).

2. Meanwhile, in deep skillet or deep-fat fryer, slowly heat salad oil or shortening (at least 2 inches) to 375F on deep-frying thermometer.

3. Roll banana chunks in flour; shake off excess. Then, with fingers, dip in batter, coating evenly. Deep-fry a few at a time, turning once, 3 to 4 minutes, or until golden-brown on both sides. Drain on paper towels. Serve hot, sprinkled with confectioners' sugar, along with slightly thawed frozen sliced strawberries or with Caramel or Rum Sauce (page 384).

Makes about 24 fritters, or 6 servings.

※

PEACH FRITTERS

1. Make Basic Sweet Batter, adding ¼ teaspoon nutmeg to dry ingredients. On paper towels, drain 2 cans (1 pound, 13 ounces) peach halves.

2. Meanwhile, in deep skillet or deep-fat fryer, slowly heat salad

oil or shortening (at least 2 inches) to 375F on deep-frying thermometer.

3. Roll peach halves in flour; shake off excess. Then, with
fingers, dip in batter, coating evenly. Deep-fry a few at a time, turning once, 3 to 4 minutes, or until golden-brown on both sides.

4. Serve fritters hot, sprinkled with confectioners' sugar, with
Almond Cream or Rum Sauce (below).

Makes 16 fritters, or 8 servings.

PINEAPPLE FRITTERS

1. Make Basic Sweet Batter. On paper towels, drain 1 can (1
pound, 13 ounces) pineapple slices. Cut in half crosswise.

2. Meanwhile, in deep skillet or deep-fat fryer, slowly heat salad
oil or shortening (at least 2 inches) to 375F on deep-frying thermometer.

3. Roll pineapple in flour; shake off excess. Then, with fingers,
dip in batter, coating evenly. Deep-fry a few at a time, turning once,
3 to 4 minutes, or until golden-brown on both sides. Drain on paper
towels. Serve hot, sprinkled with confectioners' sugar, with Cardinal
Sauce (page 384).

Makes 16 fritters, or 4 to 5 servings.

SWEET SAUCES FOR FRITTERS

ALMOND CREAM

1 cup chilled heavy cream   ½ teaspoon almond extract
2 tablespoons confectioners'
     sugar

In small bowl, whip cream only until it holds its shape. Fold in
sugar and extract. Refrigerate until serving.

Makes 2 cups.

CARDINAL SAUCE

3 tablespoons cornstarch
1 pkg (10 oz) thawed frozen
   raspberries

1 pkg (10 oz) thawed frozen sliced
   strawberries

In saucepan, combine cornstarch with 1¼ cups water until smooth. Bring to boiling point, stirring until thickened and translucent—5 to 8 minutes. Stir in berries. Let cool.
Makes 3¼ cups.

CARAMEL SAUCE

1½ cups sugar
1 cup hot water
1 tablespoon butter or
   margarine

⅛ teaspoon salt
½ teaspoon vanilla extract

1. In large, heavy skillet, heat sugar, over very low heat and stirring, until it's melted and light golden-brown.
2. Remove from heat. Very gradually stir in hot water. Bring to boiling point; reduce heat, and simmer until it thickens slightly or reaches 228F on candy thermometer. Remove from heat. Add butter or margarine, salt, and vanilla extract. Let cool.
Makes about 1¼ cups.

RUM SAUCE

⅓ cup butter or margarine
1 cup light-brown sugar, firmly
   packed

2 tablespoons light corn syrup
⅓ cup heavy cream
2 tablespoons white rum

Over low heat, melt butter or margarine in small saucepan. Stir in sugar, corn syrup, and cream; bring to boiling point. Remove from heat. Let cool; then stir in rum.
Makes 1 cup.

※

BEIGNETS SOUFFLÉS

2 tablespoons granulated sugar
½ teaspoon salt
¼ cup butter or regular
   margarine
1¼ cups sifted* all-purpose flour
4 eggs
1 teaspoon vanilla extract

* Sift before measuring.

Salad oil or shortening for
   frying

Apricot Sauce:
1 jar (12 oz) apricot preserves
2 tablespoons lemon juice
½ tablespoon kirsch

Sweetened whipped cream

1. In heavy, 2½-quart saucepan, combine sugar, salt, butter and 1 cup water. Bring to boiling; butter will melt. Remove from heat.

2. Quickly add flour all at once; beat with wooden spoon until flour is moistened. Cook over medium heat, beating vigorously until dough forms ball and leaves side of pan. Remove from heat.

3. Add eggs, one at a time, beating with electric mixer at medium speed after each addition. Continue beating until the mixture is smooth, shiny and satiny and forms strands that break apart. It should hold its shape when beater is slowly raised. Beat in vanilla.

4. In electric skillet or large, heavy skillet, slowly heat oil (1½ to 2 inches) to 350F on deep-frying thermometer.

5. Drop batter by rounded tablespoons into hot oil, six at a time. Fry about 7 minutes, or until golden, turning several times.

6. Lift out with slotted spoon. Drain on paper towels. Keep warm in oven while cooking rest.

7. Melt preserves with lemon juice; strain; add kirsch. Serve with warm beignets and whipped cream.

Makes 12 servings.

Index